Permanent Economic Disorder

All schools of thought in economics, explicitly or otherwise, have referred to economic disorder as a self-evident fact. They have also unanimously considered it to be a temporary state. By contrast, this book contends that economic disorder is an interminable condition of human existence.

From this perspective, the present study brings to light the misunderstanding of successive generations of economists on economic disorders. This book provides an alternative exposition of economic disorder and correctional measures that can be taken in order to correct these misconceptions. The analysis offered in this book is a scholarly work that provides a thorough explanation of the hidden dimensions and multiple aspects of economic disorders. Much of this book is devoted to uncovering the origins of such dimensions to further refine our understanding of the development of contemporary economies. To this end, this book also outlines how to tackle some of the most intriguing issues of our time. It seeks to provide a refreshing recount of the tenets of economic disorders.

This book is a major contribution to the literature on economic disorder and crises and will be of great interest to readers of economic theory, philosophy of economics and the history of economic thought.

Shahzavar Karimzadi is Senior Lecturer in Economics at the University of Hertfordshire Business School, UK.

Routledge Frontiers of Political Economy

Macroeconomic Modelling, Economic Policy and Methodology
Economics at the Edge
Edited by Mikael Randrup Byrialsen, Hamid Raza and Finn Olesen

Economics, Anthropology and the Origin of Money as a Bargaining Counter
Patrick Spread

Bernard Schmitt's Quantum Macroeconomic Analysis
Alvaro Cencini

Blockchain and the Commons
Vangelis Papadimitropoulos

Globalization and the Decline of American Power
The Political Economy of the American Fall
Cyrus Bina

Marx and *Le Capital*
Evaluation, History, Reception
Edited by Marcello Musto

Permanent Economic Disorder
Shahzavar Karimzadi

Temporary Economic Crises
Shahzavar Karimzadi

Money and Capital
A Critique of Monetary Thought, the Dollar and Post-Capitalism
Laurent Baronian

For more information about this series, please visit: www.routledge.com/Routledge-Frontiers-of-Political-Economy/book-series/SE0345

Permanent Economic Disorder

Shahzavar Karimzadi

Routledge
Taylor & Francis Group
LONDON AND NEW YORK

First published 2023
by Routledge
4 Park Square, Milton Park, Abingdon, Oxon OX14 4RN

and by Routledge
605 Third Avenue, New York, NY 10158

Routledge is an imprint of the Taylor & Francis Group, an informa business

British Library Cataloguing-in-Publication Data
A catalogue record for this book is available from the British Library

ISBN: 978-1-032-38699-7 (hbk)
ISBN: 978-1-032-38700-0 (pbk)
ISBN: 978-1-003-34636-4 (ebk)

DOI: 10.4324/9781003346364

Typeset in Bembo
by Apex CoVantage, LLC

Contents

Abbreviations

AD	Aggregate Demand
CWK	Collected Writings of John Maynard Keynes
DCP	Disease Control Prevention
GDP	Gross Domestic Product
IS/LM	Investment-Savings/Liquidity Preference-Money Supply
MEC	Marginal Efficiency of Capital
MPC	Marginal Propensity to Consume
MPS	Marginal Propensity to Save
MPX	Marginal Propensity to Export
OCC	Organic Composition of Capital
TCC	Technical Composition of Capital
TUC	Trade Union Congress
VBMP	Voice for Baloch Missing Persons
VCC	Value Composition of Capital
WHO	World Health Organisation

Acknowledgements

Many people helped me with their comments and suggestions when I wrote this book. Arthur Dyirakumunda read and provided his feedback on Chapter 1. I wish to thank Maciej Bancarzewski for his comments on Chapter 2. As ever, my toughest critic was my partner, Angela Harvey. Her ongoing feedback has been truly invaluable. Andy Humphries and his colleagues, from Routledge publishers, were very cooperative, patient and understanding. Frank Currie, the head of my department, has made every effort to make my heavy teaching schedule easier to bear. I am deeply indebted to all for their support and input.

Acknowledgements

Introduction

One of the recurring themes in economics has been economic disorder. For good or ill and by common admission, all schools of thought in economics, explicitly or tacitly, have referred to economic disorder as a self-evident fact. Lurking beneath this presupposition there is a deep-rooted inconsistency. The prevailing preconception recourses to the realm of an implicit world. In doing so, the postulate is a refutation of itself. It does not convey what is intended. Only one inference can be drawn from this tacitly assumed stipulation and that is the verdict that economic disorder is a temporary state.

In this book, contrary to the commonly accepted view, it is contended that economic disorder is an interminable condition of human existence. From this perspective, the present study brings to light the misunderstanding of successive generations of economists on economic disorders. The book provides an alternative exposition of economic disorder and redressive measures that can be taken in order to correct these misconceptions.

A cursory glance at the world around us can corroborate the fact that everything is in a state of continuous change. Nothing is constant. The universe, with all its contents, is not frozen in a timeless stationary mode. The human species is only infinitesimally relevant in the grand scheme of things. Considering everything at a fundamental level, the human species is susceptible to all sorts of indeterminate risks in their day-to-day existence. An average human life is merely an imperceptible dot, in the never-ending passage of time. In this big picture, everything is changing and when we put things in perspective, nothing is static. Disorder is the permanent sequence of events. The life span of humans is very short: we are born, grow up and die. The geographical location and time people are born, and die are different. There can be no two human societies with exactly identical levels of political, economic, cultural, ethical, environmental, technological and scientific development. We cannot get away with such diversity. Different parts of the world are not alike and will never be absolutely identical. Much like geographical variation, different generations of people are not alike. Each generation has varied life experiences that are adapted from their actual living conditions. To us, what is normal is an ongoing state of constant and unpredictable changes that we experience in our daily life. When we look deeper into the everyday world of commonsense experience,

DOI: 10.4324/9781003346364-1

we find the element of change being crystallised in every particle of our existence. In its more complex and open-ended form, change is an integral part of each constituent of natural and social worlds. Endless change is an unbeatable force. It is the cause of permanent economic disorders.

In its most rudimentary sense, permanent economic disorder is encapsulated in every individual's limited knowledge. There are two parts to human knowledge: the first part is, individual knowledge. The acquisition of individual knowledge is very limited. It depends on whether one has access to books and other learning materials or even if one can read and think freely. Supposing one has access to all existing human knowledge—no individual has the time and mental capacity to absorb all human knowledge. No one can be an encyclopaedia of everything for all time: no one can be a master of physics, biology, chemistry, philosophy, law, economics and history, and so on. As a matter of fact, no one can acquire all knowledge on a subset, in any discipline. A biologist or an economist, at their best, can only be specialised in a very small area of their subject and may claim some authority on it: however, from this, it does not follow that they know everything about even that minute area they claim to be specialised in. Nevertheless, one does not need to be an expert in criminal law to prevent oneself from committing a crime, or an airplane engineer to use an airplane, or an economist to use money to buy goods and services. One does not need to be a medical doctor to seek a cure when one is in pain and this goes for the rest of human activities. As individuals, we do a lot of things without having full knowledge of what we do. All living human beings are involved in economic activities and affairs, but all human beings are not economists. Most of all, economists do not know everything about the economy: the fact is that we act in a state of partial ignorance.

The most effective way to act in the state of partial ignorance is to be insured against any unexpected contingencies. The most important line of defence in this respect is discerning the ethical values of right and wrong spontaneously in the family circle, and the social surrounding, in a free, open and democratic atmosphere in a rational way. The way one is brought up is a stronger protector in preventing someone from doing unethical and illegal acts than mastering all the knowledge about ethical and legal theories and principles, whilst remaining unscrupulous. These values are formed in one's childhood from one's parents, community, education, culture and society. This defence mechanism is a much stronger force in prevention of embezzlement of the assets of one's clients and in distinguishing, ethically, right from wrong, and from knowing or not knowing the legal codes and regulations word-for-word. To someone who is brought up with the conviction of making money by any means, the door is open for any type of corrupt and illicit activities. The rule of the game in this context is "survival of the fittest." The wheels on which this unprincipled device spins would be deliberate deceit, fraud, embezzlement and misconduct. The truth of the matter is that human intelligence is a double-edged sword: It has been the source of all good and wonderful inventions and discoveries in all walks of life for the common good but, at the same time, it has also been behind all the corruptions, bloodshed, genocide, wars, and destruction. In the state of partial ignorance, human intelligence cuts both ways: It can be a blessing as well as a curse; it helps but can also hurt. It is freedom of thought in an open and democratic society, state, culture and environment, based on the rule of law, that can compensate for much of our ignorance. That can, in turn, reduce the extreme edges of our ignorance and their callous and damaging outcomes.

Insurance companies are formed because of our ignorance. They represent a promise to safeguard our ignorance against the loss of life or property. We are certain that we will die one day but do not know when or how. We are also certain of the occurrence of natural, social and political disasters, that is, hurricanes, volcanic eruptions, floods, disease, revolutions, wars, accidents, fire and theft at some time, somewhere, but we simply do not know when, where or for whom. When we are insured against such risks, it means we are mitigating our ignorance. We buy a partial safeguard and safety net for lacking knowledge. Life insurance is paid for not knowing when we will die, and we buy other types of insurance policies to cater to our lack of knowledge in other areas. Another way of dealing with the unknown is preparation for it, for example, preparation for coping with floods, hurricanes, earthquakes, extreme cold, heat and rain in those areas where these events are frequent occurrences. When we do not know the exact time of such occurrences, we have only one line of defence and that is to be prepared for these eventualities, namely the construction of suitable homes, commercial and non-commercial buildings, roads, means of transport and communications. We have to have proper clothes, shoes and other types of protection in dealing with such situations.

In the realms of truths, economic disorders are contingent truths. Each type of truth has its own implications. A necessary truth is true, and we cannot alter it; it is always true. By contrast, a contingent truth could be different. Analytic and synthetic judgement share the same core attributes to that of necessary and contingent truths respectively. A synthetic judgement is a contingent judgement; likewise, it is true within certain times, places, conditions and environments but an analytic truth does not depend upon these elements. Analytic knowledge is an example of priori knowledge. It comprises facts of reason that we get from our intuition and demonstrates them by means of deduction. These are self-evident truths that are inferred from distinct sets of axioms, which are true in all possible worlds. Synthetic truths are posteriori judgements; they are the work of our sense experience and are acquired, assembled, justified and are both applied and validated by means of sense experience.

As we can see, there is a discrete contrast between the necessary, a priori or analytic mode of knowledge from empirical synthetic modes of knowledge. On the one side, we evidently observe and find the attribute of permanency, demonstrable on the basis of definition and principles of logic, which can be validated intuitively and incontrovertibly whereas on the other side, we detect the attribute of impermanency and change that can be disputed. One is compatible with logical laws and the meaning of the terms used and the other is true, being dependent upon matters of fact. One is true in all possible worlds whilst the other is only true in the actual transient world. These two worlds are markedly different. There is a clear demarcation line between truths that are fixed and remain the same in all possible worlds, and truths that are not predetermined and permanent. The dividing line is the subject of our interest in this book and not the validity and invalidity of the distinction between each designated pair of terms.

Humans' constant adaptation and struggle for survival are the ceaseless reminders of the mastery of permanent economic disorders. We struggle to adapt to the demand of the ongoing economic disorders. Resilience in the face of adversity is something that humanity can stand up to and can manage. The relentless struggle to survive and adapt in different times, and in different natural and social conditions, is testimony to human capacity to deal with economic disorders. In the accompanying book, *Temporary Economic Crises*, it is argued that under conditions of permanent economic crises human survival is not sustainable over the long term.

This book is divided into six chapters. Chapters 1 and 2 are intended to explain the factors of permanent disorder in nature generally, and economy in particular. Permanent disorder is a self-evident fact; it can be found in just about every reality. Every aspect of life and nature is encapsulated in the working order of disorder. Chapter 1, Permanent change and disorder, describes the fundamental constituents of nature that are constantly changing. The direction of flux is unpredictable: The reality of endless uncertain changes means that nature, human societies and economies are always in a state of disorder. This imperative of continuous variation entails the fusion of natural activities with human activities. Their interaction is mutual, but the reciprocal relationship is not on an equal basis. Natural events and human activities are not mutually reinforcing; the relationship is unilateral that is skewed towards the force of nature. In this chapter, we will demonstrate that these unreciprocated and unpredictable relationships and interactions of nature with humans are the constant sources of disorder to which humans are perpetually subjected. This is the reality, which leaves no room but to cope with the contingencies. The outbreak of the Covid-19 pandemic towards the end of 2019 is one such natural contingency that will be discussed in this chapter in confirmation of the view that we live in a state of permanent disorder.

In Chapter 2, Permanent economic disorder, we address the issue of continuous disorder in human societies and economies. With the help of many examples, we shall demonstrate that disorder is the norm about how things really are. In view of this fact, it necessarily follows that no single economy can be standing apart from nature, time and place. Whatever goes in nature, whether directly or indirectly, positively or negatively, will influence the economy. No economy functions detached from human conditions: institutions, scientific and technological progress, customs or legal and moral constraints. Put simply, economies are never static: They do not stand still at their most desirable peak condition or any other level of economic activity. No economy approaches its full potential. The needs and wishes of all economic agents will never be maximised all the way to reach a perpetual balance and perfection. Such an ideal economy is untenable.

As things go, we are forever at the mercy of unpredictable forces of nature, random changes, and unintended consequences of our activities. Given that things are never the same, then the inertia of disorder is embedded in everything that exists. Even though all schools of thought in economics recognise change, this change is not set side-by-side with permanent economic disorder. In this chapter, it will be argued that economic disorder has been the chief catalyst for all ground-breaking economists in fostering and shaping their radical ideas. There is no current, nor has there ever been, an economist who has endorsed everything completely about the economic structure and organisation of his or her time. No economist has accepted the economic system of his or her time as the most perfect system that is to be preserved for eternity. They all, irrespective of their ideological persuasion, refer to defects of the system. There are those who intend to repair the defects by means of reform and others who redress the defects by dismantling the entire economic system. Nevertheless, all economists, implicitly or explicitly, admit to economic disorder and it is this disorder that triggers the overriding reason in their search for the remedy to fix what they see as the defect.

The following four chapters (3, 4, 5, and 6) encompass one group with a recurring theme. The common thread that binds all four chapters is the implicit or the explicit confession to perpetual economic disorder. This cross-cutting issue is the generic base from which nearly all economic analyses stem, and the policy solutions that are prescribed and put into practice. In general, there are three world views in economics that are all-encompassing. These overarching schools encircle all shades of economic thought, narratives, policy prescriptions, remedies and measures. The subject matter of these four chapters is to explore the key tenets of these economic world views, to address in detail their inconsistencies and to elucidate their susceptibility to banality.

Chapters 3 and 4 will provide a detailed account of the natural order. Nature has been the chief source of inspiration for all critical, curious, and creative minds since the descent of humans. The order of things, the harmony and the balance that are found in nature, have been used to construct human norms and then justify such norms on the authority of natural order and laws. The natural order of things means the things and their order are as they are of necessity: That is, it is the best possible outcome. Defying such an order is not only violating nature and breaking the laws of nature but discarding the perfect choice of the best of all conceivable worlds. Modern economics, from its inception, has derived many of its cardinal principles from the precept of the natural order. These precepts are said to be in conformity with the laws of nature. These two chapters explain how natural order was adopted in social and moral landscapes and in economics.

In these two chapters, social, moral and economic orders are considered as being integrally formed with the natural orders of things. In Chapter 4, we will show how the modern age utilised the idea of the natural order as a stepping stone to break free from the repressive tentacles of medieval times.

In every changeable phenomenon, there is a visible part and a hidden part: Harmony is unthinkable without disorder. In this matching pair, harmony is the obvious side and disorder, the concealed side. The violation of order is an ongoing process; breaking the order occurs when the invisible side in the set of two becomes visible—that is, when disorder in the realms of social, moral and economics can occur. In Chapter 3, Free markets and economic disorder, we will try to unwrap and elucidate these issues. The obvious regularity in the planetary system was taken in by economists beginning with physiocrats, was elaborated upon by the classical school and has been adopted by mainstream economics ever since.

The most vivid expression of natural order and harmony in economics is the state of equilibrium in the market where the conflicting interests are reconciled and the perfect harmony between the supply and the demand is restored. At the equilibrium point, the market is at rest. Right at the centre of this world view is the idea that in the natural course of events, disorders may occur, but disorders are self-correcting. In other words, self-corrections are also the natural order of things. Market regularities and self-corrections are of such order. As conformity to natural order results in the best outcome, a market order is revered as the most advantageous system of production, distribution and allocation of scarce resources. Economic disorder is a permanent condition and all schools of thought in economics either implicitly or explicitly acknowledge its presence. In the case of economic crises, right at the end of the prevailing school of thought in economics, an economic disorder with economic crisis is perceived as one. Accordingly, everything is left to the divine self-correcting nature of the market mechanism to rectify. Two other trends in economics will be examined in Chapters 5 and 6. Chapter 5 ventures on shades of opinion that consider the deep end of economic disorder as something that is curable. On the other side, Chapter 6 tries to cover the body of opinion that considers no end in the deep end of economic disorders and no cure to the unremitting economic disorders. One economic disorder after another will eventually destroy the very system.

Chapter 4, Self-correcting economic order, will outline the characteristics of the natural order as defined and expressed by the thinkers of the Age of Enlightenment. The best order is represented by the best of all possible worlds, a world that is self-contained, harmonious and self-adjusting. The success of natural sciences in revealing these hidden orders of the natural world attracted other social and moral thinkers to this branch of human endeavour. They became captivated by discoveries, innovations, theories and the methodology of research of natural sciences: Newtonian Physics was the proof of this automated order. This chapter delves into the areas that have attracted the attention of different schools of thought in economics to the achievements of natural sciences.

Chapters 5 and 6 are the continuation of the discussion of the two preceding chapters. In those two chapters, we have established that there is an ongoing state of economic disorder—something that is expressly or, by implication, recognised by all schools of thought in economics. In these two chapters, we shall examine the most enduring legacies of Keynes and Marx. The idea that dominated formal education in economics before the Great Depression was that modern complex economies were generally stable. It did not anticipate chronic mass unemployment. The common direction and accepted practice were strict adherents to Smith's teaching of markets. The basic element underpinning Smith's market is the market's natural working mechanism. This elaborate system consists of individuals who pursue their self-interest where prices of factors of production are flexible and responsive to market price and forces. Under such circumstances, unintended outcomes of economic activities of different economic agents are coordinated in a way that will result in harmony rather than in havoc. Smith likened the automated process to the working of the metaphoric invisible hand. The essence of this automated order is what we have, in all variations of economic equilibrium, general and partial equilibriums, which have been presented by different branches of classical and neo-classical economics. To put it briefly, except for a few unorthodox economists, including Marx, the prevailing idea before the 1929 Great Crash was that a self-regulating capitalist economy is firmly grounded in a harmonious and adaptive order. Its self-balancing mechanism ensures that all factors of production are fully employed and that the complete downfall of the economy and mass unemployment were not a cause for alarm. In a self-regulation economy, the law of markets would not allow for the possibility of a general glut or shortages of goods and services to cause a great depression and mass unemployment. The flexible price system removes the market saturation and shortages and restores the economy to its equilibrium position at the point where we have full or nearly complete employment.

The 1929 Great Crash vindicated Marx's view of the market system and evoked Keynes to re-consider his initial ideas. In Chapter 5, we shall evaluate Keynes' long-lasting legacy. Keynes acclimatised the theory of chronic economic disorder with the aid of and by the strength of the 1929 Great Depression and accommodated it into mainstream economics. He published his epoch-making book about 7 years after the Wall Street Crash. Although classical and neo-classical economists have all referred to one or another type of irregularities in economic activities, they rejected the idea of the total breakdown of the economy. Such irregularities were considered to be in the ordinary course of economic activities, but these schools were of the opinion that imbalances will heal naturally with time. Each economic disorder adjusts itself automatically; market equilibrium will always be restored due to the dominance of perfect information and price flexibility. At the going market price, all factors of production will be put to work. Keynes refuted spontaneous and self-regulating characterisation of modern industrialised economies. He broke from what was sacrosanct in the prevailing economic tradition and sought out the malaise as being inherent in the nature and structure of the capitalist economic organisation. Keynes hesitantly acceded to Marx's theory of capitalism but as a saviour to rescue it by means of managing aggregate demand.

The last chapter, Chapter 6, is on the long-lasting legacy of Marx's teachings on lifelong capitalist mode and relations of production. Marx was a visionary thinker. Like all prophesiers, he made every effort and tried every possible course to find a single panacea to remedy all human ills—a cure-all forever. To this end, he invented an economic system—capitalism as a definite historical mode of production and distribution, with laws as inevitable as laws of nature. His mission's greatest achievement has been to convert his friends and foes to capitalism as an article of faith. Around the world today we find hardly any educated person who does not take capitalism on trust, either as a supporter or as an adversary. Consequently, all contemporary theories of the economic disorder and crisis are locked up in different perspectives of capitalism. According to Marx, we have continuously worsening economic disorders because we have the capitalist mode and relations of production.

In Marx's vision, history has an end: Before reaching this end, we cannot eliminate economic disorders. The end is communism, and it is then that all economic malaise will be uprooted. For this purpose, Marx needed a social and economic construction that is degenerative, an invention that he could apply his dialectical laws of unity of negations and negation of negation, and eventually the formation of his imaginary communism. This invention was his capitalism, which he pre-supposed to be a transitory period in history. The capitalist system of production will crumble because with its own development it digs its own grave. Over time, it accelerates its rate of exploitation and the size, unity, organisation and consciousness of the working class. It is this class—the universal class—that has a natural and historical mission to lead the world. Its mission is to overthrow the capitalist system and to put an end to all forms of class structure, oppression, and exploitation, forever, everywhere.

1 Permanent change and disorder

Introduction

Our world is constantly changing. Everything that exists is in a state of motion and transformation, but the pace and nature of change varies in different times and places. The earliest idea about constant change is credited to Heraclitus (535–475 BC) of Ephesus. In his view existence means change. Heraclitus supported his view by saying that at any moment in time "we are and we are not" (Bury 2015: 320). In a similar manner the economy cannot remain in one permanent form. Just the opposite: Intermittent disorder is the permanent order of the economy. All wants and wishes of economic agents can never be completely realised and attained to the full.

A situation in which all potentials in the economy are realised, synchronised and utilised spontaneously is contrary to all facts of life. Therefore, the act of balance in the economy is untenable. A balanced economy presupposes a world where we are endowed with abundant resources, where we have omniscient economic agents and a flawless legal and political system, technological maturation and impeccable institutions and infrastructure. In this chapter we will argue that such a seamless situation is not possible.

In this chapter we address the issue that human societies and economies are in a perpetual state of disorder. In the same strain we will show that the world, the natural as well as the social world, are inextricably interrelated. The overriding theme of this chapter is to show that the change never ends. Moreover, in relation to human societies, the pace of change, in all its possible shapes and forms, will keep accelerating on a level with greater accumulation of knowledge, scientific discoveries and innovations. But the pace of change cuts both ways. Change is directly related to the advances in human knowledge; science and technology, economic development, globalisation of markets, spread of education, freedom, democracy, the rule of law and many other things. On the other hand, it encroaches on the planet's life-support systems. Human population growth and overuse of the planet's resources is a fragile relation. To sustain the ever growing number of human populations requires the application of increasingly advanced technologies. This will deplete the earth of its resources,

DOI: 10.4324/9781003346364-2

which in turn leads to deforestation, desertification and pollution that may get to a defining moment in human history.

This chapter is divided into five parts. In part one we will discuss the two most basic factors of production—land and labour. It is hard to imagine an economy without these two factors. The traditional economic theory maintains that there are four primary factors of production: land, labour, capital, and entrepreneurship. The outstanding fact is that capital and entrepreneurism cannot exist independent of land and labour. It is argued that these factors are only a derivation of the primary factors. The bulk of this part, however, is a brief outline of some major events, from natural disasters to epidemics, which have shaped the course of human history. The second part is related to the growth of population since the industrialisation and the conditions that necessarily followed. The point of emphasis in this part is the process of deforestation and how human population has impacted the process of deforestation and the effects of deforestation on global warming and loss of habitats. One of the costs in economics unaccounted for is the subject matter of this section. In the section on untold costs of idiocy, we shall take a look at a category of economic costs that are caused by human folly. Part four deals with the legacy of political philosophy from antiquity to the mid-20th century—the age of consecutive conquests and empires. This chapter draws to its close with a critical examination of the legacy of the European Empires that started with the discovery of the new world in the late 15th century. Much of what can be said about the legacy of empires is summarised in the context of the two case studies that are selected for this study.

Nothing stands still

The two most important prerequisites of a human society are the earth in its totality and the human species in its entirety. Economic writers in the 17th and beginning of the 18th century correctly acknowledged these factors as the cradles of the primary factors of production. These are the building blocks of any human society. Thomas Hobbes (1588–1679) was one of the first social critics who linked production to these primary factors. Hobbes spoke of two sources from which we acquire commodities. These are "from the two breasts of our common mother, land and sea . . . or for Labour selleth to mankind" (Hobbes 1976: 230). Along the same line John Graunt (1620–74), the founder of the science of demography, affirmed that "Hands being the Father, as Lands are the Mother and Womb of Wealth" (quoted from Whittaker 1950: 367). Much like Graunt, two other leading essayists of the period, William Petty (1623–87) and Richard Cantillon (1680–1734), held land and labour as the principal factors of production. According to Petty "Labour is the Father and active principle of Wealth, as Lands are the Mother" (Petty 1899: 68, vol. 1). Whereas, in the same strain, Richard Cantillon (1680–1734) purported that the "Land is the Source or Matter from whence all Wealth is produced. The Labour of man is the Form which produces it" (Cantillon 2001: 5).

Amongst later distinguished economists who are of the same opinion, Eugen von Bohm-Bawerk (1851–1914) stands out from the rest. Bohm-Bawerk, a leading member of the Austrian school of economics, maintained that production is a function of two key factors, land and labour. He argued "all that we get in production is the result of two, and only two, elementary productive powers—Nature and Labour. . . . There is no place for the third primary source" (Bohm-Bawerk 1930: 79).

The Physiocratic school of economics, founded in the mid 18th century in France, contended this view. The school was started by a French medical practitioner, Francois Quesnay (1694–1774). As a physician, Quesnay was inspired by William Harvey (1578–1657), the English physician who discovered the circulation of the blood in the human body in 1616. Quesnay saw some striking similarities between Harvey's discovery of the circulation of blood in a human body and his discovery of the flow of money and goods in the economy. With this insight, Quesnay presented his Tableau Economique as a mirror image of the circulation of blood around the body. The Physiocratic economic analysis is characterised by two core beliefs. The first one is a direct reflection of the French society, which was predominantly agricultural, and the second was their belief in natural order. The term, Physiocracy, borrowed from the Greek, means "government of nature." It describes a sense of faith in the power of nature that is self-regulating and self-healing. Physiocrats' writings bear the imprint of the French reliance on land. They glorified land because in their view wealth only consists of the products of the land. They believed that only the soil adds to a nation's wealth. Quesnay remarked: "let the sovereign and the nation never forget that land is the only source of wealth and that it is agriculture which multiplies it" (quoted from Whittaker 1950: 368).

Adam Smith (1723–90), the founder of modern economic science, expounded his ideas in opposing the Physiocrat and the Mercantilist precepts. The main target of Smith's attack was mercantilism. The Mercantilist school of economics consisted of a broad range of writers on economic matters that dominated western European thought from the 16th to the 18th centuries. They viewed the procurement of precious metals, gold and silver as the source of wealth. From this fundamental principle they inferred that the primary factor that leads to a nation's prosperity is a favourable balance of trade in precious metals (Gray 1957: 74–5).

Smith found fault in both Mercantilists' reasoning and their inference. He denounced it for the reason that "it was not by gold or by silver, but by labour, that all the wealth of the world was originally purchased" (Smith 1979: 133). Smith articulated his theory of the nature and cause of creation of wealth in two phases. In the first phase, which he described as the "early and rude state of society," labour alone is the source of wealth. Smith states:

> If among a nation of hunters, for example, it usually costs twice the labour to kill a beaver which it does to kill a deer, one beaver should naturally exchange for or be worth two deer. It is natural that what is usually the

> produce of two day's or two hours' labour, should be worth double of what is usually the produce of one day's or one hour's labour.
>
> (Smith 1979: 150)

But Smith also entertained the proposition that this measure of wealth is untenable in advanced economies. In such societies capital and land are also included in the value of commodities. In addition to the cost of labour (wage), the cost of land (rent) and the cost of capital (interest) will also comprise the costs of production (Brue and Grant 2013: 79).

It is to be remembered that from Smith onwards the theory of value took two different directions. Karl Marx (1818–83) diverted it in one direction and the mainstream economics led it to another route. Marx embraced the account of Smith's labour theory of value that considers labour as "the real measure of the exchangeable value of all commodities" (Smith 1979: 133). In a similar vein Marx remarked that "as values, all commodities are only definite masses of congealed labour-time" (Marx 2007: 46). Commodities are objectification of abstract labour. In elaborating his labour theory of value, Marx divided the value of a commodity into three components: constant capital (C), variable capital (V) and surplus value (S). He then classified the constant capital or the means and tools of production as dead labour. As the expression implies, the dead labour is inactive. At best it only carries its own full value to the new commodities being produced. In contrast to variable capital, constant capital does not add any extra value to commodities. Marx designated the variable capital as the creator of wealth. He calls the variable capital the living capital, the form of capital that oversees creation of surplus value (S). In the capitalist mode of production, the most advanced mode of commodity production, Marx says labour power (V) also becomes a commodity. He then went to say that as the dead labour (C) is owned by the capitalist class, the living labour (V) has no other choice except for selling their labour power to the owners of the means of production. The time that the labour power is employed is divided between the wage that a labourer will get and the surplus value (S) that is passed to the owners of the means of production. To follow his argument to its furthest conclusion, consistent with his central premise, Marx established that "capital is dead labour, which, vampire-like, lives only by sucking living labour, and lives the more, the more labour it sucks" (quoted from Pack 2010: 130).

Mainstream economics differs on this issue. Their account is best expressed in popular economics textbooks. The substance of the idea goes back all the way to David Ricardo (1772–1823). Ricardo endorsed the Smith's theory of value fully and said very little about it but succeeded to put it very briefly and clearly. The centrepiece of his theory is that he integrated the labour theory of value in his system of production and distribution of national income. In his economic system, the three factors of production—land, labour and capital—obtain a portion of national income for the part they take in production. The fourth factor of production, entrepreneurship, is credited to Jean-Baptiste Say (1767–1832). In the words of Say an entrepreneur is someone who "shifts economic resources out of one area of lower and into an area of higher productivity and greater yield" (quoted from Skousen 2010: 279).

The foregoing traditions all are missing a crucial point on the role of factors of production in an economy. The error here is in the assumption of considering land and labour as only two factors of production. Marx reduces all factors of production to one factor, labour power, whereas the mainstream economics put land and labour on a par with capital and entrepreneurship. Much of what can be said in criticism of the one also applies to the other side. One cannot curtail land and labour exclusively to two factors of production. In fact, they are more than that. There can be no human society and economy without the planet earth in its present setting. Likewise, without the human species there can be no human society and economy. These are the most indispensable requirements for human species to live and form their societies. Therefore, land and labour are far more than two factors. They are the most important building blocks of life and existence. Capital and entrepreneurship are simply an offshoot of these two fundamentals.

These core elements, however, are changing. On one side, this relentless process of change stems from human desire to own and subordinate nature to their will to serve their needs and fulfil their wishes. In the realisation of this endeavour the impact of human actions on nature has been overwhelming. The list of impacts of human species on nature is boundless. The effect of labour on land is extraordinary. A few examples will suffice to qualify this point. Human interactions with nature are both constructive and destructive. On the constructive side, Homo sapiens have been responsible for the construction of many impressive societies, scientific, technological inventions and discoveries. On the destructive side, they have been constantly engaged in war, conquest and colonisation of new lands and different communities. Humans have invented weapons of mass destruction, caused widespread deforestation and have obliterated, either partially or completely, many nations, cultures and living species.

Nature is a dynamic wonder, which is always changing. There is disorder in all its micro and macro spheres. The internal layers of the planet earth are continuously shifting, causing earthquakes and volcanic eruptions. The currents in the sea change direction, altering weather and causing hurricanes, cyclones and storms. The chemical activities taking place in the centre of the sun cause turbulence in its surroundings and in our atmosphere. The living species are continuously mutating and evolving to adapt to their new environments. Many have already vanished and many more will become extinct. Others may migrate and colonise and in time marginalise native species. New diseases and viruses are coming into being and others may mutate and disappear. Therefore, nature is in a state of perpetual disorder. Humans are merely a speck in this grand scheme of chaos and commotion.

Since its formation the earth has experienced many drastic changes, from the very extreme of the drop in its temperature to asteroid collusions, to comet attacks and massive bouts of volcanic activity. In the last 500 million years, the earth has also experienced five mass extinctions. At one time the earth accommodated between 5 to 50 billion organisms and species. Currently it is estimated to accommodate between 5 to 50 million (Raup 1991: 3–4).

It is necessary to start our study with the Cretaceous-Tertiary extinction. This was the last of the five major mass extinctions (Cloudsley-Thompson 2005: 189). This event occurred about 65 million years ago. It led to the extinction of the entire population of dinosaurs. Whatever the cause of that cataclysm might have been, that is, an asteroid or comet or a massive bout of volcanic activity—that event was as a direct result of the blocking of light and energy from the sun. This caused the end of the Cretaceous period and the beginning of the Paleogene period.

During the life of the earth, rapid changes in global temperatures have engendered calamitous droughts, famines, the alteration of the ecosystem, the migration of animals and destruction of plants. Equally, severe flooding, storms and lack of rainfall alter the way humanity is compelled to adapt to the far-reaching changes that have taken place. The rise and fall of the sea level and the drying up of rivers or their direction have drawn or repelled the human population from their original settlements. Such changes have forced them to seek new land and dominion.

The earth has experienced uncountable drastic events. One of these events is wildfires. From recent records we can deduce that their impact on all species can be devastating. Their impact can have everlasting impact on people's settlements and the landscape. They can cause widespread destruction. In modern times we have seen a terrible example in the form of the Black Friday Bushfire in Australia's Victoria State. In January 1939 a wildfire consumed a huge area and burnt about 5 million acres. In summer 2003 a large fire engulfed Iberia's taiga forest burning 27,181,000 acres. In summer 2004 a series of large fires burned about 5 million acres in Alaska. There was the Great Peshtigo Fire in October 1871 in northern Wisconsin. The fire consumed about 3.8 million acres of land and killed around 1,500 people. Another unforgettable fire was the great fire of 1910 in Idaho and Montana. These are only a few haunting examples of fires that have occurred in the earth's history. Small scale fires are very frequent but their impact on the local species and environment is also drastic. Their impact on the rest of the planet's atmosphere and environment, although less visible, is gradual and the balance of evidence suggests that they facilitate further reaction and disorder.

In ancient texts, we are constantly reminded of drought and human migrations. From the deadliest examples of modern time, we can form an image of the extent of devastation of unrecorded droughts and famines in the past. In 1769, India experienced a severe drought. The famine followed by the draught killed over 10 million people, almost one third of the Indian population. The Irish Potato Famine of 1845–8 was of the same scale of disaster, even though the cause was too much rain rather than the lack of rain. A late blight water fungus destroyed the crops that gave rise to 1million people perishing and another 2 million immigrating. The 1876–79 China drought took over nine million people and displaced many more. More than 20 million Chinese people died in the 1959–61 famine. The later famine was mostly man made; nevertheless, harvest failure also played a significant role in the disaster. The 1981–4 African drought engulfed 20 countries and resulted in the death of over a million people.

Nowadays floods are daily occurrences. No daily news is complete without a report of a flood somewhere. Such events have always been happening but not on the same scale and frequency. A few examples suffice to demonstrate their fatal impacts. In July to August 1931 China experienced heavy rains as result of which the Yangtze, Yellow and Huai rivers flooded, killing 4 million people, and affecting another 51 million. A combination of heavy rain and famine during the 1995 to 1998 period cost the lives of 3 million people in North Korea.

Earthquakes are very frequent. It is estimated that about 50,000 earthquakes take place each day. Most of them are benign with only a few very destructive. Earthquakes have contributed to the collapse of civilisations. The collapse of the Harappan civilisation is one example of this (Nabhan 2017). The earthquake that shook present-day Egypt and Syria in July 1201 is regarded as one of the deadliest ones. It killed approximately 1.1 million people in the region. Plague often coincided with major wars. The victorious, while recounting the track record of their glories, also pointed to the many types of disease that claimed many lives of their "victorious" soldiers. It is said that about 300,000 to 800,000 of Xerxes's army died from plague in the 5th century BC when the King of the Achaemenid dynasty of Persia invaded Greece (Koehler 2000). The three worst recorded world pandemics of plague are the 541, 1347, and 1894. The first one was the Justinian Plague. The epidemic started in Ethiopia and spread to Egypt and then to the Mediterranean region (Rosen 2007).

In his book, *History of the Wars*, Procopius of Caesarea (2015), gives a vivid account of the symptoms of plague and its devastating effect. He paints the situation as being so terrible that "the whole human race came near to being annihilated." The epicentre of the Justinian pandemic was Constantinople. It is reported that 5,000 (others estimated up to 10,000) people died per day in the spring of 542. In the end one-third of the population of the city perished from the disease. It then spread to Italy, southern France, the Rhine valley and Iberia, Ireland, Denmark, Africa, the Middle East and Asia Minor. Within a period of 4 years, from 542 to 546, the plague killed about 100 million people and to the imperial ruler's annoyance destroyed the Empire.

At about 200 BC Sumerians witnessed outbreaks of plague. Around 400 BC Hippocrates (460–370 BC), a Greek physician, sketched a chronicle of the outbreak of mumps on the island of Thasos. Similarly, Thucydides (460–395 BC) a historian from Athens described in detail the 430 BC plague in his city. He reported that the plague had killed one-fourth of the army. One outbreak after another outbreak of plague epidemics revisited the Roman Empire regularly. The deadliest one was the 166 AD outbreak, which killed one-third of the population of Rome (Bernstein 2009: 135).

Many believe that the Tatar armies may have helped to disseminate the 1347–52 Black Death in Europe. The event took place when Khan Jani Beg, the Khan of the Golden Horde (1342–57), surrounded Kaffa (Feodosya in Ukraine). As his army could not break into the town, in an act of revenge, his army retaliated by catapulting infected dead bodies of soldiers over the walls of Kaffa. The plague-ridden Genoese traders who survived the siege fled to Constantinople, from there to the Mediterranean, Messina and Sicily. By 1350 the plague spread to France, Germany, Spain, England and Norway and later to Russia and India (Zeigler 1969).

It is estimated that from 1347 to 1350 about 25 million people, a quarter of the European population, died because of the plague. The same number perished in Asia and Africa. Another 10 to 20 per cent of Europe's population perished in 1361 when plague resurfaced again. Michele da Piazza in his chronicle presented a vivid account of the Black Death in Italy in October 1347. The disease ravaged Northern Italy. In Europe at the same time one in every three to four people lost their lives. The outbreak reoccurred intermittently, and one-third of Venice's inhabitants were wiped out in the 1575–77 outbreak (Bernstein 2009: 142–3). Some blamed the Jewish community for the outbreak. The hysteria of targeting the vulnerable Jewish community resulted in many Jews being arrested and subjected to severe torture for something that they were totally blameless. Many innocent Jews under much distress confessed to the imaginary crime that they were being accused of. After admission many of the victims were burnt or were crashed on a wheel. In one incident in Constance, Germany, on 4 January 1349, 330 Jews were gathered in two of their own houses and were burnt alive. In the end the Black Death consumed about 12 to 15 million out of the 50 million population of Europe (Bernstein 2009: 144–5). Ibn Khaldun (1332–1406), the eminent Arab historian, wrote:

> In the middle of [fourteenth] century civilization in both the East and the West was visited by a destructive plague which devastated nations and caused populations to vanish. It swallowed up many of the good things of civilization and wiped them out. It overtook the Dynasties at the time of their senility. . . . Cities and buildings were laid waste, roads and way signs were obliterated, settlements and mansions became empty, dynasties and tribes grew weak.
>
> (Ibn Khaldun 1958: 64)

One localised outbreak of plague was that of London in 1665. Samuel Pepys (1633–1703) described it in his famous diary. In this epidemic alone about 7,000 people died per week in September 1665. The plague wiped out a fifth of London's population, 100,000 people, between 1665 and 1666 (Zeigler 1969).

The other worldwide pneumonic plague originated in Yunnan in 1894. It soon spread to Hong Kong and India and then to Europe. The plague reached Bombay by 1896 and by 1900 it spread to all ports worldwide that were connected to the international trade routes (Cregg 1985). This was the last worldwide plague endemic. By 1959 plague had killed over 15 million people, mostly in India. Undoubtedly, the occurrence of such pandemics has changed the course and directions and fabric of human societies. The flu pandemic of 1918–19 killed between 35 and 75 million people globally and over 16 million individuals just in India. A catastrophe of such magnitude is often accompanied with other misfortunes. It may well create other diseases such as smallpox, infantile diarrhoea and dysentery. It breaks the moral, social and economic fibres of the society being affected. Masses lose hope and their rational faculty becomes tainted with superstition and desolation.

Deadly viruses are not uncommon. Most probably, only a small number of them are known to modern science. Many of them are not known and born yet. To paint a picture of their lethal effects we provide a short list of contemporary deadly viruses that are relatively more common. Even this short list is a sufficient indicator of the fragility of human existence. Humans are engaged in a perilous journey in combating these dangerous germs. Hundreds of thousands of people have died from being infected by the Marburge, the Bird flu, the Ebola, the Zika, the Hantavirus, the Lassa virus, the Junin, the Crimea-Congo fever, the Machupo, the Keyasanur forest and the Dengue fever.

Animal epidemics can also be deadly. An outburst of lethal diseases in domesticated animals can also undermine or destroy the affected communities. Animal and plant diseases are numerous—even those that already have been discovered. There are out there probably many more dangerous viruses that we do not know or the conditions for their growth has not been created yet. Arbovirus infections, febrile illnesses, haemorrhagic fever, epidemic neprosonephritis, encephalitis, animal-pox, paravaccinia, Q fever, Orf, erysipeloid, vibriosis and brucellosis are just a few examples of them.

Farming is a risky and yet a vital undertaking for the survival of humankind. It is at the mercy of weather that can change without any warning. Besides, it is also at the mercy of plant diseases. This can come from all sorts of directions from fungal diseases, fusarium, and verticillium, wift, beetle blights and other causes. The fact of the matter is that farming is a very uncertain adventure. If farming is affected adversely it can result in a chronic shortage of food and the bankruptcy of many farmers.

The earth's habitable land is limited. The steady increase in human population has driven many to dwell within the vicinity of volcanoes. According to World Bank 2009 data, about 600 million people live in risky volcanic zones (Auker et al. 2013: 1). Auker et al. gathered a database of 1,115 volcanic eruptions of different volcanoes covering the 4350 BC to 2011 period (Auker et al. 2013: 6). The fatal incidents recorded for the period of 1600 to 2010 are 533 instances. The total fatalities only for these incidents are calculated to be about 278,880 death tolls (Auker et al. 2013: 9). Volcanic eruptions can cause large numbers of injuries, evacuations, economic damage, and destruction of the social fabric of a society that are impossible to quantify.

Volcanic eruptions can also cause floods. It is estimated that 5 out of the 27 largest global floods were caused by volcanic eruptions. Floods, like earthquake, volcanic eruptions, epidemics and climate change are among the most powerful forces of nature that have destroyed and effectively reshaped human societies over time. Meteorologists divide the largest and most powerful floods into two groups: quaternary and meteorological floods. The quaternary period goes back to about 1.8 million years ago. The glacial dams that were formed over thousands of years gradually jammed midcontinent drainage systems and eventually broke with earth-shattering consequences. The ancient drainage network gave way to mountains of ice sheets discharging over 20 million m3/s. These tall dams could be as high as 600 meters as in the case of the Uray flood in Asia and Missoula in North America.

In the second category are the meteorological floods. The largest floods of this kind are in tectonically active regions of the earth. One example is the Mediterranean Basin. The creation of the Straits of Gibraltar is due to the existence of this Basin. These floods can be formed by the blocking the natural flow of large rivers. In the same category are the massive landslide dams, many of which are caused by earthquakes. On the list of the largest landslide dams on earth we have Usoi dam in Tajikistan that was formed in the 1911 earthquake. The Usoi dam is 550 meters and it created Lake Sarez. The flood can also be caused by gradual ice-jam. This is what happened to the Lena River in Russia or to the Missouri river in North Dakota in April 1952. The meteorological floods are quite common. Their effects can be catastrophic. In many cases—as in the Mississippi River in 1927, the Columbia River in 1948 and the Yangtze River in 1931—they can be very devastating. The death toll just for the Yangtze River flood was about 4 million people (O'Connor and Costa 2004: 8).

Earth has a dynamic chemical and physical structure. The climate and topography of earth are variable. At times these changes can be very violent and destructive. Fire, flood, tsunamis, earthquakes, droughts, volcanic eruptions, hurricanes, deforestation, extreme cold and heat waves are elements that are inseparable from the very configuration of the earth. The very intrinsic nature of the earth is essentially formed of many unpredictable forces of destruction and construction. These forces are in constant battle of elimination and regeneration. This battle defines the turbulent life of the planet and the environment of living species.

Humans' history on earth is comparatively a very short period. From a geological time-scale point of view, it is a minor time interval. It is a little over a hundred millennia. As settled communities, our history goes back to the discovery of agriculture. This happened about 10,000 years ago (Rabie 2001: 25). Many species have come and then became extinct due to the dynamic nature of the earth and our universe. In effect, it was earth's dynamism that gave birth to the human species. Our dwelling on earth is probably temporary. It is quite possible that the fortune of the human species could change suddenly with an unexpected catastrophic event. This could be triggered by a natural calamity or even a man-made folly. The fact of the matter is in the not very far geological distant future time, the earth and our entire solar system may cease to exist.

A point that we need to emphasise is the fact that once planet earth did not exist. It is also a matter of great importance to understand that it will not be here forever. The earth is one of several planets in the solar system that orbit the Sun. All these planets and the Sun are constantly changing and are influencing each other. The earth is a sphere that orbits the Sun. While orbiting, one pole of the earth constantly tilts towards the Sun. This slight shift of earth's position is responsible for the formation of the seasons. Moreover, there is an irregular swaying motion of the earth called the mutation of the earth's axis. This is accountable for the irregular heat waves in the earth's atmosphere.

As a very dynamic entity the earth has experienced periodical cycles of heat waves and ice ages. The last ice age was about 11,000 years ago. Within two millennia of the last ice age, agriculture was discovered that enabled large groups of people to settle in one location. As the thick glaciers melted and retreated in Eurasia and North America, they caused worldwide floods and the sea level to rise by 110 meters.

In the time in between the major ice ages, the earth also has mini cycles of climate changes. The two so called "little ice age" occurred during the 15th and 18th centuries. Barbara W. Tuchman (1978) in her storyline of the 14th century attributes the drop in temperature as the chief cause that triggered much of the social and political conflicts in the century. The reason given is the drastic drop in the temperature reduced production of food radically. The severe shortage of food in turn increased competition for food and hence led to more wars and diseases and starvation.

According to the National Oceanographic and Atmospheric Administration, since 1900 the climate has been getting warmer. The rise in temperature in 20th century is estimated to be 1 degree Celsius. The causes of this increase in temperature are not fully understood but its effects are evident almost everywhere. One of the effects is the recurrence of heat waves, which have become more frequent and intense over the course of the century. Since the turn of the millennium, there have been three major heat waves in 2002, 2003 and 2015 with death tolls of 1,030, 1,210 and 1,826 respectively. Europe has experienced two heat waves, one in 2003 with 71,310 death tolls and another in 2006 with death tolls of 3,418. The death toll in Russian heat wave in 2010 was 55,736 (International Disaster Database). Other parts of the world have also experienced frequent deadly heat waves that are not recoded. The climate is changing, and it is damaging the ecosystems of the planet.

The role of the human species in global warming cannot be overrated. There is an overwhelming body of evidence that human actions have been fuelling the deterioration of the climate. Their economic activities are at least partially responsible for the emission of vast quantities of greenhouse gasses, carbon dioxide, methane and nitrous oxide. The effects of global warming can be devastating to the planet and its inhabitants. Higher temperatures destroy food production in water-scarce regions of the world and make water even scarcer in many other parts of the world. It makes farming much harder, forcing large populations of people and animals to migrate and search for food. It erodes large segments of soil and transforms fertile lands into arid waste. Consequently, strong winds become more frequent in some parts of the world while rain and floods occur in other parts. Higher temperature follows with the incubation of more diseases and pests. In turn this leads to the wider obliteration of natural habitats. It depletes the ozone layer and harms biodiversity. In time this instigates the further extinction of a wide variety of plants and animals.

At this juncture, it is necessary to look at a few examples of recent epidemics. The outbreak of epidemics, although sporadic, can occur at any moment. On 5 June 1981, the US Centres for Disease Control Prevention (DCP) published a report, describing a rare lung infection among five young men. The infection promptly weakened the immune system of these men. This was what was to be called the AIDS epidemic that soon spread throughout the world. According to the UNAIDS Fact Sheet November 2016, by the end 2015, 36.7 million people were living with HIV globally, 2.1 million were newly infected. Approximately 35 million have died since the outbreak of the epidemic.

In some parts of the world the AIDS epidemic ravaged entire nations. The hardest hit has been in the nations of sub-Saharan Africa. The spread of the disease has taken a devastating toll in the countries that were worst affected. According to UNAIDS in 2005, AIDS took lives of 3.1 million and 2.4 million of the victims were from sub-Saharan Africa. The most affected age group has been the 20 to 49 age group. The ramification of this was that it did not end in losing the productive working population but also the primary caregivers of the communities. Many children in these communities were left to fend for themselves. Mothers infected with HIV transmitted the virus to their children. By 2005, in Lesotho, one fourth of the population were infected with HIV. It is enough to mention here that in 1991–5 in Lesotho, the life expectancy was about 60 years. By 2005 it plummeted to 34 years. No one was left untouched in Lesotho. The epidemic crippled the entire fabric of social and economic life of countries such as Kenya, Malawi, Tanzania and Zambia.

The Ebola is another recent outbreak of a deadly virus. It is a viral family of Filoviridae, first detected in Sudan and Congo in 1976. The earliest case was reported in Gueckedon in Guinea in December 2013. The Ebola virus is transmitted by animals and humans. It causes inside and outside bleeding with extreme pain and fever. The outbreak if not prevented immediately would ravage the entire population. Ebola resurfaced in West Africa in March 2014 and afterwards spread rapidly. From March 2014 to January 2016, 28,637 people were infected and 11,315 died from the disease (The Economist, January 2016). Most of the victims were from Liberia, Sierra Leone and Guinea. The Ebola epidemic shattered the economic and social structure of the region. Had it not been for the world's immediate and resolute response, the impact of the disease could have been even worse.

Another very recent outbreak of epidemic virus was the outbreak of the Zika virus. The virus was discovered among monkeys in 1947 in Uganda. In humans it was identified in 1952 both in Uganda and Tanzania. But it was not until it resurfaced in Brazil in 2014 that it caught the world's attention. The Zika virus is a mosquito-borne flavivirus and is transmitted mainly by Aedes mosquitos. The virus also can be passed from a mother to her unborn child. By October 2015 there was unusual increase in newborn infants suffering from the microcephaly condition in Brazil. From 2015 to January 2016 the virus spread rapidly. More than one half million cases of Zika were reported worldwide at the start of 2016, the vast majority of which were reported in South and Latin America.

Human beings are not, therefore, armed with a complete knowledge to cope with the earth's surprises. Of equal importance is to know that we are at the mercy of the effects of the unexpected. Epidemics, infectious diseases, famines, wars, conquest, colonisation, religious strife and many other forms of contingencies have all led to various types of very intense disorder. The frequency of these eventualities varies but when natural and social disasters go side by side the result for the people affected can be very devastating.

Evidently, advances in human conditions, either by means of our improved understanding or by luck, have taken place since the Age of Enlightenment. Many infectious diseases are controlled. Sicknesses such as plague, leprosy, syphilis, smallpox and malaria can now be treated successfully. Some progress, on average, has also been made in dealing with earthquakes, floods, hurricanes, famines and epidemics. This also applies to life expectancy due to the improvement in conditions of life, nutrition and medicine. Despite this, the ultimate triumph of human reason over nature is still rudimentary. Our fate continuously depends on a perilous and ever changing natural and social world. The world we inhabit is essentially defined by unexpected disorderly and volatile events and patterns.

Deforestation and population

The anthropogenic impact on land is indisputable. Land is the factor that life begins with. It is the most vital precondition for the evolution and sustenance of the human species. The earth is the protector and the provider of all species. This interaction between the earth and the human race is an inter-reliant relation. Human beings are the ones who are at the mercy of their living environment. The relationship between land and labour in this sense is not reciprocal. The earth does not need us for its survival, and it does not forgive the folly of its inhabitants. It is our host, and we are her guests. An ancient myth has taken root in our psyche that we are superior to other species. The irony is that among all living species it is humankind that behaves like the master. There is a difference between being intelligent and claiming the title of the master of the universe. The doctrine that man is the master of all things is effectively self-defeating. The failure to grasp this fact with sufficient clarity will pave the way for our own demise. Instead of realising our dependency on our provider we have labored to subdue, alter and rule our provider. In early human societies the human impact on nature was insignificant. All that has changed with the industrial revolution and rapid increase in human population.

The most primitive forms of technology are our limbs, senses, and brain. Technological inventions, in effect, are improvements of these capabilities, capacities and faculties. Humanity expands their power of action on their surrounding environment by relying on the materials extracted from land. All inventions and discoveries aim to enhance these capabilities. The tools used in the Stone Age obviously impacted the environment. However, human impact on the environment in the Stone Age is not what it is at the present time. The impact of the use of stone was inconsequential. First and foremost, the human population was too small, and the tools used were very rudimentary. In this respect, industrialisation and its aftermath changed the course of human history. The rapid increase in human population together with application of highly entropy-increasing technology led to mass production for mass consumption. This has intensified agricultural production that in turn has led to deterioration of the only life-support that exists (Costanza et al. 1997: 3).

The human impact on planet earth is widespread and long-lasting. Nowadays we find human waste everywhere from the center of Antarctica to Mount Everest. In all ocean water there is a sign of human wastes, and it is estimated that "one fifth of the world's population breathes" more poisonous air than the standard recommended by the World Health Organization (Costanza et al. 1997: 7–8).

The earth's climate is a very complex wonder. It is a delicate system that is constantly shifting and changing in nature and rhythm. The earth's climate is evolving in a profoundly dynamic manner. The entire essence of this change is unpredictable. Pollution makes this very delicate balance even less stable. The biosphere is not infinite. Its absorptive capacity of carbon dioxide, methane, CFC, nitrous oxide and other damaging pollutants is limited. The cumulative impact of these pollutants is virtually irreversible. It is argued that each year about 7 billion tons of carbon is released into the atmosphere (Costanza et al. 1997: 11). As a direct consequence of human activities wildlife habitat is shrinking. The rate of the extinction of endangered species is faster than at any time in human history and it is accelerating. Human activities have already led to the extinction of millions of species. About 55 per cent of tropical forests, the chief inhabitants of the world's species habitat, have already been destroyed (Costanza et al. 1997: 13).

Sustainability of future generations is questionable. Serious damage will be caused by the increase in human population, pollution of the biosphere, deforestation, destruction of wildlife and soil erosion. Over the course of time the cumulative effect of reckless human actions will put human survival itself in critical jeopardy. David Ricardo (1772–1823) aptly demonstrated in his theory of rent how people farm the fertile land first and as their population grows, they move to the less fertile land. As land is limited in supply eventually the growing population will take over all the land (Ricardo 1992: 221–2). The implication of this scenario is that the population has the potential to grow more than the availability of land to sustain it. Secondly, the more land is reserved for production of food and shelter the more the soil will be deteriorated. That means banking ever more on agrochemical, monocultural techniques in farming, which harm biodiversity (Costanza et al. 1997: 26). In addition to this problem, a considerable portion of the fertile land is increasingly used for production of drugs and other illicit substances (Pomeranz and Topik 1999: xv). Due to combinations of all these activities 35 per cent of the earth's land has already been degraded (Costanza et al. 1997: 13).

The earth's forests are its lungs. Forests cover about 4 billion hectares of the earth. That is about 31 per cent of its surface. Forests are vital for all living species. They are not only the protector of biodiversity but also over 1.5 billion people live and depend on them (Leakey 2017: 389). Forests are sources of food, shelter, medicine, paper, as well as being filters of water. They absorb carbon dioxide and release oxygen into the atmosphere. Every year around 50,000 square miles of the forests are cleared for agriculture, logging for timber, for housing and settlement, for ranching and development purposes.

When Thomas R. Malthus (1766–1834), published his essay on population (in the year 1798), the world population was about 8 hundred million people. Now it is over 7.5 billion. Sustenance of this figure was inconceivable for Malthus. Such a dramatic increase in population does not fit well in his natural law of population. A law that states that when population is not checked it "increases in a geometrical ratio" but subsistence only increases "in an arithmetical ratio" (Malthus 1985: 71). Malthusian law is evidently in the wrong. Human population showed that it does neither grow exponentially nor does it always grow everywhere at the same rate. Moreover, neither food production follows a uniform arithmetic increment growth nor population a geometric ratio. At its base the theory was an agenda-driven assertion. Nonetheless, there is an important message in Malthus's observation. That is, economic resources and population cannot advance sequentially at the same rate incessantly.

All natural resources are not renewable. Moreover, the application of more developed technology, education, management, new scientific innovations and discoveries improve efficiency in using both renewable and non-renewable resources. The fact of the matter is that all economic resources are limited in supply. Inevitably a serious strain, in the end, falls on the renewable resources. Since there is one earth, the irreversibility law applies to all resources that can be extracted from the land.

The period of post-industrialisation has witnessed a significant reduction in mortality due to improvements in education, nutrition, medical and health care, and overall economic conditions. Fewer children are dying at birth and many more people live longer. Increasing life expectancy requires both more economic and medical care. Classical economists saw an end to this trend. Fixed land determines this end. Stationary state creeps in the contest between humans and the earth prior to approaching this eventual frontier. Population growth means that natural resources become even scarcer. It means there will be less land to cultivate but more consumption and an increase in emission of carbon dioxide. In addition, it results in climate change, drought, floods, congestions, hunger, arm races and wars. It is quite clear that in the foreseeable future the world's population will be increasing. Another worrying trend according to the UN projection is that by 2050 about 4 billion people will be living in the areas that are already experiencing a shortage of water (Blanton and Kegley 2017).

Hunger is an indefensible misfortune. One of its unintended consequences, however, is invention of ways and means, tools, schemes and institutions of tackling it. Probably, it is the mother of invention. It is positively a curable debility, and yet it has never left the side of humankind. The greatest strive to end hunger was after the Second World War. Those nations that embraced a social and liberal democratic policy, to a certain degree, succeeded to do away with hunger. Introduction of a system of the welfare state has been pivotal in overcoming hunger in these nations but in developing countries hunger is still widespread. In their estimate for the years 2014–16, the United Nations Food and Agriculture Organization has calculated that about 795 million people worldwide were suffering from chronic hunger.

Similarly, wars have continued to blight human life. All wars, by definition, create havoc. Wars have brought humanity to the brink of potential destruction. Wars have become more frequent, vicious and lethal. Human history is full of tales of long and catastrophic wars, many of which have wiped out nations and communities completely. The 20th century was the most violent and murderous one in human history. The death toll for the First World War alone was about 17 million. In the Second World War it is estimated that the death toll exceeded 60 million. In addition, in a selected few of more localised conflicts such as in Pakistan-Bangladesh (1971), Sudan (1985–2004), Iran-Iraq (1980–8), Cambodia (1970–80), Vietnam (1960–75), China (1949–75), Germany (1938–45), Soviet Union (1926–53), Korea (1950–3) and Congo wars, more than 1 million people in each were killed.

Untold costs of idiocy

One of the most important elements, in the broadest sense, in economics is cost. A significant portion of economic analysis is devoted exclusively to this concept. An economic transaction is the first necessary step in discerning the meaning of cost. Without economic transactions, there can be no cost. Scholars from ancient times have emphasised different elements of economic transactions. These elements are needs, scarcity and the costs of labour and material in production. These transactions were then divided into just and unjust trade or exchange, which were presented in forms of just or unjust prices. From Aristotle to the medieval scholastic writers this outlook was the single most important concern about economic transactions. In one way or another the father of modern economics, Adam Smith, has tried to update the notion of just price and make it compatible with Newtonian cosmic harmony. Smith's real costs of production in the developed economies are costs of wages, rent and profit. The combination of these costs is denoted by such expressions as "natural price" or "normal price." Over time different types and terms of cost have been added to Smith's list, beginning with total costs that consist of fixed and variable costs. At its very basic level, the cost of land and the tools used in cultivating the land is considered to be the fixed costs, and the labour employed is the variable cost. In modern economic textbooks, the term cost is a much-elaborated concept that entails costs of all factors of productions, resources and the services that are employed in the production of a commodity or a provision of a service. The total cost is defined as all expenses incurred to produce a good or service. The fixed cost is the cost of all inputs that do not vary in production of output in the short run, that is, technology is an example of the fixed cost. In comparison to the fixed cost, variable costs vary with the production of output and labour is an example of a variable cost. In Marxian parlance, these costs are identified as costs of constant capital and variable capital or cost of the dead labour and cost of the living labour.

The marginalist school has introduced another type of cost. This is the marginal cost, which is the change in total cost by producing one extra unit of output. The significance of this type of cost is the point of making decisions and the point at which the firms maximise their profits. According to this school, all rational economic choices are made at the point of margin. A firm's optimising point of production is where marginal cost is equal to the marginal revenue. Opportunity cost is another important form of cost that has been added to the corpus of economic literature. This is the cost of doing one thing instead of carrying out many other activities. Strictly speaking, it is the cost of the next best opportunity and alternative that is given up. Opportunity cost is a central concept in the prevailing bulk of written works in economics. With the rise of welfare economics, the cost has been divided into private and social costs. In this case, it is said the private economic activities may lead to some external costs or benefits. Private costs are costs that are borne by an individual and a firm and the social costs are the extra costs that as a result of the activities of individuals and firms a third party is going to be affected negatively. In this case, it is said as long as the gainers fully compensate the losers the problem of social costs can be resolved. Another cost worth mentioning here is the sunk cost, the expenses that cannot be retrieved.

Total cost, in all its variations, does not include all categories of cost in economics and it can never include all the possible costs for the reason that at any one time there are known costs and there are unknown costs. There are those sets of costs that are palpable and we have clear information of, which are itemised and detailed in the traditional economic theories. These are the explicit costs that are different from the unintended implicit or hidden costs incurred because of our ignorance. It means the body of human knowledge, the depth of our understanding, and the level of our ability, readiness and know-how have not advanced to such a degree to be mindful of such costs.

These types of costs can be carried out with good intention because we see only the benefits but not the unintended consequences of economic activity. There is not much we can do about such costs. The only thing we can do, like in the case of other random elements, is to mitigate the extreme effects of such costs by being prepared for such accidental events. A partial weapon of defence for the unforeseen circumstances is to create a social, economic, legal, cultural and institutional safety net that can stand as the agencies of calamity abatement. To put it succinctly, the most effective safeguard and coping mechanism for the unexpected in this case is the creation of a civil, democratic, open and accountable society that cultivates a framework for the protection of its most affected and vulnerable members. A truly democratic society plays the role of the outer shielding mechanism that serves as a safety net during unexpected difficult times and makes the most of the rainy days.

The purpose of this brief account of costs is to introduce another type of cost that is overlooked in economics entirely. This is a known cost, which is incurred on purpose. The appropriate term to denote this type of cost is the cost of idiocy. Let us paint a clear picture of this type of cost with the current Covid-19 pandemic as a prototype of such costs. The World Health Organisation (WHO) was informed only on 31 December 2019 about this respiratory disease, while several weeks before this date the virus was discovered in Wuhan city in China. Dr Li Wenliang (1985–2020) was the first Chinese ophthalmologist who became alarmed by the seriousness of the disease. Out of good faith, he made the outbreak of the virus public towards the end of December 2019 in a chat room with his former classmates. He alerted them of a mysterious virus and asked them to be vigilant. Dr Li posted his warning about this deadly virus on 30 December 2019. The Chinese communist inquisition summoned him 4 days after Li's warning was posted. Just by coincidence, it was in December that the Catholic Church summoned Galileo Galilei for contradicting the scripture by saying that the earth revolves around the sun. Galileo was put on trial by inquisition on 23 September 1632 and forced to renounce his heliocentric view of the solar system. The condemnation of Galileo has a cost for all humanity. With one glance through Galileo's telescope, the leaders of the Catholic Church could discover the truth. In consequence, they could allow people to have more freedom to think, write and acquire knowledge. All incalculable possible potential that was lost as a result of the restrictions that the inquisition imposed on free thinking and the fear that they created is a cost against human progress. Galileo instead of advancing our knowledge was secluded and barred from thinking and from telling the truth. For fear of facing the same fate the rest of the other unorthodox thinkers kept silent, resulting in unnecessary scientific, social, economic, and political stagnation for decades to come.

Totalitarianism in all its forms is a cost and it develops into a form of cost of idiocy when there is a proven alternative political system that is more rational, humane, democratic, legal, open, accountable, peaceful, all-inclusive and efficient.

This is since human knowledge and understanding, in general, are more advanced than what is permitted in a totalitarian system. So the gap between the potential and what is rationally, humanely, democratically and legally allowed is much greater in a totalitarian system than in a democratic society. Under totalitarian rule, all of the human potentials due to the lack of freedom are not fully and effectively utilised. The tragedy of Dr Li Wenliang and the trial of Galileo Galilei are forms of such a cost that with the least effort could have been avoided. In the case of Galileo, it was enough to observe through his telescope the rotation of the planets and in the case of Dr Li to examine his patients who were suffering from corona symptoms. The cost, human and otherwise, of failing to do so in both cases is beyond measure. The Chinese communist inquisition, on the fourth day of Li posting his warning about the pandemic, summoned Li to their Holy Office and forced him to renounce his warning. Not only was Dr Li was humiliated and forced to deny the plain fact, but he was accused of spreading false rumours and the breach of peace. He was reprimanded and punished for telling the truth. Despite all intimidation and indignities that he suffered from the authorities, Dr Li continued treating patients contracted with the coronavirus. He was infected by the same virus and died at the age of 34 on 7 February 2020.

The human and economic costs of the Covid-19 pandemic are inconceivable. The potential costs simply cannot be measured. About actual costs, we can only have a rough estimate of the human death toll, negative global economic growth, bankruptcies, unemployment, pauperism, the time and resources allocated for combating the pandemic, students missing their education, children losing their parents and many other less pronounced miseries. The Congressional Research Service Report (2021) has estimated the global negative economic growth to be between 3.4 per cent to 7.6 per cent. The Covid-19 death toll worldwide by July 2021 according to the data compiled by Johns Hopkins University is over 4 million people. The pandemic is not over yet and the time it can be brought under control is up in the air. Covid-19 like other pathogenic viruses evolves and adapts to different environments and orientations. The antiviral drugs to treat the virus create new habitats and in the course of resisting drug treatments the virus mutates and develops into new forms to adapt to its changing environment. So, far from its original Chinese strain, it has evolved to several other strains in Britain, South Africa, Nigeria, and India. Had the Chinese authorities paid due attention to Li's stark warning and treated the matter seriously and earnestly and informed the world of the outbreak immediately, the human and economic costs of the pandemic would not have been on such an enormous scale and scope. The virus could have been contained within the original place of the outbreak. The worldwide cost of Covid-19 is rooted in the Chinese totalitarian system. This is a cost that has descended from secrecy, deception and autocratic rule of the present-day Chinese political system. However, such costs are not unique to the Chinese totalitarian regime. All autocratic, theocratic and fascist states bear similar costs in the course of their time in power.

The cost of idiocy presents itself in different forms, in its tragic and comic forms. One of the ludicrously disastrous forms was the 1958–62 Chinese communist party campaign to eliminate sparrows in China. This campaign is known as "smash sparrow." Chairman Mao decreed four pests—flies, mosquitoes, rats and sparrows—to be eradicated because they are causes of many diseases and destroyers of crops. The reason for eradicating sparrows was because they eat off a portion of annual crops. The hysteria of the massacre of sparrows started by shooting sparrows, catching, and killing them, destroying their nests and eggs. The sparrow frenzy massacre depleted China from its sparrows in the subsequent years (Kasambe 2020: 23). As a result of this campaign, other pests, particularly locusts, in absence of their main predator propagated fast and disturbed the ecological balance, which caused greater crops failures in the following years. This, combined with other similar calamitous decisions, was responsible for the subsequent great famine in China that resulted in the deaths of many millions of Chinese people. Slavery, colonialism, subjugation of women, dictatorship, absence of rule of law and equal opportunity are some examples of the cost of idiocy. To be more specific about our examples, we can put the Sykes-Picot agreement (1916) and the partition of India (1947) as very compelling evidence of the cost of this nature that is totally overlooked in economics. Due to these imperial acts many artificial borders were drawn that led to the creation of several Frankenstein states like Syria, Iraq, and Pakistan. These colonial geopolitical structures since their creation have been marred into a downward spiral of bloodshed, militarism, despotism, religious fundamentalism, corruption and poverty. Those powerful states, democratic and undemocratic, that support and maintain such colonial geopolitical structures by either protecting the regimes or backing equally dreadful fundamentalist groups in these countries share the cost of idiocy in such colonial geopolitical structures.

The cost of idiocy transpires in all spheres of life and all strata of society. In this section, we have merely highlighted a few extreme cases. Among similar cases, we can also include all wars in general and the two world wars in particular. If a disagreement, contest, hostility and conflict can be resolved in a rational, humane, democratic, peaceful and moral way then why should one resort to war? Costs borne in this way are costs of idiocy because appropriate means and mechanisms are known and available to us to resolve the problem rationally, democratically and peacefully. In a comparable band of cost of idiocy, we can include the production of nuclear weapons and weapons of mass destruction. Either way, if these weapons are being used or are kept until they become obsolete and then destroyed, they are a cost to society and a waste of scarce resources. In the same league are the destruction of the environment, deforestation, depletion of natural resources, thinning and depletion of the ozone layer and desertification. Parallel to this group but in a different set we have the cost of idiocy when people are prevented from having access to the major advances in science, technology and different ground-breaking advances in other scientific fields. For instance, preventing people from using the internet due to the fear that people will be informed and as a consequence rebel against repression can only prolong despotism. The cost of idiocy in nutshell is the cost that occurs due to preventing economic agents from overcoming a problem in a rational, humane, democratic, legal, open, accountable, and moral, peaceful and efficient manner. As we have the capability and capacity to resolve difficulties in this way, when we resort to other irrational, undemocratic, repressive and deceptive means that involve loss of human life and wasteful use of resources which could have been prevented, we bear the cost out of our folly.

Feat of aggression

Humankind have been searching for food, shelter and safety from one location to another since their beginning. This necessity, over the course of time, formed a variety of human settlements in different parts of the world. The clustered settlements were set against each other in a race for more scarce resources. In this competition the stronger groups defeated the weak to prolong their own survival. But the very act of aggression put the victorious groups at risk of greater insecurity. For the very reason that success in aggression necessitates further aggression, the aggressors always live in a state of perpetual war. Often the ecstasy of being triumphant in a war fosters conceit and calls for higher prizes. So, the impulse of invincibility leads the way for more ambitious conquest. On the opposite side, the fate of defeated communities depends on how many of them are killed, displaced, enslaved or assimilated.

This mode of thought and conduct was the commonly accepted norm till the age of enlightenment. Every relatively stronger community or nationality went to subjugate the weaker ones if they had the power to do so. Conquest and the formation of empires were not just the norm but were highly praised. The conquerors were held in high esteem as great heroes. Their nations were regarded as civilised by the leading religions and the sages of the time for violently defeating and enslaving others. The invaders looked on the timidity to consent to submission as a divine right. The conquerors censured the people of occupied nations as unwise and uncivilised for the very reason of being subjected to invasion and subjugation. In effect, human cruelty and violence was rewarded with the vain notion of superiority.

Every human community has experienced some form of conquest and subjugation in its history. The prevailing notion of imperialism does not admit to this reality. The term is restricted, predominantly, to the characteristics of the European empires. The implications of this presupposition are far reaching, which we shall examine later in this chapter. On this account the world's first empire is said to be the Sargon Empire, which was established about 2250 BC in Mesopotamia (Demand 2011: 89). The empire included the Sumerian cities of the Tigris-Euphrates Delta. After conquering these territories, Sargon went into Syria and to the Taurus and chose Agade (Akkad) as his capital city. The Akkadian empire is named after this city. Numerous empires since then have come and gone but in this book, we confine our study to a few, mainly,

European empires. For this analysis, we mark the date of the rise of modern European empires with Christopher Columbus's discovery of the new world in 1492.

The general characteristics of all empires can be summarised in the use of violence, appropriation of property, forced labour and displacement of natives. Much of empires' wealth is acquired, in effect, from theft. Empires disregard the rights of their subjugated peoples. This was how the ancient empires—the Babylonians, Assyrians, Egyptian, Maya and the Roman—financed their states and armies (Pomeranz and Topik 1999: 147). Certainly, the form and the way different colonial constructions have taken shape have important distinctions and outcomes. However, the essential nature of their exploitation methods and systems of brutality remains similar.

Below we shall look at a few examples of empires that were at their extreme and are reasonably contemporary. We shall begin our brief description of these empires with the Mongol invasions in 13th century. Almost two centuries earlier than the discovery of America, the Mongols raided a vast area in Asia and Europe. They rapidly established their empire across these regions of the world. On one occasion in a matter of five days they transformed the city of Samarkand into a ruin (Grousset 2002: 239). During their brutal conquest, the use of torture was commonplace. Whoever resisted them were blinded with molten silver. The Mongol army killed about 40 million people, 11 per cent of the entire world population at the time (Hinkley 2015: 123).

However, the Mongols' conquest, as violent as it was, was not globally as world-shattering as Columbus's discovery of the new world in 1492. The Spanish empire grew as a result of the exploitation of the new world by plundering mercilessly the new world's precious metals. The conquest decimated just about the entire native population of South America, exterminating the entire indigenous population of the Island of Hispaniola. Over 5 million Native Americans were killed within a period of 3 years (Smith 2015: 108). In Tenochtitlan in 1521, the Spanish invaders massacred about 200,000 Aztecs. One favourable pass-time of the colonists is reported to be burning their victims alive. Another source of their amusement was the head crusher. They placed the head of their victims in the head crusher and then compressed it by a screw until the head of the victim was destroyed. Next to that was the knee-splitter. The knees and legs of the victims were put in this device and were crushed to cripple the victim permanently. The Spanish mercilessly exploited the Aztecs. They enslaved the natives to work around the clock. A typical example of forced labour was in the Cerro Rico peak. The native Indians were gathered in large numbers, about 14 to 16 thousand, to extract silver from the mine. A priest who visited the mine described it as a "portrait of hell" (Pomeranz and Topik 1999: 156–7).

The Portuguese too began their conquests in the 15th century. Their empire spread to South America, Asia and Africa. It was the Portuguese who were the first to initiate the transatlantic slave trade. According to the Transatlantic Slave Trade Database, from the 16th to the mid 19th century, about 12.5 million

Africans were shipped to the new world. About 36 per cent of them were shipped by the Portuguese. More than 5 million slaves died in their colonial escapade. In the first 3 years of the transatlantic slave trade, from every 100 slaves shipped only 30 of them survived (Pomeranz and Topik 1999: 154). Slaves were routinely lashed, assaulted sexually and were burnt with hot wax. The colonised people were forced to convert to Christianity. In Goa (India), the Hindus who refused to convert to Christianity were burnt alive or boiled to death in molten oil. At this juncture, it is necessary we say a few words about the Ottoman Empire, a non-European empire, which was concurrent with the Spanish and Portuguese Empires. The Ottoman Empire reflected the mindset and the deeds of its contemporaries. It was as cruel and merciless as the rest of its competitors. In 1876 when they invaded Bulgaria, they burnt and beheaded at least 5,000 Bulgarian civilians (Clodfelter 2017: 195). Towards the end of the empire, the Ottoman rulers turned against their Christian subjects. Over a period of 3 years, 1915–18, Ottoman colonisers slaughtered up to 2 million of their Armenian subjects (Kelly 2005: 230). This slaughter is characterised as a formal "genocide" by some historians.

The French empire emerged in the 16th century. The death toll just in Napoleonic wars is estimated to be about 5 million people (Malešević 2017). In Haiti, for example, the French colonisers starved their slaves and forced them to wear tin muzzles while collecting sugar cane. Whoever rebelled against their order was roasted over fire. Many were blown into pieces with gunpowder. Others were taken to amphitheatres and were ripped apart by wild dogs. It is alleged that the French imperial authorities on one occasion poisoned 100,000 Haitians with sulphur dioxide gas. Sulphur was extracted from nearby volcanoes (Markham and Zarzeczny 2017).

The Belgium Empire started in the 1880s and lasted until mid-20th century. Within the time frame of 50 years of their colonial rule about 10 million people were killed (Hochschild 2006: 225–33). Belgium's worst atrocities took place at the time of Leopold II (1835–1909). Leopold II ruled from 1865 to 1909. His colonial rule in Congo is characterised by relentless ruthlessness and exploitation. Leopold's army, Force Publique, mobilised the natives and forced them to work to their last breath. Those who disobeyed or could not achieve the quotas assigned to them had their limbs cut off. Summary executions were commonplace across their colony. Local women were sexually assaulted in massive numbers. The Belgium colonialists created the Hutu and Tutsis divide, defining the Hutus as inferior. The Rwanda genocide in the 1990s was very much a legacy of this colonial divide. In this ethnic cleansing at least 800,000 Tutsis perished (Cordell and Wolff 2010: 171).

The emphasis here has been on European Empires. The most powerful empires from the 16th century onwards have been the European empires. There were obviously other empires from outside of Europe. One of them was the Japanese Empire. The Japanese empire was shaped in the mid 19th century. It lasted until its defeat at the end of the Second World War in 1945. It was one of the most brutal empires of all time. Millions of people died under its colonial rule. In their march to Nanking in China the Japanese imperial army killed one-third of the city's population, about 200,000 people (Judgement: International Military Tribunal for the Far East: 1948). They sexually assaulted around 80,000 Chinese women from the age of 8 to 70 years old. After assaulting their victims, they often killed their victims to eliminate the evidence of their terrible crime. Other captives were subjected to an unimaginable pain. Many were soaked in gasoline and burnt alive or used as Guinea pigs in their biochemical warfare research centres. In one of their research units, unit 731, they killed 3,000 people in their ongoing experiments (Kristof 1995). The captives were dissected without the use of anaesthesia, and many prisoners were locked in pressure chambers until their eyes popped out. Others were frozen and then defrosted in boiling water.

The European Empire that outmanoeuvred all its rivals during this period was the British Empire. The British Empire emerged in the 18th century. The British Empire eclipsed its main rivals. The death toll for the British Empire is estimated to be between 100 to 150 million people (Daudi 2014: 181). This figure encompasses the death toll ensued from application of their various colonial policies, ranging from forceful occupation of new territory to civil wars to famine. The British were responsible for one of the deadliest famines of all time in India. At the same time of looting the rice and grain of India, they increased the harvest taxation. This policy eventually resulted in widespread famine. Twenty-five million Indians are estimated to have died during this man-made famine. In the British campaign against the Boer in South Africa at the turn of the 20th century about 10 per cent of the Boer population died in the British concentration camps. In another test of their power in 19th century, British colonisers wiped out virtually the entire Tasmanian male population.

Two other European Empires that are worth being mentioned here were the empires of the Soviet Union and Nazi Germany. They were relatively short-lived empires. Although ideologically they were poles apart, they had a lot in common. In the Soviet Union Empire (1922–89), the most and worst acts of atrocities were committed under Joseph Stalin (1878–1953). Under his regime about 30 to 40 million people were killed (Law 2006: 70). During his forceful policy of collectivisation, Stalin ordered Kulaks and even smaller farmers to give their assets to the state. As people resisted these policies, the state militias seized their grain and other crops and closed the routes, preventing people from transporting their products. This policy soon caused a mass famine. This famine is believed to have resulted in the deaths of approximately 7 million people. Several million people lost their lives in Stalin's labour camps and prisons.

The Empire of Nazi Germany only lasted slightly over a decade from 1933 to 1945. During this period, Germany occupied several European nations and applied their extreme theory of racial purity. Within this short period of time, they constructed 20,000 concentration camps and built the largest number of gas chambers ever seen in human history. By 1941 they were sending about 6,000 people to the Auschwitz gas chambers every day (Harees 2012: 335). They experimented on their prisoners in the cruellest manner imaginable. Many of their victims were frozen to death, others were injected with tuberculosis and malaria. Many were subjected to nerve and limb transplants without anaesthetic. The number of Nazi's victims is estimated to be approximately 30 million people. Out of this figure 6 million were drawn from Europe's Jewish community.

The worst of all possible worlds

The discovery of the new world heralded a new momentum in the predatory conquest of assailable lands and colonies. This was one-of-a-kind aggression and with it a new epoch in human history began. This was the ascendancy of European Empires, which inaugurated the beginning of an era of European world dominance. Spain and Portugal were at the forefront of this war of aggression and acquired great wealth to the detriment of the Native Americans. They used the wealth appropriated from the new world and spent it in the emerging nations of Europe, in Holland, France and England. Squandering the plundered wealth in the latter nations, they embarked on a markedly different mode of production and consumption in both the spending and the producing countries. It installed the foundations of the modern age mass production for mass consumption. The discovery of the new world also set in motion the age-old law of "might is right." With the dominance of this faith and the code of conduct, the world was divided between commanding economic and military powers of Europe. The competition between European imperial nations in seizing and settling in new territories was fierce and very violent. In this contest Britain rose to the very top.

The idea of the inferior and a superior culture was one of many inventions of this period. Any mention of colonialism today immediately but misleadingly conjures up white European nations as the only offenders. This image has been fixed in the minds of those who suffer from guilt by association, those who use it as an instrument of repression and those who are oblivious to contemporary world history. Hidden in this preconceived portrayal of one template form of empire is a gross mistake. The root of this myth goes back to the imperial rulers' depiction of non-Europeans as barbarian people who are incapable of assuming the status of a colonial state. From this misreading of imperialism, a few far-reaching implications will follow. The first implication is that it can grant to the European nations the right of nationhood but not to their ex-colony nations that were artificially divided and incarcerated in somewhat fake borders. In addition, the right of breaking free from subjugation and the exercise of the democratic right of freedom and self-determination implicitly would be restricted to some nations, but not many other nations. The latter nations are the nations that, due to a colonial policy, have been divided arbitrarily. Their borders were drawn against their democratic consent. In view of that, neither the nations subjugated are recognised as being colonised nor are the nations that dominate these nations classified as colonial powers. In other words, the colonial geopolitical constructions, the ones that are inherited from the European empires, are sanctioned as binding for the fact that they exist.

We have already pointed to legacy of colonisation of the new world and subsequent decimation of Native American nations. Two other constructions, among other colonial constructions, worthy of mention to qualify our argument are the colonial boundaries drawn in Africa and in the Middle East. Robert L. Paarlberg blames the ongoing violence and conflicts in Africa to the artificial boundaries that were drawn by the European colonial powers. The boundaries south of the Sahara were drawn at the Berlin conference in 1885 (Oppong 2006: 35). The European colonial powers drew these boundaries and divided the region with total disregard to the ethnic, national, cultural and linguistic composition of the native people. Paarlberg purports that "the boundaries were drawn for the purpose of avoiding a war between European colonizers, not to preserve peace among Africans" (Paarlberg 1999: 508). These boundaries were kept almost untouched after the European colonial powers left the region from the 1960s onwards.

The Middle East's map too was defined by the European colonial powers. It is a work of arbitrary dissection and dismemberment of the nations of this region. The European imperial powers drew the map to serve their needs at the time. The current map has contributed much to instability, wars and the development of Islamic extremism in the region (Kirazli 2016: 124). In a secret agreement, the leading imperial powers planned and engineered the political geography of the Middle East. They disregarded completely the topography, demography, national and cultural identities of the peoples of the region. When the occasion arose, they exploited such divisions to the full. When the Ottoman Empire was on the verge of collapse, the British, French and Russian imperial powers cunningly aimed to take full advantage of the situation. In a secret plan in November 1915, the Franco-British-Russian pact produced the blueprint for the Middle East. It aimed to secure their sphere of control over the region. The agreement was signed in 1916 and was named after the British and the French negotiators, Mark Sykes (1879–1919) and Francois Georges-Picot (1870–1951) respectively. The agreement came to be known as the "Sykes-Picot Agreement." This secret treaty was exposed by the Bolsheviks after the October 1917 revolution in Russia (Goldschmidt 1991: 190). The division of the Kurdish nation and its annexation by different colonial forces is a by-product of this agreement.

To have a more accurate understanding of the detrimental implications of arbitrary borderlines we have taken two case studies as the representation of these colonial geopolitical structures. The two countries that are discussed here are Iran and Pakistan. The main reason for selecting these two countries as typical colonial constructions is the author's direct affiliation with and his continuous study of these two countries for several decades. The borders of both countries were drawn after the world wars. The borders of Iran, then Persia, were drawn after the First World War and Pakistan was created after the Second World War. The British Empire had a great deal to do with the creation of these borders. Borders often change, either in the beginning or the end of empires. For this reason, the beginning and the end of empires tend to be the most savage and turbulent phases of the life cycle of empires. The beginning is marked with aggression and the end with demolition. Disaster looms at both ends of their life cycle. Usually, the bigger the empire the greater the mayhem it creates and the damage that it is responsible for. The British Empire was one of the largest empires the world has ever seen. Consequently, its negative legacy can be detected in numerous regions around the world.

Iran acquired its current shape in the 1920s. In the early 1920s the Persian king, Ahmad Shah was overthrown and Reza Khan Mir-panj assumed monarchical power. Reza Mir-panj (1878–1944) was an illiterate man (Cordesman 1999: 21). He was born in a village in Mazandaran but left his village and went to Tehran where he worked as a horse handler. As a stableman, he was employed to take care of the horses of the European commissioners in Tehran (Ludington Daily News 1926, 26 April).

The British considered the collapse of the Qajar dynasty and the disintegration of the Persian Empire as a major threat to their interests in the region. Another threat arose because of the Bolsheviks seizing the power in Russia. The British believed that India was under serious risk from the expansion of the Bolsheviks to central Asia. The prospect of the disintegration of the Persian Empire and the formation of several republics was a very palpable possibility then. The alliance of the liberated Iranian republics with the Soviet Union, by the same token, was expected and feared. The pace of events in these parts of the world alarmed the British. The British rulers needed a strong and ruthless individual to protect their interests in Iran. They assigned this duty to Reza Khan Mir-panj. By this time Reza Khan was a senior military officer in Ahmad Shah Qajar's defence force. In the British orchestrated coup d'état of 21 February 1921, Reza Khan ascended to the highest political power (Gholi Majd 2001). His rise to power was as the commander in chief of the army first, then the commander of the army and minister of war and finally, on 12 December 1925, he was enthroned as the King of Persia (Rieffer-Flanagan 2013: 19).

Reza Khan's vision of a political system was a "one man system" (Adel, Elmi and Taromi-Rad 2012: 15). To discard his humble past, he selected the pseudo surname of "Pahlavi." The term is taken from the language of ancient Persia. This deception was an attempt to connect his lineage to ancient Persian kingdoms and dynasties. After consolidating his power, Reza Khan turned his imperial ambitions to the neighbouring nations. He invaded several independent nations including Baluchistan, Kurdistan, Azerbaijan, Al-Ahwaz, and Turkmenistan. These invasions and wars were completed by the early 1930s.

In a work of this scope, we cannot survey in full the invasion and colonisation of all these nations by Reza Khan. To serve the main task of this book we have selected one nation and have briefly described the sequence of events that led to its colonisation. This history will corroborate our hypothesis that was stated previously. The example we have selected is the Baluch nation. Baluchistan is the homeland of the Baluch nation. The total area of Baluchistan is about 560,000 square kilometres. The British Imperial army invaded the independent state of Baluchistan on 13 November 1839. Subsequently, by drawing two arbitrary lines, the British divided Baluchistan into three parts. The first line, the Goldsmid Line, was drawn by Maj. General F. J. Goldsmid (1818–1909) in 1871, and the British granted western Baluchistan to Persia. That said, the British kept the eastern part of Baluchistan under their own control. The second arbitrary line, the Durand Line, was drawn by Henry Mortimer Durand (1850–1924) in 1893. This line is known as the Duran Line. Author Henry McMahon (1862–1949), another British official extended this line in 1904. As result of this line a segment of the northern part of Baluchistan was granted to Afghanistan.

The Qajar rulers of Iran upheld their colonial authority over western Baluchistan up until the outbreak of the First World War. By this time, the balance of power shifted in the favour of the Baluch rulers. The British acknowledged this and officially recognised Bahram Khan and later his nephew Dost Mohammed Khan as the de facto rulers of western Baluchistan. In a report by J. Ramsay on 25 January 1927, he describes Baluch sentiment towards the occupying forces as follows:

> there is not a vestige of Persian authority existing, nor has Persia any means of asserting her theoretical claims to sovereignty over an area in which Persians are aliens and . . . are detested by the people [Baluch] . . . Not only has the country under discussion [western Baluchistan] slipped out of Persian grasp, it has been so hostile to Persia.
>
> (quoted from Breseeg 2004: 185)

Reza Khan was inspired by the German Nazi's belief in in racial purity and by the founder of modern Turkey, Mustafa Kemal Ataturk's (1862–1949), policy of forced assimilation of non-Turkish nations in Turkey in aiding his political ideology. He became a close ally of fascist Germany (Goldschmidt 1991: 213). Driven by the racist belief of the fascist cult, Reza Khan renamed Persia to Iran on 21 March 1935. The designate, Iran, means the land of Aryan race. The choice of this designate then was firmly grounded in the fascist's notion of Aryans as being the superior master race compared to other nationalities and communities.

The monarchy in Iran was toppled in 1979, and the masses suddenly erupted into open revolt against the Pahlavi dynasty. The Shia clergy took advantage of the power vacuum and of the sudden outpouring of mass rage against the old system. In deposing the Shah, Ruhollah Khomeini (1902–89) assumed the leadership of revolution in Iran. Amid the heat of the revolution, Khomeini promised the public to end political repression, cronyism and poverty in Iran. He promised freedom of thought, economic prosperity and justice. On 24 January 1979 in his reply to Diana Johnstone about political freedom including expression of anti-religious views and communist political parties, Khomeini promised that in his Islamic state everyone "would be free to express his own ideas and to decide his own destiny" (Johnstone 2002: 262). Khomeini promised free oil to be brought at peoples' doorsteps, free electricity, water, and transportation (Noraiee 2011: 50). But after assuming political power, he did not only not fulfil his promises, but his rule was the start of a new dark age in Iran. Not long after the revolution, Khomeini called those who demonstrated for freedom and justice "wild animals" who deserve to be executed and burnt in public (Baqer 2000: 219). Khomeini, in his speech on 24 August 1979, said that people's priority should not be economics. Because economics is "for donkeys."

Political executions in Iran under the Islamic regime just for the period of 1979 to 2003 are estimated at 11,000 individuals (Keddie 2003: 370), which is way below the actual number. In one of Khomeini's orders in 1988 it is said that about 30,000 political prisoners were decimated (Lamb 2001). According to Hussein-Ali Montazeri (1922–2009), who was Khomeini's successor prior to his protest to this massacre, within 2 weeks of enactment of Khomeini's order 3,800 political prisoners were executed in Iran (Lamb 2001). The number of political prisoners killed extra-judicially or under torture can never be known. The Islamic regime instigated the war with Iraq which lasted for 8 years, from September 1980 to August 1988. The cost of the war was enormous for the whole region. For Iran it is estimated about 1,050,000 to 1,930,000 dead and economic costs of about 69 billion dollars. In case of Iraq the death toll is said to be around 550,000 to 1,040,000 and the economic costs about 159 billion dollars (Murray and Woods 2014: 242). Over 4 million Iranians have left Iran over the past four decades (Axworthy 2017: 1981). The exodus of most learned and skilled members of society has crippled the entire fabric of social, political, economic, legal and cultural order in Iran. In the last four decades Iran has progressively been infested with chronic corruption, cronyism, religious fundamentalism, mismanagement, continuous purge of any rational dissent and ceaseless trampling on human rights.

The best time in the Pahlavi regime was from 1960 to 1976. During this period economic growth per annum on average in Iran was 9.8 per cent. For the same period the consumer price index was 5.7 per cent and per capita income increased by 7 per cent. In the year that the Shah's regime was deposed, in March 1979, $1 exchanged to 7 Tomans. For most of 2019 the exchange rate was $1 for over 10,000 Tomans. The official inflation rate has on average been in two-digits. Not to mention the costs of the regime's other misadventures such as billions of dollars being spent every year for the last four decades in spreading Shia fundamentalism in Iraq, Syria, Yamen, Lebanon, Bahrein, Afghanistan, Pakistan and many other countries.

The ruling clerics of Iran and their disciples dream of the creation of a Shia Empire. For that purpose, they have tried to organise an army of "20 million soldiers of Islam." To achieve this aim, the ruling clerics have encouraged high birth rates and within a short period of time the population of Iran more than doubled. The total population of Iran in 1979 was about 37 million and it increased to over 80 million after three decades. According to the 2018 Misery Index, Iran was number 15 out of 126 as the most miserable and according to Transparency International 2017 it is ranked at 130 out of 175 most corrupt countries in the world.

Iran is a colonial construction. Both regimes, the monarchy and the Islamic, have dealt very harshly with other non-Persian nationalities in Iran. The Baluch in western Baluchistan have been one of these colonised nations that have borne the brunt of this policy. Mahmud Khalatbary, then foreign minister of Shah, in 1977 openly admitted the Persian colonial policy in Baluchistan. In an interview with S. Harrison, he described his government policy towards the Baluch nation, and stressed that Baluch have always wanted "to create their own independent state." So, it has been the Iranian regime policy to keep the Baluch "as politically weak, disunited, and as backward as possible" (Harrison 1981: 159).

Discrimination against minority groups and nationalities is considerably far worse under the Islamic regime of Iran than under the former regime. Any democratic demands by the minority nationalities and groups are treated not just as an existential threat to the Islamic government but also as a threat of disintegration of Iran. A few examples suffice to demonstrate the way the Islamic regime treats the Baluch. According to Amnesty International reports for the period 2004 to 2009, the number of executions in Iran were about 1,481 individuals. This number at the time was out of the total population of Iran of 75 million people. During the same period, about 800 Baluch nationals were killed in western Baluchistan. The trend of the most historical data about the population of western Baluchistan suggests a figure of 3 million. Taking 3 million as the closest rough estimation of the Baluch population within the boundary of Iran, it follows then for the same period, 55 per cent of all executions in Iran were from western Baluchistan. This was the highest number of executions per population for this period in the world (Karimzadi 2015: 80). The Islamic regime also executed the entire adult male population of several Baluch villages in Iran. The vice president for women and family affairs of the Islamic regime, Shahindokht Molaverdi, confirmed this mass murder for only one of those villages in Baluchistan (The Guardian 2016, 26 February). After one year in power, the Islamic regime seized complete political power and banned all its political opponents. The regime crushed all political, human and civil rights organisations all over Iran including in Baluchistan. Most members of these organisations have either been arrested and imprisoned or executed or have left the country. Yaqub Mehernahad, a 28-year-old Baluch journalist, was the first blogger to be hanged in the world. The blog that he was running was granted the right and in Persian parts of the country running a similar blog was a normal activity. But Mehernahad was arrested in May 2007 and after enduring many months of torture was hanged on 4 August 2008.

As for eastern Baluchistan, the wheel of fortune turned against them in 1948. A combination of circumstances led to eastern Baluchistan regaining its independence from Britain on 11 August 1947. The news of Baluchistan's independence was reported in the *New York Times* on 12 August 1947. Eight months after this date, on 26 March 1948, the Pakistan army invaded eastern Baluchistan (Baloch 1975). Ever since, the Pakistani army have conducted five nationwide military operations in Baluchistan. These took place in 1948, 1958, 1962, 1973–7 and 2002.

Baluchistan is another familiar casualty of British colonial policy. British attempts to defend their crown jewel from the emerging Russian empire followed by its many spillover effects. One of these ill effects was recolonisation of eastern Baluchistan. The British knew well enough that leaving India was equal to the end of their empire. Thus, British rulers wilfully disfigured India and left it ruined. No wonder that we have the adverse after-effects of British policy lingering to this day. To hold back the Indian liberation movement, on 20 December 1906, the British and their Indian collaborators set up a religious political party by the name of the Muslim League. The first article of the party reads that the main goal of the party is "to promote among the Mussalmans (Muslims) of India, feelings of loyalty to the British government" (quoted from Ikram 1992: 99). The close collaboration of British colonial rulers with the elites of Indian Muslims was a key factor in perpetuating British colonial rule in India and in dividing India. But the events of the two world wars weakened British colonial power significantly and tipped the balance in favour of the United States and the Soviet Union power. The end of the Empire was imminent, and Winston Churchill (1874–1965) was anxious about the growing influence of the Soviet Empire around the world, in particular in Asia. The British rule in India for Churchill was not just a necessity for saving the empire but it was a natural thing to do. Indians, in his eyes, were incapable of governing themselves, and he believed if "India is granted freedom, power will go to the hands of rascals, rogues [and] freebooters" (quoted from Sharma 2012: 314).

Indeed, no colonial power wishes to terminate its colonial rule by choice. One hallmark of the dying empires is their last raid and ransack of the colony that they are forced to flee from. The deadliest empires are those which are at end of their lives. It is when they leave behind their most atrocious legacies. In case of the British Empire, it was the partition of India and the creation of the Frankenstein Islamic state of Pakistan. The declassified British government secret files are the witness of this very fact. The British aimed to divide India for no other reason but to inflict as much harm as possible to free India. The harm could have not been any greater than dividing India on religious grounds. The classified military documents made public in 1988 show that the British government was expecting a full-scale war with Russia at the end of the Second World War. In laying the groundwork for war Churchill ordered a series of secret plans under the code name of "Operation Unthinkable." The British were also worried that an independent India would not allow Britain to use India for their political and military influence in the region. The "War Cabinet-Top Secret-Post-Hostilities Planning," from 1945 shows that Churchill believed giving independence to the whole of India would be tantamount to giving the whole of Asia to Soviet Union dominance. In view of that he ordered to "keep a bit of India" (quoted from Herman 2008: 545).

A bit of India that they had in mind was those parts of India with the majority of the Muslim population. Pakistan, therefore, was an end product of this policy. The tag "Pakistan" was coined in the 1930s. It was an idle fancy of an Indian Muslim student while he was studying English literature in Cambridge. The term is deeply offensive. It has no foundation and does not designate any nationality. Choudhary Rahmat Ali (1897–1951), born in Balachaur India, invented the term in 1933. The term is borrowed from Iranian languages. It literally means the "land of the clean people." The intention and thought behind it is extremely xenophobic and loaded with racial and religious hatred. The crucial thing to understand about designates such as Pakistan and Iran is the political, social and historical settings in which these terms were invented. The decade that these terms were used was the decade of the ascendency of fascism in Europe. It was a period which witnessed a battle of ideological and religious fanaticism. The spectre of fascism was sweeping all over the landscape of Europe and beyond. The advocates of Iran and Pakistan were immersed deeply in fascist ideology. The fundamentalist Muslims admired the fascist racist creed in the 1930s (Payne 1995: 352).

In their very hasty exit, the British set up a commission and assigned Cyril Radcliffe (1899–1977) to divide India in the name of Islam. Radcliffe knew almost nothing about India, and the complexity of the task that was assigned to him. The two provinces of India that were the subject of dispute were the provinces of Bengal and Punjab. Radcliffe arrived in India on 8 July 1947 and drew the boundary lines in these provinces on 15 August 1947. The Commission responsible for the partition was composed of two members from the Muslim side of east Bengal (Abu Saleh Mohamed Akram and S. A. Rahman). From the western side of Bengal (the Indian side) the commission consisted of C. C. Biswas and B. K. Mukherji. On the Punjab side the commission consisted of Din Mohamed and Muhammad Munier from western Muslim part. From the eastern, Indian part there were Mehr Chand Mahajan and Teja Sing. East Bengal and west Punjab were thousands of miles apart. The representatives of these provinces could not agree on any point, and in the end Radcliffe dictated the boundary lines of partition of the relevant provinces.

M. A. Jinnah (1876–1948), leader of the Muslim League, opposed creation of a separate state for Indian Muslims so long as the British establishment was sure of their stay in India. The unequivocal British decision about leaving India heartened Jinnah's demand to go down the line of breaking India. With such powerful backup Jinnah dismissed any sensible suggestion or compromise between him and other Indians who were against the partition. Those who negotiated the terms of partition with Jinnah found him as a man bereft of reason and humanity. Jawaharlal Nehru (1889–1964) described him as a man short of a "civilised mind" (quoted from Khilnani 2009: 267). Mahatma Gandhi (1869–1948) called him a "maniac" and "an evil genius" (Ghose 1991: 319). Lord Louis Mountbatten (1900–79), the last viceroy of British India, called him "a psychopathic case" (Ray 2011: 16).

The partition of India in August 1947 has led to, if not the largest but one of the largest, forced mass migrations in human history. The people of the same nation went for slaughtering each other in the most vicious way. The estimate of civilian deaths is about one and a half million. In addition, 12 million people are believed to have been uprooted from their birthplaces (Bulliet et al. 2015: 619). Let us take the city of Karachi as an example to show the dimension and scale of this mass displacement. The population of Hindus in Karachi, the first capital city of Pakistan, pre-partition totalled about 48 per cent. After the partition it has been reduced to less than 1.5 per cent. Partition led to widespread murder, rape and arson. Armed mobs marched back and forth hacking to death those with different religious beliefs. The "pregnant women had their breasts cut off and babies hacked out of their bellies, infants were found literally roasted on spits" (Hajari 2015: xviii). The very essence of the state of Pakistan was moulded in the middle of all these atrocities during the partition.

The Punjabi Muslims are as much Indians as Sikh and Hindu Punjabis. Drawing an arbitrary line between them does not miraculously make them two separate nations. Moreover, Islam is not a nation. Islam is merely a religion, which has many sects. Conversion to Islam is not coequal to creation of a new nation. But this is what the Punjabi army, political and religious establishment from west Punjab have used to justify the creation of Pakistan and their colonial power over other nations under their domination. With this background, Pakistan cannot be anything but a continuous succession of violence, Islamic fundamentalism, poverty, corruption, militarism and war. From the first day of its existence, Pakistan launched its first war against India in 1947. It also instigated the 1965, 1971, 1999, 2001/02 and 2019 wars with India.

The antagonism between the two founding wings of Pakistan, the west Punjab and east Bengal, began in the first year of creation of this state. The conflict came to its head in January 1971. In the General Election of Pakistan that year the east Bengalis won the election. Out of 300 total seats, east Bengal won 162 of the seats, 54 per cent of the total votes. The Punjabis, with less than 30 per cent of the votes, prevented the Bengalis from forming the government. General Yahya Khan, the head of the Pakistan army and the state, in his February 1971 conference, threatened the Bengalis with grave consequences if they did not concede to his terms. He said in case Bengalis do not concede to his orders "kill three million of them" (Payne 1973: 50). This is what the Punjabi army of Pakistan did in East Bengal, then East Pakistan. Within a period of 267 days the Punjabi army of West Pakistan killed about 1,247,000 Bengalis in East Bengal (Rummel 1994: 331). One weapon of the Punjabi troops of Pakistan to subdue the Bengali resistant movement was gang rape. The number of Bengali women being raped during the same period is estimated to be about 200,000 to 400,000 women (Brownmiller 1993: 81–3).

Bangladesh, East Pakistan, broke away from Pakistan in September 1971. After their defeat in East Bengal, the Pakistan army have turned their guns against the Sindhi, Pashtun and Baluch nations. Pashtun society, under the colonial rule of Punjabi Muslim rulers of Pakistan, has regressed to medieval times, into one of most violent and apocalyptic territory that one can imagine. The Pakistan army have turned the Pashtun areas to their workshop where they groom their Jihadist crusaders and export them all over the world. This is where the idea of Taliban was conceived, born, nurtured and thrived. All Jihadist groups, predominantly though by no means completely, including Al-Qaeda and the Taliban have been mobilised, trained and armed under the umbrella of the Pakistan army. There are more than 50 different Islamic extremist groups that work under their protection. Many of these groups are set for specific purposes (Palmer and Palmer 2008: 128). Bin laden, the notorious leader of Al-Qaeda, was found and killed near a military compound in Punjab on 2 May 2011.

It is more important to know that the Baluch case, compared to other nationalities in Pakistan, is entirely different. The Baluch nation is one of the Iranian nations. Besides, Baluchistan was an independent entity and after the British occupied Baluchistan, Baluch continuously fought against British colonialism. For which purpose, soon after the First World War, they organised political parties to regain their independence through legal means. Baluch fell victim to their own naiveté. They wanted to resolve the Baluch issue through colonial legal means. To this end they hired an Indian lawyer in 1936. The lawyer in question was M. A. Jinnah. Jinnah defended Baluchistan's case for over 10 years and signed the Standstill Agreement on 4 August 1947, endorsing Baluchistan independence (Siddiqi 2012: 59). The agreement was signed by the representatives of Britain, Baluchistan and the forthcoming state of Pakistan. Following this the British left eastern Baluchistan and Baluch declared their independence on 11 August 1947, the news of which was reported in the *New York Times* on 12 August 1947.

Pakistan, the first ever Islamist state, was created on 14 August 1947. A few months after its making Pakistan invaded the independent state of Baluchistan in March 1948. Baluch launched a campaign of resistance from the first day of occupation, which continues to the present day. Pakistan so far has carried out, as noted earlier, five major military operations in Baluchistan to pacify the Baluch struggle for independence. From the very beginning of occupation of Baluchistan, the Pakistan army has targeted the most informed, secular, conscientious and educated section of Baluch society. Subsequently, thousands of Baluch have been arrested, imprisoned, disappeared, displaced and killed. During the 1973–7 conflict, Pakistan deployed more than 90,000 of its troops in Baluchistan to crush the Baluch war of liberation. The armed conflict between the Baluch and Pakistan ended with over 25,000 Baluch being killed and hundreds of thousands were either internally displaced or sought sanctuary in Afghanistan and the Gulf states (Karimzadi 2015).

From 2001 to 2013, according to the Voice for Baluch Missing Persons (VBMP) about 18,000 Baluch were abducted and disappeared by the Pakistani military. Out of this number, it is estimated, 2,000 of them were killed (Nazish 2014, 6 January). Pakistan also tested their nuclear bombs in Baluchistan on 28

May 1998. Five tests were carried out in the Koh Kambaran range and Chaghai hills. The sixth test was on 28 May 1998. These tests have contaminated a vast area of Baluchistan with toxic nuclear radiation. The vicinity is under total control of the Pakistan army. So far, there has not been any independent study of the effects of these tests.

Nations such as the Baluch and Kurdish nations share a common plight. They are the casualty of colonialism. In their existing socioeconomic order, their progress is undeniably impeded if not totally debilitated by being colonised. Past and present colonialism has paralysed and blocked their potential development. The most elemental fact about such nations is that their future is shaped and conducted into two opposite directions. The course along which these nations are ushered is set off by two exogenous monocratic authorities. Initially, European empires conquered, divided and ruled these nations. This has altered and retarded their natural process of progress and evolution. The fate of all stateless nations is sealed in this deep-seated misdeed. The second exogenous catalytic agent that aggravates the situation and has sanctified the present order as eternal is the existing artificial colonial geopolitical constructions that these nations are willy-nilly annexed to. The choices for such nations are seriously restricted.

These nations are the hostages of the prevailing world order; sanctified norms sanctioned by the mainstream ideologies, misinformation shrouded in the cult of irrationality and vested interest be it political, economic or in the military arena. Baluch and other stateless nations are compelled in their selection of a panacea to have the worst of all possible worlds. In the realm of possibilities, their choices are restricted to either fight or regain their freedom or gradually degenerate and being crushed under forces of colonialism and subjugation. In the existing quasi-legitimised international political order, there are too many artificial states. The share of the world's land and the population living within these borders is quite extensive (Alesina, Matuszeski and Easterly 2011). These spurious countries are colonial geopolitical constructions that live in a permanent state of social, political, economic, and cultural instability and crisis. The nations that suffer the most under these artificial boundaries are scarcely prioritised and discussed in mainstream economics. All schools of mainstream economics dwell in a parochial world, a world that legitimises the existing international political order and a world that is compatible with the interests of the developed countries. Here the criteria of truth are seriously subverted. Preconceived assumptions and theories have taken the place of the facts. Many intricate and distant facts and relations are coloured to hide the reality. Not only has the open and impartial inquiry lost its meaning but also pseudo-reality on such issues is regarded as a settled norm of conduct. This view is widespread in economics. No fact, data, idea and conclusion can be considered reliable and valid if the bases of existing colonial geopolitical construction are dismissed out of hand. Any theory that is content with the existing colonial geopolitical order and does not include factors cited previously objectively in its analysis will fail to explain the true state of permanent social, political instability in these fake boundaries.

Conclusion

We live in a chaotic world because the chain of cause and effect is interminable. The world is unpredictable and is constantly changing. Every moment in time is pregnant with unknowns. We will never have social, economic, cultural, political and legal systems that are perfect. A significant part of the world even today is still under the sway of colonial geopolitical construction of the past empires. Political entities that are invented by empires can never be free of violence and suffering. Religion is still a commanding destructive force in the world. Blaise Pascal (1623–62) pointed out the destructive power of religion by saying that "men never do evil so completely and so cheerfully as when they do it in the name of their religion" (Pascal 2018: 171).

We do not live in an ideal world. There are millions of people worldwide who are unemployed or have no access to the most basic means of subsistence. Many millions are forced to flee from persecution or in search of a better life. The economy and institutions of most nations are either under-utilised or they are grossly inefficient. By virtue of the fact that modern economies are the legacy of the past empires and their arbitrary division of the world, the distribution of resources is gravely unjust. For instance, about 20 per cent of the world's richest people "consumes over 70% of the world's commercial energy" (Costanza et al. 1997: 14).

Science and technology by their very nature are dynamic. New innovations and discoveries lead to more innovations and discoveries. The practice is a self-propelling process. The more scientific innovations and discoveries we have the faster will be the pace of scientific achievements. That may be so, but technological progress makes the old technologies also obsolete. This is the very point that J. A. Schumpeter described as the process of "creative destruction" (Schumpeter 1994: 83). This cycle of creative destruction is endless. In the course of time with the greater spread and accumulation of knowledge, this process will accelerate too. Progress and change cannot be halted. Alongside the acceleration and accumulation of human knowledge arises the paradox of the dearth of knowledge in the midst of the ocean of information. Individual knowledge progressively will be reduced to particulars in the ever-expanding ocean of knowledge.

It should be borne in mind that we are forever at the mercy of the forces of nature. The earth is in perpetual turmoil. At any moment in time many parts of the earth are either too cold or too hot. Many countries experience devastating hurricanes, floods or droughts or political and social instability. The danger of the cosmic commotions from meteorite and comets always looms over our heads. The earth's climate has oscillated from one extreme to another extreme over the years. The earth will never be free of deviations in the earth's crust, earthquakes, volcanic eruptions, damaging winds, drought and water shortage, hurricanes and floods, thunderstorms and tornadoes, hail and ice storms, landslides, wildfires, sinkholes and tsunamis, pestilence and many other unexpected events.

In addition, human actions have precipitated the pace of change in the natural world. People are responsible for overexploitation of natural resources, destruction of habitats and the extinction of many species. Mass deforestation has destroyed the habitats of unknown numbers of animals, birds, insects and plants. The increasing loss of biodiversity will have irreversible effects. The effects of global warming from the burning of fossil fuels and depletion of ozone are far-reaching. The global warming will cause the earth's temperature to rise. That will precipitate climate change. This could lead to the destruction of vegetation, wildlife, melting of polar-ice caps and the prospect of bigger and more violent hurricanes and floods. The depletion of the ozone layer will allow the UV rays from Sun to enter the earth's atmosphere. The UV rays are very harmful to humans, plants and animals. UV Rays cause non-melanoma skin cancer, damage eyes (eye cataract and snow blindness), and weaken and impair the immune system. The impact of these effects on social, political and economic arenas are incalculable.

Besides all these activities there are unintended consequences of human actions. These actions can broadly be divided into two distinctive categories. In the first category are production of arms in general that are used in wars, which are patently destructive or are kept and then destroyed. That means they are wasted. There are all sorts of weapons. Among them are weapons of mass destruction—the chemical, biological and nuclear weapons. These weapons are very expensive to produce. When used they cause mass devastation and if kept, they become obsolete. Either way the capital invested in such weapons is wasted. The effects of these weapons on polluting the environment are also long lasting and costly. In the second category is the consequences of well-intended actions. For example, consequences of genetic engineering. Besides many advantages of genetic engineering, it also has its side effects. The effects of chemical pollution eventually decay and disappear, but the same thing is not applicable to genetic pollution. In the latter case, it stays and multiplies forever (Ausubel and Harpignies 2004). Above all, introduction of new species and new plants through genetic engineering could be the bearer of new diseases or being susceptible to much mundane bacteria or viruses that could modify and transform them into more deadly ones later.

Therefore, when we delve into the real world, we observe a state of disorder everywhere. We live in a state of permanent disorder. Granted that everything is changing, there can be no fixed, eternal, immutable and indestructible things that can be frozen in time perpetually. That being understood, we can infer that the notion that all can rest in equilibrium is unthinkable and counterintuitive. Bearing this in mind, that everything is in a perpetual state of motion, then change and fixed order cannot be compatible and reconciled with one another. The two stand opposite of each other. Recognising all this, in the last analysis, necessitates a complementary constituent. Simply put, an isolated change does not exist. All changes take place in connection to other things. Change, therefore, is universal.

Things are neither isolated nor free from motion. Moreover, there is infinite diversity of things, motions and interdependency and interconnection of processes that cause the continuous change that is prevailing. Everything is bound by the conditions of existence, an infinite process of interdependent relationships. Under these conditions of existence things come into being and go out of being. New things are conceived, develop, born, decay and die. The potency of change is embedded in every phenomenon. It is of profound importance to discern the inner process of self-motion and change. The cycle of change is eternal. Each change in the cycle is neither identical nor orderly. Nothing remains the same. Therefore, we have a constant process of eruption, evolution and development. How can it be otherwise? The occurrence of change is recognised by all economists. In general, they all confirm those changes that we have explored in this chapter. What has been said in respect to both the natural and social world is not incompatible with much of what has been written about economics. Although this proposition may sound too obvious. Nevertheless, it is included and accounted for in the most general terms in all schools of thought in economics. In light of this general confirmation of change we can conclude that all schools of thought in economics share the theory of permanent disorder in economic and social development. This theme will form the subject matter of the next chapter.

2 Permanent economic disorder

Introduction

No writer about economics, in the past or at the present, has endorsed in a complete manner the economic organisation of his or her time. There has never been a system of production and distribution that has been unanimously approved by all economists. Likewise, no sound economist, hitherto, has accepted an economic system as the most perfect and ideal system to be preserved in its entirety for eternity. Far from it. The belief in a perfect economic system is ill-founded. A perfect economic system is essentially a delusion. All pioneering economists have responded to what they considered to be the symptomatic of the crucial problems of the economic system of their time. The original thinkers questioned the conventional arrangements as well as the prevalent economic ideas. They have never taken for granted the existing economic organisation as the most perfect and ideal arrangements that must be kept intact forever. Neither have the features of the system that the prevailing belief beheld as unassailable been the initial inducement to entice their ground-breaking writings. The attempt to refute the conventional wisdom and escape from the old ideas is evidence to the contrary.

Irrespective of their political, ideological or religious persuasion and irrespective of the time of their writings, all serious economists' writings are triggered by what they regard as the defects of the system. This reaction stems from two opposite directions. One is from the perspective of defending the status quo. This approach is driven by the belief that the alternative will be damaging or unworkable. The other approach derives from the perspective of desiring to radically change the economic system altogether. In either case the centrepiece of both perspectives, implicitly and explicitly, begins with the issue of economic disorder. By underlining the drawbacks of the system, they attempt to define solutions either to defend or reject the prevailing economic system. Either way, the economic reality is incompatible with their beliefs. The purpose of pointing out the drawbacks of the economic system is also professed from two contrasting outlooks. One inclines to reform the system and the other to dismantle and replace it.

DOI: 10.4324/9781003346364-3

In this sense economics is the science of economic disorder. It is about discerning and managing economic disorders. Economic disorders are the symptoms from which economic theories are extracted, articulated and prescribed. After all, economic disorder is a permanent state of order of every known economy. No economy operates in its full capacity. No economy is characterised by complete efficiency. Furthermore, no economy is fortified within the walls of total harmony and order. Constant change results in disorder. Being habituated to the contrary belief would impede our reasoning by a multitude of errors. That is not all. This is by no means as simple as it sounds. Although this description contributes to a better direction to economic inquiry, this cannot by itself be taken to imply a causal relationship. From this perspective we can form a clearer vision upon which we can base our judgement of economic inquiry. Thus, it has been the perpetual presence of economic disorders that has inspired and sustained creative studies in economics.

In this chapter and next chapter, we shall show that economic disorder is a common theme that is shared in the writings of all critical economists. We shall show that economic disorder is a permanent condition. Economics in its true sense of the word means endless disorders. It is only in a utopian economic system that we can envisage a society that is unified, orderly and in total harmony. Only in a utopian model does an economy operate in total optimum efficiency. At no time in history have we been free from economic disorders, and we will never be free from them in the future.

This chapter is divided into four sections. Section one poses the argument as to whether there has ever been or there will ever be an economy that could feasibly be defined as perfect. It fosters the idea that perfect efficiency cannot be applied in an existing economy. A perfect economy does not exist, and it will never be materialised. The best of all possible worlds' economy is a utopian ideal that we can envisage in our imagination but cannot put into practice. The second section of the chapter examines ancient economic thought and economic disorder. Ancient economic thoughts are very sketchy. Such considerations were prompted by the economic problems that authors of the ancient world perceived and reflected in their writings. In section three, we shall discuss the canonical teaching in economics and the transition from ecclesiastic economics to the secular teaching of the real-world economy. In this section we shall also discover that what prompted these authors to write about the economy is what they considered to be the defects that needed to be remedied or improved. The last part of this chapter draws to its close by examining the works of the first two schools of thought in economics. This part will show how Mercantilists and Physiocrats were influenced by what they perceived as economic malfunctions and the policy prescriptions that they suggested to cure the economic disorders that they believed they had identified.

The best of all possible worlds

Consider a perfect world where everything is complete and flawless. Everything is where it is meant to be in its most optimum condition. Assume that the entire system is in its most desirable and efficient state. All its activities are created in accordance with the most perfect laws that are designed eternally to provide the best possible outcomes. This is an economic system that is free from any defect or disorder. The system is programmed in the most perfect way. It is a complete and everlasting system. The same could be said of all constituents of this economic universe. Overall, they are faultless and timeless. This being so, it follows that all constituents of this wonderland are also perfect. The economy: social relations, culture, law, language, technology, institutions, political system and so on—all sound and work perfectly well. This is analogous to saying that all individuals that form this social and economic community must also be totally flawless.

Human beings create their own societies. Claiming these societies are perfect, then it should follow that the creators of these societies must also be perfect. They are complete and convey in perfect terms what is intended. Their values sustain humanity in the best and most perfect manner possible. By the same token, one can infer that human species are supreme beings who are endowed with infinite power, knowledge and goodness, a supreme species that recognises all possibilities, risks and is fully prepared to deal with any crisis. Such a species must constitute a perfect form of being. The fact of the matter is that such a world has never existed. It is not simply achievable. Moreover, neither the ancients nor the thinkers of other ages have prophesied the feasibility of such a social system. Only in the theistic world is there a perfect divine abode for the dedicated disciples to enter after they leave the mortal world.

One important implication of the conceptualisation of this utopian society is to delve into economics writings and see if we can find a similar line of thought in economic literature. What is amply evident from the past economic narratives is a lack of perfect economy and society. This line of thought is fundamentally at odds with the works of pioneering economists. The indispensability of economic disorder is the predominate feature of writings of most inventive economists. Contrary to popular belief, it is not the confirmation of the prevailing economic orders that has inspired their writings but rather the reverse. It has been the recognition of the prevailing economic disorders that has inspired economists' quest for solutions. Without giving serious thought to this aspect of inquiry in economics we would lack a comprehensive understanding of the evolution and development of thought in economics. Economic ideas are the product of the economic disorders of specific times. In meeting the social and economic challenges of their times, innovative economists seek to explain the causes of such disorders. They undertake this in order either to maintain and secure the status quo fully or partially or discard it wholly.

In this chapter we shall demonstrate that disorder is a perpetual situation in society and economy. This characteristic of the economy has been referred to by all pioneering thinkers in economics. This is the common denominator that all schools of thought in economics share. From the mere fact that economists of every ideological persuasion refuse to accept a perfect economic and social order we can deduce that economic disorder is an indispensable constituent of their discourse.

In Chapter 1 we have discussed, in a very general way, some aspects of the world both natural and social that are not just unpredictable but also integral parts of the ever-changing world. In this chapter and the next chapter, we shall review the idea of permanent disorder in the writings of economists. Irrespective of the time and place of writing, all ground-breaking economists have this trait in common in their economic analysis. In other words, there is not a single stage in human history at which the thinkers in general and economists in particular have regarded the social and economic organisation of their time as perfect and flawless. In the same way, there is not a nation that has succeeded to adopt a political, social, economic and legal structure that is so perfect that it cannot be refined or improved. Therefore, we can draw the conclusion that economic disorder is a permanent state of affairs. Such a situation is found in all societies to a different extent. The least contentious part of the argument is that the difference in economic disorder is a difference of degree rather than a difference of kind.

Ancient thinkers were clearly mindful of the forces of creation and destruction in human societies. In India and Hindu mythology, Brahma, Vishnu and Shiva are three gods of creation, preservation and destruction. Brahman (600 BC) professed that all beings are created, sustained and then destroyed (Marballi 2014: 293). Buddha (563–483 BC) projected life as one of ceaseless suffering (Grimm 1999: 264). Nagarjuna, a Buddhist sage, in the second century AD, talked about the limitation of human knowledge, claiming that we can never sufficiently explain the reality around us. Ramanuja (1017–1137 AD) maintained that bondage stems from ignorance. He considered devotion as the remedy for breaking from ignorance (Potter 1991: 156). Belonging to the same line of thought, another Indian thinker, Rabindranath Tagore (1861–1941) regarded disorder in the economy as being triggered by greed and the private accumulation of wealth instead of giving priority to common well-being.

Ancient Chinese thinkers also referred to this state of disorder in their writings. For Confucius (551–479 BC) economic disorder is to be reflected in human character. In his view we can correct such disorders with effective education. Thus, the aim of education is the attainment of Ren (jen) or human heartedness. Ren exists as the highest form of virtue. It is acquired by practicing Li or social norms. But social norms are not fixed in a formal sense. They are different in distinct times, places and individual situations. Taking on Li necessitates Yi. A proper character is epitomised in Yi. That in turn is the embodiment of rationality. A peaceful and ordered society cannot be achieved unless these teaching are fully and precisely implemented (Ivanhoe 1991).

Lao Tzu (sixth century BC) was a Chinese thinker who questioned the claim to complete knowledge (Bedrij 2007: 253). He reasoned that we cannot precisely define the patterns and processes that exist in the objective universe. Our understanding of the world is always indeterminate. All things consist of opposites that are complementary and inseparable. Mozi (470–391 BC) spoke of social conflict resulting due to the fact that no one can be impartial (Rothlin and McCann 2016: 43). Partiality is regarded as the primary cause of social tension and unrest. This is like the ideas of Shotoku Taishi (574–622 AD), an ancient Japanese thinker. He asserted that people act in pursuit of their interests. Pursuit of self-interest is inherently egoistical and one-sided. In pursuit of self-interest, people become narrow-minded. Their self-interest limits their faculty of reasoning. This conduct would undermine their ability to discern and distinguish the right from the wrong. Shotoku suggested that important matters should be resolved through consensus. Han Fei-tzu (280–33 BC), another Chinese thinker also thought that human beings are essentially selfish (Ekelund and Herbert 2007: 23). Due to this innate predisposition, individuals react to reward and punishment.

Another Chinese thinker, Zhuangzi who was born in the 4th century BC argued that the world is constantly changing. As a result of this flux, our experience of the world also adapts and changes (Kjellberg 1996). He infers from this assumption that any slavish pledge to dogmatism is degenerative and will lead ultimately to conflict. To Guo Xiang, who was born in the 3rd century AD in China, the world is synonymous with change. Liezi who lived in the 5th and 4th century AD also echoed a similar perspective. He argued that a spontaneous and harmonious life requires us to break free from empty preconceptions and conventional norms. He reached the conclusion that one's life is too short so one should submit to the external circumstances and follow a hedonistic way of life.

The ancient economic thought and economic disorder

The ancient Greek thinkers drew inspiration from the earlier Asiatic civilisations. However, their contribution to ancient thought is without equal. The Greek thinkers dramatically advanced most branches of science in ancient times and found shortcomings in all fields of inquiry. They examined and criticised many academic spheres of thought including mathematics, epistemology, philosophy, politics, ethics, natural science, cosmology, medicine and many more. The predominant theory in Greece was that all forms of matter consist of atoms. They referred to the essential roots of geometry and arithmetic to verify this supposition. The ancient Greek thinkers believed geometry commenced from a specific point and arithmetic was the primary basis of science.

One area of economic disorder that the ancient Greek philosophers touched upon was the division of labour. They tacitly contended that the division of labour was not fully utilised. Xenophon illustrated how the division of labour augmented productivity in the urban economy. In comparing the division of labour in a small town with a big city, Xenophon remarked:

> In a small city the same man must make beds and chairs and ploughs and tables, and often build houses as well; and indeed, he will be only too glad if he can find enough employers in all his trades to keep him. Now it is impossible that a single man working at a dozen crafts can do them all; but

> in the great cities, owing to the wide demand for each particular thing, a single craft will suffice for a means of livelihood, and often enough even a single department of that; there are shoemakers who will only make sandals for men and others only for women. Or one artisan will get his living merely by stitching shoes, another by cutting them out, a third by shaping the upper leathers, and a fourth will do nothing but fit the parts together. Necessarily the man who spends all his time and trouble on the smallest task will do that task the best.
>
> (quoted from Sedlacek 2011: 102)

Xenophon then explained the advantages of the division of labour. He stated that "he who devotes himself to a very specialized line of work is bound to do it in the best possible manner" (quoted from Gray 1957: 32). In substance Xenophon's argument for the advantages of the division of labour is essentially very modern in conception and tone. His successors, from Plato to Hutcheson, Hume and Smith merely elaborated on and applied his approach to the ever-expanding commercial society of their own time. Much of what can be said about Plato's account of the division of labour in the *Republic* is almost a verbatim reiteration of Xenophon's narrative. He examines the advantages of the division of labour and reaffirms that "Quantity and quality [of goods] are . . . more easily produced when a man specializes appropriately on a single job for which he is naturally fitted" (Plato 1965: 103).

In ancient Greece the division of labour was restricted by powerful social, legal, cultural and conventional obstacles and norms. The whole social system rested on slavery and a kind of caste system. The Greek city state ran, predominantly, on slavery social standards (Gray 1957: 14). Slavery was a matter of fact. It was viewed as a subordination to the will and regulation of nature. Any formal denial of slavery was deemed counterintuitive. Even for most systematic thinkers and scholars, it was a necessary and natural institution. Aristotle ranked slaves as the "lower sort . . . by nature." Then he proceeded to say, "it is better for them as for all inferiors that they should be under the rule of a master" (Aristotle 1984: 1990).

Aristotle alleges that inequality is entirely consistent with nature. He believed that social disparity cannot be evaded or avoided. He argued that inequity should be defended. In his criticism of Plato's ideal state, Aristotle contended that it was unworkable. Aristotle regarded communism, in essence, unnatural. He regarded concept of equality to be incompatible to human instincts. He argued that in a social structure defined by communism there would be endless disputes between those who work more and earn less and those who work less and earn more. In Aristotle's perspective communistic social organisation results in the abolition of private property. Aristotle regarded this as a perverted idea that was against human natural instincts. Aristotle defined communism as essentially unnatural and unworkable. He argued "the love each individual bears to himself is not purposeless." By accentuating the advantages of private property, Aristotle defended it because he proclaimed that it increases people's pleasure immeasurably. He says:

> When a man feels a thing to be his own; for the love of self is a feeling implanted by nature and not given in vain. . . . No one, when men have all things in common, will any longer set an example of liberality or do any liberal action, for liberality consists in the use which is made of property.
> (Aristotle 2016: 30)

Aristotle also pointed to the danger of undue disparity of income, insisting that extreme poverty "is the parent of revolution and crime" (Aristotle 1996: 41). In stark contrast, for Plato, common ownership is not a cause of conflict. Plato contends that the absence of common ownership among equals results in conflict. For this reason, according to Plato, the "servants and masters never can be friend, nor good and bad" (Plato 1871: 273).

Slavery is unproductive since it involves forced labour and is totally dishonourable from an ethical perspective. Throughout antiquity, the work of the slaves, artisans, craftspersons and serfs was regarded as the opposite of a virtuous or honourable life. In all traditional and underdeveloped societies work is generally regarded with inordinate contempt. However, working on the land has been seen as an exception. Slaves inevitably despise work because it is a forced and obligatory labour. Those who carry out the work receive practically nothing in return from the fruits of their labour. Deep seated resentment against work is embedded in the very nature of slave labour. Pliny referred to the inefficiency of slave labour in ancient times. He asserted that the worst plan is when you "have land tilled by slaves" because slaves "live without hope" (quoted from Gray 1957: 37).

In ancient societies we see both a disapproval of work as well as a powerful social current against the acquisition of wealth. This perspective is very strongly expressed in Homer's household economy where trade and excessive wealth are also censured as undesirable. Trade is faulted "as a secondary, and inferior, way of acquiring wealth" (Backhouse 2002: 11).

The Greek philosophers sought the good life neither in slave labour nor in the acquisition of wealth. Excessive wealth also will result in inefficiency. In a dialogue in book four of the *Republic*, Plato enquired: "when a potter becomes rich, will he . . . any longer take the same pains with his art?" He replies that this specific individual "will grow more and more indolent and careless" (Plato 2010: 261). Plato professes that getting rich and happiness are mutually incompatible. In his view a rich person's wealth cannot entirely be attained by just means. Going by this assumption, a rich person is not faultless. Plato states:

> The citizen must indeed be happy and good . . . but very rich and very good at the same time cannot be. . . . For they mean by "the rich" the few who have the most valuable possessions, although the owner of them may

> quite well be a rogue. And if this is true, I can never assent to the doctrine that the rich man will be happy . . . the very rich are not good, and, if they are not good, they are not happy.
>
> (Plato 2010: 261)

Epicurus (341–270 BC) held the view that there is one life. He argued that it exists in the "here and now." Epicurus defined freedom as the primary aim of human life. He believed that liberty can be accomplished by narrowing down one's life to bare necessity. Freedom from want is thus regarded as the highest form of freedom for Epicurus. The followers of the Cynic school and the Stoic school were the devotees of this way of life. Another disciple of this way of thought was Marcus Aurelius, Roman emperor from 161 to 180 AD. In this tradition happiness is not indemnified in the acquisition of wealth. Happiness should be sought in virtue. Valued and ethical good deeds are regarded as more important than the accumulation of wealth. Carrying out good deeds is tantamount to enjoying a clear conscience and a sense of human fulfilment. In the light of this interpretation, what you do should leave no room for remorse or a guilty conscience (Backhouse 2002: 26).

Aristotle divided economic activities into natural and unnatural activities. Everything was seen to have a natural predisposition. If a thing is taken out of its formal nature and placed somewhere that is contrary to its nature, then that act would be classified as entirely unnatural. Aristotle claims that "nature makes nothing without some end in view, nothing to no purpose, it must be that nature has made all things specifically for the sake of man" (Aristotle 1970: 40). For example, the nature of a shirt is to be worn. So, it is contrary to its nature for the shirt to be eaten. Aristotle applied the same rationale to economic activities. From this standpoint, Aristotle separated two natural attributes of goods. They are either used and consumed or exchanged with other goods to be consumed. Anything outside of these conceptual boundaries is regarded as unnatural. For example, making more wealth out of the exchange of goods is unnatural as there can be no limit in the acquisition of wealth.

The economic activity that is compatible with nature is the one according to which "either the goods must be there to start with, or this art of acquisition must see that they are provided; goods, that is, which may be stored up, as being useful or necessary for providing a livelihood" (Aristotle 1970: 40). What is exchanged in this manner can be defined as true wealth. Aristotle identified another important form of exchange. This was the act of making money out of money. There is no limit in the acquisition of wealth in this way. Payment of interest on loans falls into this category. Aristotle maintains that charging money is the most disliked acquisition of wealth:

> for interest is a yield arising out of money itself, not a product of that for which money was provided. Money was intended to be a means of exchange; interest represents an increase in the money itself . . . of all ways of getting wealth this is the most contrary to nature.
>
> (Aristotle 1970: 46)

Plato's perspective on the payment of interest is a somewhat confused view. In the Law in one place, he says "no one shall lend money upon interest" (Plato 2010: 261). In another place he describes interest as a penalty for the delay in making contractual payments. He states:

> let him who, having already received the work in exchange, does not pay the price in the time agreed, pay double the price; and if a year has elapsed, although interest is not to be taken on loans, yet for every drachma which he owes to the contractor let him pay a monthly interest of an obol.
>
> (Plato 1981: 518 — An obol was valued at one sixth of a drachma)

The ancient Greek writers' hostility to the payment of interest reflected the general sentiment of the time. Aristotle was essentially a populist. In this he articulated the public sentiment. He succeeded in fostering a misleading belief within the province of philosophical investigation. In the ancient world the payment of interest in relation to loans was not uncommon. Borrowing and lending was not for productive purposes but mostly for personal needs (Galbraith 1991: 12). Besides, interest rates were very high and those who could not repay the loan were enslaved (Whittaker 1950: 516).

The first formal laws on the payment of interest were decreed by Hammurabi in ancient Babylonia in about 1800 BC. The first written contracts for loans date from this period. These contracts were written in the presence of official witnesses. Hammurabi set a maximum rate for the payment of interest. Loans, by and large, were secured by pledging land, slaves, wives, concubines or children. In addition, the legal codes restricted slavery to 3 years for those who were unable to pay their debts (Homer 1963: 4).

The next major reform in the credit system occurred around 600 BC. By this time the Greeks had "developed an economic system that was commercial, urban, and monetary. Credit came to facilitate trade. There was extensive borrowing at interest, especially on ship loan . . . Pawn credit was widespread. Debt had become an insupportable burden" (Homer 1963: 34). The main cause of the economic crisis of 594 BC was excessive debt. After assuming power, Solon introduced several economic reforms. He reduced many debts, abolished limits on payment of interest and cancelled debts for many who could not pay. His most significant reform, however, was abolishing slavery as a punishment for the inability to pay debt (Homer 1963: 4).

Romans also made some attempts to regulate their credit system. The Twelve Tables, dates from 450 BC. They are like Hammurabi legal code. Hostility towards the payment of interest was not exclusive to Ancient Greece or Rome. It was a common trend in all ancient societies. Homer says:

> The Israelites did not permit lending with interest. As late as 450 B.C. the Iranians considered that the taking of interest on a loan dishonoured a man. Ancient Indian literature reviled usurers and set interest maxima.
>
> (Homer 1963: 21)

Excessive debts were not the only problem that the ancient cultures had encountered. For instance, during the Hellenistic period, Greeks experienced great instability, wars, revolutions and conquests. Alexander III of Macedon (356–23 BC) conquered Persia and appropriated its immense gold and silver treasures and dispersed the war bounty throughout the Mediterranean region. This mass inflow of coins in the Mediterranean region consequently resulted in high prices and lower rates of interest (Homer 1963: 38–9).

Ancient religious texts also refer to credit irregularities and transgressions. Loans based on real estate or pawns are cited in the Bible, the Zend Avesta, and the Veda. Rejecting payment of interest on loan in these texts are ad hoc and somewhat incoherent. The first expression of such hostility can be found in India. The Brahmanic law regulated usury. The law restricted lending on interest by the higher castes, that is, Brahmanas and Kshatriyas. In Vasishtha we read that one "who acquiring property cheap, gives it for a high price, is called a usurer and blamed among those who recite the Veda" (quoted from Haney 1922: 38).

The Hebrew and Hindu interpretation of the payment of interest is very similar. In both cases there is a limit on the maximum rate. In both cases in the event of the king's death or doubling of the principal or the jubilee year the interest is cancelled (Haney 1922: 39). In the Old Testament there are a few passages that relate to the payment of interest. It forbids the payment of interest for some specific group of people. In one extract it states, "if thou lend money to any of my people that is poor by thee, thou shalt not be to him as a usurer, neither shalt thou lay upon him usury" (Exodus 22, v. 25). In another extract it says "if thy brother be waxen poor and fallen in decay with thee; then thou shalt believe him: yea, though he be a stranger, or a sojourner; that he may live with thee. Take thou no usury of him, or increase: but fear thy God; that thy brother may live with thee. Thou shalt not give him thy money upon usury, nor lend him thy victuals for increase" (Leviticus 25, vv. 35–7). The Old Testament has a provision on its general rule of unacceptability of charging of interest on loans. Irrespective of how one can interpret the term "brother" either as a sibling or fellow believer, either way receiving interest on loans is not permitted. The provision that has been added is granting loans to strangers and receiving interest on these loans. This is how another passage of the Old Testament clarifies its last dictum on usury. It instructs its followers that "unto a stranger thou mayest lend upon usury; but unto thy brother thou shalt not lend upon usury" (Deuteronomy 23, vv. 19–20).

The Gospel of Luke taught the Christians to "lend, hoping for nothing again" (Luke 6, v. 35). Islam adopted most of these Judo-Christian doctrines on the issue of interest. Several passages in the Quran express more rigid attitudes towards the payment of interest. The clearest passage in the Quran that deals on usury is 2:275 where it declares:

> Those who charge usury are in the same position as those controlled by the devil's influence. This is because they claim that usury is the same as

> commerce. However, God permits commerce, and prohibits usury. Thus, whoever heeds this commandment from his Lord, and refrains from usury, he may keep his past earnings, and his judgment rests with God. As for those who persist in usury, they incur Hell, wherein they abide forever.
>
> (Quran passage 2:275)

In the Christian world legal bans on interest became more rigid as Christianity became a state ideology. The critical event was the Roman Empire's conversion to Christianity. This took place after the outbreak of plague in the 3rd century. The epidemic wiped out approximately one third of the Roman population. Because of the epidemic the empire retreated. Roman conquests subsided. Inevitably there was a profound decrease in the flow of precious metals gained from the wars of conquest. The Empire lost a primary source of revenue. To uphold the imperial army and the extravagant expenditures of the emperor and his elite entourage, the Roman authorities increased taxation and debased their coinage. The content of silver coins fell by 40 per cent by 250 AD and to 4 per cent by 270 (Backhouse 2002: 30).

It was amid such economic and political upheavals that the Roman Empire found salvation in Christianity. In 312 Constantine (272–337 AD) converted to Christianity. He created the Council of Nicaea in the year 325 AD. It was this Council that denounced payment of interest as being un-Christian. Although the church's first declaration against usury was in (305–6 AD), it was not legally enforceable. The emperor who made Christianity the official religion of the Roman Empire was Emperor Theodosius (346–95 AD) (Backhouse 2002: 29). The status of Christianity was transformed after being adopted as the official religion of the empire. It was no longer the voice of the oppressed. It had become an instrument of conquest and repression. Christian teachings became more rigid and repressive as they blended with the rules of the state machinery. Harsh measures were needed to guard and expand the empire. Payment of interest on loans was one of these key measures. At first the Tertullian priests denounced it as immoral. However, they only barred Christian priests from accepting interest on loans. Two Bishop brothers; Basil, Bishop of Caesarea, and Gregory, Bishop of Nyssa, in the 4th century designated interest as one of the deadly sins (Whittaker 1950: 519).

As the western part of the Roman Empire declined, the eastern part of the empire resumed its hostility to the payment of interest. The most notable regulation of usury in this period was that of Justinian legal code. Justinian was the Emperor of the Byzantine during 527–65 AD. The Justinian code classified loans into two distinct types. The loans used in business paid a higher rate of interest. If a debtor failed to pay his debt on due dates, he was charged a penal rate (Whittaker 1950: 518). The next canonical debate on usury came after Arab academics introduced many of the Greek works to Western Europe. This instigated some interest about usury again among scriptural theologians and secular scholars alike. Aristotle's argument for a ban on usury well suited the ecclesiastic conviction. Thomas Aquinas (1225–74) in *Summa Theologica* overruled usury on the same grounds as Aristotle. He said, "to take usury for money lent is unjust in itself, because this is to sell what does not exist" (quoted from Worden 2010: 80). The upsurge of interest in the subject of credit and payment of interest on loans eventually led Pope Clement V in 1311 to denounce all forms of interest as sinful and heretical (Whittaker 1950: 518).

Payment of interest on loans has never been stamped out totally. Forbidding interest on loans resulted in underground illegal markets. This in turn resulted in the payment of higher rates of interest. Desperate individuals and families were compelled to borrow on interest just to survive. One fact that we must not forget is that people of means and power, kings and nobles, were never barred from borrowing or lending on interest. It was after the Reformation that the actual conditions of the business world modified the attitude towards the payment of interest.

Money has been expressed in different forms (Karimzadi 2013). All forms of money are subject to debasement and devaluation. The form of money that has exposed its debasement trait most noticeably is money in the form of coinage. Coinage is dated from the first millennium BC (Homer 1963: 17). It developed to standardise the medium of exchange. Different forms of money have been invented because the traditional forms of money could not answer the new requirements of the economy and commerce. Historians record the Lydian Starter as the first standardised coin in the world. According to Herodotus the Lydian Starter became the official coin of the Lydian Empire in the 7th century BC during the reign of King Alyattes (619–560 BC). The Lydian Starter was an electrum. It was an alloy consisting of both gold and silver. Originally it consisted of about 55 per cent gold, 45 per cent silver and a little copper. In the course of time not just this proportion changed but the metal content of the gold and silver also diminished.

Not long after the standardisation of coinage the rulers and the fraudsters alike began to tamper with the metal content of the coins. All sorts of tricks such as clipping, sweating, hoarding and counterfeiting were deployed to reduce the precious metal contents of the coins. This process continued until coins lost all their intrinsic value and were modified to token or fiduciary forms of money. We must add that monetary debasement is not exclusive to metallic forms of money. All forms of money are subject to debasement from time to time. I. A. Moosa (2014) has shown that monetary debasement has occurred all the way through history from ancient Rome to the monetary debasement of Zimbabwe in recent decades.

The Lydian Starter predates the Athenian drachma. When Solon assumed power in 594 BC, he only debased the drachma partially. When Greece became a part of the Roman Empire the silver content of drachma was reduced to 67 grains. By the time of Alexander, it was reduced to 65 grains of fine silver. The Persian Sekka, a metallic coin, was introduced by Darius (521–486 BC) in the 5th century BC. By the time of the Sasanian conquest the metal content of the Sekka was reduced to about one gram.

The Denarius is another good example of the way in which the metallic content of the coin form of money was tampered with. Emperor Caesar Augustus ordered in 15 BC that the silver content of Denarius should be about 95 to 98 per cent. Nearly three centuries after that it lost all its silver content (Homer 1963: 49). Punch marked coins were issued in India in the 7th and 6th century with a full metal content. These coins were also debased and lost their metallic content with the passage of time (Sarkar 1978: 122).

In the Old Testament there are three main indicatives of economic disorder. These are the idea of progress, the economic cycle and the arrival of the saviour. Economic progress covertly implies disorder. In one sense the economy improves with time. In other words, at any given time, the economy is not operating at its full capacity. Sedlacek states that time in the Old Testament is linear. It started sometime in the past and it is heading to a more improved future. The progress continues till the coming of the messiah (Sedlacek 2011: 47).

The arrival of the messiah implies that the social and economic conditions are very bad and will inevitably improve with his coming. Sedlacek remarks that the Jews were the first that rose against the god, the pharaoh. The invisible god called Moses to come to the world to end wickedness and tyranny and bring justice on earth (Sedlacek 2011: 55). Sedlacek also links the first account of the business cycle to the Hebrew writers. This account of the economic cycle is a by-product of the notions of good and bad. These are core concepts in the Old Testament (Sedlacek 2011: 62). Hebrew writers demonstrated the first proposition of the business cycle with the pharaoh's dream of the seven fat and seven lean cows. The seven fat cows represented years of economic plenty. The emaciated cows represented the years of scarcity and starvation. According to Genesis (41:1–4):

> Pharaoh had a dream: he was standing by the Nile, when out of the river there came up seven cows, sleek and fat, and they grazed among the reeds. After them, seven other cows, ugly and gaunt, came up out of the Nile and stood beside those on the riverbank. And the cows that were ugly and gaunt ate up the seven sleek, fat cows. Then Pharaoh woke up.
>
> (Genesis 41:1–4)

In another passage we have Joseph's interpretation of the dream, which reads:

> Seven years of great abundance are coming throughout the land of Egypt, but seven years of famine will follow them. Then all the abundance in Egypt will be forgotten, and the famine will ravage the land.
>
> (Genesis 41:29–30)

The first economists were the Greeks. Hesiod (750–650 BC) was, possibly, the first economist. Most probably he was the first thinker to recognise the problem of scarcity. He pointed out that permanent scarcity exists in an economy. According to Hesiod the desire of the Gods to punish their subjects leads to the existence of scarcity. In *Works and Day*, Hesiod claims that "the Gods keep the means of life concealed from human beings. Otherwise, you would easily be able to work in just one day so as to have enough for a whole year even without working" (Hesiod 2006: 91).

The next notable discussion on economics is the work of Xenophon. In his dialogue, Oikonomikos, he discusses the principles of efficient estate management. The important assumption in Xenophon's writings is that he assumes that the economy is not fixed. Economy is defined as a dynamic entity. The economy oscillates from good to bad or vice versa. He states, "when husbandry flourishes, all the other arts are in good fettle; but whenever the land is compelled to lie waste, the other arts of landsmen and mariners alike well-nigh perish" (quoted from Gray 1957: 30). The land is productive, but it does not provide without the toil of men and women. There is a limit on how much a given land can produce. Adding more labour on given land leads to diminishing returns. Xenophon claims that "the landowners could all tell you how many teams and how many labourers are required for their estates. If anyone employs hand in excess of requirements, it is reckoned as a loss" (quoted from Gray 1957: 30). Xenophon deliberated, in a very rudimentary way, the law of increasing returns and business cycles. In silver mining, he argued, by employing more people the rate of return of mining silver will increase. In his short tract, "The Ways and Means to Increase the Revenues of Athens," he noted that excess in any market can lead to bankruptcy, including when there is excess of entrepreneurs. War booties seized in conflicts are no more than passing gains. It is during periods of peace that we can enjoy prosperity and wealth can be accumulated. It is in the war that the wealth is spent, and the economy deteriorates (Xenophon 2013).

Three other areas of economics that the ancient Greek considered were the subjects of money, interest and the state. All these themes implicitly relate to the issue of economic disorder. We have already looked at their work on money and interest. Discussion and examination of the state is a very significant part of Greek classical writings. In his book, *Republic*, Plato laid down his blueprint for an ideal state, a state that came into being out of economic necessity. Plato speaks of the state as something that was invented as a necessity. It was invented because in one sense nobody is self-sufficient. People have distinct needs. For the provision of these needs they form social organisations that would clear the way for greater cooperation. With this economic cooperation in mind the state was invented (Snooks 1997: 52). Aristotle in his book, *Politics*, regards the state as a natural necessity. He seeks its inevitability in the division of human societies into rulers and subjects. To show how the state came into being he discusses the concept of human social evolution. Aristotle maintains that the state has evolved from the household to the village and then to much larger associations (Gray 1957: 24).

The Roman Empire was formed by the force of armies and conquerors. Its wealth, by and large, derived from its numerous conquests. Roman thinkers investigated and explored the nature of the economy in three key areas of inquiry. These were from legal, philosophical and agricultural viewpoints (Haney 1922: 68). Nevertheless, the law was their overriding concern and sphere of investigation. The Roman jurists made a distinction between human law and natural law. This is the same trend that later influenced subsequent medieval thought. The jus civile law constituted national law and the jus gentium law related to the legal status of foreigners (Haney 1922: 68). From this distinction there emerged the freedom of contract, the separation of personal from the non-personal assets and the departure of law from religion (Haney 1922: 69).

The great thinkers of this period were Cicero, Seneca, Pliny (elder and the younger), Marcus Aurelius and Epictetus. These writers questioned the prevailing disorders in the empire. The chief among the social faults that these thinkers identified were the lust for money, opulence and conspicuous waste. The excesses of the empire appalled these writers. Their revulsion from greed and excess led them to embrace a simple, more modest lifestyle. They longed to simplify their lives by going "back to nature" (Haney 1922: 71). Likewise, these writers viewed usury from this standpoint. Marcus Tullius Cicero (106–43 BC) condemned usury by equating it to homicide (Haney 1922: 71). Cicero came straight to the point by saying "what is wrong is never expedient" (Haney 1922: 71). In essence, this means the law must be universally applied.

As we have noted earlier Varro regarded slave labour as inefficient. But, in his view, the same does not apply to the farmworkers. Since they are free labourers, they are more efficient. Freedom lessens their sense of inferiority, and fair treatment encourages them to work harder. Farmworkers compared to slave labour become more efficient by enjoying such rights as "occasional exemption from work, or the permission to graze a beast of their own on the farm, and by other privileges of the same kind" (quoted from Flower 2012).

The only productive sector in the ancient caste economy was agriculture. Cicero classified different industries based on what he called their propensity of respectability and vulgarity. Tax gatherers and usurers were the least respectable vocations. Hired labourers who are unskilled and paid wages are vulgar and disrespected. Merchants are also in this vulgar category. In contrast, agriculture was not seen as having these disadvantages. It was regarded as the most pleasant and productive industry in the economy (Belliotti 2009: 48).

Excesses in all affairs, including the public debt, contributed to the decadence and fall of the Roman Empire. The insatiable craving for more conquest, power and conspicuous waste drained the treasury of the empire. Pliny describes one example of Nero's conspicuous waste. He remarks "good authorities declare that Arabia does not produce so large a quantity of perfume in a year's output as was burnt by the Emperor Nero in a day at the obsequies of his consort Poppaea" (quoted from van der Veen 2011: 40). Intense dislike of such excesses and greed drove people like St Jerome (347–420 AD) to be banished into the world of self-reliance, privation, pauperism and retreating to life of solitude (Backhouse 2002: 30).

From theocratic to secular economics

Economics, as a scientific subject, is a by-product of the age of enlightenment. We shall explore the role that the age of enlightenment has played in formation of economics as a scientific subject of inquiry in Chapter 4. In this section we will look at the events, social and political upheavals, that paved the way for the establishment of the first schools of thought in economics. We will also show the relationship between these ideas, which were somewhat extemporaneous and unsystematic, and the economic disorders that they intended to explain. From the 15th century onwards, Europe went through some major social, political, cultural and economic cycles of revolutionary transformation. Europeans discovered America and used gunpowder on a large scale in their conquest of new colonies. They invented printing, conceived and launched the Renaissance and the Reformation revolts. These events had far-reaching consequences that broadened the horizons of humanity to a point of no return to the old orders.

These events shook the core foundations of commanding beliefs, customs, privileges and obligations of the archaic ecclesiastical world view and power. The things that once were considered heretical became much in vogue and respectable. Scholasticism and canon laws gradually gave way to pursuit of self-interest, secularism and individuality. The new era opened the minds and eyes of those who wanted to see reality as it was. Those with a critical disposition saw disorder in all constituents of the economy and society of their time.

In what is described as the Dark Ages in Europe, the economic activities were dominated by Biblical laws. Pivotal to canonical law is the transitory world. This world is the testing ground. For the believers this world was a subordinate to the world after death. So nothing was worth having was the upshot of this creed in this world. Most of all, when this tenet was applied, one could not own anything including land because everything belongs to God. In view of that, accumulation of wealth was considered undesirable since it could keep people away from their main duty of serving God. In the Old Testament the pursuit of wealth and exploitation are interdependent. Prophet Amos, dated about 8th century BC, advised his followers against the danger of the pursuit of wealth. He says:

> Listen to this, you who grind the destitute and plunder the humble, you who say When will the new moon be past so that we may sell our corn? When will the Sabbath be past so that we may open our wheat again, giving short measure in the bushel and taking overweight in the silver, tilting the scales fraudulently, and selling the dust of the wheat; that we may buy the poor for silver and the destitute for a pair of shoes?
>
> (Amos 8: 4–6)

The New Testament embraced the same teaching. Jesus and his early disciples "came from the poorest parts of Jewish society . . . Thus, he required his followers to give up their possessions . . . and taught that rewards for righteousness would be found in heaven rather than on earth" (Backhouse 2002: 33). St Paul, who is basically the founder of Christianity, predicted Christ's second coming. He described this event as connected to the impending end of the world. Why then accumulate wealth? Influenced by this doctrine "many of the scholastic writers [became] mendicant friars who were committed to a life of poverty. They did not consider wealth to raise the quality of life" (Backhouse 2002: 44). The Church leaders advocated a simple life of poverty for the masses. Furthermore, they prohibited them from lending or borrowing money. This environment was neither conducive to economic development nor to the development of economic thought.

The 14th century was a period of great tumult and instability. This was the century of the Hundred Years' War, the Black Death, the decline of population, a rise in wages and fall in prices of agricultural products. At the same time, civil and religious discontent crippled the leading nations of Europe. These events had a lasting impact on the social, economic, political and cultural progress and development of the upcoming European empires.

Economics is essentially related to the issue of price. Understandably, the issue of price has been central to economic analysis from the past until now. In medieval times, it preoccupied most of the scholastic examination and discussion of economics. These writers tried to define a common meaning for the just price. Similarly, price inflation has been an intermittent disorder throughout history (Horvath 1983: 50). One of these outbreaks of inflation took place towards the end of the13th and beginning of the 14th century. Brenner correlates the cause of series of inflation to an increase in population and urbanisation (Brenner 1983: 94). Van Cauwenberghe also links this spate of inflation to the growing population and takes grain prices as an example to show the extent to which prices had increased. He remarks that "at the beginning of the fourteenth century, grain prices were four times what they had been at the end of the twelfth century" (Van Cauwenberghe 1983: 147).

One important factor that has been largely overlooked in respect to inflation in this period is the rise in wages caused by the Black Death. This huge epidemic caused a significant fall in the labour force. As result of the Black Death, it is believed that the population of Europe fell by approximately a third. In some areas the population decrease amounted to almost half of the labour force. Labour became scarce and conflicts between labourers and landlords became endemic. Pillage of the precious metals of America, mainly from Mexico and Peru, and an influx of precious metals in Europe revolutionised the price system in western Europe. This led in turn to high inflation in the economies of this region (Nicolini 2009: 124). The huge increase in prices during this period effectively undermined the religious concept of the just price. The traditional teachings of the church in relation to price was undermined by a sharp increase of up to 400 per cent in general prices.

In the 13th century the powerful tentacles of the Mongol Empire stretched as far as the seashores of Europe. The expanding Mongol Empire created a trade route between the Far East, the Middle East, Central Asia and Europe. During the same period Christian forces reclaimed control of Spain from Arab rule. The expansion and development of international trade linked a very wide area of Asia, Europe and Africa. Trading cities soon spread across the eastern Mediterranean. This was a new reality that could not be explained by the established doctrines and teachings of the church. The rising urban population in turn created an educated class. This learned section of society then discovered Greek literature, which had originally been introduced to Europe by Arab thinkers and poets. Subsequently, the social gulf between critical thinkers, the church and the state began to widen.

Several key factors impacted medieval thought. In turn this development led to the birth of the European cultural renaissance and theological reformation. The march to modernity could not have been possible had it not been for the fracturing and final dissolution of the Christian Roman Empire. Another crucial factor was the exodus and escape of many scholars to Italy after the fall of Constantinople in 1453. These scholars brought with them the cultural knowledge and philosophy of a range of Greek and Arab writers and thinkers. This soon initiated a revival in classical inquiry and learning. Another key factor was the innovation of the mariner's compass. This technical development facilitated the exploration of distant parts of the world. Another vital development was European access to gunpowder. The invention of printing spread literacy and knowledge. The combination of these factors weakened the old bonds and provided the necessary elements for the formation of city-states, national identity and expansion of trade and commerce.

Renaissance thinkers and artists took advantage of these new changes. Secular humanism lay at the heart of the Renaissance movement. Men of letters such as Dante, humanists such as Desiderius Erasmus and Leonardo da Vinci spearheaded this dynamic movement. The proponents of this movement were driven by a belief in human dignity and syncretism. The quest for truth was brought to the centre of academic and philosophical investigations. The Renaissance thinkers repudiated a life of penance as the most ideal and noble human duty. They refused the teaching of fatalistic inaction encouraged by the church. Followers of Renaissance defined humanity in new terms and liberated themselves from conservative fatalism. They deserted the sedentary passive bystander. Individuals were encouraged to inquire, understand and exert control over the forces of nature, and not bend their necks to predestination. Critical analysis and rational consideration displaced blind faith. Renaissance thinkers and artists advocated a new spirit of free thinking and inquiry. The Renaissance was a springboard for new ideas and challenges. It was a spark in the frozen minds. The Reformation movement was one of these sparks in western Europe in the 16th century that was led by Martin Luther (1483–1546) and John Calvin (1509–64). This was a mild protest, but its effects were rather dramatic.

Martin Luther nailed his 95 theses to the door of the Castle church in Germany on 31 October 1517. He was not happy with the Church's over-indulgence, the Pope's authority in relation to the issue of purgatory and with the reliability of the saints in the gospel. Except for these minor objections, Luther was prepared to work under the papacy authority. John Calvin, another leading figure of the Reformation movement, fled France after raising similar objections against the monopoly of papal authority. He fled to Basel in Switzerland. It was there in 1536 that he published the first theological treatise of the Protestant movement. The Reformation fractured and undermined the established authority of the church. This new philosophical approach came to gain a foothold among the monarchs and rulers of northern Europe. It was because of the reformation that Henry VIII of England repudiated Papal authority in 1534. He then deepened the rupture with Rome by remarrying against the canonical doctrines of the established Church. This movement, unintentionally, weakened a major barrier against human rational inquiry and economic progress.

From the beginning of time people have observed far-reaching changes both in natural and social spheres of their surroundings. Draughts, floods, heatwaves, pandemics and many other disasters were nothing new. They have caused shortages and famines on an intermittent basis throughout history. In the social sphere, wars, subjugation and tyrannical rulers destroyed economies and caused famine and shortages. All nations have experienced such difficulties at one time or another in their histories. Evidently, in a subsistence economy, matters are significantly less complicated than in an economy of extensive division of labour and employment. In advanced economies one factor that progressively gets entangled and impenetrable is the nature of exchange. Advanced economic structures are dominated by the issue of exchange. The exchange system in turn becomes more complex with the increasing specialisation of employment and the increasing number of goods produced and the services offered. The enormous inflow of precious metals from the new world radically expanded the system of exchange of goods, services and money in the leading nations of Europe. It also resulted in four other long-lasting changes to European economies. The new influx stimulated production and expanded international trade. The Kings and Queens of the leading empires of Europe less and less counted on their national tax revenue and more on plundering the resources of their colonies and on international trade. The huge inflow of wealth also resulted in an inflationary revolution in the northern and western parts of Europe.

The desire for gold drove Christopher Columbus to the new world. He described gold as "a wonderful thing!" To possess gold, he boasted, empowers one to be the "master of everything he desires" and with it "one can even get souls into paradise" (quoted from Ruggiero 2013: 29). The influx of inordinate gold and wealth led to greater excesses in other domains of life. One of these excesses was the slave trade. From 1519 to the late 1860s about 9.5 million African slaves were shipped to America (Bernstein 2009: 275). The mortality rate among the slaves was very high. A testimony to Parliament of the one vessel called the Alexander ship provides a tiny glimpse of the harrowing conditions which the slaves experienced. We read in the testimony:

> When employed in stowing the slaves, he made the most of the room and wedged them in. They had not so much room as a man in his coffin, either in length or in breadth. It was impossible for them to turn or shift . . . [one] cannot conceive of any situation so dreadful and disgusting as that of the slaves when ill of the flux: in the Alexander, the deck was covered with blood and mucus, and resembled a slaughterhouse. The stench and foul air were intolerable.
>
> (quoted from Bernstein 2009: 275)

Gold as a form of money has intrinsic value. So it can be debased. Nicole Oresme (1320–82) in the 14th century referred to some adverse effects of debased money on the economy. The Kipper und Wipper was one form of debasing money. It was one type of scales that moneychangers used to identify debased coins from undebased ones. In the course of identification, they withdrew undebased coins from circulation, then combined them with less valuable metals and re-issued them into general circulation. Nicole Oresme regarded money as a public good and argued against arbitrarily debasing it. He reflected on the fact that when two mediums of exchange are in circulation at the same time and have the same designation but different value, the debased currency would drive out of circulation the medium that has the higher value. Nicolaus Copernicus (1473–1543) rediscovered this point and years later it was reclaimed by Thomas Gresham (1519–97). In his treatise, Oresme denounced any form of debasement of coins, and described anyone who debases coins as a liar who:

> commits perjury; he bears false witness; for it is clearly a shame for a king to certify that a thing is gold when it is not gold, or that it weighs a pound when it does not do so. The gain which flows from such practices is not merely dishonest, it is also unnatural.
>
> (quoted from Gray 1957: 63)

Jean Bodin (1530–96) was one of the earliest writers of the period, writing in 1576, who observed a causal relation between the inflow of precious metals from the new world and high prices in Europe. He said "I find that the high prices we see today are due to some four or five causes. The principal and almost the only one . . . is the abundance of gold and silver" (quoted from Galbraith 1991: 35). Irrespective of the accuracy of such claims and counter-claims, one fact that these writers were acknowledging from their close observation of their society and the time is the apparent economic disorder that they witnessed.

The reality is always ahead of established conventions and ideas. This is what happened in relation to the culture of the payment of interest on loans. Charles Dumoulin (or Molinaeus, 1500–66), a French jurist published a book entitled *Tractus Commerciorum et Usurum* in 1546. In this book, he argued that the payment of interest is a legitimate return on money lent. Calvin agreed with Dumoulin and professed in a letter in 1575 that acquiring interest should not be regarded as sinful. His position is tentative but wavers between two essential positions. On the one hand, he permits payment of interest in some cases and on the other hand he prohibits it in other cases. He states:

> usury should not be demanded from men in need; nor is it lawful to force any man to pay usury who is oppressed by need or calamity . . . he who receives a loan on usury should make at least as much for himself by his labour and care as he obtains who gives the loan.
>
> (quoted from Cohen and Cohen 2002: 166, footnote 27)

Economics detached itself from the established theocracy during the age of enlightenment. Several preconditions were fulfilled to facilitate this break up. The first prerequisite was the recognition and definition of a person all on its own in his and her own rights. We must add that initially this right did not apply to all individuals but only to male individuals. The slow recovery of the rights of the individual came to separate him from his adherence to a particular religion or a specific community. Obtaining this right in turn brought forth a new setting for a different form of economic structure and relationships. It was said that an individual on his own is rational and capable to understand, decide and pursue his interests. Spinoza, in his *Tractatus Theologico-politicus*, in 1670 argued that the individual mind belongs to no other entity but the individual himself or herself. The mind of everyone cannot be separated from the individual and controlled by anyone else. Spinoza remarks:

> If men's minds were as easily controlled as their tongues, every king would sit safely on his throne, and government by compulsion would cease; for every subject would shape his life according to the intentions of his rulers, and would esteem a thing true or false, good or evil, just or unjust, in obedience to their dictates. However . . . no man's mind can possibly lie wholly at the disposal of another, for no one can willingly transfer his natural right of free reason and judgement or be compelled so to do.
>
> (Spinoza 2007: 257)

Likewise, Hobbes extended this crucial notion of everyone in one's own right. Hobbes stated that individual desire is indivisible from each person. He claimed that a man's selfish desires do not stop with his escape from anarchy into formal, political society. In Hobbes's view it is against human nature to be satisfied at all. This is because human happiness lay not in the attainment of some definite objective but in perpetual progress from one new satisfaction to another (Whittaker 1950: 95).

On the list of other prerequisites for establishment of the new social and economic setting we have the works of Thomas Hobbes and John Locke and their implementations. Their ideas contributed a great deal to the Revolution of 1688 in England. This revolutionary period terminated the absolute power of the monarchy and transferred political authority to a representative legislative body. The revolution and its achievements created a new social, political, legal and cultural context in which the objective rule of law became difficult to defeat. The monarch's arbitrary decrees or noxious divine laws were gradually replaced with secular laws. The representative government claimed legitimacy for the protection of its citizens. It proclaimed its legal right to raise revenue for its expenditures through a transparent and just taxation system. The taxation system operated in an objective and legal manner. Tax revenues were raised to pay for the state's expenditures and debts. That legitimacy brought about a more stable and conducive economic environment for individuals to have mastery over their economic activities. This stability clearly benefitted individuals, particularly in relation to the security of their property. This new stability worked to reduce interest rates as well as encouraging further economic and commercial activity (Bernstein 2009: 248). This environment also enabled individuals to observe the nature of reality in a more objective manner. Reality did not need to be defined in deference to divine scriptures or obscure, ancient texts. The sense of newly founded individual freedom of course encouraged continued questioning of the assumptions and habits of the old world. Consolidation and interactions of all these changes severely weakened the old rules, the rigid customary codes and the hegemony of blind faith.

Mercantilists, physiocrats and economic disorder

Economics became an established scientific discipline in the 18th century. Since its establishment as a discipline, economics has branched out into several schools of thought. The most widely acknowledged schools are Mercantilism, Physiocrats, Classical Political Economy, Marxian Economics, the German Historical School, the Marginalist School, the Institutionalist School, the Neoclassical School of Economics, the Austrian School, the Keynesian School, the Post-Keynesian School and the Monetarist School. On the periphery, there are branches of economics that deal with specific subjects or areas in economics such as environmental economics, feminist economics, welfare economics, and econometrics and so on. Moreover, there are many variations of opinions within each of these schools of thought. One can hardly find two economists even from the same school who agree on everything about their own school. Continuous divergences of opinion among economists are yet another indication of a state of permanent disorder in the economy. In the last section of this chapter, we will show how Mercantilist and Physiocrat writers had acknowledged the state of permanent disorder in the economy in their economic analyses.

The term Mercantilism was coined by Victor de Riqueti Marquis de Mirabeau (1715–89). It describes a collection of opinions of many writers that spreads from the 16th to the 18th century. Galbraith states that Mercantilism was "a marked break with the ethical attitudes and instructions of Aristotle and Saint Thomas Aquinas and the Middle Ages in general" (Galbraith 1991: 37). The pursuit of self-interest and not a pursuit of a better life in another world is a striking distinction of the work of these writers. The acquisition of wealth moved to centre stage as a social goal. This primary aim superseded the previously dominant ethical and religiously inspired conventions and expectations. People were no longer required to strive for some dubious religious reward based on ancient books. Mercantilist core beliefs were drawn from common sense and the race for wealth. Wealth during this period was seen to be comprised of precious metals such as gold and silver. A richer merchant was the one who possessed more gold. Formal virtue or commitment to divine laws was no longer the key to an individual securing esteem and success. Adherence to the stated rules of a religious text bore no relevance to an individual's sense of importance or wealth. The acquisition of gold defined the social status of an individual and his place in the world. In crude terms the pious lessons formerly embodied in ancient books had been displaced by an earthlier focus. Wealth was the great indicator of status and self-worth. An individual had to develop his own skills and know how to achieve success and security.

One implication of adhering to this idea was the growing distance between the state and theocracy. At the same time the compatibility between the economic interests of merchants and the state became closer. This congeniality of interest of the rising merchant class facilitated the rise of modern national states. For a national state to become affluent, self-sufficient and powerful, it had to rely more on its merchants than on the church. This greater dependency of the state on the merchant class can be seen from the policies and privileges that the states adopted and implemented to serve the interest of this upcoming social class. The policies that called for self-sufficiency, export of manufacturing goods, low wages, import of precious metals, patents and monopolies and acquisition of more colonies were all calculated efforts to serve the interest of the emerging merchant class. Mercantilists "valued gold and silver as the avenues by which power and strengths were to be attained" (Gray 1957: 79). Thomas Mun wrote:

> The ordinary means . . . to increase our wealth and treasure is by Forraign Trade . . . This ought to be encouraged, for upon it hangs the great revenue of the king, the honor of the kingdom, the noble profession of the merchant, the school of our arts, the supply of our poor, the improvements of our lands, the nursery of our mariners, the walls of the kingdom, the means of our treasury, the sinews of our wars, the terror of our enemies.
>
> (quoted from Leonard 1993: 24)

Mercantilist writers could not agree with Aristotle's view of interest. Thomas Mun was in favour of charging interest on loans. Loans, Thomas Mun (1571–1641) argued, enable the young and merchants without funds to borrow and invest and hence create employment and trade (Haney 1922: 122). Most writers of the Mercantilist period looked to the Netherlands to validate their views. They correlated greater economic activities and growth with the lower rates of interests in Netherlands. Josiah Child remarked that "we shall never stand on even ground with Dutch in trade till interest be the same with us as with them" (Child 1751: 29).

Charles Davenant (1656–1714) described the usurers as individuals "who are the true drones of a commonwealth, living upon the honey without any labour" (Davenant 1695: 111). John Locke regarded the cause of lower interest rate in supply of plenty of money. From this supposition he argued that interest rates cannot be regulated by fixed rules (Homer 1963: 80). Mercantilists advanced the debate on interest and succeeded to make the payment of interest on loans to be accepted as necessity and not as a sinful act. Indeed, the payment of interest on loans was now deemed to be free of sin. The argument then shifted to what determines the rate of interest.

More rigorous thinkers such as William Petty and John Locke reasoned that in any nation for any given level of trade there is a proportion of money that is naturally required for that level of trade. Greater or lesser amounts from what is naturally required would adversely affect the level of trade and the fluctuations in the rates of interest. Petty argued "money is but the Fat of the Body-Politick, whereof too much doth as often hinder its Agility, as too little makes it sick" (quoted from Bowley 1973: 20). Likewise, Locke maintained that a certain amount of money drives a certain level of trade. If much of the money is taken out of circulation that would reduce the level of trade (Locke 1824: 12). Locke points to a specific rate of interest that is most suitable for a given economic circumstance and calls it the natural rate of interest, the rate of interest which will be formed when the quantity of money required is the most appropriate to a given level of trade. Locke extrapolated from this supposition that the thing that:

> constantly raises the natural interest of money, is, when money is little, in proportion to the trade of a country. For in trade everybody calls for money, according as he wants it, and this disproportion is always felt. . . . It is in vain, therefore, to go about effectually to reduce the price of interest by law.
>
> (Locke 1751: 6)

On the same subject Duddly North (1641–91) speculated that:

> as plenty makes cheapness in other things, as Corn, Wool . . . when they come to Market in greater Quantities than there are buyers to deal for, the Price will fall; so, if there be more Lenders than Borrowers, Interest will

> also fall; wherefore it is not low Interest makes Trade, but Trade increasing, the Stock of the Nation makes Interest low. It is said, that in Holland Interest is lower than in England. I answer . . . because their Stock is greater than ours.
>
> (North 1997: 45)

Mercantilists also applied the everyday common-sense experience to business fluctuations. Josiah Child examined the situation of the poor in England. He compared their living conditions with those of the poor in different countries. He concluded that the poor are better off in countries in which goods are more expensive than in countries where goods are cheaper. In the same way the poor are better off in years when things become more expensive than when the prices are lower.

Richard Cantillon (1680–1734) linked the business cycle to the supply of money. He commented that:

> If more money continues to be drawn from the Mines all prices will owing to this abundance rise to such a point that not only will the Landowners raise their rents considerably when the leases expire and resume their old style of living, increasing proportionally the wages of their servants, but the Mechanics and Workmen will raise the prices of their articles so high that there will be a considerable profit in buying them from the foreigner who makes them much more cheaply. This will naturally induce several people to import many manufactured articles made in foreign countries, where they will be found very cheap: this will gradually ruin the Mechanics and the Manufacturers of the State who will not be able to maintain themselves there by working at such low prices owing to the dearness of living.
>
> (Cantillon 2001: 68)

The mercantilist's take on permanent economic disorders can be viewed from two main perspectives. In the first place, it is from specifying the defects of their contemporary economic system. Secondly, it is from both their intended and unintended implications of execution of their policies. Mercantilists' doctrines were proposed to serve the interest of the merchant class. They were aimed at restricting competition and granting monopoly privileges to a few companies such as the British East India Company. Mercantilist policies called for the colonisation of new territory on the one hand and on the other hand for the centralisation of political power in the form of a powerful national state, endorsing political absolutism and despotism (Haney 1922: 106–7).

Mercantilists narrowed down definition of the wealth of a nation to the quantity and extent of its precious metals. In this manner they curtailed the basis of international trade and reduced scales of exports and imports to levels which were favourable to the merchant class. Most of all, what was good for the merchants was regarded as being good for the nation and the state. All sorts of tariffs and duties were imposed to restrict export of precious metals. Mercantilists considered international trade as a form of relationship that what one country gains is at the exact expense of its trading counterpart. It goes without saying that these ideas and policies restricted trade, allocation of resources, economic development and employment. The mercantilist period was the time of the emerging European empires. This was the period which saw the subjugation of America, Africa and many Asian nations. Colonisation, militarism and ongoing wars between rival empires were distinctive characteristics of this period.

The Physiocrats lasted only for a very short period. The school is dated from 1756 when Francois Quesnay (1694–1774) published one article in the Grande Encyclopédie to the publication of the *Wealth of Nations* in 1776. The school was the product of France in the mid 18th century. At that time the agricultural sector dominated French economy. Agriculture "was more than an occupation, it was . . . a way of life" for French people (Galbraith 1991). The actual economic conditions of France could not fit well with the mercantilists' concept of the source of wealth. The Physiocrats rejected precious metals as the source of wealth. Their common-sense experience pointed to a different source of the origin of wealth. From his experience of French economy, Quesnay formulated the Physiocrats' chief maxim that "agriculture is the source of all the wealth of the State and of the wealth of all the citizens" (quoted from Aspromourgos 2009: 21).

A common-sense observation shows that when a farmer plants one seed of wheat, in due course, he reaps many seeds at the time of harvest. From this observation the Physiocrats concluded that the land must be the most productive sector of the economy. They argued that wealth cannot be produced by any other economic activity except from cultivation of land. They believed that wealth cannot be created in exchange because trade is sterile. Trade is merely the exchange of commodities of equal value. In their view, trade was not only neutral but ultimately harmful. They considered that trade can grant excessive power to merchants. These merchants could then employ their power and influence to increase prices artificially. Industry at best is neutral. It only reshaped the primary materials taken from land and remade them into actual products. Therefore, agriculture must be the only source of surplus product. As landlords own the land, the surplus product expressed in the form of rent will enrich the landowners. Given that there is one source of surplus product and one social class who seize the surplus, the Physiocrats concluded that there should be only one type of tax. This is a tax on the land itself, and this tax should be levied on the landowning class.

Physiocrats criticised the mercantilist ideas, policies and the old system in France. In France at the time, the state regulation of the economy was excessive and exhaustive. The French economy was undermined by all sorts of taxes, tolls and tariffs. The nobility and the clergy were exempt from paying tax, so the burden of taxation was on only small landholders and peasants. The French government prohibited the export of grain from France. Domestic trade was subjected to many strict regulations. The extent of regulation was such that it even "specified that number of threads per inch in the manufacture of cloth" (Fusfeld 2002: 18).

Quesnay's background had also a profound influence on his observation of the economy. He was influenced by William Harvey's (1578–1658) discovery of the circulation of blood in living animals. In his classic work *Tableau Economique* in 1758, Quesnay tried to extend the mechanism of the circulation of the blood to circulation of income and products in the French economy. He strove to equate the economy to a natural organism and argued that like an organism circular flow of income conforms to the rules of nature (Brue and Grant 2013). Quesnay believed that just as interfering in nature would disturb the natural order, interfering in the economy would also lead to disharmony and disorder in the natural order of the economic system.

In the Physiocrats' view, the economy is not immune from natural imperatives. Deviating from a natural economic order can cause disorder in the economy. Therefore, Physiocrats argued for the implementation of the economic policy of the Laissez-faire, laissez-passer. This phrase was coined by Vincent de Gournay (1712–59). It essentially means that the government should refrain from formal interference in people's private business or commercial affairs. In the final analysis, the Physiocrats called for the minimum interference of the government in the economy. They argued that except for the protection of life, property and freedom of contract, the government should refrain from any other intervention in the economy.

Conclusion

When studying any aspect of human life, we soon encounter the spectre of disorder, either in the form of natural disorders or in terms of social disorders. We have looked at several natural disorders in Chapter 1. The focus of this chapter has been on economic disorders. Different schools of thought in economics have emerged in reacting to the economic disorders of their times. This general positioning of economics trains of thought applies as much to the pioneering schools as to the succeeding schools of thought in economics.

It cannot be open to doubt that there has not and there cannot be a perfect economic system. Any economic system that has existed so far has had its distinctive faults. In view of this fact, we have designated these faults or defects as economic disorder. Thus, economic disorder is a permanent constituent of all economic systems.

Economies exist in a continuous state of flux. Perfect economies would not change, either progress or regress. Without flaw means being free from the seeds of its own destruction. Lacking perfection tacitly implies disorder. Causes of permanent economic disorders cannot be fully known at any given time. Among these causes, we find the issue of scarcity. By scarcity we are referring to its general and relative forms. In its general forms all economic resources are scarce. Whereas in its relative form scarcity exists in relation to the level of one's wants to his or her income. There are two catalysts within the zone of wants and income that nurture economic disorders. The first one is the insatiability of human wants and the second one is the inexhaustible potential capacity of human knowledge and skills to improve the organisation of production and distribution. These elements are never constant and for this very reason economic disorder is a permanent state of affairs. It is to be remembered that we cannot have everything we want at any moment in time. If all things were not limited in supply, then "there would be no scarcity—no economic goods—no need to economise—no economic problem" (Stanlake 1976: 3).

Obviously, the old and the new things and situations are not the same. As there is nothing constant, the transition from the old to the new involves disorder. The shifting conditions of business changes as well as our social outlook. In the course of time the force of circumstances change economic ideas. Economic conditions and economic ideas are interdependent. The old economic systems, for good or ill, change and create a new reality. In the light of the changed reality and ideas the entire situation will alter. We can understand that the whole process is related to an endless chain of permanent disorder.

It was changing economic realities that brought about the Renaissance and the Reformation. Thus, we can be confidant when we assert that political and cultural concerns influence the nature of economic activity. The Renaissance and the Reformation produced new patterns of cultural, political and economic behaviour. The ideas behind these social movements in turn exercised a profound effect on the economic reality and modified the predominant reality. The core requirement in the diminishing power of the church was the force of circumstances and the ideas that accompanied that changing reality. The church was not just in charge of divine and political power but was also "the greatest of feudal lords" (Roll 1983). The power of the church began to break down step by step. This process culminated finally in the Reformation. In the course of time, it retrieved and succumbed to wordly matters of progress, natural law, rational and scientific investigation. In Machiavelli words "necessity not virtue" became the guide for economic action (Roll 1983).

The steady and incremental undermining of the social influence of religious rules and traditions exercised a profound influence on economic development. The two forms of development are intertwined in countless ways. The issue of acquiring interest on loans was a crucial factor to the development of new economic activity. What had previously been regarded as sinful and unethical came to be viewed as an essential element in the life of an expanding economy. Religious assumptions and norms of behaviour were steadily displaced by an increasingly materialistic society.

Nobody knows for sure where the economy is heading ultimately. The answer is in the distant future. Knowledge of everything can neither be condensed within the remit of a single person nor in the minds of everyone collectively. The conditions of life are continuously changing. Consequently, our ideas and interests adapt and change too. Our ideas and interests are never the same. Whatever these ideas and interests might be, they merely mirror the condition of the society in which we live. These ideas and interests are always based on a mixture of truth, fiction, mysticism, ritual, intended and unintended consequences of our daily actions. We cannot simply know the causes and effects of all these activities in their entirety. One might contest the analogy but cannot disregard the manifestation of permanent economic disorders.

Modern, industrialised societies are highly complex. The intricacy of advanced economies is an exponential process. It is a process that is self-perpetuating. It inflates the division of labour. The essential point to be understood in this context is that economic improvement requires bigger and more sophisticated organisations, that is, greater cooperation. Closer examination of advances in economy reveals that economic agents increasingly become vulnerable with greater economic development. On the one hand, individuals enjoy greater wealth due to greater cooperation and on the other hand, they become more dependent. They become more specialised in much smaller economic tasks. The more sophisticated the division of labour, the less the members of a society can survive single-handedly. Let us take world trade as an example. An increase in world trade results in more prosperity but it will also intensify individual economic agent dependency on a greater number of people, products and markets. This economic dependency and the vulnerability of individuals augments with greater economic development and trade. This is yet another general indicative of perpetual disorder in the economy.

The wealth of industrialised societies has increased because of the improvement in a host of other components of the economy. Underpinning this development is the development of science and technology, development of infrastructure, appropriate institutions, rule of law, property rights, freedom of thought and association, improvement in financial markets and institutions and so on. The history of all these aspects of the economy is marked by their gradual and interdependent development. Moreover, they take place within the given context of the exercise of power. Such matters cannot be detached completely from some degree of ignorance, misinformation, corruption and mismanagement. In other words, they are not perfect and will never be perfect.

The pioneers of modern economics have experienced a wide range of general economic disorders and have reflected this in their writings. Their views relate to what they considered to be wrong and right at the time and the society in which they lived. Their general ideas and strategies are in effect products of their unique experience in certain historical phases. The first two schools of thought in economics, the Mercantilists and the Physiocrats, described some of these economic defects. Both schools of thought examined their societies and attempted to prescribe policies to improve the situation. They either detected disorders within the actual organisation of the economy or in the conventional wisdom that imposed its policy prescriptions.

3 Free markets and economic disorder

Introduction

One idea that has attracted the attention of mainstream economics since the publication of the *Wealth of Nations*, has been the idea of a market-driven economy. This is the devotion to the idea of a hands-off approach or self-managed economy as the most efficient economic system. The standard pro-market analysis depicts free markets as if they are encoded naturally to deliver the most perfect results, as if markets track the regularities of Mother Nature. Subordination to the will of the markets, it is held, is not just a natural process but it is the most advantageous and optimal mechanism for the allocation of scarce resources.

However, on further reflection we can detect two overriding misconceptions in this perspective that are generally overlooked. The generalisation, overall, does not convey what is intended totally. The first fallacy is that it equates free markets or economy to natural economic progression, order and optimum efficiency. This is a misreading of the subject that is advocated by both the proponents and the opponents of mainstream economics. Both sides imply that free markets are contradictory or even mutually exclusive in relation to economic disorders. As we shall find out in this chapter, nothing could be further from the case. This perspective is fundamentally at odds with the reality as well as the mass of economic literature. There is also an unspoken assumption of economic disorder within the model of the free market economy.

The second misconception is the failure to distinguish the difference between economic disorder and crisis. In this chapter we shall explain that economic disorder and economic crisis are two materially different conditions. We shall demonstrate that economic disorders are a permanent condition of every organised economy. After all, contrary to the general belief, economic disorder has tacitly or overtly been admitted by all schools of thought in economics. Not just that, every pioneering economist has launched his or her study from delving into one or another form of economic disorder.

This chapter is divided into six parts. The first two parts will establish how the classical political economists initiated their study of the economy based on the economic disorders of their time. The third part is on economists' response

DOI: 10.4324/9781003346364-4

to the economic disorders and the challenges that the industrial revolution had thrown at them. From part three onwards we shall examine various contests against the theoretical inadequacy of classical political economy. These theoretical inadequacies are also a testimony to the economic disorder that disconnects the theory from the formal economic reality. Different schools of thought that thrived after the era of classical political economics either accepted its core doctrines or rejected them entirely. In both cases they foster a different creed to the political economy. This is not the contentious part of our argument. Forming a new school involves denial, at least partially, of the validity of the preceding doctrines. Take the marginalist school for example. The marginalists did not reject the core principles of the classical political economy entirely. However, they regarded them as unscientific because they were not mathematical.

Part four of this chapter relates to two schools of thought that studied the economy from an entirely different standpoint from that of the classical school and their followers. These are the German Historical School and the American Institutionalist School. The followers of these schools consider economic disorders in contemporary economies as wholly unavoidable. Most of the studies by supporters of these schools focus on the issue of the economic disorders of contemporary economies and the failure of mainstream economics to explain or overcome such disorders. The chapter closes with a brief review of the Austrian and the Monetarist schools. The exponents of these schools are among the most ardent protagonists of free enterprise. However, they too are distinguished for underlining the economic disorders and for rebutting the fallacy of predominant economic doctrines.

Classical political economy and economic disorder

Adam Smith's crowning work, *The Wealth of Nations*, is marked as the beginning of modern economics. This work is regarded as the holy writ of the free market economy. At its core it regards the free market economy as consistent with the natural order. It regards the free market economy as a system assumed to be orderly and efficient. The depiction of classical economics in this way is somewhat incomplete. The work of Smith and his successors, on the contrary, are exemplary demonstrations of economic disorder. Their works, by and large, describe the versatile disorders that they witnessed in their time. It is to be remembered that Adam Smith did not only refute the views advocated by Mercantilists and Physiocrats but also reiterated the drawbacks of the prevailing economic system. Nonetheless, out of the two schools, he found his views to be closer to the views held by Physiocrats. Physiocracy, Smith argued, "with all its imperfections . . . the nearest approximation to the truth that has yet been published on the subject of political economy" (Smith 1976a: 199).

As a leading member of the age of Enlightenment, Smith rejected the old scholastic traditions. He did not put his faith in divinity and ancient scriptures. He relied on the way the ordinary people conducted their lives. It was the recognition of this fact that enabled him to escape from the old ideas. His approach was based on the power of reason and the natural order. Just like Newton's scientific revolution, Smith was captivated by natural order. Newton disclosed the order and harmony of the physical universe and Smith tried to find a similar kind of order in the economy.

Smith in his book, *The Theory of Moral Sentiments*, wrote that human conduct rests on the motives of self-love and sympathy—the desire to be free and a sense of propriety, and the habit of labour and the propensity to exchange. This classification of human motives was pivotal in his economic analysis in the *Wealth of Nations*. He places sympathy above all human passions. It is sympathy that unites individuals to one another to form a society. Smith held that it is the sense of fellow-feeling that "humbles the arrogance of self-love" and the predisposition that enable us to act as an impartial spectator (Smith 2006: 83).

Smith contested the conventional view in relation to moral sentiments of vice and virtue. He was enticed by the one unorthodox idea of Bernard Mandeville (1670–1733). Mandeville discussed his paradox of private vice and public benefit in his work, *The Fable of the Bees* (1989). He rebutted the idea that self-interested egoistic passions like vanity, greed and pride would always work against public benefit. In other words, acts of benevolence are always beneficial whereas acts of self-interest are publicly disadvantageous. Mandeville's sense of irony could not fit in well with the established morality of his time but to Smith it was a revelation. The common good would be accomplished, Smith postulated, when people are left free to pursue their self-interest. Most people would benefit from "the uniform, constant, and uninterrupted effort of every man to better his condition, the principle from which public and national, as well as private opulence is originally derived" (Smith 1976b: 343). To Smith the pursuit of self-interest in a free society and economy is a two-way track. In one direction individuals buy goods because they need the goods and are either unable or unwilling to produce them themselves. In the opposite direction the sellers of goods make profit because there are people who are willing to buy their goods and services that they offer.

Smith reiterated this relationship in his most quoted extract. He describes the mundane occupations of a butcher, a brewer and a baker in a free market and the unintended consequence of their trades. Smith states:

> It is not from the benevolence of the butcher, the brewer, or the baker, that we expect our dinner, but from their regard to their own interest. We address ourselves, not to their humanity but to their self-love, and never talk to them of our own necessities but of their advantages.
>
> (Smith 1986: 119)

In the former times, the pursuit of self-interest was judged as vice. It was fundamentally at odds with the core beliefs of religion. It was deemed as a completely perverted notion. However, it is very hard to envisage an organised economy without the quest for self-interest. Smith realised that one cannot play down or dismiss this fact. To follow his argument to its furthest conclusion, he needed a thorough clarification of the relationship between modern organised economies and the pursuit of self-interest. It was from this bare fact that he has inferred his far-reaching conclusions in relation to modern economies.

The difficulty was how to rescue the intensely disliked but much needed concept of self-interest from the grip of vice. If, indeed, it was true that self-interest does not belong to the realm of virtue then Smith required a very thorough and strong analysis to qualify his argument. Clearly it was a difficult hypothesis to substantiate. He had to find a safe sanctuary to outline and explain his heretical view. Smith placed his trust in what was described as the state of natural liberty, an idea that was much in vogue then. As in the state of natural liberty every individual behaves in accordance with one's self-interest. The idea was neither original nor profound. Its history went back to the ancient times. Hugo Grotius (1583–1645), however, in the 17th century used it in his book *The Law of War and Peace* (1625).

To Grotius, natural order and the civil society are regarded as compatible (Bates 2012: 56). This provided adequate ammunition for Smith to seek a similar kind of natural order in the economy. Smith was more concerned with the obstacles that prevented the application of natural order in the economy than the nature of the term itself. In relation to this very issue, he laid the blame at the doorstep of the state. According to Smith, government interference blocks the natural order of the economy. The natural order is embedded in economic freedom, free trade, laissez faire and free competition. Natural liberty is regarded as a self-healing mechanism that robotically directs the haggling of the buyers and sellers into organised orders. In this way "the wisdom of nature . . . [has] . . . made ample provisions for remedying many bad effects of the folly and injustice of man" (Smith 1976a: 53).

Smith argued at some length that interaction of cooperation and pursuit of self-interest is orderly. This is how he explained the process:

> As every individual, therefore, endeavours as much as he can both to employ his capital in the support of domestic industry, and so to direct that industry that its produce may be of the greatest value; every individual necessarily labours to render the annual revenue of society as great as he can. He generally . . . neither intends to promote the public interest, nor knows how much he is promoting it . . . he intends only his own security; and by directing that industry in such a manner as its produce may be of the greatest value, he intends only his own gain, and he is in this, as in so many other cases, led by an invisible hand to promote an end which was no part of his intention . . . By pursuing his own interest, he frequently promotes that of the society more effectually than when he really intends to promote it.
>
> (Smith 1827: 184)

Nevertheless, Smith assigns a very important role for government in his system of natural liberty. There are three functions of government that in the absence of which the natural liberty is defective. These are the establishment and maintenance of justice, national defence and public institutions. In a completely unregulated economy, monopolies will be formed. The lack of competition will create barriers to entry and diminish the control of the "invisible hand" over the market, resulting in monopoly power and monopoly prices. Besides, monopolies restrict individuals' needs and reduce their wealth and well-being. Smith censured the monopolists for "keeping the market continually understocked" and by selling "their commodities much above the natural price" (Smith 1986: 164).

Smith also pointed to several other limitations that would hamper the normal process of the system of natural liberty and enterprise. One of these limitations is the division of labour. Two determining causes of economic disorder for Smith are the division of labour and improvement in labour skills and education. Both factors will work to augment labour productivity, in particular the division of labour. However, the division of labour is also limited by the size of the Market. Besides, all labour is not equally productive. There is productive labour and there is unproductive labour. Government officials and professions such as priests, lawyers, physicians and singers, in his view, for example, are unproductive employment.

Smith's natural liberty and enterprise is based on a Universalist outlook. Natural liberty is not just applicable to domestic trade but also to international trade. In his critique of mercantilism, Smith puts forward a compelling argument for international trade. He refuted mercantilists' zero sum theory of trade. Smith reasoned that international trade is mutually beneficial. In another celebrated passage, Smith specified that:

> It is the maxim of every prudent master of a family, never to attempt to make at home what it will cost him more to make than to buy. The tailor does not attempt to make his own shoes but buys them from the shoemaker. The shoemaker does not attempt to make his own clothes but employs a tailor. The farmer attempts to make neither the one nor the other but employs those artificers. . . . What is prudence in the conduct of every private family, can scarce be folly in that of a great kingdom. If a foreign country can supply us with a commodity cheaper than we can make it, better buy it of them with some part of the produce of our own industry, employed in a way in which we have some advantage.
>
> (Smith 1869: 29)

Smith postulates a natural world. For Smith the economy of the natural world has a natural order. Let us take the relationship between value and price to demonstrate this point. For Smith, value and price are distinct. So how are the two distinguishable? The answer rests in Smith's labour theory of value. Labour is the measure of value. To qualify this assertion, he gives an example of "a nation of hunters." He adds if it "costs twice the labour to kill a beaver which it does to kill a deer, one beaver should naturally exchange for or be worth two deer. It is natural that what is usually the produce of two days' or two hours' labour, should be worth double of what is usually the produce of one day's or one hour's labour" (Smith 1986: 150).

Smith, in elucidating the distinction between use-value and exchange value, discloses an embedded potential disorder in the economy. He declares that value:

> has two different meanings, and sometimes expresses the utility of some particular object, and sometimes the power of purchasing other goods which the possession of that object conveys. The one may be called "value in use"; the other, "value in exchange." The things which have the greatest value in use have frequently little or no value in exchange; and on the contrary, those which have the greatest value in exchange have frequently no value in use. Nothing is more useful than water, but it will purchase scarce anything: scarce anything can be had in exchange for it. A diamond, on the contrary, has scarcely any value in use; but a very great quantity of other goods may frequently be had in exchange for it.
>
> (Smith 1986: 131–2)

The potential disorder does not end in the difference between use and exchange values but also in the difference between the natural and the market price. Smith equates the natural price to the costs of hiring labour, land and capital in a developed economy. That is sum of the wages, rent and profit. He then stipulates that "when the price of any commodity is neither more nor less than what is sufficient to pay the rent of the land, the wages of the labour, and the profits of the stock employed in raising, preparing, and bringing it to market according to their natural rates, the commodity is then sold for what may be called its natural price" (Smith 1986: 158). The natural price is the central gravity that all prices tend to gravitate towards.

Two points are worthy of note in this respect. Firstly, the size of each factor of production that is shared in production of a commodity also has a natural price. Natural price is transitory and occurs only occasionally. This is the crux of Smith's argument. In this way, Smith tacitly admitted a state of permanent disorder in the economy. Deviation from the natural price can be caused by different factors. The price can increase or decrease due to scarcity or abundance of the factors of production. It could also be caused by the conflict of interest between different social groups in society. Smith saw the possibility of such conflict between masters and workers, merchants and manufacturers, farmers and landlords. In this battle, Smith clearly indicated that the social classes who receive rent and profit are the privileged ones. They have monopoly power and hence will benefit at the expense of wage labourers. As a result, none of the social groups are priced at their natural level. In view of this implicit assumption, it can be said that economic disorder is permanent.

David Ricardo (1772–1823) read the *Wealth of Nations* in 1799. The book left a lifelong impression on Ricardo. It made him, in effect, become an outstanding economist. Ricardo's formative years were a time of great change and extreme social and economic upheaval. Europe was in the grip of the French Revolution and the Napoleonic wars. In this period the French and the British allocated much of their resources to their protracted wars. In addition to mass military expenditures, from the mid-1790s to 1825, England experienced several bad harvests and economic crises. Monetary crises progressed to such a height that the Bank of England suspended the convertibility of currency in 1797, only to be restored in 1819–21. Adding to all those difficulties was the unprecedented rise in England's population. English society saw a sharp increase in the number of dispossessed wage labourers.

The suspending of the convertibility of currency and the ensuing increase in bank credit led to a new economic debate. Many economists discussed the causes of the increase in prices and the depreciation of the pound in Britain. These discussions came to be known as the currency and the banking school's debate. This discussion went on until the 1844 Banking Act.

In his article, *The High Price of Bullion: A Proof of the Depreciation of Bank Notes* (1810), Ricardo argued that the increase in the volume of bank notes was the cause of the increase in the level of prices. Ricardo believed gold constitutes real money. Paper money is nothing but a form of representative money. The Bank of England in turn was the central custodian of the gold reserve. It had the power to control the gold reserve and hence the volume of money in the economy. Ricardo concluded that as the bank suspended its convertibility policy it supplied more notes than the gold reserves in the bank. So, oversupply of notes caused the prices to rise and the Pound to depreciate. The British House of Commons then appointed the Bullion Committee to study the situation. The Committee leaned more on the authority of Ricardo's reputation rather than conducting a critical investigation of the actual problem. Subsequently, they called for repealing the Bank Restriction Act.

Ricardo also joined the debate on the Corn Laws controversy in 1815. The Corn Laws were passed after a decline in wheat prices in Britain. The British Parliament passed these laws to restrict the import and export of grain. Parliament raised the tariff on import of wheat. In response to this policy, Ricardo wrote his *Essay on the Influence of a Low Price of Corn on the Profits of Stock* in 1815. In this essay, Ricardo criticised the policy and maintained that the increase in tariff will act against the industrialists and would benefit the landlords. It would increase the rent and decrease the profit of the industrialists. Ricardo's book *The Principles of Political Economy and Taxation*, 1817, is a product of such controversies and such a tumultuous period. The basic theme in all these works points to a multitude of defects and disorders in the economy and economic policies.

Above all, Ricardo was a humanist. His main concern was the determination of the laws and regulation of distribution of income. To this end he argued that:

> The produce of the earth—all that is derived from its surface by the united application of labour, machinery, and capital, is divided among the three

> classes of the community; namely, the proprietor of the land, the owner of the stock or capital necessary for its cultivation, and the labourers by whose industry it is cultivated.
>
> (Ricardo 1992: 3)

Thus, the element of economic disorder can be found in every strand of Ricardo's economic analysis. However, he is more explicit in relation to some economic disorders than others. For instance, he is very clear on the scarcity of fertile soil. The supply of land in general and the supply of fertile land in particular is limited. He points, with sufficient precision, to scarcity of fertile land as the source of rent. So, payment of rent is not a necessity but merely an aberration. Payment of rent is due to monopoly ownership of fertile land. Accordingly, rent varies with the quality of land in use. It corresponds to the quality of land. Rent will increase:

> When in the progress of society, land of the second degree of fertility is taken into cultivation, rent immediately commences on that of the first quality, and the amount of that rent will depend on the difference in quality of these two portions of land. When land of the third quality is taken into cultivation, rent immediately commences on the second, and it is regulated as before, by the difference in their productive powers. At the same time, the rent of the first quality will rise, for that must always be above the rent of the second, by the difference between the produce which they yield with a given quantity of capital and labour.
>
> (Ricardo 1992: 3)

The implicit assumption in this excerpt is that over time the economy will progress. Parallel to economic progress we will see rapid population growth. To keep pace with high rates of population growth, the less fertile lands are brought into cultivation. That in turn will result in a rise in the rent of the more fertile land. Such economic disorders are inexorable. They will continue until the law of diminishing returns sets in. Eventually, because of the combination of various factors the economy will approach its stationary state. The class that will benefit from this development is the landlord class. The reason for that is:

> in the progress of society and wealth, the additional quantity of food required is obtained by the sacrifice of more and more labour. This tendency, this gravitation as it were of profits, is happily checked at repeated intervals by the improvements in machinery connected with the production of necessaries, as well as by discoveries in the science of agriculture, which enable us to relinquish a portion of labour before required, and therefore lower the price of the prime necessary of the labour. The rise in the price of necessaries, and in the wages of labour is, however limited; for as soon as wages should be equal . . . to . . . the whole receipts of the farmer, there must be an end of accumulation; for no capital can then yield

> any profit whatever, and no additional labour can be demanded, and consequently population will have reached its higher point.
>
> (Ricardo 1992: 71)

Another major cause of economic disorder that Ricardo wrote about is the restrictions that were enforced against free trade. In his response to such restrictions, Ricardo provided one of the most compelling deductive justifications for free trade ever conceived of in economics. Ricardo put forward the idea that:

> Under a system of perfectly free commerce, each country naturally devotes its capital and labour to such employments as are most beneficial to each. This pursuit of individual advantage is admirably connected with the universal good of the whole. By stimulating industry, by rewarding ingenuity, and by using most efficaciously the peculiar powers bestowed by nature, it distributes labour most effectively and most economically: while, by increasing the general mass of productions, it diffuses general benefit, and binds together by one common tie of interest and intercourse, the universal society of nations throughout the civilized world. It is this principle which determines that wine shall be made in France and Portugal, that corn shall be grown in America and Poland, and that hardware and other goods shall be manufactured in England.
>
> (Ricardo 1992: 81)

Ricardo erected his economic system based upon Smith's doctrine of the laissez faire. Even this central premise is subject to constant disorder. It is subject to the iron law of wages as they defined it. The conviction is that wages at any period are determined at the subsistence level. Any attempt to increase real wages would therefore be entirely futile. Improvement in real wages is a self-defeating endeavour. It would not just increase the working population but also decrease the profit of manufacturers. In either case, wages ultimately would be reduced to the subsistence level.

Paupers struggle for survival

Thomas Robert Malthus (1766–1834) is best known for his theory of population. As a distinguished member of the classical school, he more than any other member of the school attempted to disentangle many economic disorders of his time. Malthus was not as optimistic about the future of humanity as most of his contemporary thinkers were. Optimistic confidence in a bright future was articulated most cheerfully in the work of William Godwin (1756–1836). Malthus' father was an eager disciple of this view. Godwin articulated the belief that one day in the not-too-distant future all misery, famine, inequality and injustices would disappear. But there was one major hurdle in attaining such an ideal society for Malthus. It was the rapid growth of human population and the incapacity of scarce resources to keep up with it.

This was the same conundrum that had preoccupied the mind of Charles Darwin (1809–82) for some years before reading Malthus's book on population. It was in Malthus's book, *An Essay on the Principle of Population* (1798), which he discovered the way out. Malthus's ideas cleared the way for Darwin to formulate his celebrated theory of evolution in his ground-breaking book, *The Origin of Species* (1859). Darwin in his Autobiography wrote that:

> In October 1838, that is, fifteen months after I had begun my systematic inquiry, I happened to read for amusement Malthus on Population, and being well prepared to appreciate the struggle for existence which everywhere goes on, from long-continued observation of the habits of animals and plants, it at once struck me that under these circumstances favourable variations would tend to be preserved, and unfavourable ones to be destroyed. The result of this would be the formation of a new species. Here, then, I had at last got a theory by which to work.
>
> (Darwin 1958: 120)

Malthus's theory of population states that land is limited in supply but there is no limit to population growth. Malthus commences his theory with two postulates: "First, that food is necessary to the existence of man. Secondly, that the passion between the sexes is necessary, and will remain nearly in its present state" (Malthus 1996: 4). He then extrapolates from his premises that "assuming, then, my postulate as granted, I say, that the power of population is indefinitely greater than the power in the earth to produce subsistence for man. Population, when unchecked, increases in a geometrical ratio. Subsistence only increases in an arithmetical ratio" (Malthus 1996: 5).

Based on these two postulates and their effects, Malthus construed his laws of population and his policy recommendations. Malthus claimed that population grows at a geometric rate, at the rate of 1, 2, 4, 8, 16 and the food supply increases at an arithmetic rate, at the rate of 1, 2, 3, 4, 5, 6 and so on. If this situation is unchecked, Malthus concluded that it eventually would lead to famine, misery, plague and war. He considered two solutions to the problem. He argued that nature will sort it out itself and adjust the level of population to the supply of food or we could reduce its impacts with support of some positive laws. In practice both forces are involved. Malthus asserts that:

> It is an evident truth that, whatever the increase in the means of subsistence, the increase in population must be limited by it, at least after the food has once been divided into the smallest shares that will support life. All the children born, beyond what would be required to keep up the population to this level, must necessarily perish, unless room be made for them by the deaths of grown persons. . .. To act consistently therefore, we should facilitate, instead of foolishly and vainly endeavouring to impede, the operations of nature in producing this mortality; and if we dread the too frequent visitation of the horrid form of famine, we should sedulously

> encourage the other forms of destruction, which we compel nature to use. Instead of recommending cleanliness to the poor, we should encourage contrary habits.
>
> (Malthus 1872: 411–12)

Malthus's final opinion on the matter was that poverty and misery are like a natural punishment for the "lower classes" who do not restrain their reproduction. He was opposed to any form of relief to the poor provided either by the government or charitable organisations. Such aids, in his view, do not just remedy the situation but would encourage the poor to increase their reproduction. He held the poor responsible for their terrible conditions and wrote:

> A man who is born into a world . . . if he cannot get subsistence from his parents on whom he has a just demand, and if the society do not want his labour, has no claim of *right* to the smallest portion of food, and, in fact has no business to be where he is. At nature's mighty feast there is no vacant cover for him. She tells him to be gone and will quickly execute her own orders.
>
> (Malthus 1989: 127—Italics in original)

Malthus sensed an inbuilt tendency of permanent disorder in the economy. He embarked on a quest to answer this question in his *Principles of Political Economy*. This was the tendency of insufficient effective demand, a theorem that was later instrumental in J. M. Keynes' refutation of the laissez faire doctrine. Contrary to the long-established view that all savings would be spent one way or another, Malthus argued that this is not necessarily the case. Provided that workers receive wages at the subsistence level, effective demand would be insufficient to buy all the goods produced. Reasoning that workers produce goods at a value greater than their wages, the surplus income created in production goes to the employers. Since the workers' wage income is insufficient to buy all the output produced, the demand for the surplus output should be provided from another source. If it does not come from wage income it must then come from the social classes whose incomes are greater than their consumptions. The manufactures and landlords, even though their populations are relatively small, were the social groups with considerable positive savings that could be channelled indirectly to consumption. This line of reasoning led Malthus to legitimise conspicuous consumption of affluent social groups as a needed curse to create extra demand for the surplus output, or else surplus products would stay unsold which would hamper further investment and cause economic crisis.

To overcome this problem, Malthus suggested that it would be implausible to disregard what was then considered as unproductive consumption. Malthus proceeded that:

> There must therefore be a considerable class of persons who have both the will and power to consume more material wealth than they produce, or

> the mercantile classes could not continue profitably to produce so much more than they consume. In this class the landlords no doubt stands pre-eminent; but if they were not assisted by the great mass of individuals engaged in personal services, whom they maintain, their own consumption would of itself be insufficient to keep up and increase the value of the produce and enable the increase of its quantity more than to counterbalance the fall of its price. Nor could the capitalist in that case continue with effect the same habits of savings.
>
> (Malthus 1986: 400)

Nassau William Senior (1790–1864) was a lawyer who moved into the field of economics. In spite being a radical conformist, he too spoke of many defects of the economy and took part in the designing and execution of many economic policies throughout the first half of the 19th century in Britain. The policies revolved around the Poor Laws, working time and population. To begin with, it was the state of the poor that drew his attention to economics, intended to improve the standard of living of the poor. In the latter years he allied the chief causes of poverty with the poor themselves and with the poor laws, maintaining that the government by assisting the poor would prevent them from liberating themselves from their long-standing poverty. In 1832 Senior was appointed to lead the Poor Law Inquiry Commission. The commission presented its report in 1834. In this report Senior articulated his recommendations about the Poor laws. The report attributed the blame for poverty to the poor themselves and held them responsible for their own misfortune. As the draconian recommendations of the report were implemented, the conditions of the poor deteriorated even more (Edsall 1971: 5–7).

Eric Hobsbawm (1917–2012), the eminent British historian, described Senior's recommendation and its implementation of the 1834 Poor law Act as:

> an engine of degradation and oppression. . . . There have been few more inhuman statutes than the Poor Law Act of 1834, which made relief "less eligible" than the lowest wage outside, confined it to the jail-like workhouse, forcibly separating husbands, wives, and children in order to punish the poor for their destitution, and discourage them from the dangerous temptation of procreating further paupers.
>
> (Hobsbawm 1999: 67)

Senior opposed the reduction of the working time to 12 hours per day as proposed in the 1833 Factory Act. It was not unusual then to employ large numbers of children to work in factories (Brue and Grant 2013: 145). Senior cast doubt about the validity of Malthus's theory of population and was less convinced about the scientific strength of the dominant economic theory. He put forward four general propositions in his book, *An Outline of the Science of*

Political Economy, upon which to erect the science of economics. These principles are:

> 1. That man desires to obtain additional wealth with as little sacrifice as possible.
> 2. That the population of the world, or, in other words, the number of persons inhabiting it, is limited only by moral or physical evil, or by fear of a deficiency of those articles of wealth which the habits of the individuals of each class of its inhabitants lead them to require.
> 3. That the powers of labour, and of the other instruments which produce wealth, may be indefinitely increased by using their products as means of further production.
> 4. That agricultural skill remaining the same, additional labour employed on the land within a given district produces in general a less proportionate return, or, in other words, that though, with every increase of the labour bestowed, the aggregate return is increased, the increase of the return is not in proportion to the increase of the labour.
>
> (Senior 1939: 26)

Classical political economy started with Adam Smith, and it concluded with John Stuart Mill (1806–73). Mill was a polymath, a prolific writer, and a fully enlightened liberal thinker. Mill's main contribution in economic theory was his distinction between production and distribution, contending that the two follow different laws. Production operates according to the laws of nature and distribution according to moral laws. Mill declares that:

> The laws and conditions of the production of wealth, partake of the character of physical truths. There is nothing optional or arbitrary in them. . .. It is not so with the Distribution of Wealth. That is a matter of human institutions solely. The things once there, mankind, individually or collectively, can do with them as they like.
>
> (Mill 1985: 349–50)

Mill, like the rest of the classical school, prophesised the eventual fall in the rate of profit in the industrialised economies. Granting that the economy rests on the principle of the laissez faire system, it eventually will reach a state in which production will approach a stationary level. The economy will reach its physical limits and economic growth will remain static. Production will meet its ultimate boundaries. That may be so, but to Mill this was not a bad thing. Unlike other members of the classical school, Mill believed that the stationary state has its own merits. It could divert our devotion to other much more fulfilling activities. Instead of going for profit, economic growth and a ferocious competitive life, we could spend our free time in pursuit of art, education, leisure and creativity.

Mill criticised the system of distribution of income in the laissez faire economy. He particularly censured the policy adopted against the rights of the workers and women. Their rights were blatantly violated. Women, as half of the population, were disenfranchised and workers worked long hours in terrible conditions. In defence of the political and economic rights of women, Mill remarked that:

> Let every occupation be open to all, without favour or discouragement to any, and employments will fall into the hands of those men and women who are found by experience to be most capable of worthily exercising them. There need be no fear that women will take out of the hands of men any occupation which men perform better than they. Each individual will prove his or her capacities, in the only way in which capacities can be proved—by trial; and the world will have the benefit of the best faculties of all its inhabitants. But to interfere beforehand by an arbitrary limit, and declare that whatever be the genius, talent, energy, or force of mind of an individual of a certain sex or class, those faculties shall not be exerted, or shall be exerted only in some few of the many modes in which others are permitted to use theirs, is not only an injustice to the individual, and a detriment to society, which loses what it can ill spare, but is also the most effectual mode of providing that, in the sex or class so fettered, the qualities which are not permitted to be exercised shall not exist.
>
> (Taylor and Mill 2004: 9)

Before closing this section, we should note that as the pace of industrialisation quickened, classical economics appeared less plausible and credible language of economic prescription. The rift between economic theory and economic reality widened. The class distinctions became much sharper. It became obvious that there was increasing wealth in fewer hands. Mounting acquisition of wealth went hand in hand with the rapid increase in the number of dispossessed labourers, poverty, insecurity, employment of women and children in workhouses. Shanty towns grew in cities near these workhouses and factories. In these vicinities, slums, vice, crime, disease, hunger and misery were the normal way of life. Workers were deprived of any formal rights and trade unions were illegal. It was against such a background that subsequent economists questioned the moral ethos and the epistemic adequacy of the classical economists' instructions and remedies.

Mechanisation and economic disorder

The industrial revolution broke up the previous social order and introduced the middle class in Britain. It widened the gap between social classes and different sectors of the economy. It sharpened the contrast between the landlords, industrialists, bankers, merchants, workers and other social groups. Each group competed not only in the same industry and sector but also in other industries and sectors too. As industrialisation took off and positioned into its safe trajectory, it fostered two superseding classes. These were the capitalist and the working classes. Neither group was homogenous. Both groups varied according to the wide-ranging industry and the sector of the economy. Collectively, however, despite their in-class diversity, the interest of the two classes was not compatible. An ongoing struggle between these classes developed. During this struggle the capitalists strived to reduce the cost of labour. Inevitably the working class fought to reduce labour time and increase their wages. Workers attempted to secure an improvement in the conditions of the workplace. The application of new machinery, procurement of higher profits and greater economies of scale over time gradually concentrated capital in fewer hands. The combination and interaction of all these forces resulted in the periodical cycle of over-production and under-consumption. This development had a series of consequences. It produced an army of the unemployed and a glut of unsold commodities. At this time there were more resources, capital and more advanced technology, capital accumulation and production compared to any other period in the past. However, in real terms the economy kept fluctuating, contracting and expanding. It happened so often that it even alarmed the British prime minister in the 1840s. Benjamin Disraeli defined England during this period as "the two nations" country (Glassman 2002: 2).

This period was a transitional epoch. It was a time of great social, political and economic upheaval. It was a period of severe social contrasts and violence. The advanced European nations were plunged into a revolutionary mode. The 1789 French revolution proclaimed "liberty, equality, fraternity" and the 1848 revolution formed the Paris Commune. The old political and religious order looked vulnerable to new ideas of social justice and change. Many traditional forces were ousted from power. The pace of scientific and technological progress was fast. The gap between the classical instructions, prescriptions and prognoses and the new economic reality was widening sharply. The good old days of classical political economy were clearly over. This economic school had run its course and passed its golden age. The new conditions and environment resulted in the formation of three new schools of thought in economics. These were the Marxian school, the German Historical school and the Marginalist school. We shall return to the Marxian account of economic disorder and crisis in Chapter 6. What follows next is the German Historical and the Marginalist schools, and their implicit acknowledgement of economic disorder respectively.

The German Historical school was established in the 1840s. It is drawn from the works of Friedrich List (1789–1846) and Wilhelm Roscher (1817–94). Among the pioneers of the school were also Bruno Hildebrand (1812–78) and Karl Knies (1821–98). These writers echoed the political and economic complications of Germany after the Napoleonic wars. J. K. Galbraith describes the German situation then as "a politically disorderly, economically backward melange of princely states" (Galbraith 2017: 100).

The victorious powers had a different plan for Germany after the war. Austria wanted to keep it weak and divided. Britain wanted a strong Prussia to counter France. Russia was yearning to usurp parts of Poland. In short, Germany was very weak, divided and primarily an agricultural society. Germany was encircled by many enemies and hostile neighbours. Its economic and political conditions were significantly different from those of Britain. Classical doctrines offered very little comfort for the difficulties that Germany was facing. Germany did not even have a unified identity. German patriots were preoccupied with such issues as the unification of Germany. They aspired to the formation of a national state. They yearned for constitutional political reforms. Strategic economic schemes and policies were not their priority.

It was under these conditions that German Historical writers supported government intervention in the economy. Without government assistance, they maintained, Germany could not catch up and compete with Britain. Their experience of an ever-changing Germany made classical economic doctrines appear rather irrelevant. It was obvious to all that there was a huge disparity between the British and the German economies. The contrast also indicated that nations develop at different speeds. Members of the German Historical school stipulated from self-evidential experience that stages of economic development are cumulative. They inferred that economic development should not be dissimilar to that of Darwin's evolutionary biology.

The German Historical school's system is based on the conviction that the state is the hallmark of social cohesion. Focal of a society is not the individual, the focal of a society is the state. A nation has interests of its own and these interests can be different from those of individuals. The State is the guardian of both the nation and individuals. The German Historical school proposed an inductive/historical approach in their study of the economy. They established a method that regarded the economy as a historical process. For them the economy was a part of an integrated whole. They argued that economists must not confine their analyses to economic motives. They believed that economists must analyse the moral merit and outcomes of economic activities as well. Overall, the German Historical school endorsed conservative reforms to divert the working class from revolution and socialist ideology.

Wilhelm Roscher maintained that societies begin with a state of immaturity. In time society then develops to maturity. Eventually, they decline, decay and perish. Friedrich List identified five crucial stages of development. These are original barbarism, pastoral condition, agricultural condition, agricultural manufacturing condition and agricultural manufacturing commercial condition. List in his influential book argued that "history teaches us how nations . . . may and must . . . modify their systems according to the measure of their own progress" (List 2005: 141, vol. I). He continues to say that we cannot detach each nation from its historical context. This is because the present state of any nation:

> is the result of the accumulation of all discoveries, inventions, improvements, perfections, and exertions of all the generations which have lived before us; they form the mental capital of the present human race, and every separate nation is productive only in the proportion in which it has

> known how to appropriate these attainments of former generations and to increase them by its own acquirements.
>
> (List 2006: 29–30, vol. II)

The German Historical school rejected the classical doctrine of the harmony of interest among diverse social groups in society. List resisted the view proclaiming that private interests of certain members may or may not be compatible to the highest good for the whole community. Certain individuals may become too rich, for example, by importing manufacturing goods while the nation's manufacturing industry may suffer because of it. In turn this may lead many workers to lose their jobs. So laissez faire economic theory cannot be applicable universally. For List, laissez-faire is "a maxim which sounds no less agreeable to robbers, cheats and thieves than to the merchant" (quoted from Gray 1957: 231). List argued that free trade works only among equals. Thus, "in order to allow freedom of trade to operate naturally, the less advanced nations must first be raised by artificial measures to that stage of cultivation to which the English nation has been artificially elevated" (List 2006: 20, vol. II).

Knowing that an economy develops in stages, then it was obvious that Germany was lagging behind Britain. For Germany to catch up it had to close the gap. Accomplishing this aim required state intervention. Adam Muller (1779–1829) assumed that the state "is not merely a fundamental human need; it is the supreme human need" (Gray 1957: 219). List also professed that a statesman who is not proactive is not a statesman. "A statesman will know and must know . . . how the productive powers of a whole nation can be awakened, increased, and protected, and how, on the other hand, they are weakened, laid to sleep, or utterly destroyed" (List 2006: 34, vol. III).

To many German social critics, it became obvious that the gap in economic development between the two nations could not be overcome without the protection of the infant industries. The social critics had to change their approach of inquiry to back up their economic evolutionary theory. The economy could not, in their view, be studied as a static entity. It had to be investigated as a dynamic process. Hence, the classical method was ineffective. The classical school looked for universal laws. This did not match well with a historical approach.

Gustav Schmoller (1838–1917) went as far as assigning the task of the study of the economy almost entirely around collecting self-evident historical and factual truths. The disagreement on what method is more appropriate to the study of an economy instigated an ill-tempered debate between Schmoller and Carl Menger in 1883. Schmoller was so hostile to the method of deductive reasoning that he accused those who used this method as being unfit to teach in a German university. He argued that such academics had to be ostracised and ousted from their teaching positions in German universities. Menger in his response to Schmoller's criticism published a pamphlet entitled, *Errors of Historicism*. Menger retorted that:

> The historians have stepped upon the territory of our science like foreign conquerors, in order to force upon us their language and their customs,

> their terminology and their methods, and to fight intolerantly every branch of enquiry which does not correspond with their special method.
>
> (quoted from Brue and Grant 2013: 216)

At this point we can digress and safely skip to the Marginalist School. The founders of this school targeted the classical economics from a different angle. They claimed that they had discovered the solution to the classical paradox of value in use and value in exchange and used the example of the water and diamonds paradox. In this equation the total utility of water is greater than that of diamonds, but the marginal utility of diamonds exceeds that of water. It follows then that as we consume more units of a good, our total utility will naturally increase. However, the consumption of any additional unit does not add equal utility to our total utility. Marginal utility decreases as we consume one additional unit of a good. The more units of a good we have, the lower price we are prepared to pay for it.

There are two elements of economic disorder in this line of thinking. First the alternative theory openly regards the classical view of exchange as incorrect. Secondly it concedes that our satisfaction diminishes as we have more of the same goods. In other words, value or price is not static. Value is a dynamic entity. It decreases with the quantity of goods available.

William Stanley Jevons (1835–82) says that "final degree of utility . . . varies with the quantity of [the] commodity, and ultimately decreases as that quantity increases. No commodity can be named which we continue to desire with the same force, whatever be the quantity already in use or possession" (Jevons 1871: 62, vol. I). John Bates Clark (1847–1938) extended the constituent of the diminishing marginal returns to production in his theory of distribution. Clark pointed out that "the last tool adds less to man's efficiency than do earlier tools. If capital be used in increasing quantity by a fixed working force, it is subject to a law of diminishing productivity. . .. The diminishing productivity of labour, when it is used in connection with a fixed amount of capital, is a universal phenomenon. . .. The action of the general law . . . becomes the basis of a theory of distribution" (Clark 1899: 48–50).

We must add that the concept of the margin was not the invention of the Marginalist school. Antoine Cournot and Jules Dupuit (1804–66) in France and Johann Heinrich von Thünen (1783–1850) in Germany, and David Ricardo, all used the concept in their works. Friedrich von Wieser (1851–1926) coined the term "marginal utility." The Marginalist school made the idea the centre of their economic system. This school of thought was the work of three talented economists. William Stanley Jevons (1835–82) published his book *Theory of Political Economy* in (1871). In the same year Carl Menger (1840–1921) independently discussed the idea in his treatise of *Principles of Economics*. In 1874 Marie-Esprit-Léon Walras (1834–1910) also raised the point in his book *Elements of Pure Economics*.

The focus of the Marginalist writers is the individual. The Marginalist's economics begins and ends with the individual. Economic agents are individuals. Economic agents are rational and utility maximisers. We find the clearest expression of the economics of individualism in Menger's works. Menger professes, social sciences can be as reliable as natural sciences if we apply a correct method of ontological individualism. Menger reduces complex society to its most basic element (Cubeddu 1993: 85). The individual is the base and the essence of the economy and is an indivisible rational unit. The individual's actions are an ontological necessity. A rational economic maximiser, according to Herbert Simon, is someone "who will settle for nothing less than the best" (quoted from Teraji 2016: 9).

From this point of view individuals do not have a unified sense of value. It is different from one individual to another, as such value depends on utility. Jevon argued that the costs of production occur in the past. When a good comes to the market its value depends not on the costs of production but upon the utility the buyers think they get by having the good. Jevons states "the fact is, that labour once spent has no influence on the future value of any article: it is gone and lost forever. In commerce bygones are for ever bygones" (Jevons 1888: 164). Then deducing from this assertion that value depends on utility and its unit of measurement are pleasure and pain. Exchange conveys the same level of satisfaction in that the counterparties maximise their satisfaction. In Menger's words: "the principle which leads men to exchange is the same principle that guides them in their *economic* activity as a whole; it is the endeavour to ensure the fullest possible satisfaction of their needs" (Menger 2007: 180, Italics in original).

Sale and purchase, in each transaction, is determined by the last unit of utility or profit. Jevons remarks that "we shall seldom need to consider the degree of utility except as regards the last increment which is consumed" (Jevons 1871: 61, vol. I). Two goods are exchanged when marginal utility of a good (X) divided by its price is equal to the marginal utility of the other good (Y) divided by its price. In Jevons' notation MUx/Px = MUy/Py. This approach was proposed to counter the classical and Marxian theory of exchange.

Jevons branded classical economics as pre-scientific. For economics to become scientific, he declared that it "must be mathematical" (Jevons 1871). Francis Y. Edgeworth (1845–1926) entitled his book *Mathematical Psychics* (1881) to give the book an air of scientific respectability. He derogatively described nonmathematical economics as the "zigzag windings of the flowery path of literature" (quoted from Khwaja 2013: 476). The remarkable accomplishments of mathematics in natural sciences deeply impressed these writers. Philip Mirowski contended that

> the progenitors of neoclassical economic theory boldly copied the reigning physical theories in the 1870s. The further one digs, the greater the realization that those neoclassicals did not imitate physics in a desultory or superficial manner; no, they copied their models mostly term for term and symbol for symbol and said so.
>
> (Mirowski 1999: 3)

All the same, the Marginalist revolution did not achieve definitive authority over a single period. It secured a long-lasting dominance in mainstream economics.

Alfred Marshall (1842–1924) fused classical cost theory with marginalist utility theory. Marginalism was firmly grounded in the modern neoclassical economics. It was due to the influence of the marginalists that Marshall switched the title of the subject from "political economy" to "economics." This can be seen as an attempt to disengage economics from political philosophy. In his acclaimed textbook, *Principles of Economics*, Marshall alleges that we "cannot create material things." We simply produce "utilities" (Marshall 2009: 53). When Marshall inserted the utility theory into production, he had two targets in mind. His first objective was to marry the classical cost theory (supply) to the marginalist utility theory (demand). This concept framed his partial equilibrium theory.

The cost of production in normal conditions in classical economics is identical to the market price. It is the cost of labour-time. It is something that is on the supply side of the market. For the Marginalists, the market price is determined by the utility of the goods. The desire of consumers for the goods is significant. Market demand is crucial. Marshall contested both inferences of the supply and demand sides of the argument. He reasoned that:

> We might as reasonably dispute whether it is the upper or the under blade of a pair of scissors that cuts a piece of paper, as whether value is governed by utility or cost of production. It is true that when one blade is held still, and the cutting is affected by moving the other, we may say with careless brevity that the cutting is done by the second; but the statement is not strictly accurate and is to be excused only so long as it claims to be merely a popular and not a strictly scientific account of what happens.
>
> (Marshall 2009: 290)

Marshall argued it is a mistake to assume that price can only be determined either by supply or demand. It is determined by both sides, supply and demand. He regarded economics like biology that follows the path of Darwinian evolution. The method of inquiry in economics should therefore be an essentially evolutionary method since "nature does not make jumps" (Gordon 2002: 253). Marshall's background was in mathematics. The application of mathematics in his analysis is negligible. In 1906 he wrote:

> [I had] a growing feeling in the later years of my work at the subject that a good mathematical theorem dealing with economic hypotheses was very unlikely to be good economics: and I went more and more on the rules—(1) Use mathematics as a shorthand language, rather than as an engine of inquiry. (2) Keep to them till you have done. (3) Translate into English.

> (4) Then illustrate by examples that are important in real life. (5) Burn the mathematics. (6) If you can't succeed in (4), burn (3). This last I did often.
> (Marshall 1996: 130)

Exodus from supply and demand

By the late 19th century, the US economy had been transformed into a mature industrial economy. The course of economic development in the United States undermined the authenticity of classical and neo-classical theory. Economic growth, of its own accord, did not improve workers' living conditions. Workers worked hard and for long hours but experienced not much improvement in their living conditions. Their jobs were insecure and there were no or very few health and safety regulations in the workplace. Workers and their children were deprived of education, especially access to higher education. Mass migration into the country kept labour supply high and wage rates low. Credit markets were underdeveloped and were crippled by extensive usury laws. Regressive taxation dominated the taxation system. The working population and the poor were under constant economic pressure to make ends meet. The first generation of American economists were drawn from among these immigrants. Most of them were from Germany and had their training in the German Historical school.

The school that Thorstein B. Veblen (1857–1929) founded, the Institutionalist school, rejected the assumptions and conclusions of the Marginalist and New Classical schools. He regarded these schools as being untenable. The Institutionalist writers disagreed with the proposition that economic activities are the sum of the activities of individuals motivated mechanically to maximise their pleasure. They considered this definition as too narrow and unreal. Economic activities, they argued, are not the work of isolated individuals but are social activities. In turn, social activities form patterns in action that create collective behaviour. This collective action is greater than the sum of its parts. The combined interaction of such activities in each time and place develops specific modes of thought, character, ideology and relations of production and exchange. Thus, economics is not a self-contained subject. It does not exist in isolation. It is not detached from politics, sociology, law, morality, custom, ideology, tradition, history, institutions, science and technology.

The matters of economic facts on which economic judgements are based cannot be deduced by the study of isolated individual behaviour. Such judgements require the study of institutions (Commons 1931). Institutions determine the society through the means of collective actions. Collective actions shape and control individuals' actions. Such actions also liberate individuals. John R. Commons (1862–1945) states that collective action would free the individual and is "liberation and expansion of individual action" (Commons 1931: 651).

Two implications follow from this approach. Both are overlooked in neoclassical economics. In the first place, collective action requires cooperation.

Human societies cannot function without cooperation. This is the least contentious part of the argument. Any lasting and relatively complex social cooperation requires group formations. In these formations the members of the group collaborate in pursuit of their mutual self-interest. The second implication that can be deduced from this inference is that different individuals can exercise different economic, social, legal and political power in the group. That is, a society is composed of conflict of interests between various social groups. For instance, there are conflicts of interests between big business and small business, consumers against producers, employers against workers and so on.

The Institutionalists contested the neoclassical supposition that the economy is composed of rational, atomistic and hedonistic individuals. The Institutionalists did not agree that such individuals are acting in a harmonious manner in an economic setting that is perfectly competitive. John R. Commons confronted the supposition that collective actions among diverse social groups with different economic, social, cultural and political power are harmonious. Collective action of diverse interests cannot be harmonious. By its very nature the diversity of interest and power in one social setting entails order. That does not counter the fact that under such a situation all participants would not benefit from the management of conflicts. Laissez faire is incapable of achieving that. In complex societies it is only partially attainable through the mediation of government. Market prices are not adequate indices of individual and social welfare. Nor are they a true reflection of an effective and efficient use of resources. The Institutionalists called for reform to erase some excesses of free market forces of supply and demand. They desired reform not only to overcome the failings of the market but also to reconcile the clashes of interests for the common good. The most effective institution that is capable of meaningful mediation, from their perspective, is a representative and impartial government.

The Institutionalists went head-to-head with the neoclassical method of analysis. Economic activities from the Institutionalist perspective are not stationary. In the evolutionary contests, those sides that are best suited to the changing environment would survive and proliferate and the opposite sides would stagnate and perish. From this perspective economic equilibrium is unattainable. The Institutionalists charged the neoclassicals as being ahistorical and from the Institutionalist standpoint there will be "no understanding of economics without an awareness of its history" (Galbraith 2017: 1). Economics, Galbraith noted, "is obsessively concerned with the future . . . and . . . the present, in turn, is profoundly a product of the past . . . what we now believe in economics has deep roots in history" (Galbraith 2017: 4–5). In this battle between the future and the past there are those who want to move forward and there are those who benefit from the status quo. Understandably, economic agents "who benefit from the *status quo* resist change, as do economists who have a vested interest in what has always been taught and believed" (Galbraith 2017: 2—Italics in original).

Veblen designated the neoclassical theory as teleological and pre-Darwinian. He defined it as teleological because equilibrium is its ultimate end. It is not just that—they also imply that equilibrium is socially beneficial. It is taxonomic because it classifies the economy into parts that are fixed and unchanging. In its price theory buyers and sellers have complete knowledge, which is unfounded. Many factors such as tastes, preferences, technology, organisations and institutions are fixed. Contrary to neoclassical belief, real individuals are not driven by the desire to maximise pleasure and minimise pain. Neither does the pursuit of self-interest necessarily promote social interest. Instead, Veblen says, "man is not simply a bundle of desires but rather a coherent structure of propensities and habits which seeks realisation and expression in an unfolding society" (Landreth and Colander 1994: 323).

Veblen in his book, *The Theory of the Leisure Class*, argues that in a market economy all actions are judged by money and wealth. The institutions of the market change the patterns of consumption. The accumulation of wealth in the language of the market is not for satisfying physical, spiritual, aesthetic or intellectual wants. The intention is to display one's wealth. The wasteful consumption cultivates reputation, power, prestige and honour. The market economy is an economy of the pecuniary culture that involves the pursuit of conspicuous leisure and pecuniary emulation. We see no distinction between production for use and production for profit in the culture of the market. Business prevents production for use. This is because the nature of business is:

> to "make money" not to produce goods. The production of goods is a mechanical process. It is incidental to the making of money. The making of money is a pecuniary operation, carried on by bargain and sale, not by mechanical appliances and powers. . .. The highest achievement in business is the nearest approach to getting something for nothing.
>
> (Veblen 2005: 92)

The leisure class is not interested in useful and productive work. This is because:

> These occupations are government, war, sports, and devout observances . . . the ordinary and ostensible motive of the leisure class in engaging in these occupations is assuredly not an increase of wealth by productive effort. At this time as at any other cultural stage, government and war are, at least in part, carried on for the pecuniary gain of those who engage in them; but it is gain obtained by the honourable method of seizure and conversion. These occupations are of the nature of predatory, not of productive, employment.
>
> (Veblen 1943: 40)

In the market dominion a public-spirited businessperson who disregards profits will be put out of business before long. The Constitution of the market is private property. Veblen deliberates that "human nature being what it is, the struggle of each to possess more than his neighbour is inseparable from the institution of private property" (quoted from Reisman 2012: 101). Therefore, the formation of monopoly is most favourable in the culture of unrestricted private property. Monopolies restrict production and raise prices. In doing that they reduce investment and may cause economic depression.

To Institutionalist writers the lever of change is technology. Technology has its own dynamism. Scientists, engineers and inventors always try to improve technology, methods of production and organisations. The business class do not share this view. The prospect of profit is their main priority. Hence with the development of the economy the conflict between technology and the business class will tend to grow. For Veblen this conflict will eventually result in a significant rift in society. The upshot of this rift is socialism. Veblen argues that the new arrangement would be dominated by science and technology. Production then will be planned to serve the needs of the community and to promote the welfare of the society.

Institutionalists presented a detailed analysis of business cycles. Wesley Clair Mitchell's (1874–1948) study of business fluctuations is among one of the most thorough and insightful early studies in the field. His book on business cycles was published about two decades before the Great Depression. Mitchell attributes cycles to the extensive use of money in the economy. He commented that "it is not until the uses of money have reached an advanced stage in a country that its economic vicissitudes take on the character of business cycles" (Mitchell 1930: 75). Sharp economic fluctuations occur in monetary economies as they are complex and interdependent arrangements. In monetary economies the failures or successes of firms and sectors of the economy are continuously communicated within the labyrinth sensorium of industrial, commercial and financial ties.

In short, according to Mitchell, business cycles are regular events. Trade cycles are integral parts of a pecuniary commercial society. This is because in this form of economic arrangement profit is the primary focal motive of any economic activity. Business fluctuations will follow the pattern of the prospect for profit. Businesses are set up in anticipation of awaited profits. The motive of expected profit is a more powerful incentive than the concern for past profits or losses. Firms look forward rather than backward for profit. There will be more investment when the anticipated profits are higher. A business cycle commences when there is an outbreak of optimism. As the trail of optimism spreads, output, employment and profit begin to rise. Profits continue rising as long as the prospect of making profit is positive. Then other forces set in and prices begin to rise. An increase in prices fuels the orders for more goods. In the meantime, as profits keep rising, credit expands. One of the reasons that profits keep rising is that wage and overhead costs fall behind rising prices. The increase in profit leads to more investment in capital goods. This can in turn lead to an economic boom. This process will increase the costs of conducting business. The costs of raw materials, wages and interest will begin to rise.

Towards the end of the boom the increase in demand for goods compels the firms to employ overtime labour. The best resources are employed first. The most effective management is applied during the first period of growth and the most efficient workers were employed then. At the peak of the cycle, inputs of production will be less efficient but more expensive. This is followed by the increase in sticky prices such as rents and rates. The increasing costs of production eat into the firms' profit. Interest on loans will increase and creditors will demand their funds to be repaid all in good time. Eventually the situation will run out of control. Mistrust will spread and vast liquidation will change the whole direction of the economy. Firms dump their goods into the market to avoid the looming prospect of bankruptcy. That extenuates the rate of bankruptcy by spreading economic despondency and gloom. That leads to a drastic reduction in investment. In turn the economy dives into depression with many of the workforce being thrown out of the employed labour market.

Mitchell's sketch of the business cycle was imaginative and one of a kind for its time. The Great Depression of 1929, however, changed the standard view about the market-driven economy. It shook the very foundation of conventional economics. The Wall Street crash occurred in October 1929. In the United States the output of capital goods in 1932 was a quarter of what it was in 1929. Within the same period industrial production dropped to half of what it was a couple of years earlier. Output plummeted to roughly two-thirds of previous levels. In 1929 unemployment in America was half a million. It increased to 12 million in 1932. Just in industrialised countries unemployment climbed to 30 million by 1933 (Stewart 1991: 55–6).

Business cycles as regular sequences that could spiral out of control did not fit within the established classical and neoclassical economic paradigm. The random fluctuation in a sector of the economy was possible but not a general glut or the collapse of the whole economy. There was an unbending faith in the self-regulating market and full employment as a natural condition. The periodic increases in unemployment were viewed as an aberration. By defining an economic concept as natural meant it accorded to the tenets of a free laissez-faire economy. In Say's law there can be no general surplus production (Sowell 1972: 4). The occasional over- and under-expansion of capital goods is merely caused by the unbalanced structure of production. This issue is seen to remedy itself automatically. The increase in wages leads to a decrease in the number of workers being employed. The unemployed workers then push wages down. Unemployed workers are then re-employed on lower wages. The marginal productivity theory reinforced this view. In a nutshell, workers were blamed for being unemployed as they could obtain employment if they accepted market wage rates.

However, this is not what happened in the Great Depression. Unemployed workers looked for work at lower wages but could not find a job. Despite this reality, conventional economics called for lower wages. Their remedy was to reduce the level of wages even further. They believed this would be followed by a balanced budget. Just leave the economy to its own devices and it by its own efforts would take its natural course. The Great Depression left a profound mark on J. M. Keynes (1883–1946). After the depression, Keynes realised that there was something seriously wrong with the accepted economic theory. He concluded that neither an unregulated economy nor orthodox remedies could fully be relied on to maintain full employment. Keynes's magnum opus, *The General Theory of Employment, Interest and Money*, constituted a significant break with his past. It was "a repudiation of the foundations of laissez-faire" (Dillard 1966: 1). Keynes's book revolutionised economic theory in the 20th century. We shall return to Keynes's discourse on economic disorder and crisis at length in Chapter 5.

Praxeology and individual action

Two new schools appeared contemporaneously. These are the Marginalist School and the Austrian School. Both schools were born in the 1870s. Their core principles share a great deal of common ground. Carl Menger (1840–1921) is one of the pioneers in both schools. The Austrian School was also a product of its time. It emerged as an alternative paradigm in the face of the failure of dominant economic theory to explain contemporary economic disorders. Carl Menger's book, *Principles of Economics*, marks the beginning of the school. The book was published in 1871. It represented a departure from the German Historical school. Carl Menger led the first generation of the school. Ludwig von Mises (1881–1973) dominated the second generation and Friedrich von Hayek (1889–1992) the third generation.

Methodological individualism can be regarded as the guiding principle of the school. The basic position of this school is most succinctly enunciated by Israel M. Kirzner. He says,

> society is made up of numerous individuals. Each individual can be viewed as independently selecting his goal program . . . and each individual adopts his own course of action to achieve his goals. It is therefore unrealistic to speak of society as a single unit seeking to allocate resources in order to faithfully reflect "its" given hierarchy of goals. Society has no single mind where the goals of different individuals can be ranked on a single scale.
>
> (Kirzner 2007: 35)

Thus, if the aim is to improve efficiency, Kirzner remarks "efficiency for a social system means the efficiency with which it permits its individual members to achieve their several goals" (Kirzner 2007: 35).

The concept of "fact" has a specific meaning in Austrian methodology. From their perspective, facts in relation to the natural sciences are what the actors think and believe. In social sciences fact can be defined in a distinct manner. Facts relate primarily to the purposes and plans of individuals. Thus, in the natural sciences our key aim is to understand and then to predict. By contrast, the aim of the social sciences is to render human action intelligible.

Since individuals act, the focus of economics should be on individuals. Mises reasons that:

> In our view the concept of man is, above all else, also the concept of the being who acts. Our consciousness is that of an ego which is capable of acting and does act. The fact that our deeds are intentional makes them actions. Our thinking about men and their conduct, and our conduct toward men and toward our surroundings in general presuppose the category of action.
>
> (Mises 2003: 15)

Individuals' actions are values that can only be fully known to the individual who acted. Mises holds that "no sensible proposition concerning human action can be asserted without reference to what the acting individuals are aiming at and what they consider as success or failure, as profit or loss" (Mises 1962: 80). Moreover, individuals' values, plans, expectations and understanding are entirely subjective. The subjective valuation of goods creates economic value. The subjective valuation implies individuals making choices. Hence, society cannot choose of its own accord. It is the individual who exercises choice. The aim of economic analysis should focus on the intelligibility of individual purposes, plans and actions. As a complementary task, economists should study and map out the unintended consequences of individual choices. We have no facts as such but subjective values. These subjective values are our data. Such data cannot be measured mathematically. Value, ultimately, is the measure of the intensity of an individual's desire for a thing.

To the Austrian school human knowledge is a subjective evaluation. As such it can never be defined precisely. There will always be an element of the unknown in economic activities. The unknown will never disappear. This reality makes our knowledge of the economy imperfect. For this reason, economic agents speculate, out of practical necessity, in everything they do. F. A. Hayek asks the question:

> How can the combination of fragments of knowledge existing in different minds bring about results which, if they were to be brought about deliberately, would require a knowledge on the part of the directing mind which no single person can possess?
>
> (Hayek 2014: 5)

If we cannot achieve perfect knowledge, what then is the function of economic theory? Can there be any valid economic theory? In Austrian economics, the most valid economic theory is the one that is derived deductively from human action. However, this method should be supported with praxeology and an interpretive understanding of history. Praxeology is used to deduce economic laws that encompass all human action. The interpretive approach questions a specific historical episode (Udehn 2001: 113). The implications of this methodology are that the individual actions take place in a specific time and place. An economic agent selects a desired end. Then the economic agent adopts a means to achieve that specific end. No other person would be more informed about the choice of the end and the means than the individual who has acted. Even the same individual would not be fully informed about his or her action, let alone those who would attempt to study his or her action. Therefore, no economic decision is fully rational. In a market, all economic agents have diverse desires, plans, ends and means. All these agents act under conditions of uncertainty. They do not know the plans, ends and actions of other individuals totally. The outcomes of these actions will be known only after the action has taken place. The issue is more complex than it first appears. In the first instance we have the outcomes of actions that cannot be predicted. This is followed by the interval of time between the desire, plan and action to the outcome of the action. During these intervals the economic agents would influence each other. The economic agents alter what was intended. Consequently, what was desired and planned may not be attained.

According to this argument we cannot have equilibrium in the economy. In an economy based on an equilibrium, the goods are willingly produced, supplied and cleared. So the supply of goods will be equal to the demand for goods. At this equilibrium market price, producers maximise their profit and consumers maximise their utility. In this perfect and optimum state of affairs, all the resources are allocated most efficiently. In a world of continual change, Hayek purported, equilibrium is a virtual impossibility.

Within the confines of these parameters the Austrian school argued for a free market economy. It regarded the free market economy as the most effective economic system known hitherto. They have opposed any form of planned economy and defended private property as one of the most fundamental and vital constituents of the market economy. The private ownership of the means of production is indispensable in their economic view. Private ownership is crucial for the effective application of the market price and for economic calculation. The market price is not only a price. It is the signal, the information to make decisions to buy or to sell. Market prices summarise the required information for market participants to make timely and sound decisions. Markets decentralise economic decision making. By means of trial and error, markets will coordinate economic activities. This process creates a harmonious order among numerous individuals with diverse interests and demands. Kirzner states that the price system will emerge whenever "a profit opportunity exists wherever a given resource or a given product can be bought in the market at one price and sold again for a higher price. [Therefore,] a possibility for profit exists wherever there is a price discrepancy" (Kirzner 2007: 302–3). Market price acts as a signal that directs the allocation of resources where more profit can be made. Kirzner continues,

> a price discrepancy means a chance to make profits. By definition entrepreneurs seek profits; thus, the very situation that symptomizes the

> need for a correction creates the force capable of inducing such actions. Moreover . . . the entrepreneurial search for profits implies a *search for situations where resources are misallocated.*
>
> (Kirzner 2007: 303, Italics in original)

The proponents of the Austrian school took a strong stance against the command economy. They opposed the economic system that was implemented in the Soviet Union. They were also very critical of the Keynesian theory of management of aggregate demand. Mises argued that the first task of economists should be to tell the government what it cannot do. Everyone would be better off if the government is prevented from influencing economic activity. Murray N. Rothbard comments that:

> *no government interference with exchanges can ever increase social utility* . . . whenever government forces anyone to make an exchange which he would not have made, this person loses in utility as a result of the coercion. But taxation is just such a coerced exchange . . . since all government actions rest on its taxing power, we deduce that: *no act of government whatever can increase social utility.*
>
> (Rothbard 2011: 323 Italics in original)

Socialism, Mises argues, is flawed because it "cannot be realized . . . it is beyond human power to establish it as a social system." Mises reckons "a man who chooses between drinking a glass of milk and a glass of potassium cyanide does not choose between two beverages; he chooses between life and death. A society that chooses between capitalism and socialism does not choose between two social systems; it chooses between social cooperation and disintegration of society" (Mises 1998: 676).

The Austrian school presents two main reasons for the failure of the command economy. First, we cannot have perfect knowledge. Logically, perfect socialism requires perfect knowledge. In any economic system, economic activities cannot be free from the element of uncertainty. All economic activities involve elements of uncertainty and risk. Therefore, there can be no perfect economic plan. The calculation and implementation of a strategy or plan cannot be perfect when our knowledge is imperfect. Mises gives details as to why economic measurement in socialism is largely impractical. Impossibility of measurement, he maintains:

> is not due to the lack of technical methods for the establishment of measure. It is due to the absence of constant relations. If it were only caused by technical insufficiency, at least an approximate estimation would be possible in some cases. The main fact is that there are no constant relations. Economics is not, as ignorant positivists repeat again and again, backward because it is not "quantitative." It is not quantitative because there are no constants. Statistical figures referring to economic events are historical data. They tell us what happened in non-repeatable historical cases.
>
> (Mises 1998: 56)

Monetarism and monetary disorders

The history of monetary disorders dates to time immemorial. These disorders comprise many diverse causes and factors. These include the absence of a generally accepted medium of exchange, lack of standardisation of the medium of exchange, debasing the medium of exchange, fluctuations in exchange rate, the usury interest rates, the usury laws and inflation to that of underdevelopment of credit institutions and instruments. There are written records of such matters in the earliest religious scripts as well as in the works of the ancient social critics and philosophers.

Aristotle's view on money dominated the theory of money for over two millennia. He identified three functions of money. These were as a unit of account, a store of value and a medium of exchange. Aristotle regarded money as a veil, something that is barren by nature. Aristotle saw money as an instrument that is neutral. Nonetheless, it facilitates the exchange. This is the foundation upon which Aristotle based the centrepiece of his theory of exchange and interest. Exchange is in real terms the swap of equivalence. So, the payment of interest on money is deemed unnatural since the creditor pays the lender more than the amount borrowed.

The theory of money stagnated for about two millennia. There was not any significant advancement in Aristotle's theory until the discovery of the new world. The discovery of the new world transformed Western and Northern Europe. Gold effectively changed the world. Gold was the main medium of exchange. The massive influx of gold into Europe amplified the role of money and interest in the economy. It helped to create a new reality that required new interpretation and theory.

The departure from the old doctrines was slow and vigilant. More daring enlightened social critics confronted the old way of thinking. David Hume (1711–76) was amongst most systematic thinkers who drew his analyses of monetary matters from the new reality. In his essay *Of Interest*, Hume explained causes of high or low rates of interest not from the old texts but from existing economic conditions. He wrote:

> The rate of interest . . . is not derived from the quantity of the precious metals. . .. High interest arises from three circumstances: A great demand for borrowing; little riches to supply that demand; and great profits arising from commerce . . . low interest, on the other hand, proceeds from the three opposite circumstances: A small demand for borrowing; great riches to supply the demand; and small profits arising from commerce: And these circumstances are all connected together, and proceed from the increase of industry and commerce, not of gold and silver.
>
> (Hume 2003: 127)

It was this realistic scrutiny of the actual economy that retracted the Aristotelian supremacy. The educated approach paved the way for the expansion of modern credit systems. Without this prerequisite large and modern business organisations would not have been possible. Jeremy Bentham (1748–1832) denounced the old beliefs and attitudes towards monetary matters. He challenged the misleading rationale by explaining that:

> Among the various species or modifications of liberty, of which on different occasions we have heard so much in England, I do not recollect ever seeing anything yet offered on behalf of the *liberty of making one's own terms in money-bargains* . . .
>
> In a word, the proposition I have been accustomed to lay down to myself on this subject is the following one, viz. that *no man of ripe years and of sound mind, acting freely, and with his eyes open, ought to be hindered, with a view to his advantage, from making such bargain, in the way of obtaining money, as he thinks fit: nor (*what is a necessary consequence*) anybody hindered from supplying him, upon any terms he thinks proper to accede to.*
>
> (Bentham 1816: 3 Italics in original)

These days one cannot imagine the operation of any developed economy without a sophisticated credit system. That is, interest on loans is not just accepted but it has become an integral part of modern economies. The field that is hard to form consensus on is the right rate of interest. To the classical economist, interest was the matching instrument between investment (demand) and savings (supply) of loans. It was the amount that was paid for saving. Even though the neoclassical theory of interest varies in form, in essence it conveys the same message. N. W. Senior (1790–1864) articulated one form of it. He defined interest as a reward for abstinence. That is, saving is abstaining from current consumption and interest is the reward for it (Senior 1939: 59–60).

The marginal productivity is a variation of the neoclassical theory of interest. The borrowed money here is for productive purposes. The rate of interest is determined where the marginal product of capital is equal to the rate of interest (Brown 1913). Dennis Holme Robertson's (1890–1963) loanable fund theory of interest also fits well within this boundary of the neoclassical theory. Interest from this point of view is the money paid for the loanable funds and its rate is determined by demand for and supply of loanable funds (Hansen 1951). The Austrian or Agio theory of interest is part of this spectrum of thought. Eugen Böhm von Bawerk (1851–1914) first proposed this theory. Böhm von Bawerk argued that the reason that we receive interest for the money we lend is that we give preference to present goods. We give priority to present satisfaction over future satisfaction. Thus, unless we get a premium in the form of interest, we would not delay our consumption. We prioritise current goods over future goods. Interest is nothing less than deferring one's consumption to the future (Brown 1913).

We shall return to Keynes and Marx and examine their theories of interest at length in Chapters 5 and 6 respectively. Here we will briefly make a few supplementary remarks to illuminate the historical context in which the theory of interest has evolved. Interest is an indivisible fragment of Marx's theory of surplus value. For Marx workers create all the surplus value in the economy. Subsequently, surplus value is divided between the different types of the capitalist classes. Interest is the share that goes to the money lending capitalists (Fine 2012: 120). The Keynes theory of interest stems from his premise that money in the form of cash earns no interest. We do not receive interest if we carry our money in cash. Thus, interest is the money paid for parting with one's cash. For Keynes, interest is not the price for abstaining from consumption and for hoarding. Interest is paid for parting with one's cash (Blaug 1996: 521).

The other two noteworthy complications in relation to money have been the forms and the quantity of money in circulation. It was the issue that had preoccupied the minds of many scholars and sages in ancient India, China, Babylon, Persia, Greece and Rome. As for the issue of money, many correlated the chronic inflation rate to the overissue of money. One example of ancient monetary disorder occurred in Greece in the 4th century BC under Dionysius of Syracuse. Dionysius "borrowed from his subjects in the form of promissory notes, issued a decree that all money in circulation was to be turned over to the government" (Reinhart and Rogoff 2011: 174). Those who declined were sentenced to death. Dionysius then stamped two drachmas on each drachma coin collected and paid his debt.

Monetary disorders in ancient times were mainly localised but sporadic. The ancient economies were not developed monetary economies. The situation, however, radically changed towards the end of middle ages. It was at this time that we saw the sharp rise of population and the discovery of the new world. The use of a medium of exchange became a necessity. It was not a minor matter anymore. From this period there was an ever-growing collection of literature regarding monetary disorders. It is in the beginning of the new age that the French scholastic philosopher Nicole Oresme (1320–82) laid the foundations of the modern quantity theory of money. Oresme found a direct relation between debasing the content and weight of coins and inflation. He noted:

> for all money is called artificial wealth, as indeed it is, since a man might have an abundance of it and yet die of hunger . . . what is still more harmful is the way people disregard the clipping of the King's moneys and pass them at the same rate as good ones of full weight. This cannot last long, because of the confusion which may result.
>
> (Oresme 2006: 81, 88)

Jean Bodin (1530–96), the French political philosopher, correlated the vast inflow of precious metals from the American mines with the extraordinary increase in prices in Europe. He commented:

> I find that the high prices we see today are due to some four or five causes. The principal and almost the only one (which no one has referred to until now) is the abundance of gold and silver, which is today much greater in this Kingdom than it was four hundred years ago. . . . The second reason

> for the high prices arises in part from monopolies. The third is scarcity, caused partly by export and partly by waste. The fourth is the pleasure of Kings and great lords, who raise the price of the things they like. The fifth has to do with the price of money, debased from its former standard.
>
> (Bodin 2006: 127)

The growth of an economy based on money in Europe created many controversies. These issues were based on the relationship between the quantity of money and the economy in the 17th and 18th centuries. Many authors and pamphleteers discussed and revised the quantity theory of money. In the mid 18th century David Hume (1711–1776) provided the clearest description of the theory. He says, "suppose that, by miracle, every man in Great Britain should have five pounds slipped into his pocket in one night; this would much more than double the whole money that is at present in the kingdom; yet there would not next day, nor for some time, be any more lenders, nor any variation in the interest" (Hume 1998: 181). Hume examines two effects of the expansion in the money supply. After some time as an additional quantity of money trickles into different sectors of the economy, one portion of money causes demand to increase. Another portion causes general prices to rise.

The quantity theory of money has reappeared whenever inflation has reemerged. The Bullionist and the Anti-bullionist controversy in the 19th century was one such occasion. The bullionist proponents were David Ricardo and Lord Overstone (1796–1883). They attributed the rise in prices in Britain to the overissue of paper money. The currency school, as they were known, linked the cause of the depreciation of the pound to the overissue of notes. They considered paper money as representative money (Schuler 1992: 33). They held the bank of England responsible for issuing far more paper money than the gold reserves in its custody. To reduce inflation, they recommended, the Bank should restore convertibility and issue notes to the amount that corresponded to the bank's gold reserve.

The Anti-bullionists, the banking school, saw the matter in a different light. The leading figure in this camp was Thomas Tooke (1774–1858). The banking school did not correlate the cause of inflation to the bank's policy of overissue of notes. It detected a causal link to the wars and massive government expenditures abroad. The debate continued until the 1844 Bank Charter Act. The act adopted the currency school line. Money supply in Britain was centralised. The Bank of England became the central monetary authority with an overriding function to protect the nation's bullion reserves.

Marx, arguably, was the first economist who systematically integrated the monetary with the real sectors of the economy. Among non-Marxian economists, John Gustav Knut Wicksell (1851–1926), the eminent Swedish economist, was the first who adopted a similar approach. John Gustav Knut Wicksell based his ideas in the neoclassical semantic. Wicksell's deliberation, however, surpassed Marx in his demonstration of the crucial role of interest rates in the complex developed credit economies. The pivotal downside of his inquiry is that he circumscribed his quantity theory of money and interest rate to the neoclassical equilibrium price. This fact has prevented his innovative theory from achieving its full potential. However, he succeeded in demonstrating how fluctuation in interest rates engenders cumulative inflationary or deflationary cycles (Kasper 2002: 54). He showed how changes in interest rates change the balance between savings and investment and described how the central bank can manage this disequilibrium to promote price stability.

Wicksell was trying to discover why prices collectively in complex credit economies rise or fall every so often. The answer, in his view, related to interest rates. He started his inquiry from the point when prices do not rise or fall collectively. From this assumption he deduced two kinds of rate of interest. These were the natural rate and the bank rate (Wicksell 2007: 171–2). The natural rate of interest is the rate that depends on supply and demand for real capital that has not been invested yet. Therefore, the supply and demand of credit determine the natural rate of interest. The nature of the credit system is not the same as it was before the establishment of the banking system. The creation of banks profoundly transformed the credit system. Before that time, the credit system was dominated by individual money lenders. Money lenders merely lent their own money, whereas this is not the case in the modern credit system. Money lending is not restricted to a bank's own funds. One of the key factors in transition from individual money lenders to the banking system is that banks would lend other people's money. Banks create credit out of their depositors' money. Under this new credit system, the bank rate can be higher, lower, or equal to the natural rate. The natural rate is the rate that balances savings and investment. When this happens, it does not result in a change in prices. If the bank rate is higher than the natural rate there will be more savings and hence less investment. Therefore, prices will decrease. However, if the bank rate is lower than the natural rate there will be an increase in investment and hence prices will rise.

Besides the integration of real and monetary aspects of the economy, Wicksell's greater theoretical originality related to his discussion of interest as an instrument of economic policy. By altering the interest rate correctly and methodically, he suggested that the central bank can control the general price level. This is how Wicksell described the whole process:

> *So long as prices remain unaltered the banks' rate of interest is to remain unaltered. If prices rise, the rate of interest is to be raised; and if prices fall, the rate of interest is to be lowered; and the rate of interest is henceforth to be maintained at its new level until a further movement of prices call for a further change in one direction or the other.*
>
> The more promptly that these changes are undertaken the smaller is the possibility of considerable fluctuations of the general level of prices. If prices are kept fairly stable, the rate of interest will merely have to keep step with such rises or falls in the natural rate.

> In my opinion, the main cause of the instability of prices resides in the inability or failure of the banks to follow this rule. . . . I should like then in all humility to call attention to the fact that the banks' prime duty is not to earn a great deal of money but to provide the public with a medium of exchange—and to provide this medium in adequate measure, to aim at stability of prices. In any case, their obligations to society are enormously more important than their private obligations, and if they are ultimately unable to fulfil their obligations to society along these lines of private enterprise—which I very much doubt—then they would provide a worthy activity for the State.
>
> (Wicksell 2007: 189–90—Italics in original)

The debate about the relationship between the quantity of money and general prices has remained current. In the early decades of the 20th century Irving Fisher (1867–1947), the renowned American economist, apportioned most of his study on monetary matters. In his book, the *Purchasing Power of Money*, Fisher formulated a version of the quantity theory of money that has continued to be the standard model for subsequent works. Fisher discerned five determinants of the purchasing power of money. These are: (1) the volume of currency in circulation, (2) its velocity of circulation, (3) the volume of bank current account deposits, (4) its velocity and (5) the volume of trade (Fisher 1997: 63–4). In the light of these assumptions, Fisher assembled his equation of exchange. In his equation we have, MV = PT, where M stands for the quantity of currency, V for velocity of circulation, P for the average level of prices and T for the quantity of goods and services that are exchanged. Fisher's equation of exchange is a truism, a tautological relationship whereby it declares that the money supply corresponds proportionately to the changes in prices.

Cambridge economists, led by Alfred Marshall, attempted to alter the equation of exchange from a simple truism into a causal relationship. They reformulated Fisher's equation into the equation of exchange. That is M = kY. The Cambridge equation was intended to be regarded as a behavioural relationship (Hawke 1980: 93). In this equation k is known as Marshallian k, which is the reciprocal of V. It stands for the proportion of the public's income that is maintained in the form of cash balances. The hyperinflations that ensued immediately after the First World War and the Great Depression repudiated the validity of both equations. Neither equation was relevant as a policy instrument to remedy the situation, nor could they explain the difficulties that the advanced economies were facing.

These events not only questioned different interpretations of the quantity theory of money but also discredited the neoclassical laissez-faire economy. The events shifted the climate of opinion in favour of government intervention. The idea of the Keynesian management of aggregate demand gained many new supporters. It was after this economic turmoil that John Maynard Keynes (1883–1946) cast doubts on the capability of advanced industrialised economies to adjust automatically at the level where full employment can be safeguarded. To this end he invented his theory of aggregate effective demand—relating unemployment to insufficient effective demand and inflation to excessive effective demand.

Keynes won the battle of his time. However, on the periphery there were a minority of economists who remained loyal to the old traditions. Milton Friedman (1912–2006) was one of the sceptics. In his 1957 work, Friedman resurrected the quantity theory of money, correlating the price level to supply of money. In this and his subsequent works, he made the Fed responsible for the Great Depression. He blamed the bank's ill-conceived monetary policies. None of these arguments were the main source of his subsequent fame. Alban William Phillips's (1914–75) findings promoted Friedman's reputation. Phillips, a statistician and economist, was a Keynesian supporter. In his study of money wages in Britain from 1861 to 1957 he extrapolated an inverse relationship between the rate of unemployment and the rate of inflation. This trade-off became to be known as the Phillips' curve. The curve offered the policy makers a profound choice. They could either stick to a lower rate of unemployment by stimulating aggregate demand with higher inflation or lower the inflation rate and have a higher level of unemployment.

In the 1970s both inflation and unemployment soared in most developed economies. Economists borrowed stagflation, a term that Iain Macleod coined in his speech to the British parliament in 1965, to characterise this situation. Monetarists regarded the Keynesian policy of management of aggregate demand responsible for the stagflation. Monetarists argued that using government expenditures to stimulate aggregate demand would influence the economy in two main ways. These are the factors that have a short-term and long-term influence for the reason that boosting aggregate demand in the short term will augment both prices and the rate of employment. In the long term, there will not be any trade-off between unemployment and inflation (Dwivedi 2005: 454). The Keynesian policy of managing the economy, monetarists argued, is self-defeating. It eventually results in stagflation.

In the context of the business cycle, Friedman regarded the increase in employment during the first phase of the cycle as unexpected. It is caused by the fall in the real wage rate because of the increase in prices. As soon as the workers learn that their real wages have fallen, they begin to make demands for higher wages. Two forces interact as a catalyst to increase prices. The first factor is the initial increase in wage rates and the second one is the expectation of higher prices in the future. This is a trend that will last until the unemployment rate returns to its natural rate (Galbraith 1998: 174). The natural rate of unemployment corresponds to the intersection where the actual and expected rate of inflation are equal.

Fiscal policy, the preferred Keynesian macroeconomic policy to solve the situation under such circumstances, would in fact make the situation worse. Friedman was suspicious of the intention of bureaucrats and politicians who endorsed Keynesian diagnoses. Secondly, because politicians are self-promoting groups who aim to be re-elected. Keynesian economics in the short term is deceptively effective. It is in harmony with the obvious aim of politicians to be re-elected. This short-term surge of economic activity results in short-term political popularity. In the short term it can result in the possible re-election of these politicians. Concluding that there could be no trade-off between inflation and employment in the long run, in the long term the Phillip curve is vertical.

Freidman regarded stagflation as a government syndrome. He believed it was caused by excessive and reckless government expenditure. Freidman argued that the authorities should abstain from Keynesian strategies. Such strategies would raise inflationary expectations. Arguing the policy makers need to convince the economic agents to earn back their eroded trust, it is then that the quantity theory of money proves valid as an effective macroeconomic policy. Since the movement of nominal income is assumed to be correlated to the expansion and contraction of the stock of money, then the direction of causation is from the left to the right side of the equation of exchange. Given that the velocity of circulation (V) is constant or predictable, then the change in money supply after some time lag will affect the level of production, employment and prices.

Friedman's only grand economic prophesy is price stability. He hoped the government could be responsible in this regard. To achieve this objective, authorities should discard fiscal policy. They must embrace monetary policy. The control of the growth of money supply would ensure price stability. Friedman stipulated a strict relationship between the gross national product and the money supply. He believed this close correlation can be predicted, apprehended, and managed. The rule that simultaneously synchronises the expansion and contraction of the economy, irrespective of the phase of the business cycle, is a specific rate of money supply and rate of growth of output per annum. Friedman estimated a constant ratio between the two. He estimated, on average, the rate of growth of real output over time to be about 3 per cent. So, if monetary authorities authorise to increase the money supply by 3 to 5 per cent over the same period, then general prices would be kept under control and stay at about 1 to 2 per cent (Handa 2000: 452).

Conclusion

References to economic disorder can be observed in both conventional and marginal economic literature. Economic science is dependent on a wide spectrum of views and debates. Economic disorder is an obvious state of affairs. It cannot be ignored. Wherever there is change there is disorder. Economies are constantly changing. The cause of changes can sometimes be natural, social or a combination of the two. Changes in the economy cannot be dismissed or be taken for granted. There will always be new scientific and technological inventions and discoveries. There has never been such pace of change in human history than what is currently under way. No human society can be immune to conflict and change. The pattern of social conflicts between those who enjoy more wealth and those who have less, or nothing, inevitably develops into a conflict. Inequality of income is virtually a constant characteristic of economic life. Uneven development and the distribution of natural resources are such matters that cannot be eradicated entirely. Such problems can be improved with global cooperation of the nations that are free and democratic. However, these problems cannot easily be eradicated. Our knowledge is and will always remain partial. Irrationalism, superstitions, mysticism and religious strife have their roots in everything we do. The quagmire of current and past injustices, wars, repressions and colonialism have incapacitated a significant number of nations. A large portion of the human population, as a direct result of these legacies, are deprived of employing their potentials fully and effectively. The legacy of repression and imperialism has distorted the economic destiny of many nations. There is not an aspect of a society that is completely developed. We cannot say that the economic, legal, cultural, artistic, political, social and managerial aspects and institutions of a particular society have reached their full development and potential. The centrepiece of our theory is that economic disorder is inevitable and is permanent.

Economic disorder and instability can hardly escape one's view. In this chapter we have demonstrated how the reservoir of economic literature has widened and deepened over time. Economic thinkers have engaged in a process of discerning, reacting, anticipating and criticising the paradoxes, inconsistencies, difficulties and shortcomings of unexpected events and economic ideas. Economic literature expands by adapting old theories to new realities. It strives to explain these new realities with narratives that are innovative, informative and correspond to new facts.

The ideas of monetarism in the 1970s and 1980s enchanted the devotees of the free market economic model. They offered virtually nothing new on the merits of free markets but were able to win political influence and popular support, so their crusade was effective. Monetarists succeeded in converting the political establishments of Britain and the United States to their creed. In the United Kingdom the Conservative Party under the leadership of Mrs Margaret Hilda Thatcher (1925–2013) assumed political power in 1979. About 2 years later in 1981 the Republican Party under the leadership of Ronald Wilson Reagan (1911–2004) was elected in the United States. The ideas and values of the Monetarists and the Austrian theories suited best the new political environment. Their discourse was seized upon with almost religious fever.

Monetarists acknowledged tacitly the disorders in the economy. They acted to remedy what they considered to be economic defects and flaws. Ironically, they employed the state machine to reduce the role of the state in the economy. This developed into a wider trend that spread to many countries. These ideas even conquered the eastern European countries after the collapse of the Soviet Empire. The core ideology of monetarism found expression in a range of policies. In a number of countries key industries were privatised, taxes were cut, government expenditures in certain sectors of the economy and services were reduced, financial markets were deregulated, the inequality of income was encouraged and private incentives were promoted.

Milton Friedman, who crystalised the monetarist argument, explicitly refers to economic disorders. Freidman collected a vast amount of empirical information about the United States economy. He aimed to reveal the extent of disorders between money, prices and interest rates. He reinterpreted the quantity theory and argued strongly that the old theory was inadequate. Freidman challenged the Phillips' curve, which was generally accepted as a truism. He said that in the long term the natural rate of unemployment is compatible with any rate of inflation. He argued that the Fed was largely responsible for the severe recession in the United States and asserted that "throughout its history, the Fed has proclaimed that it was using its powers to promote economic stability. But the record does not support this claim. On the contrary the Fed has been a major source of instability" (Friedman 1972: 65). Monetarism lost its credibility as soon as its policies were put into practice in the early 1980s. Its influence has diminished during the period between the 1987 financial crisis to the 2007 global financial crisis. Many attributed the economic crisis of 2008 to their policies and ideas.

4 Self-correcting economic order

Introduction

In the last three chapters, we have shown that economic disorder is the permanent course of events. The perpetual disorder is instigated by the relentless pattern of change. Everything is changing. Both the natural world and human societies are subject to endless change and transformation. All schools of thought in economics admit to this central fact either implicitly or explicitly. One way or another it is acknowledged in their writings. All the various schools across the ideological divide in economics are attentive to the issue of change. The admission of change entails an acknowledgement of disorder. Order is a form of perpetuity of the sameness with no end. Deviation from sameness is in effect a form of disorder. In this sense, there is a formal inconsistency in many economic theories. How can such economic theories profess belief in a permanent harmony and self-adjusting economy while accepting the reality of unending change? How can we assume that any form of economic system is permanent? Can an economic system always be self-adjusting? This opinion is highly debatable. The ideal economy with this perfect characteristic is said to be a free market economy. Some claim that the free market is an economic system that is harmonious, orderly and self-adjusting. In this system, everything works because it is meant to work according to a self-contained, pre-established fixed order of nature. In the strict sense, this corresponds closely to Leibniz doctrine of the best of all possible worlds. Leibniz argument of the best of all possible worlds is based on his "principle of sufficient reason." This principle stipulates that "nothing happens without a reason." So, "why it should be . . . otherwise" (Leibniz 1989: 682). Anything out of the remit and trajectory of this principle is argued to be a contravention to the law of nature.

Economics as a scientific discipline can be regarded as a relative latecomer. It was not at the forefront of the scientific revolution. Economics was an offshoot of the age of enlightenment. The scientific revolution chiselled its mark on virtually every aspect of human endeavours including economics. The critical thinkers of the age were very impressed with the success of the natural sciences. They were captivated with scientific discoveries, innovations, theories and the methodology of research. The age of enlightenment revived the Stoic approach

DOI: 10.4324/9781003346364-5

in which everything is viewed as essentially interconnected. The plain truth is that within the compass of scientific inquiries everything is connected. Science does not exist in a vacuum. It is a social activity that is applied within a certain social context. It is vitally important to understand this. A disassociated, disconnected mono science is a pseudo-science. Such a science can be no more than a subservient aspect of an established ideological order.

The democratisation of knowledge accelerated the division of labour in scientific endeavour. The age of enlightenment speeded up this process. Different branches of studies were divided into separate scientific disciplines. Each discipline was assigned to a specific inquiry. In relation to this there are two important points worthy of consideration. Firstly, the division of employment in scientific endeavour stimulates dexterity, skill and professionalism in the given branch of inquiry. This will tend to give rise to greater specialism, time saving and more focused knowledge. This, in turn, will bring about more innovations, inventions and discoveries. These developments will relate to both the dominion of ideas and in the territory of reality. Secondly, the greater the success of one discipline the greater will be its power to set the trend among other disciplines. The Newtonian revolution in Physics in the 17th century and the Darwinian revolution in the 19th century in biology are key examples. Of all the social sciences, economics has imitated the natural sciences the most. This was a recurring theme also in other social sciences. Other social sciences that were a step behind in their academic credential have copied what economics had mimicked from natural sciences.

The nature of the different scientific endeavours is not the same. So why is it the case that the form substitutes the essence to the nature of the subject? There are overbearing eye-catching attractions and powers that can subordinate many disciplines to one discipline. Ideas or theories, right or wrong, can become fashionable. If the new idea captures the imagination and attention of thinkers then outmoded ideas or theories, right or wrong, would become marginalised. This progression is a self-propelling process. The more people adhere to the overriding view the more attractive it becomes. With time the new idea appears more and more credible. The second factor in promoting the tide of fashion is the veil of ignorance.

This is due to the herd mentality. It is the mob psychology that fosters ignorance. The trend comes to obscure objective facts. The fashionable perspective can be neither accurate nor illuminating. Most individuals follow the crowd because conformity is an easier path to pursue. Besides, there is a vested interest in all ideas. Adhering to the ideas that are in vogue can offer better prospects in employment, promotion, income, research funds, social status, prestige and general social acceptance.

It is the purpose of this chapter to evaluate how the great achievements in natural sciences acted as an inspiration to social sciences, and to economics. In view of that, this chapter discusses the enticement upon which each school of thought in economics describes its system of thought as being scientific. The rest of the chapter contains a critical examination of the way in which social and cultural trends have played their role in economic thinking. These trends have tended to imitate the methodology of the natural sciences. The chapter will demonstrate how economic matters have been perceived as well-balanced occurrences. Furthermore, economic matters have been regarded as factors that are essentially in harmony with timeless natural laws.

The chapter is divided into five parts. Part one examines the issues of the unity and harmony of ideas. It shows how humanity, and these ideas are inextricably linked. These ideas are fundamental to the very nature of being human. We find the desire for balance, harmony and equilibrium in the earliest thoughts. The idea of harmony has been addressed in various cultural and intellectual forms. These forms have included music, mathematics, philosophy and aesthetics.

Part two deals with the idea that nature is the master of all things. In this section, we will examine the fundamental principles which underlay this doctrine. We will strive to trace back this doctrine to the point of its origin. We will consider the rationale, multiplicity of forms, essence and the logical implications of this idea. We will reflect on concepts such as justice, the perfect number, harmony, equilibrium, natural law, universal reason and human dignity. In demonstrating the complex connections between these concepts, we will develop and outline the focus of this section. Our central theory will detail how all these developments spin around one absolute and eternal point.

In part three, the rediscovery of reason, we shall explain the key role of reason in the foundation of the modern age. We will examine its role in the Axial Age and how it was revived in the age of enlightenment. We will discuss the realisation that reason is crucial and central to knowledge, humanity and progress. Reason came to be seen as the hallmark of sure and certain knowledge. Reason was regarded as something that was indispensable to rational statement and a deeper understanding of the world. Reason informed and guided the conduct of scientific investigation. Reason was central to the development of human understanding. Reason enabled humanity to begin to unlock the secrets of the world. This was the striking feature and seminal achievement of the Age of Reason. This was a serious departure from old philosophical traditions. Reason was a concept that could be said to have rendered knowledge accessible to the common person. Everyone became capable of acquiring knowledge. Reason as a concept in society effectively liberated knowledge. The implications of this autonomy were very profound indeed. Consequently, there was greater freedom of belief and conscience. In time we saw the separation of religion from the state, equality before the law and consensually legitimised government.

Part four is concerned with science, order and progress. We will probe more deeply into the humanities departure from their past. Prior to the Age of Enlightenment, Europe was dominated by the central concept of the "original sin." This world view is eternally gloomy and it stands against reason. These two visions, the world of original sin and the world of enlightenment, were two distinct world views. The first world view was degenerative. It was dominated by popular myths, superstition, fatalism, baseless speculation and esoteric learning. The upcoming vision, on the contrary, was founded on a mood of optimism. It was a vision that yearned for progress and looked to the future. The desire for free thought and scientific inquiry became stronger and stronger. The new approach understood that nature and human behaviour are subject to certain patterns and rules. The new optimism was based on a longing to decode the mysteries of nature. The aim of this part is to examine the link between optimism, the direction of history, natural regularity, progress and objective truth. All these factors made the break with the past possible.

Part five is devoted to the influence of the Age of Enlightenment on the foundation of modern economics. This part provides an outline of the interaction between the general principles of the Age of Reason and the formative ideas of economic theory. The forerunners of modern economics were enthusiastic disciples of the Age of Enlightenment. They rejected conventional ideas and searched for systematic regularities in the sphere of economic conditions and human behaviour. These laws and regularities were presumed to be consistent and universal. They saw these laws as following a natural course manifested in the laws of cause and effect. Buying, selling and the motive to make profit were regarded in a similar way. They regarded the economic concept of laissez-faire as compatible with natural liberty. In this philosophical approach individuals are perceived as essentially rational. As such, individuals should be permitted to pursue their enlightened interest. The rational individual earns the right to be free to utilise his material income as he wishes.

Unity and harmony of higher order

The idea of harmony dates to ancient times. Many ancient civilisations including those of India, China, and Greece, all produced detailed discussions in relation to the concept of harmony. This was central to their attempt to understand the person, society and nature. The term "harmony" is derived from Greek. Apuoyia or Harmonia in Greek means "a fastening or join." In the teaching of ancient India, Gautama Buddha (563–483 BC) assigned harmony as one of his three interdependent concepts. Cause-effect, compassion in conjunction with harmony are the foundations of Buddha's philosophy. "Sangha" is a term in Sanskrit that bears a close analogy to the idea of harmony. In Buddhism, it is synonymous with the concept of order. The phrase "samagra-sangha" is commonly used in Buddhist texts. This phrase means "harmonious order" (Akira 1998: 60).

Buddha regarded harmony as something that is socially and economically desirable and beneficial. In one of his dialogues, he says "have you heard that the Vajjians meet in harmony, break up in harmony, and carry on their business in harmony? . . . Ananda, as long as the Vajjians meet in harmony, break up in harmony, and carry on their business in harmony, they may be expected to prosper and not decline" (Buddha 2005: 138).

Confucius (551–479 BC) was Buddha's contemporary. The idea of harmony in China predates Kongfuzi K'un Fu-Tzu's teaching. His account of harmony has dominated Chinese philosophy. These thinkers contemplated the idea of harmony at a time of extreme turmoil. Confucius lived during a very turbulent and eventful time in China (Juntao 200: 75). Extremism, chaos, unrest, violence and conflicts were widespread. The thing that was in short supply was unity and harmony. Confucius wanted to restore an imaginary stability. Confucius associated this stability with ancient China. He longed for the time when the Chinese were united and lived in harmony. He felt nostalgic for China of the Golden Age and intended to achieve this philosophical goal by means of virtue (de) and correct ritual (li).

Music is the base on which the Confucius notion of harmony (he) stands. The book of Zhuangzi clearly makes the link between music and harmony. "The Book of Music speaks of harmony" (quoted from Yao 2000: 171). As in music, harmony is an inner order. Confucius detects a sense of interdependency between human emotion and music. Emotion is not something that can be expressed in due time. The timely and proper expression of emotion requires nurturing and the cultivation of good character. That, in turn, requires inner harmony. Those who succeed in nurturing harmony within will become virtuous. They live at ease with themselves, with others and their environment. Harmony is entrenched in the essence of music. In addition, "music expresses the harmony of the universe, while rituals express the order of the universe. Through harmony, all things are influenced and through the order, all things have a proper place" (Price 2010: 129).

For Confucius music is unique. It is the heart of harmony. Above all, music is necessary for cultivating good character. By fostering good character individuals become virtuous. To save society from chaos attitudes, ideas and feelings must be harmonised. Existence consists of a great many opposing forces. The cumulative interactions of these opposite forces, if channelled correctly, can be brought to the ideal situation. Then we would have complete unity and perfect harmony. Confucius regarded harmony as the point of equilibrium. For Confucius harmony is a state of accomplishment that is interdependent, fulfilled, whole and impeccable. All in all, it is the manifestation of the mean. Zisi, Confucius's grandson, described equilibrium as "the great foundation of the world, and harmony its universal path. When equilibrium and harmony are realized to the highest degree, heaven and earth will attain their proper order all things will flourish" (quoted from Chen 2017: 53).

It is not hard to imagine a balanced, unified, harmonious and perfect order. One of humanity's most profound hopes is to achieve harmony. A cursory examination of our daily activities is sufficient to confirm our instinctive demand for harmony. We perceive the existence of harmony in many aspects of the world around us. We detect a sense of harmony in culture and nature. At the core of the experience of being human is a sensitive appreciation of the existence of harmony.

The Chinese were the first who articulated such a common-sense experience of harmony. The Guoyu is a collection of anecdotes or speeches that dates from about the 6th and 7th centuries in China. According to these ancient writings, "harmony is that by which things are usually generated; whereas through sameness things are unable to continue. Bridging different things together so as to arrive at equilibrium is called harmony" (quoted from Chen 2017: 51). Examples of harmony are also provided in cooking, in seasons, in poetry and music. It is said that "harmony is like making soup. One cooks fish with water, fire, vinegar, meat sauce, salt, and plums, and heats it with firewood. The masterful chef combines these harmoniously, adjusting its various flavours, adding where insufficient and subtracting where excessive" (quoted from Chen 2017: 52). It is also recorded that the Emperor Shun asked his minister of music to compose a piece of music using a poem so that "the eight different kinds of musical instruments can be adjusted so that one shall not take from or interfere with another; and spirits and men are brought into harmony" (quoted from Chen 2017: 52). Confucius's sense of order and equilibrium are rooted essentially in the harmony of music.

In ancient Greece, Pre-Pythagoreans perceived the world in terms of a physical unity. In fact, Pythagoras (born in 569 BC) condensed the whole essence of the world into a number. Numbers are pivotal in Pythagoras' cosmology. It was Pythagoras who coined the term "Kosmos" and described it as the "sum of the whole" (Stamatellos 2012: 37). Cosmos in its entirety is described as a harmonious whole. Aristotle wrote that Pythagorean "supposed the whole heaven to be a harmonia and a number" (quoted from Christian 2009: 501). When all parts of a whole work together there is harmony. For instance, when all parts of a structure "vibrate" together that structure, even though it is in a state of motion, is in harmony. Pythagoras regarded the soul as equivalent to a mini cosmos. He believed the soul is in harmony. The unity of the harmony of soul and "the music of the sphere" are represented by a number. That number is number 1 (Christian 2009: 501).

The use of scales dates to antiquity. All human settlements have employed scales for weighing. The people of the ancient world must have known the general principle of scales. Scales can be either balanced or unbalanced. When scales are balanced the pans contain the same weight. The scales, in effect, represent a kind of mathematical dualism. It may well have been the dualism of the scales that initially inspired the Greek concept of cosmic dualism. One well-known proponent of this view in Ancient Greece was Pythagoras. He argued that the physical universe is balanced by a unity of opposite forces. He regarded the presence of conflicting forces at the same time as not contrary to the state of order and a sense of balance. In his view, despite simultaneous opposing forces, there is order in everything. These orders are explained in mathematical terms (Loposer 2008: 93).

One distinguishing tenet of an ideal state is the condition in which everything is balanced. This is the point of equilibrium. One way to demonstrate a sense of equilibrium is through music. The point of equilibrium in music is expressed at the point that there is a proportionate combination of various tones. This is when the audience hears a pleasant and harmonious melody. Such a balanced situation is equally required for the creation of an ideal situation in everything else. To Pythagoras illness, for example, is a deviation from the point of equilibrium. At the equilibrium level, all elements in a body are balanced and coordinated to create a unity. The restoration of equilibrium will, therefore, reinstate one to his or her full health (Hergenhah and Henly 2014: 32). Accordingly, a person in an ideal state of health is in equilibrium. Pythagoras postulates that the illness transforms the person both biologically and socially. The illness disturbs the biological balance. It detaches him or her from the normal balance of social life. The restoration of equilibrium restores the biological balance. It also brings order and normalcy in his or her social life (Keane 2015: 67).

The unity of whole as the ideal state constitutes one of the principal subjects of discussion in the philosophical writings of ancient Greece. Stoics regarded a good life as a life of order and harmony. It is a life of virtue. Acting virtuously meant living in harmony with nature. The unity of whole as the finest expression of harmony also occupies the writings of Plato and Aristotle. Plato maintained that all parts of the body are interrelated. In the event of illness, no part can be treated in isolation. The entire body, in which he includes the soul, is a whole unit. Unless this whole is balanced in its state of equilibrium, we cannot obtain our full health. In the laws, Plato sought such an equilibrium and harmony in an ideal and balanced constitution (Jayapalan 2002: 156).

A human body has many parts. The parts that constitute a person must work in unity and harmony for the individual to be healthy and happy. For Plato, there is a basic parallel with this concept and the understanding of the state. A state is a body that consists of different parts. Plato perceives a profound parallel between the ideal equilibrium of health and happiness within an individual and that of an ideal political state of unity, harmony and balance. Plato desires to see the different parts of the state functioning in harmony and balance. Disharmony amounts to injustice. The different parts of the whole must exist in equilibrium, both united and harmonious (Schrems 2007: 118). Aristotle too was enchanted with the idea of order, balance and harmony. Aristotle emphasised that nature exists as an ordered structure. His concepts of physics are based on this idea (Long 1998: 291). Aristotle links this sense of unity and harmony in his application of justice in society for a harmonious and good life. This balancing position is the same as the balancing position of a scale or lever. Aristotle's references to levers are brief and sporadic. Nevertheless, they preceded that of Archimedes who explained the mathematical principles of the lever. He referred to the mathematical equilibrium of the levers to exemplify his notion of equilibrium (Tabak 2004: 32). Archimedes (c. 287–212 BC) is commonly credited with defining the general mathematical principle of equilibrium. This general principle states that "equal weights at the equal distance are in equilibrium" (quoted from Tabak 2004: 32).

The philosophy and science of ancient Greece represents the foundation of western thought. With the rise of Islam Greek science and philosophy later infiltrated the Arab world. These ideas were reintroduced to the western world by the Arab thinkers from the middle of the 12th century. Muhammad

(c. 570–632), the founder of Islam, established a new political order in Medina in 622. Muhammad's political philosophy and religion were inspired by the political, cultural and economic environment of his time. He drew inspiration from many sources. The tribal customs and codes of the Arab world provided the context in which his ideas developed. Muhammad adopted many Jewish and Christian doctrines and beliefs. He drew on their essentially monotheistic faith. Monotheistic religion is founded on the belief that it enjoys a particular and unique insight. The sense of subjective truth revealed particularly and completely informs the nature and identity of all monotheistic religions. Truth becomes a concept that is established without critical challenges or rational examination.

Monotheistic religions regard themselves as being the last refuge and only guardian of truth. Those outside the devoted members of the religion are judged as being wrong. Such a world view leaves no room for doubt or free will. Compelling the whole world to convert to only one unique belief is the inevitable consequence of this philosophical approach. Thus, Mohammad's theocracy was an imperialistic movement from its very inception. Immediately after it had secured its base, the followers of Islam instigated a series of bloody conquests. These wars culminated in the forced conversion of the populations of the colonised nations. Invasion and war became core elements of religious zeal.

Within a few decades, a large territory in the Middle East fell under authority of the Muslim empire. Eventually, Islamic imperial power extended to all the Arabian Peninsula, the Iranian plateau, north Africa and southern Europe. Governing such an extensive colonial territory required organisation, management, control, defence, production and trade. Many more activities that involved understanding, intelligent planning and the execution of macro policies were also essential to the new empire. These necessities drew the Imperial rulers and their intelligentsia to the classical Greek texts. The Greek texts were exploited extensively to govern, defend and maintain the Islamic Empire.

The height of the Islamic Empire came in the 9th to the 11th centuries. It was at this time that most of the translations of Greek classics into Arabic took place. In the 12th century the Arabs occupied parts of southern Europe. As a result, they reintroduced elements of Greek philosophy and science into Western Europe. The next tide took place when the Ottoman Empire occupied Constantinople. Many scholars escaped to Western Europe. These scholars were instrumental in spreading Greek literature. This process in turn helped facilitate the ongoing Renaissance in Western Europe.

The Renaissance can be seen as a rebellious upheaval against medieval Europe. The movement defied the dominant ideas of Western and Central Europe. It questioned in a very profound way the supreme authority of theocracy. The exponents of the Renaissance advocated liberal humanism. The Renaissance was a transitory period that revived Greek philosophy. It revitalised interest in ancient Greek and Roman science, philosophy, art and culture. The Renaissance scholars, thinkers and artists, by and large, were fascinated with the idea of harmony. Most specifically, they were immersed in the Pythagorean sense of cosmic harmony (Stuckrad 2014: 16). Leonardo da Vinci (1452–1519) was one of the key men of the Renaissance. Pythagorean equilibrium and harmony are central to nearly all his encyclopaedic contributions.

Although the idea of God was central to Renaissance thinking, the concept was distinct from that of the dark ages. God was still regarded as the creator of the universe. However, the universe of the Renaissance is quite different from that of earlier times. The universe of Renaissance thinkers resembles the universe of the ancient Greek philosophers and mathematicians. This universe is a mathematical structure. It can be defined in the precise mathematical language of proportionality. The universe is regarded as a structure with synchronised parts that are in perfect harmony. According to the thinkers of the Renaissance the universe is no longer so mysterious. Nature is no longer impenetrable. The secrets of the universe are no longer far beyond the reach of human understanding. Scientists, philosophers, poets, artists and musicians are all engaged in a process of rational discovery. Johannes Kepler (1571–1630) the German astronomer and mathematician remarked that "the chief aim of all investigations of the external world should be to discover the rational order and harmony which has been imposed on it by God and which He revealed to us in the language of mathematics" (quoted from Delitala and Marsan 2014: vi).

Equilibrium, harmony and proportionality are themes that are central to the works of Leonardo da Vinci (1452–1519), Raffaello Sanzio da Urbino (1483–1520), Donato Bramante (1444–1514), Giordano Bruno (1548–1600), Tiziano Vecelli (1488–1576), Michelangelo (1475–1564), Leon Battista Alberti (1404–74) and Donatello di Niccolo di Betto Bradi (1386–1466). The basic idea behind the writings, paintings, inventions and creations of all these painters, architects, poets, sculptors, mathematicians, philosophers and scientists is harmony. Marin Mersenne (1588–1648), a Renaissance French physicist, mathematician and philosopher demonstrated his musical system in the language of mathematics (Knobloch 2002). He attempted to show that pure beauty and harmony are derived from the arrangement of perfect proportionality.

Gottfried Wilhelm Leibniz (1646–1716) a German philosopher declared that the world, despite all its apparent diversity and variation, is a unified and harmonious unit. He criticised the atomists: both the ancient (Leucippus, Democritus, Epicurus) and his contemporary scientists such as Newton for their contrary view. Leibniz argued that they are incorrect on this point. For Leibniz, matter does not consist of indivisible particles. Matter is not made up of atoms (Freudenthal 1986: 42). He regarded God as the first designer. The process of creation by God was flawless and complete. For Leibniz, God's infinite cognitive power surpasses everything else. Leibniz upheld the view that the world consists of an infinite number of monads. God is the source of the creation of these monads. These are unique substances. They have no parts and are perfectly indivisible. Leibniz regarded these monads as the primary building blocks of everything.

Leibniz believed in a doctrine of pre-established harmony. His starting point philosophically is that God is responsible for the creation of all matter. For

Leibniz, the world is made of monads. Every existing substance only affects itself. As a result of divine design these independent substances causally interact with each other. In so doing they create unity and harmony. For Leibniz, the same causal relationship exists between body and soul. He argued that therefore they can establish unity and harmony.

Copernicus (1473–1543) undertook a quest of discovery that involved examining universal truths that are applicable in any time and place. He commenced his analysis with the inference that there is symmetry between different parts of the world. His search for universal truth led him to one of his most insightful discoveries in the history of astronomy. He argued that the planetary motions exist in perfect unity and harmony (Gassendi and Thill 2002: 105). He believed that the Sun lay at the centre of the solar system. He argued that the planets revolve around the Sun. Tycho Brahe (1546–1601), another architect of the modern science of astronomy, was a wealthy Danish scientist. He made the most accurate observation of planetary motion in his time. Brahe employed Johannes Kepler (1571–1630), the German mathematician and astronomer, as his assistant at the age of 27. Kepler helped record the planetary positions of the cosmos. This opportunity allowed Kepler to have access to Brahe's extensive data on the motions of the heavenly bodies. He utilised the opportunity given and advanced Kepler's findings significantly. His investigations led to many original discoveries.

Kepler devoted his scientific endeavour to recording planetary motions. He diligently assessed the accumulation of his observations. Among his great achievements were the discovery of his three laws of the motions of the heavenly bodies. These laws were:

> (i) The planets revolve around the sun in elliptical orbits with the sun occupying one focus; (ii) The orbital velocity of a planet sweeps out equal areas in equal times; and (iii) The squares of the periods of revolution of the planets are proportional to the cubes of their orbital major axes.
>
> (Saha 2008: 3)

Tycho Brahe and Kepler's discoveries inevitably alarmed many powerful vested interests. Their discoveries openly challenged the authority of the church. Their research undermined the domination of Aristotle's teaching. Tycho discovered a new star, the Tycho Supernova, on 11 November 1572 (Penprase 2011: 263). He observed that it was located beyond the Moon. According to prevailing belief it was not meant to be in the constellation of Cassiopeia. Such discoveries were not compatible with Aristotelian cosmology. In the Aristotelian universe, the chaos and imperfections that we perceive on Earth do not exist amongst the heavenly bodies. According to the established view of Aristotle, the whole cosmos consists of immutable and harmonious bodies. In essence the stars are perfect.

Kepler indicated that his discoveries, the laws of planetary motion, validated the harmony of heavenly bodies. God's designs are regarded as flawless, and the universe is self-contained. We cannot separate perfection and harmony from the planets and their motion. Nothing can contravene God's will. The sun only follows God's divine instruction. Kepler compared the synchronisation of planetary motion to the harmony in music. This influence is very evident in Kepler's book *Harmony of the World*. The centrepiece of his theory of the harmony of the planetary motions is compared with the "music of the spheres" (Perry 2016: 235). His third law of planetary motion echoes this harmony (Nicolson 1999: 51). It is also necessary to know that this law was indispensable for the theoretical foundation of Newtonian cosmic mechanics (Pesic 2014: 73).

The church labelled Galileo Galilei (1564–1642) as an immoral dissenter. The name of Galileo has been registered in human history forever. His conflict with the inquisition related to a very serious matter. It was the conflict between truth and superstition. Galileo was not only a pioneering scientist, but he was also an original thinker. He advocated the Copernican heliocentric cosmology. As a result, the church put him under house arrest in 1633. Galileo's contributions to the theory of motion and his methodology of research were critical for Newton's great scientific achievements. It was Galileo who formulated the law of inertia, the idea that objects continue their motion unless they are abstracted by another force. Newton's universal law of gravity owed much to Kepler's research on elliptical orbits and Galileo's law of inertia. In his monumental work, *Mathematical Principles of Natural Philosophy*, Newton outlined a unified universe. He described a complete unit that is in constant motion. For Newton, the indispensable element that regulates and controls this motion is the universal force of gravitation. All matter is subject to this universal force. It is an irresistible and constant force in the universe. This force pulls all matter to the centre. The greater the mass of a matter the greater is its pulling force. The greater the distance between the matters the weaker the pulling force is. With the help of his laws of motion and the universal law of gravitation, Newton described the earth's orbit around the Sun. He also predicted the Moon's orbit around the earth, the rise and fall of ocean tides and the changes in the seasons.

The 17th century was a landmark in human history. It was a period that saw immensely important discoveries. It paved the way for many other subsequent epic accomplishments. It was also the century that marked the beginning of modern democratic nations. Cumulative scientific endeavours, discoveries, innovations, events, methodological shifts and social and political movements all contributed to massive advances in human understanding. The combined weight of this progress marked a definite turning point in history. The human sense of their place in the universe could simply never be the same again.

The theoretical foundation of this scientific and social transformation, however, centred on the image and the light of the harmony and unity of the universe. Copernicus, Tycho, Kepler and Galileo to Newton demonstrated the unity and harmony of nature and cosmos. Their deep faith in perfect harmony and the unity of the universe was corroborated with rigorous analysis, concrete data and informed observations.

These individuals were the greatest scientists of their times. Had they questioned the unity of the divine and the perfect harmony of the world, they simply would not have achieved what they had accomplished. Articulating formal opposition to the concept of God would have amounted to committing suicide. God's central role in the construction of the universe was assumed to be true by the whole society. Accepting the divine creation of the universe was a kind of philosophical camouflage. This assumption concealed the profound meanings and implications of their revolutionary discoveries. The church treated those who questioned their geocentric astronomy openly with great cruelty. The experience of Giordano Bruno (1548–1600) the Italian astronomer, philosopher and mathematician were still very fresh to all pioneering scientists and critical thinkers in the 17th century. Bruno rejected the dominant geocentric view. Contrary to the established religious teachings, he advocated the existence of an infinite universe. The church accused Bruno of heresy. He was burned alive at the stake on 12 February 1600 (Blum 2012: 103).

Overt opposition to the idea that a perfect divine being had created a perfect and unified universe was very dangerous. To deny that the universe existed in perfect harmony and motion was regarded as blasphemous. Any such theory amounted to a direct confrontation with the established church. The realisation that there is a harmonious and unified universe that is in constant motion was significant in itself. It implied that these motions and unity are governed by natural laws. Beneath the observable chaos we can detect formal laws. The obvious disorders are therefore deceiving. Furthermore, we are empowered with a faculty that enables us to disclose the secrets of nature. To solve the riddles of nature, the pioneering scientist of the modern age suggested we needed a precise language to communicate these regularities and the harmony. That language was mathematics. The regularities of nature are transcribed in the language of mathematical relations and proportionality. Galileo famously said that the universe is a "grand book which . . . is written in the language of mathematics and its characters are triangles, circles, and other geometric figures without which it is humanly impossible to understand a single word of it" (quoted from Kennedy 2013: 194). This was what Newton most successfully applied in his masterwork. In this monumental work he "postulated three laws of motion that joined all celestial and terrestrial objects into a vast mechanical system whose parts worked in perfect harmony and whose connections could be expressed in mathematical terms" (Perry 2016: 237).

The motto of the new age was to seek the perfect truth in the book of nature. The departure from the writings of Ancient Greece and the Bible was a direct result of this outlook. These sources were set aside as being degenerative. Descartes went even a step further. Descartes was prepared to doubt everything. He entered a profound world of imagination and explored his power of intuition. He concluded that

> there is not one of my former beliefs about which a doubt may not properly be raised. . . . So, in future, I must withhold my assent from these

former beliefs just as carefully as I would from obvious falsehoods if I want to discover any certainty.

(Descartes 1996: 18)

Descartes, despite his break with the past, tacitly accepted his concept of identity and his vortex mechanics. He based the former on the idea of unity and the latter on the principle of equilibrium. He reasoned that "there are two ways in which things of which we have different ideas can be taken to be one and the same thing: either by a unity and identity of nature or merely by a unity of composition" (Descartes 2000: 195). As for his vortex of celestial mechanics it "deals with equilibrium" (Schuster 2017: 19). Descartes was in search of clear and distinct knowledge. He aimed to discover a method that led to such knowledge. His method of doubt drove him to the understanding that anything that is acquired by sense perception is probable and hence must be rejected. The only certain knowledge that is clear, distinct and certain is the one that is attained by means of intuition and deduction. This is a form of knowledge, just like mathematics, that can be derived from the stipulation and be proved conclusively. The truth is guaranteed mathematically by rules of deduction or inference.

The break with the past took place in both deductive and inductive reasoning. The critical thinkers of the age cast doubt on the tenability of divinity. They questioned the ancient texts as the ultimate source of knowledge. One radical but inevitable consequence of dispensing with the divinity and dismissal of ancient texts as indeterminate truth was giving credit where credit was due. It handed over knowledge to individuals. Individuals resumed their rightful place. Two further implications were followed by this very noteworthy fact, one that the ancient texts and the religious texts could not have the total monopoly over human knowledge. Most significant of all, they were not complete truths. Their assertions were not universally valid. Moreover, knowledge was also liberated from any one social group or sect in a society, that is, the priests, philosophers or just men. It implied that every individual had the ability to observe and study. The book of nature was open to everyone. Any rational individual could potentially discover the laws of nature. In practice that meant the exclusion of God's monopoly over knowledge. It constituted the emancipation of knowledge. Knowledge no longer existed under the restraints of theocracy and pseudoscience.

This break liberated knowledge and made it more democratic. Every individual could exercise the act of acquiring new knowledge. Human knowledge was no longer the preserve of a religious establishment. This new basis effectively freed humanity from the confinement of the medieval mind. In many ways this can be seen as the birth of the democratic age.

The new approach undermined the old method of acquiring knowledge. It regarded the practice of memorising and reciting old texts to enhance one's knowledge as degenerative and a waste of human time and potential. Such methods were held responsible for the rigidity of mind and the stagnation of society. Francis Bacon (1561–1626) denounced the Aristotelian and Scholastic methods of research as being barren and regressive. In a very influential passage, Bacon described his scientific research method along these lines:

> Those who have handled sciences have been men of experiment or men of dogmas. The men of experiment are like the ant, they only digest the use; the reasoners resemble spiders who make cobwebs out of their substance. But the bee takes a middle course; it gathers the material from the flowers of the garden and of the field but transforms and digests it by a power of its own.
>
> (Bacon 1999: 128)

The application of Bacon's scientific methodology brought immediate results. Copernicus, Tycho, Kepler, Galileo and Newton applied Bacon's methods of research. They did not only look for the real reasons and causes of the matters. They were also very proactive and systematic in what they did and achieved. They employed the latest technologies of the time to observe the motion of planets. They also observed the mundane activities of falling things or the change of tides and seasons.

Measure of everything

The idea that nature is the master of all things was among the core beliefs of the school of Hellas in Ancient Greece. Nature was said to be the measure of all things. Nature was regarded as a force that works according to its own laws. In the school of Hellas, the term law has a different meaning in relation to different contexts. In the context of geometry, it stood for something that is right, that is, the right line. In other contexts, it represented the binding and unity of men, principles and relations. Above all, it was anything that is backed by reason. The contemporary usage of law is different from that of the ancient Greeks. To Greeks law was permanent. It was sovereign and divine. Natural law was inextricably linked with human nature and reason. These laws were universal yet were not written but communicated in our deeds. The law of self-preservation, the law of morality and avoiding evil are examples of such laws. These laws were said to be innate, embedded in our nature and a priori. Most important of all, we can have knowledge of such laws.

We can detect traces of the idea of permanent law in Homer's poetry. The legendary poet lived most probably in the 8th or 9th century BC. In his epic poem, *The Iliad*, Achilles and Agamemnon became friends in accordance with the divine laws of right and wrong, justice and injustice. The term law, however, first appeared in Hesiod's (750–650) poem, *Works, and Days*. The idea of natural law kept evolving over time. Its essentials were formed by the works of Pythagoras, the Stoics, Heraclitus, Plato and Aristotle. The common trait among the works of these writers in relation to the law is its immutability and permanency. One common theme about the law among all these writers is justice. To Pythagoras justice is a universal right. It is a number with certain quantitative and qualitative attributes. Justice is a square number that is multiplied into itself (Barker 2010: 2010). Thus, justice is a whole and perfect number. As it consists of equal parts, it is completely harmonious. This concept infers that equality is the principle of justice. Equilibrium is the point of perfect justice. It is the point when all parts are equal. Opposite consideration applies to disequilibrium, when the parts are unequal. Disequilibrium is contrary to natural law. So justice and natural law are maintained when all parts are equal.

With all, the Hellas thinkers were not totally oblivious to the distinction between natural laws and human laws. Heraclitus was the first thinker who made a distinction between the two. He kept permanency and eternality. The writers of Hellas attributed these concepts to law. Furthermore, he marked the law with attributes of reason and command. Proceeding on this track he postulated that the law is the reason, and the law governs. Heraclitus gave the law a meaning in the context of regulating urban life. His primary assumption was that law is reason and reason is universal. So the laws that govern the city must be universal. For all that, Heraclitus concluded that "the people must fight for the law just as for a city wall" (quoted from Lebow 2003: 357).

The two most eminent members of the school of Hellas were Plato and Aristotle. The permanency and universality of law form a vital part of their analytical outlook. Plato in *Minos* refers to many instances of law in different societies and then equates each instance to a form of law. With this in mind, he inquires what all these forms of law have in common. He replies that all forms of law share a common essence that is absolute and eternal. Plato's description of Socrates' trial presents a good example of his distinction between incidental laws and natural laws. In this predicament, there was a choice for Socrates to make. He was compelled to choose between innate and eternal justice or an instance or a form of law. Socrates opted for the former. In his defence, Socrates says: "either acquit me or not; but whatever you do, know that I shall never alter my ways" (Plato 1992: 31).

The school of Hellas reached its high point with Aristotle. Aristotle advanced the most significant ideas of the school. The ideas, which were once considered to be firm and certain, lost much of their rigor and authority. The Greek creative period had reached its peak. It was rapidly running out of steam. Its end was imminent. It grew jaded and weary. It could not nurture new ideas within the confinement of the social, political, legal, cultural, economic and scientific framework of its time.

Aristotle was the single most dynamic thinker of the Hellas school. He belongs simultaneously to two eras. This duality of being in two periods can best be illustrated by his explanation of the law. On the one hand he discussed universal laws that are eternal and consistent. On the other hand, he described the same laws as not applicable in all times. In *Politics*, Aristotle defines natural laws as the nature of the things. It is "what each thing is when fully developed . . . whether we are speaking of a man, a horse or a family" (quoted from Reale 1990: 337). As for the concept of natural justice, it is seen as being distinct from human laws. It does not apply to slaves and women. Aristotle makes a distinction between two types of justices, the natural and conventional forms of justice. This is how he makes this distinction:

> of political justice. There are two forms of it, the natural and the conventional. It is natural when it has the same validity everywhere. It is convenient when there is no original reason why it should take one form rather than another and the rule it imposes is reached by agreement, after which it holds good.
>
> (Aristotle 1970: 157)

The kernel of the ancient Greek thinking consists of four basic elements. First, human beings are the centre of the cosmos. Protagoras (c. 490–420 BC) purported that "man is the measure of all things" (quoted from Brannigan 1981: 1). Second, the universal law is realisable and obtainable within a milieu of reason, relation and law. Third, the world is essentially orderly and harmonious forever. This natural order is expressed in all interrelated patterns and rhythms that we observe around us. Forth, justice is equality. It is harmony and equilibrium. The most dedicated disciples of these concepts were the Stoics. Zeno of Citium (c. 336–265 BC) founded the Stoic school. Speaking of the greatest good in life, Zeno said it is Logos (Goranko 2016: 18). It is the universal reason. Logos is the purpose of life. Zeno argued that what distinguishes the human race from animals is that human beings live according to reason and animals do not. For Zeno, the concept of self-preservation is central to human identity. As a corollary of this maxim, he deduced the inference that a happy life is a moral life. It is according to virtue and in agreement with nature (Annas 1993: 166).

Zeno and the Stoics held the opinion that nothing is new or random. All things are assembled in a single natural structure. Nature is predetermined. It is complete and intelligible, and the course of events are pre-set. Human instinct and passion cannot disclose the secrets of nature. Natural laws exist for a reason. Natural laws are infallible. The whole consists of the divine reason. Its parts appear and reappear following the preordained cycles of events and patterns. Zeno pointed to the beginning and the end of the universe. In his view, the universe began with fire and will end with fire.

Virtue and the universe are not two distinct entities. The two are inseparably connected. Likewise, it is subject to the same universal laws. Zeno states that "man is endowed with reason, the faculty which gives his superiority over the brute: therefore, for man "life in accordance with nature" is rightly understood to mean life in accordance with reason. Hence, Zeno's definition of the end is "to live of virtue since it is the virtue that nature leads" (Copleston 1946: 395). Nature is predetermined. From this, it follows that the universe is complete and harmonious. A good life is one that is consistent with nature. Thus, the ideal state of being is consistent with the goals of nature. Virtue is good and what is good is in harmony with nature.

Stoicism influenced the emerging Roman Empire. The Emperor Marcus Aurelius (121–80) was a notable convert to the ideals of Stoicism. Lucius Annaeus Seneca (4 BC – 65 AD) and Epictetus (50–135) also adopted the Stoics' philosophy and placed a great deal of emphasis on the demeanour of virtue. The Roman Stoics held human dignity to be the aim and purpose of virtue. The emperor regarded dignitas humana (human dignity) as the basis of the natural law. He advocated the same degree of rights and freedom as everything follows the same law.

The Roman law owes much to Marcus Tullius Cicero (106–43 BC). Cicero was a Roman lawyer, philosopher and politician. His main source of inspiration were the ideas of the Greek Stoics. He divided the law into two general branches; moral laws and positive laws (Letwin 2003: 175). He regarded the former as superior to the latter laws. Cicero argued that supreme laws are eternal. They exist regardless of whether they are written or not. These laws are right because they are well-matched to reason. Such laws are in congruity with nature. They belong to the law of nature. Such laws are general in character. Laws that are specific to a given time and a place are conditional laws. By contrast, universal laws are applicable everywhere and for all nations. One law for all, Cicero maintained, stems from a single source. God is the author, the master and the judge of the law. In Cicero's system of law, what binds people in a society is justice, which is safeguarded by the eternal law of command and prohibition.

One of most deeply ingrained of human predispositions is belief. Human beings by necessity are believers. To live and adapt to a changing environment, we are constrained by the necessity of practical life. We need to trust what we believe to act. Human knowledge by its nature is deficient. Individual knowledge is not infinite. It can never be complete. It is always limited. We cannot simply know everything. What we think we know, we know only partially. Just for this very reason, the necessity of freedom of thought and imagination becomes the absolute imperative. The ground on which we act is not based on full knowledge but partly on instinct. It is based partially on our trust in what we believe. Prehistoric societies practiced polytheism. The sources of inspiration for such varied beliefs, ideas and deities were their natural surroundings. People's imagination living under different conditions was stirred by the rhythms that they observed in nature. Human belief was profoundly influenced by the cycle of the seasons, day and night, birth and death, weather conditions, co-dependency and other factors. This aspect of ancient paganism has been passed not to modern pagans but to other deists or atheists (Magliocco 2014: 105). This is the belief in the spontaneous order in nature.

Faith in harmonious order is found among the beliefs of people in different continents (Pontineu: 279). In Ancient Egypt, such unity, balance and harmony are manifested in the term Ma'at. This name was associated with a goddess. It means straight, which also entails the attributes of order, justice and balance (Rauh and Kraus 2017: 44). The universe is portrayed as something that is perfect and orderly. Harmony also dominates the thought of the Ancient Indians. Hinduism is a pantheistic and polytheistic religion. The universe is personified in Brahman, which is the representation of everything, all reality and truth. There is a division of responsibilities among Hindu's gods and goddesses. Their purpose is to coordinate universal harmony. The second member of the Hindu Trinity is Vishnu. This god is believed to preserve and maintain unity, order and harmony in the universe (Rhodes 2011: 5). In Buddhism everything proceeds from the mind. Buddha relocated the cosmic order and harmony into mind. According to Buddha, mental cultivation enables one to obtain and maintain true harmony and order. If we pursue this pathway in good conscience, we will embrace the principle of nonviolence as the ideal universal peace. For Buddha, true harmony establishes peace between mind and the cosmos (Gomes 1992: 31).

Taoism is one of the oldest religions in China. Central to Taoism is the principle of balance and harmony, too. It is believed that the ancient Chinese thinker, Tao Tzu, who died in 517 BC created Taoism at the beginning of the 6th century BC. Harmony in Taoism can be achieved when there is a balance in the relationship between 'Yang' (male) and 'Yin' the female (Gualtieri 1994: 62). Harmony also played a pivotal role in the beliefs of the Native Americans. For the Native Americans a life based on a moral order was associated with the unity and harmony in the universe.

Gomes contends that this vision of the relationship between nature and humanity is expressed most vividly by the Navago tribe. The Native American tribes defined perfect harmony as the state when there is a profound unity and balance between human societies and nature. The result of this harmony is peace, good health and long life (Gomes 2012: 1291). To the Aboriginal peoples of Australia harmony is defined as the organic interdependency between humans and land. Harmony is achieved when "human beings are united with land and with the other forms of life on the land" (Kelbessa 2011: 576). In ancient Greece Harmonia was the goddess of harmony, peace and unity. In many ways the teaching of the Greek Stoics is rooted in the instructions of this goddess.

An image of the cosmos and all the species in their entirety, to the untrained mind, conjures the necessity of spontaneous order. This concept coexists with our wisdom of ignorance. Humanity lives, by and large, in hope of knowing. Knowledge is an eternal human goal. Exact knowledge may prove a considerable challenge to achieve. Without hope, human endeavour would be forlorn. Hope, even void of substance, cannot simply be dismissed. Hope cannot be taken for granted. If we experience despair and despondency due to a lack of exact knowledge, then all hope is lost. Destruction invokes dejection and nihilism. Humanity would face extinction if it lost the ability to hope. A plurality of heterogeneous entities demands a relation of entities that enjoys credibility and order. The concept of order is a central precept in all religions and ideologies. It is signposted, either overtly or tacitly, in all systems of thought.

Religions were formed as a direct result of the creation of rules. The centrepiece of the system of rules is law. Religion and law have developed side by side. To live in social groups and interact with each other, humanity required certain rules of conduct and behaviour. These rules exist and change in accordance with the conditions of life and environment.

For most of human history, these rules and codes of conduct were passed verbally from one generation to the next. Written rules are a relatively recent occurrence. The ruler of ancient Babylonia, Hammurabi (c. 2123–80 BC), was an inventive ruler in this respect. He introduced a written code of laws. (Somervill 2010: 41). The basic tenets of Judaism, Christianity and Islam date back to the time of Hammurabi. The instigators and the preachers of the ecclesiastic movements were among the first lawmakers.

The first forms of law related to crucial concepts such as self-preservation. Earthly laws defined the essential rules of conduct between the members of a family or a community. These laws were designed to facilitate collective wellbeing. Hence, these laws were contingent on the changing conditions and the requirements of the growing human communities. The origins of secular, moral and positive laws are rooted in these laws. With the emergence of religious beliefs, over time the clerics from different religions departed from worldly laws and created two other forms of law. These laws were defined by their relationship to the concept of a Supreme Being. There were also important laws to safeguard the role and interests of the clergy and the type of religion they advocated.

To elucidate this issue sufficiently let us take Christianity as an example. The Christian religion is of some significance since it was the dominant religion of Europe. Northern and Western Europe were transformed from a pre-medieval state to modern Europe. Christianity came to exercise huge power after the Roman emperor, Constantine I (280–337), accepted the Christian faith. Constantine was the first Roman emperor who used the apparatus of the state to defend and endorse Christianity. He issued the Edict of Milan in 313. This law embraced Christianity as the state religion. Predictably, Christian priests had to differentiate divine laws from human laws to secure their superior position. Some laws were unassailable. Other laws could be changed or adapted according to requirements and wishes of the rulers and the pontiffs. The Christian legal system is a hierarchical system. The leading teachers of Christianity such as Ambrose, Augustine and Gregory divided the law into two types. These were defined as divine laws and human laws. The divine laws were regarded as immutable and eternal. These laws derive their legitimacy from biblical scripture and revelation. Such laws exist conceptually because the deity executes a preordained order. In Christianity, human salvation depends on these laws. On the other hand, positive laws (human laws) are man-made laws. Human laws constitute a body of rules and regulations that are enacted by different governments. These laws are essentially provisional in character. They are conditional on the circumstances of each government and community.

In Augustine's (354–430), work *De Magistro and De Peccatorum Meritis*, we discover a definition of what constitutes the ideal absolute law. According to the bishop, this law dates to the "pre-fall." The bishop of Hippo refers to the fall of man in the Garden of Eden. As the story goes, Adam and Eve were corrupted by temptation. Together they transgressed God's commandments. Their actions amounted to a criminal rebellion against God. God retaliated and took his revenge by cursing humanity forever. This sin not only exposed the very dubious inner self of human nature, but it also corrupted it forever. For this purpose, it is argued, those positive laws are needed because of the sinful nature of humans. Positive laws, although imperfect, are necessary in the defence of God, church and order.

The leading theologians of medieval Europe became obsessed with the distinctions between divine laws and positive laws. The theological establishment had two central aims. Their first goal was to reinforce the supremacy of divinity. For the theologians it was key to emphasise the singularity of one God and one religion. Secondly, they hoped to confer divine legitimacy on one emperor. The most celebrated theologian of the medieval epoch was Thomas Aquinas (1225–74). He divided law into four different forms. (Schwarz 2002: 196). The first type is external law. These laws are essentially God's laws. The second type are those laws that are revealed through the medium of "reason." He defined these laws as natural laws. The third type are those laws that are revealed in religious scripture. The final type are the positive laws. The validity of any positive law, according to Aquinas, should be measured in relation to its compatibility with divine laws.

The Renaissance era in Europe began in the late 15th century. This is a period in which Europe is believed to have rejected the values and ideals of the middle ages. This period saw the revival of ancient Greek humanism in Europe.

In the philosophy of humanism, it is the human that is regarded as the centre of everything. Four constituents of the Renaissance are of critical importance in this respect. The first one is Protagoras' maxim that "man is the measure of all things." The next is the pre-eminence of the natural world. The Renaissance thinkers adopted the naturalistic approach of the Ancient Greeks. They aspired to understand the actual mechanism of the real world. The third element is the emphasis on the unity and harmony both in nature and in thought (Davidson 1994: 49). The fourth element, which is essential for the realisation of the three components, is the necessity of free, unhindered inquiry.

The European Renaissance sought to apply the Greek naturalistic approach of inquiry. Their subject of inquiry was the human condition. Hugo Grotius (1583–1645) a Dutch philosopher and jurist experienced the destructive nature of war. The Dutch war of independence against the Spanish empire (1568–1648) occurred during his lifetime. The liberation of the Dutch nation is historically significant. Holland was the first small nation in early modern Europe that gained its independence. The Dutch struggle involved 80 years of war. Dutch freedom heralded a new vision of national independence.

It effectively provided new meaning to the ideas of freedom. Dutch independence enshrined important concepts such as sovereignty, the legitimacy of political power, law and equality of rights among nations.

Grotius associated all wars with cruelty and destruction. He believed that war harmed all forces engaged in the conflict. Grotius argued that every reasonable means must be employed to prevent wars. Grotius believed that in the event of war violence and destruction should be limited. He anticipated the dawn of a new era. His experience of living under Spanish colonial rule taught him one crucial lesson, which was the illegitimacy of Spanish colonial domination in Holland. The Dutch nation fought to be free from Spain. This process did not seem, after all, contrary to natural laws. Grotius, however, did not fully recognise the legitimate and democratic lawmakers. Making peace was his aim and he erroneously presumed that peace between the colonisers and the colonised nations can be achieved.

Grotius owed his concept of the legal system to Greek and Roman natural law. It is no wonder that he held the view that justice and natural law are synonymous. A natural law is founded on the nature of things. The definition of a natural law is in one sense very simple. In the same vein, justice can be no other concept than that of what is just. From this, we can ascertain that with the proper application of rational reasoning we can discover, expose and understand these laws. Grotius described the law of nature as "unalterable, that it cannot be changed by God himself" (Grotius 2007: 22). He made a link between natural law and natural rights and professed a law that permitted slavery, conquest and colonialism. Yet at the same time he supported justice and harmony. Despite certain inconsistencies, Grotius's idea of natural law was instrumental in nurturing the approach of philosophers such as John Locke and Adam Smith.

The rediscovery of reason

Karl Jaspers (1883–1969), a German psychiatrist and philosopher, described the first creative period that was global in human history as the "pivotal age." He described it as the Axial Age. He estimated that it lasted for about a millennium from 800 BC to 200 AD. Jaspers' claim is valid, but the timescale is overestimated. Clearly human history witnessed a period of great intellectual creativity from 500 BC to 200 BC. This era revolutionised human thinking. It was a period that shaped the subsequent course of human history. It gave birth to Indian religions and philosophy, to Hinduism, Buddhism and Jainism. In the Middle East, it created the Hebrew prophets and their Hundred Schools. In China, Confucianism and Daoism were established. Among the Iranian nations, Zoroaster disseminated his vision of the world in this era. It could be argued that the single most momentous achievement of this time was found in the ideas of ancient Greece.

New approaches to thought and philosophy had profound consequences. New thinkers articulated a series of penetrating and valuable questions.

The tradition of the passive spectator was over. The axial age no longer took everything for granted. The new age stressed active investigation. The axial age produced a large body of work. The ideas of this period are extraordinary for their originality, range, scope and depth. This period undertook a profound journey of investigation and questioning.

Indian thinkers debated the relationship between Karma and Moksha (Doniger 2014: 28). They implied that embedded in each action there is a cause. Karma is the amassed effects of one's actions. Human life depends on this ever-increasing Karma. However, Karma's effects are not interminable. Moksha is defined as the cure. It constitutes a route out of Karma.

Chinese thinkers recommended their right way (Dao). This was a means to create a good society (Assandri 2014: 53). Followers of Confucius associated Dao with the promotion of a peaceful and humane society. By contrast the devotees of Zhuangzi identified the cosmic Dao as their key to a good life. Zoroaster from the Iranian Plateau identified two opposite forces that were in constant struggle (Wray and Mobley 2005: 85). Zoroaster detected a pattern of gathering and marrying forces. He regarded every force as existing in two opposite cosmic identities. This concept defines human life as a profound struggle between good and evil. People are not regarded as separate from these powerful forces. They are not passive spectators. They are active constituents of these cosmic forces. The thinkers of the Jewish world invented the idea of a powerful being that could in time emancipate their community. They longed for freedom from captivity and bondage (Allen 1977: 68). The Jewish thinkers defined a powerful entity that is supreme in every conceivable way. His moral laws are absolute. His message is written down and can be accessed in the form of a sacred text. According to the Jewish philosophers the destiny of everyone and everything is predetermined.

The thinkers of the ancient Greek world occupy an exceptional place. Their ideas and debates testify to the incredible power of human reason. The quest for truth was central to their thinking. For the Greek philosophers the process of evoking truth had an intrinsic value. The Greek philosophers commended the pursuit of truth as an end itself. For them the sense of truth was essentially knowable. They employed reason as the most effective method to acquire truth. This was the same method that Socrates recommended. Socrates advocated a philosophical method based on open and honest questioning. Socrates was devoted to the relentless pursuit of truth. Plato employed the method of Socrates to connect the real world to the eternal world of ideas. The key characteristic of the thinkers of the Axial Age was their profound commitment to reason. They believed that reason could decipher and interpret the concealed truths of the world. The process of inquiry would lead to the acquirement of insightful knowledge. By understanding reality, we can remedy undesirable situations in human society.

The gap between the Axial Age and the age of enlightenment is about 2,000 years. The absolute rule of theocracy and monarchy dominated the intervening period. In some respects, the age of enlightenment was a renewal of the Axial Age. Their fundamental tenets are the same. Their core concepts related primarily to nature and reason. Even the discussion of the nature of divinity in the Axial Age relied on the power of reason. Reason was regarded as a means to explain the essence of divinity. The age of reasoning did not just return to these fundamental ideas. It also examined the prerequisites for the effective application of human reason. Their chief aim was to understand the very nature of a thing. They strove to comprehend its essence in an objective manner.

The concepts of nature and the power of human beings to reason was the starting point of the new thinkers. Their central aim was to emancipate humanity from repression and ignorance. They inferred that everyone was entirely capable of thinking and acting independently. The reasoning individual could become free from the bondage of religion and political authority. Rationality was regarded as a property that everyone is born with. So it is natural for everyone to employ this natural ability as best as they can. The restraint or prevention of this ability is deemed as unnatural. The liberation of the power of human reason is possible only when humanity is free. The tyranny of theocracy, monarchy and ignorance had to be decidedly rejected. At the heart of this period is the belief that individuals must be free to employ their natural ability to study, interpret and critically scrutinise nature, society, authorities and traditions.

Freedom of thought was largely associated with the period of ancient Greece. After this period, freedom of thought was discouraged. Every attempt was made to silence critical thinking. In the course of time the violation and abuse of the freedom of thought were legitimised and institutionalised. The pursuit of truth became a crime. The freedom to hold a contrary view to that of the established state and the religion was regarded as sacrilege. Any free thinker was treated very harshly. Dissidents were held in harsh conditions. Punishment was vicious and unfair. This period was dominated by wars, imperial conquests, absolute monarchies and theocracy. Christianity became the dominant religion of Europe. Religious zealots as well as ruthless monarchs repressed any form of dissent. Every attempt was made to stifle progressive thought. This was a period of violence, superstition, economic stagnation and intolerance. The religious establishment combined with the tyranny of the state stifled the scope of human freedom and thinking.

With the advent of the Renaissance in Europe the dark ages stage by stage sluggishly were abandoned. In a few centuries a new philosophical approach began to appear. The discovery and exploitation of the new world gave birth to a new period. The colonisation of other parts of the world radically transformed the European colonial states. The European nations that enjoyed powerful empires became very rich. The new wealth helped create a series of affluent social classes. These new wealthy classes required valid and reliable information to pursue their dreams, adventures and conquests. Correspondingly, European conquests brought about several unintended consequences. One of these unintended consequences was the expansion of economic activities between

European colonisers and their colonies. Another consequence was the rise of wealthy social classes who enjoyed high incomes and more free time. The wealthy social classes developed a desire for education, study and research. By the 17th century such classes were very well established. They began to publish their philosophical ideas and scientific discoveries. This is a body of investigative work that has revolutionised our understanding of both the natural and social worlds.

Freedom of thought inevitably questioned the very legitimacy of autocracy and theocracy. This was one of the main causes of the underdevelopment of social sciences compared to natural sciences in undemocratic societies. Evidently, it was natural sciences that outpaced social sciences as the modern era dawned. The development of all sciences, in the modern time, are by-products of the European age of enlightenment. Economics was an offshoot of the new theories, discoveries and innovations in the natural sciences. The age of enlightenment depicted the world of nature and human societies as natural structures. These structures were believed to be ruled by natural laws. Such laws are discoverable by means of rational thinking, proper scientific methods and the application of mathematical language. Streeten noted that "just as Kepler was inspired by doctrine of harmony in the spheres to discover the laws which govern the orbits of the planets, so the early economists were inspired by the doctrine that there is a harmony of interests in a society to formulate economic laws" (quoted from Kirzner 1989: 95).

The age of enlightenment preserved and advanced the idea of natural law. This was an idea that continued its presence in western thought from the time of ancient Greece and Rome to modern times. Central to this belief was the idea that nature has got its own laws. This was a concept that grew over time. The achievements of natural scientists in discovering such laws in the 17th century strengthened the general conviction in the power of modern science. Cairnes wrote:

> What Astronomy does for the phenomena of the heavenly bodies; what Dynamics does for the phenomena of motion; what Chemistry does for the phenomena of chemical combination; what Physiology does for the phenomena of the functions of organic life; that Political Economy does for the phenomena of wealth; it expounds the laws according to which those phenomena co-exist with or succeed each other; that is to say, it expounds the laws of the phenomena of wealth.
>
> (Cairnes 1875: 35)

William Whewell (1794–1866) invented the term "scientist." The common noun, science, is roughly what used to be referred to as natural philosophy. The designate has become synonymous with truth and discoveries of universal laws. The label has been distorted in many ways. The term "scientist" has been regarded as a badge of honour. It has also been seen as a self-evident maxim.

Before the advent of modern science, human intellectual endeavours were divided into natural philosophy and moral philosophy. Natural philosophy is the precursor of the natural sciences. With the advent of modern science, terms such as "scientific" and "unscientific" replaced the former definitions. There is no universal or objective consensus on what exactly constitutes science. Science can perhaps be defined as a process concerned with the discovery of truth in accordance with certain established rules and methods. The true representative of science is said to be the natural sciences. In the natural sciences formal validity can be guaranteed. Some might argue that this is not really the case in the realm of social studies. Scholars of social studies may well question the correct academic status of their discipline.

When Adam Smith laid the foundations of the science of economics, the essential requirements of modern economics were already in place. Here we shall only point to the chief preconditions that necessitated a modern analysis of the economy.

The colonisation of America, Africa and Asia after the 15th century had profound consequences for the development of Europe. The looted wealth, exploitation and trade made many of the European states extraordinarily rich. One of the determining effects of this global event was the formation of a new social class. This class had more free time to spend on a range of creative and intellectual activities than the preceding generations. The demands and the scope of the learning classes exceeded the restrictive boundaries of religious dogmas. The learning class was able to move beyond traditional customs, theocratic and monarchic rules and regulations. The practical requirements of the changing society and economy had exceeded the confinement of the old and medieval mindset. The established feudalistic social structure and the theocratic political establishment could no longer restrain ideas and creativity.

The old outlook lost its sense of authority. Past assumptions in relation to knowledge were undermined and challenged. This period, naturally, created its spokespersons. The transitional period produced its envoys. These thinkers were able to articulate and validate the transition and its directions. These envoys were pioneering thinkers. They were hungry for true knowledge. The acquirement of reliable knowledge was their central aim. They attempted to establish the most effective methods of inquiry. They sought true and valid knowledge. Francis Bacon (1561–1626) was the forerunner of this group of thinkers. He challenged the ancient authorities and criticised them as counterproductive and unreliable. He questioned the methods upon which the theories, prescriptions and the predictions of ancient texts were based and constructed. Bacon believed that the old suppositions were neither applicable nor concordant to nature. For Bacon, scientists are not the master of nature but the "servants and interpreters of nature" (Backhouse 2002: 67). In his very influential book, *Novum Organum*, Bacon described his scientific method. A correct method, he argued, is based on "two principles: natural history, the detailed, systematic collection of facts about nature, and induction, deriving laws of nature from these facts" (Backhouse 2002: 67). Bacon compared the merit of different research methods and declared that:

> Those who have handled sciences have been either men of experiment or men of dogmas. The men of experiment are like the ant, they only digest and use; the reasoners resemble spiders who make cobwebs out of their substance. But the bee takes a middle course; it gathers the material from the flowers of the garden and of the field but transforms and digests it by a power of its own.
>
> (Bacon 1999: 128)

Bacon's approach became the most influential method of the period. The Royal Society adopted his method in 1662. It influenced greatly the leading scientists and philosophers of the time such as Robert Boyle (1627–91), Isaac Newton, Robert Hooke (1635–1703) and John Locke (Backhouse 2002: 68). Another influential philosopher who rejected the scholastic tradition was the French philosopher, Rene' Descartes (1596–1650). Descartes aimed to base knowledge on firm, clear and distinct ideas. He challenged all the established ideas of the past. He questioned all the assumptions and concepts of the past. Most specifically, he doubted knowledge that relied on sensation for its validity. He assumed that truth cannot be doubted. With this presupposition, he proposed his cogito, ergo sum (I think, therefore I am) hypothesis. Descartes' method of doubt opened the way for the critical questioning of dogmas. His method also placed trust in the power of reason. Descartes' body of knowledge is based "on a set of simple, self-evident truths" and deductive logic (Backhouse 2002: 67).

Along with the discovery of new land, the new astronomical discoveries of Tycho Brahe and Kepler challenged and undermined the ideas of the medieval world. The concept that the sun and not the earth was the centre of the universe was a critical moment. This new concept represented a profound break with the past. New astronomical instruments enabled more accurate scientific investigation. Kepler and then Galileo painstakingly observed the heavenly bodies. They carefully recorded the motion of the planets and reported their findings factually. All in all, this constituted a daring and ground-breaking mission. These scientists were under the constant surveillance of the Papal Inquisition. Taken together, both their method of inquiry and their findings were heretical. What they discovered was contrary to religious assumptions. They created new, dynamic perspectives in relation to nature and cosmology. These findings of the uniformity and harmony of the cosmos confirmed the age old view of natural law. They demonstrated that the pattern of planets' movement follows a regular direction. The theocratic rulers of the time found these discoveries and ideas deeply alarming. The tragic fates of Bruno and Galileo were still fresh in the minds of many unorthodox thinkers. The fear of encountering the same punishment intimidated many from revealing their heretical ideas.

Descartes made the most of the findings of the new, radical astronomers. He was particularly inspired by Kepler and Galileo. Descartes defined the universe as an infinite space where planets move without obstruction. His formulation of the law of inertia also marked a significant milestone in the development of modern astrophysics. It contributed to the development of Newton's theory of the universal law of gravity. These observations, findings and views altered the old world forever. Our conception of the world was fundamentally transformed.

These discoveries defined the universe as a natural phenomenon, a uniform and harmonious mechanism. The concept of God was profoundly undermined. In many senses the very idea of God had been rendered redundant. These discoveries dramatically altered our sense of the nature of the universe. These new assumptions overshadowed the role of God as the coordinator and operator of the motion of heavenly bodies. The universe could be defined as a mechanical system. It came to be viewed as a system that ran naturally according to inexorable and endless laws. These laws could be articulated and defined in a mathematical geometrical language. New ideas portrayed nature as a force that could not transgress from these laws. The new model of the cosmos ended God's monopoly. The formal sovereignty of God in relation to the universe was exposed as an invalid concept. This was a huge step in the liberation of humanity from the burden of superstition.

No transitional phase owes its creation and essence to one solitary factor. The transition from one epoch to another is triggered by cumulative causes and factors. Moreover, it cannot be the work of any revolutionary moment. Historical transitions occur as result of many diverse factors. Transitions occur in a long and gradual process. The scientific revolution in the 17th century was the outcome of such a process. Besides, each new event acts as a catalyst for many unintended consequences and ideas. Many factors contributed to the outbreak of the scientific revolution. One factor was colonialism. The colonisation of America, Africa and Asia resulted in the creation of a new wealthy class among the imperial nations of Europe. The windfall of wealth brought unprecedented demand for more goods, services and capital. Greater economic activities require more applicable scientific knowledge. This important necessity separated the new learning class from the clergy. The new class no longer speculated on divine revelation. They dedicated their time to studying the material world. They attempted to find workable solutions to pressing problems of their time. The expanding societies, economies, governments, populations, empires and trade required new ideas. A meaningful understanding of the real world without the employment of proper reason is not attainable. Therefore, the new discoveries required the use of reason and critical thinking.

In the end, the philosophy of Ancient Greece paid off. The dynamic and challenging nature of Greek philosophy had profound consequences. The medieval European mind was confronted by radical concepts. Theological dogmas were undermined. A huge gap developed between the proper use of reason and rigid scriptural speculations. More observant and critical thinkers of the medieval times embraced the tendency. They made good use of the philosophical trend and reaped the benefits. William of Ockham (1258–1349) can be regarded as one of these critical thinkers. He deliberately separated the dominion of human reason from theological revelation. He drew a clear line between the concepts of human reason and religion (Shand 2014: 47). This distinction became crucial in the age of enlightenment. This was the period that came to be described as the age of reason. Some might argue that this was not an entirely accurate description of the period. However, it was certainly a period which saw great protest against unreason and dogma.

The combination of the Renaissance, the Reformation and the scientific revolution weakened religious domination and power. The theological world view was deeply undermined. The advancing enlightenment gradually instituted its rational, naturalist and scientific alternative. Divisions in the Roman Catholic Church in the 16th century resulted in the Reformation. Protestant Christians departed from the main body of Christianity. This process weakened the domination of religion. Criticism of the theocratic establishment was emboldened. The breakup also enabled many to think in an unconventional manner. A few European nations opted for Protestantism. These nations, such as Holland and England, established relative individual liberty and greater freedom to express different beliefs.

Freedom of thought, expression and employment were among crucial factors that enabled these nations to develop more rapidly. Social, economic, cultural, political, legal, institutional and scientific advances occurred in these nations. Compared to their competitors, the new Protestant nations were dynamic and forward looking. One must not also forget the invention of printing and gunpowder and their role in dissemination of influence and power.

The relative freedom of belief was an unintended outcome of the Reformation. The Christian religion is a Universalist faith. The belief is based on the idea that everyone is born in sin. Sinful people are believed to descend to hell unless they are saved. Jesus Christ came to redeem people from their sin. So, like all Universalist religions, Christian faith is an imperialistic ideology. It wants everyone to convert to Christianity. The Roman Catholic Church mirrored this feature of Christianity. The Roman Catholic state claimed to represent God. It implemented the laws of God on earth. From this perspective, true laws were seen as God's laws. True laws had to be consistent with God's laws. God was regarded as sovereign. The sovereignty of political authorities was therefore seen as being derived from God.

A philosophical battle emerged in Europe. On one side was the new intellectual social class. This class possessed a different and alternative world view. They sought to define the sovereignty of state and law based on the people of a nation. On the other side there were the ecclesiastical forces. Their world view saw political and legal sovereignty based in God. This ideological conflict helped to pave the way to individual and national freedom. The German theologian, Martin Luther (1483–1546), could not have survived the wrath of the

Roman Catholic imperial papacy if it was not for (a) his direct personal experience of the extent of the corruption in the Roman Catholic Church and (b) by the time Luther raised his voice against the Catholic Church much work had been done to weaken the absolute power of the Roman Catholic Church. Luther's "95 Theses," which he published on 31 October 1517 was a very conservative challenge. It could have easily been absorbed within the body of the Catholic Church. Many knew that within the Catholic Church there were significant abuses of power. However, very few dared to tell the truth. For that, Luther was summoned to attend at the Diet of Worms (Monter 1999: 28). Fearing the severe punishment of the Roman Church he did not appear at the trial. Instead, wisely he went into hiding.

Subsequently, Luther was declared a heretic and excommunicated. Martin Luther and his Protestant Reformation movement could well have been destroyed in its initial stages. He was assisted by several factors. The emerging nations that opposed the Roman Catholic Church imperialism openly helped weaken the Catholic establishment. Martin Luther was also assisted by the invention and spread of the printing press.

This was the early phase of modern national consciousness. This was a form of political identity that was distinct from imperialism and colonialism. This new and evolving political outlook capitalised on trepidations of religious wars. For all intents and purposes, it became a force to be reckoned with. The growing proponents of national liberation movements protected Martin Luther from the powerful imperial Roman Catholic Church.

The age of enlightenment displaced the assumptions and beliefs of the medieval period. The emancipation from religious repression went hand in hand with a denunciation of political despotism. As Christianity was adopted as the religion of the Roman Empire, gradually Christian divine doctrines and laws superseded older political rules and jurisdiction. The primacy of absolute being overruled everything else. The church essentially controlled the actions of the state. The clergy and the civil authority combined formed the seat of deity. The temporal power, the state was demoted to one arm of the church. The absolute papal power lasted for many centuries. This resulted in a very long period of rigid conformity. Divine dogmas and religious persecution dominated society. This was a regressive phase that halted the diversity of belief and dissent. It was a period in which any nonconformist opinions were regarded as heretical.

Christianity is a totalitarian and expansionist faith. It does not just call for total allegiance and obedience. It also aims to achieve the submission of all the temporal world to its creed. Christianity works well as an imperial and colonialist ideology. Islam also employed imperialist beliefs at its core. The ecclesiastical officials believed that their faith allowed them to exercise political authority over every nation.

Durante degli Alighieri known as Dante (1265–1321) was an Italian political thinker and poet. He expressed criticism of the alliance between the church and the civil authority. While in exile he wrote *De Monarchia* (1313). In this work he tried unsuccessfully to elucidate the validation for dividing the power of these two institutions. He regarded the power of the monarchy as distinct to that of the pope. He argued that the source of the power of monarchy must not come from the pope. It must come from God. Durante failed to recall that the pope was the embodiment of God, but he found much in this union to condemn.

Secularism and the rule of religion are concepts that have been in conflict for many years. The schism dates to the time when religion began to take over the realm of political authority. The Reformation in Europe confronted the monopoly of religion over every dominion of life. The reformation requested the restoration of the old system. Nevertheless, it accidentally created a rift between the concepts of civil power and ecclesiastic supremacy. For the first time, it was the enlightenment that defied, most forcefully, the domination and exclusive privileges of ecclesiastic political power. The new age, in the territory of politics, dawned with the works of Thomas Hobbes and John Locke. These political philosophers were troubled by the concept of religious supremacy. They were uncomfortable with the idea of one religion exerting power over other faiths or ideas. They found religion to be a principal cause of most wars, conflicts, violence, socio-economic malaise and political repression. They believed that religion was a source of acrimony and disorder. One reason for their emphasis on this point emanated from their conviction that religion inherently restricts the freedom of belief. Hobbes in *Leviathan* sought salvation against such hostility, division and instability under the wing of authoritarianism. In the interest of maintaining peace, Hobbes called for the subordination of religion to the state. Both Hobbes and Locke left England and went into exile for expressing their unconventional opinions. These authors experienced personally the repression derived from the unity of religion and state.

John Locke forwarded a theory that ideas come from sensation and reflection. This idea had a few implied consequences. For Locke everyone was the source of knowledge. Locke defined the brain of a new-born infant as a clean slate (Goodson 2014: 288–9). He reasoned that during natural human growth and development people acquire knowledge through their sensory experience. Prior to sense experience, the mind is empty. Through one's senses, one receives data from the outside world. This data is a form of raw material. This raw material is channelled into one's mind. The received data is processed into complex ideas. These ideas describe and explain the real world. In view of this, each person can exercise the power of reasoning. Knowledge is rooted in each person. It emanates from the interaction of each person with the world. By implication, then it is up to everyone as to how to employ this power. Human knowledge can bloom if one's senses and brain are used correctly and effectively. One of the most important ramifications of this theory was the proposition that acquiring knowledge is not outside a person's control. Human knowledge is not a predetermined activity. It is not the work of providence. Hence, fate does not decide the course of one's life. A person's present and future is not inescapable or preordained.

Having this in mind, Locke wrote his treatise, *A Letter Concerning Toleration*. He wrote this treatise while he was in exile. In this treatise, Locke argued that belief cannot be imposed by force. Locke argued that coercion cannot change belief. A plurality of religion and beliefs creates greater tolerance, peace and stability. Moreover, freedom of beliefs and ideas will prevent one faith from dominating other thoughts and beliefs. However, Locke did not disseminate his view of pluralism and toleration to the defenders of the Catholic faith.

Two key historical events which helped to separate the state from religion were the American war for independence (1775–85) and the 1789 French revolution. The American war of independence began in April 1775. People from different parts of Europe migrated to North America. The colonists comprised people from a variety of European nationalities. They had different historical backgrounds, languages, cultures, religions and motives for leaving their ancestral homelands. Many joined colonial armies, many migrated to strike gold and exploit the economic bonanza. Many colonialists left Europe for the new world to find a safe sanctuary free of religious strife and persecution. An added motive for many new settlers was to break away with the restrictive customs, cultures moral and social values practiced in their homelands. What was fermenting in the 13 colonies of Britain in North America was a fusion of all these diverse interests, thoughts and expectations. The interests of settlers and the British imperial rulers became, slowly but surely, incompatible. The settlers relished the experience of greater political and economic freedom. With any freedom comes the demand for greater freedom. A trend of this nature could not fit in with the goals of an imperial ruler.

The conflict between Britain and its colony was predictable. The settler's desire for greater freedom was met with British restrictions. The power and the scope of colonial legislatures to deal with local matters were progressively truncated. Trade was limited, taxes increased and fair trial by a jury was disallowed. The settlers were alarmed and dissatisfied. They found themselves losing their relative political and economic freedoms. The settlers were underrepresented, overtaxed and oppressed. Additional punitive laws denied their liberty. In truth, this was only one side of the equation. The fact that these people had left their ancestral homeland, this very fact was a liberating catalyst to break away with old traditions. Old values, culture, beliefs, expectations and colonial subjugation were restraints that the settlers wished to escape from. These people were in pursuit of something new. They were in quest of greater freedom, tolerance and economic fortune.

The American Revolution occurred during the enlightenment. Many of the settlers were proponents of the ideals of the age of enlightenment. The leaders of the American war of independence were very well versed with this new train of thought. John Locke's political ideas were well timed. His political philosophy was profoundly relevant. Locke's ideas guided the leaders of the new American republic in their struggle for independence. John Locke's philosophy clearly influenced the declaration of independence. His ideas played a role in the deliberation of the new constitution. Locke's ideas of the rights of the subjects to rebel against unjust laws, questioning the divine right of monarchy, the separation of state from religion, the idea that people are created equal, the belief in the right of dissent, limited government, social contract, separation of power and the consent of the governed were crucial concepts for the new, democratic republic.

Entrenched in this new world view was the conviction that people are born with certain natural rights. According to these ideas the people are sovereign. The constitution of the new republic is initiated with this right. But the sovereignty of people does not end in the selection of constitution. It extends to freedom of selection of religion too. The freedom of religion and the separation of religion from the state are complementary. Thomas Jefferson (1743–1826), one of the founding fathers of the republic and the main author of the American Declaration of Independence, considered this separation as the basis of individual liberty. His motto was that "honesty is the first chapter in the book of wisdom" (Jefferson 1854: 112, vol. 7). He alerted that "I tremble for my country when I reflect that God is just: that his justice cannot sleep forever" (Jefferson 1854: 404, vol. 8). James Madison (1751–1836), another founding father who served as the fourth president of America, objected to the unity of state and church on the ground that giving superior privilege and having official status to any follower of any denomination of church as the state church will degenerate into corruption and tyranny. The least harmful strategy of the state towards religion is a policy that is neutral. The impartiality is one of the most critical rudiments of a democratic government. A state religion is bound to fail. State religions inevitably violate the rights of people to freedom of thought and conscience.

The founding fathers of the United States of America perceived a profound danger in all forms of power. The most obvious forms of power are political, religious and economic power. John Adams (1735–1826), the second president of the United States, cautioned his people that "there is danger from all men. The only maxim of a free government ought to be to trust no man living with power to endanger the public liberty" (quoted from Bovard 2005: 150). Alexander Hamilton (1757–1804), another founding father and the promoter of the republic constitution, advised that what people want is a just and limited government. George Washington (1732–99), the first president of the United States, prophesised that this eventuality, reverting to tyranny, is possible "if the freedom of speech is taken away then dumb and silent, we may be led, like sheep to the slaughter" (quoted from Robertson 2009: 16). Leaders of the American war of independence, if not totally optimist, were realist and pragmatist. They knew very well that there is no panacea for all social ills. However, they knew that social ills can be prevented and rectified. They believed that ignorance is not bliss. Ignorance merely multiplies the difficulties of the human condition. Benjamin Franklin (1706–90) prognosticated that "an investment in knowledge pays the best interest" (quoted from Kozuskanich 2015: 4). James Madison (1751–1836), another founder of American independence movement, added that "knowledge will forever govern ignorance, and a people who mean to be their governors must arm themselves with the power which knowledge gives" (quoted from Broadwater 2012: 184).

The 1789 French Revolution raised the flag of secularism. The revolution banished the two central custodians of tyranny and despotism. These were the divine right of monarchy and the power of the church. The revolution ended monarchy. It gave birth to a new republican state. The Republic undermined the mighty power of the church by confiscating its assets on 9 April 1790 (Réville 1905: 606). The church was deposed from the position of absolute power. It was made subordinate to the republic. Civil authority held sway over the church. Neither of these events, however, could have been successful without the demotion of religion. Religion had to become subordinate to the power of civil society. The separation of religion from the state resulted in the restoration of freedom of belief and conscience.

The leading writers and philosophers of the French Enlightenment believed strongly that religion and absolute monarchy obstructed human freedom. Religion was regarded as the main obstacle to real progress. The fulfilment of human nature was impossible if faced with religion and absolute monarchy. Religion fosters superstition and submission. It promotes ignorance and fanaticism. It creates and feeds cruelty. Francois-Marie Arouet better known as Voltaire (1694–1778) a French writer, historian and philosopher wrote that "those who can make you believe absurdities can make you commit atrocities" (quoted from Hulsey and Frost 2004: 83). The two top culprits in this category are religion and monarchy (dictatorship). Voltaire rebuked that religion "began when the first scoundrel met the first fool" (quoted from Chase 2018: 8). Against dictatorship, he warned his reader that "the sentiment of justice is so natural, and so universally acquired by all mankind, that it seems to be independent of all law, party, all religion" (Grana 2010: 47). Freedom of belief is Voltaire's remedy to overcome the tyranny of religion and dictatorship. In corroboration of his antidote, Voltaire commented that "if you have two religions in your land, the two will cut each other's throat; but if you have thirty religions, they will dwell in peace" (quoted from Dreisbach 2011: 188).

The French lawyer and philosopher, Baron de Montesquieu (1689–1755), considered the misuse of power to be the key cause of injustices. Both the state and religion are predisposed to abuse power. Misappropriation of power occurs when all power is assumed by one person, religion, or institution. Whereas, under the protectorate of liberty "there is no abuse of power" (Montesquieu 1766: 220). Moreover, "it is necessary from the very nature of things that power should be a check of power" (Montesquieu 1766: 220). The ground for religious wars is not "the fact that there is more than one religion, but by the spirit of intolerance" (quoted from Larrere 2009: 296). Misapplication of power is not an external matter. It is in the nature of the subject that exploits the power. Montesquieu qualifies this inference by attesting that "constant experience shows that every man invested with power is apt to abuse it, and to carry his authority as far as it will go" (Montesquieu 2007: 150). On this account, he deduced his doctrine of the separation of power. Montesquieu's pioneering theory argued for the separation of powers. He believed in checks and balances on political power. His ideas have had huge influence. He exercised a profound influence on the development of later political thought and democratic constitutions. These concepts have become the ideological cornerstones of the modern democratic world. The idea of the separation of powers testifies that:

> when the legislative and executive powers are united in the same person, or in the same body of magistrates, there can be no liberty: because apprehensions may arise, lest the same Monarch or senate should enact tyrannical laws, to execute then in a tyrannical manner.
>
> (quoted from Tamanaha 2004: 52)

Another member of French Enlightenment, Jean-Jacques Rousseau (1712–78), placed his trust in human nature. It could be said that Rousseau overly romanticised human nature (Masters 1976: 98). He argued that human nature is inherently flawless, but it has been corrupted by modern societies. Since human nature is good, it must then be consistent with liberty. Rousseau then concludes that the prevention of natural liberty is the cause of all social ills in modern societies.

Denis Diderot (1713–84), the co-founder and chief editor of *Encyclopaedia*, alluded that "from fanaticism to barbarism is only one step" (Diderot 2016: 72). But who are the offenders of such monstrous acts? Diderot eagerly replies they are the kings and priests. Then he pledges a sweeping generalisation that "man will never be free until the last king is strangled with the entrails of the last priest" (quoted from Palmer 2013: 195). Diderot's remedy to all social ills and ignorance is scepticism. In his effort to escape, rescue and recover from fanaticism and barbarism he advises that "all things must be examined, debated, investigated without exception and without regard for anyone's feelings" (quoted from Rata 2012: 111). The kings and priests, by the very nature of their deific rights and social positions, encroach upon the good nature of humans. Diderot censures that:

> No man has received from nature the right to give orders to others. Freedom is a gift from heaven, and every individual of the same species has the right to enjoy it as soon as he is in the enjoyment of his reason.
>
> (quoted from Sternhell 2010: 166–7)

The power of religion rests on delusion and ignorance. The herd instinct facilitates conformity and superstition. Barbarism triumphs when deluded and ignorant mobs are on the loose. David Hume (1711–76), the Scottish philosopher and historian, removed the garb of mystery and divinity from religion. Hume brought religion down to earth. In his book, *Dialogue Concerning Natural Religion*, Hume described religion as a human construction. He referred to fear and hope as the origins of religion. Man created God in his own image.

All attributes of God are manmade. These attributes are drawn from the realm of human experience. Enlightened thinkers regard religion as an instrument of repression. For Baron d'Holbach (1723–89), religion was the chief cause of submission and ignorance (Styers 2004: 56). Donatien Alphonse Francois Marquis de Sade (1740–1814), a French revolutionary and philosopher, described religion as an opium. Religion is fed to the people to obtain their submission. This is what he said in 1797. Later Marx restated this concept in a few of his famous phrases, as in religion is "the sigh of oppressed creatures," religion is "the heart of a heartless world" and religion is the "opium of the people" (Marx 1967: 250).

The concept of reason is one of the main measures of humanity, knowledge, civilisation and progress for the advocates of the enlightenment movement. Religion and absolute monarchy stand in the direct opposite to this development of human potentials. Reason is founded on critical thinking and freedom of thought. The human capacity to reason is natural, while religion and dictatorship prevent people from exercising reason. These are unnatural obstacles in fulfilling human potential and progress. The significance of the term "reason" was so important that it was employed to describe the age.

An individual no longer required religion to acquire knowledge. Moreover, the idea of living in an ethical manner no longer required a formal faith. The true nature of religion can be regarded as blind obedience and intolerance. The result of this unquestioning obedience and intolerance is constant war between ascending and descending religions. Each religion insists on a unique sense of its validity that cannot be doubted. A faith thrives out of a devotion to only one subjective truth. Absolute divine laws are by their very nature inflexible and beyond doubt. This is the binding system where truths become partial and slanted perspectives that nurture demand slavish devotion. It is little wonder that the process of rational questioning and examination is a curse in organised religions.

It follows therefore that each religion defines itself as uniquely informed and blessed with authentic insight. Each religion asserts a formal claim to possessing a particular all-encompassing validity. Religious conversion becomes a kind of duty that has divine purpose. It becomes regarded as god's will to bring others to one's selected religion. Converting others to one's religion is a divine command. Countless religious conflicts have been justified on such grounds. Tolerance is the cure for blind fanaticism, wrote the writer and dramatist of the Enlightenment, Gotthold Ephraim Lessing (1729–81). In his play, *Nathan the Wise*, Lessing tried to disclose the causes of religious fanaticism. In his work he attempted to outline the remedy to help overcome religious intolerance as one of the greatest of human failings.

The system of punishment in religion is both crude and demented. A perfect example of this punitive justice can be seen in the Abrahamic religions. The basis of this system of punishment is retribution. It is based on the concepts of revenge and retributive justice. In several proclamations, the Old Testament leaves no room for doubt in relation to its ideal form of justice. In one of its edicts, The Old Testament proclaims that "if any harm follows, then you shall give life for life, eye for an eye, tooth for tooth, hand for hand, foot for foot, burn for burn, wound for wound, stripe for stripe" (Exodus 21:23–5). We find the same fervent and unforgiving tone in Leviticus 24:19–20. Here it prescribes that "anyone who maims another shall suffer the same injury in turn: fracture for fracture, eye for an eye, tooth for tooth; the injury inflicted is the injury to be suffered." In another extract, the Old Testament orders its followers to be very firm in handling god's proclamations. It instructs them to "show no pity" and to ensure that the law of "life for life, eye for an eye, tooth for tooth, hand for hand, foot for foot" takes its course swiftly and at once (Deuteronomy 19:21).

There appears to be a shift of philosophical focus in the New Testament in relation to the basic rule of justice. In the New Testament, we read: "you have heard that it was said, 'An eye for an eye, and a tooth for a tooth.' But I tell you, don't resist him who is evil; but whoever strikes you on your right cheek, turn to him the other also" (Matthew 5:38). The New Testament describes a few somewhat futile rhetorical articles of clemency. However, in essence, revenge is the chief constituent of both the Old and New Testaments. When we examine the history of Christianity, we see the domination of the concept of punitive justice. Harsh and draconian punishment has been a core characteristic of all Christian states. The metaphysical mantras of "turning the other cheek," "love your neighbour as yourself" and "love your enemies" lack any historical validation. Christianity has certainly been one of the most vindictive and violent religions in human history.

The Christian religion has displayed a ferocious, unrestrained, ruthless and totalitarian nature. Christianity has provoked countless examples of antagonism both from within and from outside the religion. A key to understanding the age of Enlightenment is discerning the significance of this very fact. Bringing down Christian religion from power was one of the great accomplishments of the age of Enlightenment. In this respect, among the Abrahamic faiths, Islam has not been influenced by the age of Enlightenment. The Islamic system of justice at its core is the one that is outlined in the Old Testament. It is a retributive justice that is still practiced in several Islamic states. The Koran reiterates the Old Testament retaliation law virtually word for word. In Sura 5, Koran prescribes its law of equal retaliation as "life for life, an eye for an eye, and nose for nose, and ear for ear, tooth for a tooth."

The concept of punitive justice rests on arbitrary and forbidding laws. The Italian criminologist and economist Cesare Beccaria (1738–94) a writer of the age of enlightenment questioned the justification for the retributive law. He argued that a penal code that is based on torture, mutilation and capital punishment can be neither effective, legitimate nor just. In his book *On Crimes and Punishments*, he denounced such actions as barbaric and intrinsically immoral. Beccaria condemned vengeful reprisal. He called for the immediate abolition of all forms of torture and capital punishment. In unison with the spirit of the age, in line with growing intellectual tradition of natural law philosophy,

Beccaria believed that there are certain natural rights that must be protected by law. One of these rights is equality before the law. No one shall be deprived of his or her life and liberty. All individuals should be subject to the same laws and be treated fairly and humanely. He declared that "for in the eye of the law, every man is innocent, whose crime has not been proved" (Beccaria 1804: 56).

One of the unintended consequences of the relative superiority of the European nations in the age of Enlightenment was a justification of colonialism. Some proponents of the Enlightenment were oblivious to the profoundly negative nature of empire building. Others romanticised the process by which European states enslaved and exploited their new colonies. Some actively endorsed the force of imperialism, arguing that the European hegemony was inevitable and beneficial for all humankind.

Imperialism as a concept was essentially contrary to the very spirit of the Enlightenment movement. For this reason, it did not go unnoticed. Many thinkers of the age did take a firm stand against colonialism. The most outspoken critic of colonialism of the age was Johann Gottfried von Herder Her (1744–1803), a German writer and critic. He found the whole policy and the way of thinking to be contrary to reason, civilised norms, justice and equality. In his book, *Outlines of a Philosophy of the History of Man*, Herder Her articulated his views about equality under the law for all nations. He argued that there should be one law for all nations. He believed that all nations should be subject to the same laws. Accordingly, he regarded colonialism as being incongruent to this law. He perceived colonialism as a blatant violation of this law. Herder Her rejected imperialist subjugation. He believed that the rights of nations cannot be determined on the grounds of their size, power, population, location or the level of development. For Herder Her the equality of nations should be established irrespective of all these differences. Each nation must be mindful of the rights of other nations. Nations must exercise mutual respect. It follows then that each nation has the right to be free of colonialism. Each nation has the right to be independent. Each nation must be free to pursue and enjoy their arts, culture and language. Each free nation must determine their way of life. Herder Her regarded colonialism as unethical and stated that depriving a nation of "their country, you deprive them of everything" (Herder 1803: 303).

Entrenched in this perspective is faith in the right of freedom of conscience and toleration of dissent. These elements were seen as natural. What is unnatural and irrational is coercing someone to conform to a faith or an idea. This outlook was extended to the realm of self-preservation and self-betterment too. These propensities are natural as in preserving one's life or improving one's conditions of life one acts in accordance with nature. Whichever authority stands against or suppresses these rights will be acting against nature and natural justice.

Equally political orders can be natural or unnatural. A form of political order that is natural is one that has a legal legitimacy. It is based on the rational consent of people. Subjugation could not exist within the remit of natural legitimacy. The Dutch example served well in validating this stance. The liberation of Holland from the Spanish Empire was an important catalyst for the political philosophy of the Enlightenment. It was the first small nation to succeed in gaining her independence. The Dutch struggle for independence lasted 80 years (1568–1648). The Dutch engaged in a sustained and constant struggle to undermine the dominance of Spain. Dutch independence inspired a new point of view in relation to the rights of nations (Tangain 2014: 96–8). This was the idea of equal rights among all nations. There were two sides to this story. One was outlined by Johann Gottfried von Herder Her who objected to colonisation. Herder Her argued that nations had the right to live according to their own preferred culture, language and moral codes. Dutch liberation itself was a validation for equality of rights for nations. Furthermore, Dutch liberation put in the picture the connection between colonialism and enslaving the people of colonised nations. Both acts were not compatible with the philosophy of liberation. As for the slave trade, whoever endorsed colonialism sanctioned the system of slavery.

By all accounts, the Enlightenment movement, from start to finish remained faithful to the idea of natural rights. Among these rights were the core concepts of freedom: justice, freedom of thought, fair trial, equality under the law, rebelling against tyranny and constitutional government. Absolute power came to be regarded as unnatural. Absolute power leaves all political power in the hands of a single person. One individual in charge of the executive, legislative and judicial branches of the government results in tyranny. Thus, they called for a division of power among these organs of government. In addition, they argued that the judiciary organ had to be independent. An individual will not be able to enjoy his or her natural rights unless these measures are taken. The necessary precondition to protecting the natural rights of individuals from the state is when the state power is not under the monopoly of one person or institution. The advocates of the age discovered that the concept of freedom of thought, imagination and speech were the most effective weapons against tyranny and absolutism. Also, they learned that to establish freedom of thought and expression one needed to have freedom of assembly and association.

Liberty was regarded as a self-evident truth to the exponents of the Enlightenment. On this basis many leading champions of the Enlightenment opposed the slave trade. Aristotle also relied on nature to defend the institution of slavery. The protagonist of the age of reason argued against this perspective. French thinkers spearheaded this movement. Rousseau played a central role in this philosophical fight. He was the frankest opponent of the institution of slavery. He condemned slavery in the strongest terms and wrote that "the right to enslave is null, not only because it is illegitimate, but because it is absurd and means nothing. The words slavery and right are contradictory and mutually exclusive" (Rousseau 2016: 26). Montesquieu on the same subject deliberated that

> the state of slavery is bad of its own nature: it is neither useful to the master nor to the slave; not to the slave, because he can do nothing thro' a motive

> of virtue; not to the master, because he contracts all manner of bad habits with his slaves; he accustoms himself insensibly to the want of all moral virtues; he grows fierce, hasty, severe, choleric, voluptuous, and cruel.
>
> (Montesquieu 1977: 258–9)

Montesquieu, somewhat, indirectly justified slavery under certain circumstances. Voltaire condemned the institution of slavery but expressed racial prejudice against black Africans. He held that Africans are from "a different species that mated with orangutans" (Addison 2009: 46). In contrast, Abbe' Pluche (1688–1761) rejects slavery categorically. In one passage in his *Persian Letters* he describes an incident of the slave trade. He observed a mother in Africa "calmly selling her daughter to a stranger for a sum of cowry shells" (quoted from Miller 2008: 66). On another occasion two sons sold their father to European buyers. He wrote that the experience "wounded [his] eyes as much as those" who carried out the sales. Other firm opponents of slavery pursued more practical paths of action. In France Jacques-Pierre Brissot (1754–1793) created the Society of the Friends of Blacks in 1788. In Britain William Wilberforce (1759–1833) and Thomas Clarkson (1760–1846) founded the Society for the Abolition of Slave Trade in 1787.

Natural liberty was an inclusive concept. John Locke commented that,

> the natural liberty of man is to be free from any superior power on earth, and not to be under the will or legislative authority of man, but to have only the law of Nature for his rule. The liberty of man in society is to be under no other legislative power but that established by consent in the commonwealth, nor under the dominion of any will, or restraint of any law, but what that legislative shall enact according to the trust put in it.
>
> (Locke 2004: 14)

Locke derives human liberty from nature. He proceeds that:

> freedom of men under government is to have a standing rule to live by, common to every one of that society, and made by the legislative power erected in it. A liberty to follow my own will in all things where that rule prescribes not, and not to be subject to the inconstant, uncertain, unknown, arbitrary will of another man, as freedom of nature is to be under no other restraint but the law of nature.
>
> (Locke 2004: 14)

Locke's words and deeds on the issue of slavery were not consistent. In his time the slave trade was a very profitable business. Many wealthy writers and political leaders from the higher echelons of society had a stake in this lucrative trade. Locke invested in a company that was deeply involved in the slave trade. The trading organisation was called the "Company of Royal Adventures in England Trading in Africa" and was chartered in 1663. The slave trade on the west coast of Africa was under the monopoly of this company. One-quarter of the company's trade by 1665 was related to the slave trade. Locke presented three different views in relation to the institution of slavery. He vindicated slavery in terms of a "just war." Those who surrendered in war can be treated as slaves. In his, *On Slavery*, Locke discusses the issue of voluntary slaves. In this work he argues that slavery is permissible if somebody signs a contract and gives up the right to personhood willingly.

Scottish thinkers were among the pioneers of the age. Hutcheson, Adam Smith's favourite teacher, was a prominent and influential thinker of the age. He was the first among the scholars of the time who criticised the Aristotelian doctrine that some people are born slaves and some masters. Hutcheson based his refutation of the Aristotle dictum on the premise that everyone feels pain and humiliation. Thus, it is irrational to assume that there are people who are born with the capacity to endure lifelong indignity, degradation and pain. Another Scottish scholar, Adam Ferguson, in his book *Institutes of Moral Philosophy* (1769), pointed out that "no one is born a slave; because everyone is born with all his original rights" (Ferguson 1769: 201). David Hume rejected the institution of slavery but alleged that "black people were inferior to white" (Webster 2003: 486).

Science, order and progress

From the end of the axial age to the beginning of the age of enlightenment, the world fell into a very long period of stagnation. This period lasted for about 2,000 years. The most apparent characteristics of this period were relentless wars, disease, starvation, extreme human cruelty and the rule of theocracy. Mediaeval Europe was plunged into the dark ages. Theocracy was dominant in a profound and all-encompassing manner. Theocracy held sway. Religion exercised absolute power. Religion was able to exercise dominance over all aspects of life, both material and intellectual. After Constantine (272/3–337 AD), the first Roman Emperor to convert to Christianity, the Church gradually concentrated all godly and earthly powers into the hands of the Popes. They perceived their role as that of direct representatives of God. Lothario Conti, Pope Innocent III (1198–1216) on his coronation proclaimed that he was "half-way between God and man, smaller than God, Greater than man" (Scott 2011: 72).

The power of the inquisition was supreme. It was employed to control the masses and silence dissent. The common people lived under the rule and dominance of religion. The common people exercised little or no power of any kind and were excluded from education. They owned little or nothing. Religion defined what was and was not sinful. The religious powers believed that their world view was absolute. Theocracy defined the existing world in purely religious terms that required no second guessing. Rational dissent was deemed unacceptable.

The Pope was regarded as the representative of God on Earth. As such the Pope exercised supreme power and moral authority. His theocratic leadership tolerated no philosophical rival. Moral codes emanated from the Papacy, which claimed divine legitimacy. The Pope was regarded as infallible. The common people were permanently in the wrong. Their everlasting vice derived from the concept of original sin. So it was futile to attempt to improve one's living conditions. It was pointless to oppose the ruling authority. The attempt to better one's conditions was perceived as devious or even immoral. The poor were treated with contempt and considered unspiritual and vulgar. Society existed as a harsh and inflexible hierarchy.

Religion dictated the dominant vision of life. Everyone's fate was sealed in his and her destiny. The Bible was seen as the definitive book that had been transcribed by God on the day of creation. The church exercised unquestionable social power. This world view created a degenerative and stagnant society. Dissent and rational examination of the world was discouraged and even outlawed.

Those who transgressed from these norms were regarded as heretics. Dissenters were dealt with harshly. The age of Enlightenment challenged this world view. It presented a secular vision of the world. This new perspective argued that the future is unknown. The new thinkers argued that people create the future. Free individuals can determine and direct the future. The Enlightenment movement was a cumulative and gradual process. It stopped the wheels of absolute theocracy from spinning unrestrained. They replaced it with a secular democratic alternative. At the heart of this vision rests the concept of organic evolution. The Enlightenment thinkers defined an optimistic view in relation to human progress. Progress was deemed feasible both in material conditions and intellectually. Belief in human progress brought the human to the central point of understanding and action. God was relegated to the philosophical periphery. This meant that any individual could be the master of his or her own destiny. Knowledge came to require an empirical basis. This was a profoundly significant break with the past. The rational examination of the forces of the world as it existed provided a crucial new philosophical perspective.

The intellectual horizons of the interim period, the period between the axial age and the age of Enlightenment, were limited to two essential sources. These were the authority of divine texts and the ancient Greek texts. These texts were employed as the criteria to judge the validity and reliability of any intellectual output. This narrow philosophical method had the most far-reaching implications. It incarcerated all possible truth in these texts. The process of understanding was limited and restricted. Truthful insight was the domain of a very small elite. The established clergy exercised a dominant and relentless authority. The narrow class exercising control denied any wider community the validity of dissent. The clergy constituted a self-serving elite which monopolised knowledge. Without social mobility those outside the clergy class could not examine or decipher religious truths. Human knowledge was confined to aged religious texts. Doubt was deemed an invalid reaction to the philosophical certainties provided and defined by religious texts. Dissent from the established creed was regarded as heresy. The accused were imprisoned, tortured and burnt to death. Knowledge was a prisoner of dogmatic religious conservatism.

There would not be any substantial progress under this closed system. Progress in human knowledge only flourished when access to knowledge became democratic. The quest for truth became an individual concern. The process of examining knowledge critically required a distinctive, new approach. An individual could question and consider ideas in a profoundly new manner.

Two philosophers made an indispensable contribution to the new approach. They were Francis Bacon and Rene Descartes. These two scientists and philosophers defied the past beliefs. They employed new, vital methods of seeking for truth. Firstly, they cast aside the exclusivity of knowledge to a small, privileged class. Accordingly, each person can acquire knowledge. Their methods of acquiring knowledge are inclusive. Secondly, the pursuit of knowledge is desirable. The process empowers individuals. The result of this individual pursuit is to undermine ignorance. Knowledge emancipates individuals. In turn everyone becomes more independent. Thirdly, the future is not known. Indeed, the future cannot be known. Human progress is desirable. The process of improving our understanding of the world ennobles and liberates humankind. Old certainties and rules are quickly rendered vulnerable once the hunger for dissent and questioning is encouraged. Knowledge becomes accessible once the restrictions of clerical domination are undermined. Ancient texts defined the world in a series of stagnant, unshakeable truths. Once the pursuit of knowledge is defined as a process requiring critical thinking, then outdated clerical assumptions wither and fade away.

Launching a contrary trend to question the prevailing beliefs, traditions and methods was the first step towards progress. The emerging critical thinkers were great advocates of progress. They sought it in nature and history. For both Bacon and Descartes, science and technology were the engines of human progress. Furthermore, they argued that advances in science and technology can lead to an improved understanding of the world. The question was breaking the chief barrier that prevented science to advance. Bacon saw the obstacle in suppositions that are not validated by facts and reason. This was the prevailing climate in his time. Bacon wanted to liberate science from unsubstantiated assertions. He defined these assumptions as "idols knowledge." For Bacon, that knowledge which cannot be corroborated cannot be based on facts and hence cannot be verified rationally. This approach constituted dissent from established orthodoxy. Indeed, it was an approach that tactfully refuted the practice of relying on religious authority. Ancient texts were no longer the primary source of knowledge.

For Bacon the confirmation of a theory on the grounds of faith was both unreliable and irrational. The old perspective encouraged a futile cycle of stale repetition. Bacon proposed a new start. He called it a "great instauration." That is "a total reconstruction of the science, arts, and all human knowledge, raised upon the proper foundations" (Bacon 1999: 66). Bacon pointed to power as one important aspect of knowledge. In one sense human knowledge for Bacon is not an end in itself. It is a means to improve human power over nature and human conditions. Bacon coined the phrase that "knowledge is power." He carried on saying that "knowledge and power come to the same thing for nature cannot be conquered except by obeying her" (quoted from Copleston 2003: 300).

Another figure of crucial importance was Descartes. He expressed critical doubt in relation to every established truth of his times. Instead of empirical generalisation based on careful observation (induction), Descartes relied on the power of pure reason (deduction). He deduced from pure deduction his well-known proposition of Cogito ergo sum (I think, therefore I am). This was one proposition that he could not doubt. Thus, he concluded that valid scientific knowledge must be as "clear and distinct ideas" as this proposition. In a scientific theory, then, the conclusion must logically be followed from its premises.

Both Bacon and Descartes encouraged scepticism, doubt, disbelief and dissent. Their search was for a secure foundation of knowledge. They did not want to base the foundation of knowledge on religious authority. They rejected emotion, tradition, speculation, prejudice or theocracy. They embraced the scientific method. They yearned to establish freedom of imagination, contemplation and expression. These two thinkers helped provide a vigorous and dynamic new philosophical context in which to pursue knowledge.

The medieval age in Europe lost sight of the real world. It was obsessed in theistic terms about an imaginary life after death. Life before death was only a testing time. Life was no more than a preparation for the life after death. Human knowledge was cocooned in this sterile and vicious cycle. Escaping from this philosophical cage was profoundly difficult. New approaches and new ideas constituted a radical break with the past. Michel de Montaigne (1533–93), a French essayist, broke with this tradition. In a leap of imagination, he embraced the concept of the progressive liberty of human knowledge. Contrary to conventional myth, Montaigne argued, knowledge is not for "the preparation of man for a safe death" but it should be for the betterment of human conditions (quoted from Lombardo 2008: 295).

Emerging science and technology turned Montaigne's wish into a concrete reality in the following centuries. The discovery of a new continent reinforced the belief in human progress. The discoveries and scientific contributions of Copernicus, Kepler, Galileo, Descartes and Newton painted a different and dynamic picture of the world. By means of careful observation, and the application of scientific research methodology and deduction, these scientists expressed their theories and their astronomical laws. They presented a different universe. They created a new philosophical context in which the world could be understood. They discovered and defined new scientific perspectives. They outlined laws that provided an explanation of the nature of the world. These laws were physical, mechanistic and universal. The planets were understood to be bodies that were imperfect. These bodies did not move in a perfect circular motion. The existence of imperfection in the motion of these bodies had profound philosophical consequences. The process of scientific examination and exploration seemed manifestly to deny the role of a perfect and infallible creator.

The scientific methods that could describe, discover, and predict the operation of nature and universe could also be employed to understand human society. Therefore, it was feasible to improve human conditions. The scientific research methods that were proposed by Bacon and Descartes were adopted to explain, interpret and understand human societies. It was envisaged that a human society can be constructed like a machine. This entity could then be directed towards an ideal state. Science and the correct application of scientific methods would make progress possible. One of the most critical ramifications of this conclusion was to dislodge divinity in shaping the fate of humanity. The history of humanity was not predetermined. Human beings were the masters of their own future. Their future was not preordained. Human progress could logically therefore be directed and enhanced. Human society could be analysed, dissected and improved. The future was no longer defined and restricted by the clergy and those exercising absolute power. This was a pivotal shift in the direction of human history, a development that was self-propelling. This dramatic philosophical shift created its own impetus and momentum.

Newton's discoveries of the universal laws of gravitation and motion were the crowning achievements of the age. Such discoveries fostered a growing belief that humanity could form a comprehensive explanation of the universe and human society. The new ideas argued and proved that both the heavenly bodies and human societies are governed by natural laws. Other branches of science soon adopted the same scientific methods. They also attained similar impressive results. Andreas Vesalius (1514–64) and William Harvey (1578–1657) applied the same methods in their investigation of anatomy and physiology. Harvey applied the same scientific approach in his study of the mechanics of the heart and circulation of blood in animals. By carefully observing, recording and reflecting on his findings, he discovered the circulation of the blood in the human body. Harvey demonstrated how the valves in the veins carry blood around the body and return it back to the heart. Harvey described his important discovery as follows:

> It has been shown by reason and experiment that blood by the beat of the ventricles flows through the lungs and heart and is pumped to the whole body. . . . It must, therefore, be concluded that the blood in the animal body moves around in a circle continuously and that the action of the function of the heart is to accomplish this by pumping. This is the only reason for the motion and beat of the heart.
>
> (Harvey 2003: 73)

These seminal discoveries corroborated the research methods of Bacon and Descartes. They confirmed that by careful and methodical observation, experiments and deduction one can advance our knowledge of the world. These successes exerted profound influence on contemporary scientists and thinkers. It convinced them that with the systematic application of these methods human beings can amass a comprehensive and unified body of knowledge of both human and nature. From this, it follows that humanity can calculate, predict and determine their future without resorting to divinity. Religion had lost the stifling domination it had enjoyed for so long. This was a completely distinctive world view. It discredited the authority of religion and orthodox ideas. Without forsaking the authority of superstition and convention, Galileo could not have demonstrated his key discoveries. Galileo proved that objects falling to earth accelerate in velocity. This discovery would have been impossible if the authority of the church had not been undermined. Kepler would not have been able to show that earth orbits around the sun; Newton would not have been able to describe the universal law of gravity. Harvey could not have demonstrated the circular flow of blood in human body. These were natural regularities that were derived from the actual function of nature itself.

The laws of nature are expressed in regularities. Nature follows a natural course. The world is as it is meant to be. Each event in nature has a natural cause. Every cause has an effect. The law of cause and effect is also subject to natural uniformity and regularity. Cause and effect chart a natural order. The cause precedes the effect. Describing natural uniformities with the regularity theory of causation was a radical abolitionist and dangerous method against predominant conventional wisdom. It presented a materialistic vision of natural order. The ramification of revision in the epistemological method was incalculable. The theory of regularity of causation stood in stark contrast to the teleological world view.

The teleological image of the world is one in which everything is predetermined. The world is fixed. The future is pre-set. Destiny defines everything. The past, the present and the future are defined in inflexible and sterile terms. There is no sense of change and method. On the contrary, the natural law of cause and effect enables us to know the unknown. In this scheme of natural regularities, it is the past which determines the present and future. It was no longer the intended future that determined the course of events. The course of events was determined by the past and present events. After all, the law of the cause and effect was a breach of conformity and the standard analysis of the prevailing convention. On the primacy of the law of cause-and-effect Simon Laplace (1749–1827), one of the greatest mathematical physicists of his time wrote that:

> We may regard the present state of the universe as the effect of its past and the cause of its future. An intellect which at any given moment knew all the forces that animate nature and the mutual positions of the beings that compose it, if this intellect were vast enough to submit that data to analysis, could condense into a single formula the movement of the greatest bodies of the universe and that of the lightest atom: for such an intellect nothing would be uncertain, and the future just like the past would be present before its eyes.
>
> (quoted in Lawrenz 2012: 172)

The ascent of progress is the instant that went with the first human beings. Progress is related to the human struggle to survive. Social progress is built on the human longing to live more securely and comfortably. Humans desire to make sure that they have enough food, better shelter and security. In the beginning, these concerns were for one day after another, then perhaps for one month to another. With the formation of more complex societies these aims became extended to longer periods of time. In the first instance, the act of stepping out of the cave and searching for food was a symbolic sign of progress. Taking a twig and hitting a branch of a mulberry tree to collect the fruit constitutes another significant step towards progress. Picking up a stone and smashing it to create a tool for farming or hunting is also a leap forward in development. Building a shelter was another important step in human progress. Discovering fire was another, creating tools another, domesticating animals and farming another. The steps are small but signify crucial moments of development. Clearly forms of progress occur in one way or another in different ancient societies. Progress is essentially a cumulative process. The combination of seemingly small gestures and adaptations come to signify huge change.

Progress is in time and in specific place. There are diverse opinions concerning time. The theory of time in relation to progress follows two general distinct trends. Both trends date back to ancient times. In Zoroastrianism, the ancient religion of the Iranian nations, time is regarded as a linear process (Boyce 2001: 99). It advances forward into the future. Judaism and Christianity have adopted the same concept of time. The prophecy of the coming of the Messiah is related to a linear notion of time. The expectation of the second coming of Christ is a subdivision of this trend. This is an expectation that a saviour will come and will rescue humanity. The doctrine of "thy Kingdom come" is a promise of progress and a restoration of a perfect life in the future time.

We can also trace back the idea of progress to Aristotle's concept of potential and actual (Bader 2015: 193). When potentials actualise there is progress. Any dynamic connection is a chain of progress. For Aristotle, the universe has infinite potential. The actualisation of these potentials is progress. Leibniz embraced this theory fully. His theory of universal progress is essentially an Aristotelian theory. The foundation of Leibniz theory of progress is the "principle of plenitude." This principle states that everything that can be—will be. Leibniz construes his assertion of realisation of God as the ultimate perfection and beautifies from his principle of plenitude. He says that given that there is a universe with infinite potential then the ultimate progress is one that gives rise to the realisation of the perfect God. Leibniz claimed that "to realize in its completeness the universal beauty and perfection of the works of God, we must recognize a certain perpetual and very free progress of the whole universe, such that it is always going forward to greater improvement" (quoted from Nisbet 2009: 158).

There is a sense of progress in entertaining any ray of hope. The most basic impulse of optimism for a better future is the first step to progress. Humanity could not have advanced without a degree of optimism. The age of

Enlightenment stressed the positive sense embodied in human potential. There was an underlining philosophical optimism at the heart of the age of Enlightenment. The catalyst to this great optimistic upheaval was the unprecedented scientific discoveries, technological innovations and social and economic development that took place. Greater freedom of thought and inquiry encouraged an optimistic reading of the place of humans in the world. The period engendered a sense of self-belief that humanity can direct their future. Human society was perceived as being capable of changing for the better. It enhanced the faith in progress that "we surpass all the times that have been before us; and it is highly probable that those that will succeed, will far surpass us" (quoted from Lombardo 2008: 303).

In Ancient India there were both cyclic and linear concepts of history. However, the former was the more dominant one. In Hinduism and Buddhism, time is conceived of as a circular entity. The wheel of history (Kalachakra) rotates endlessly around the same orbit. The world repeats itself according to the law of Samsara. This results in the rebirth of all existence and matter. The law of Samsara emphasises the cyclicality of everything (Griffith-Dickson 2005: 365). The age of Enlightenment departed from this conception of history. It was a profound and radical break with past ideas. It was under these circumstances that economics as a new scientific discipline in its own rights laid its first foundations. Modern economics was born from the idea of human and social progress.

The founders of modern economics framed their thoughts around the idea of progress. Turgot (1727–81), a member of the French Physiocrats School who greatly influenced Adam Smith, placed progress at the heart of his economic doctrines. He outlined his economic theory in the context of a stage-by-stage development of human societies. Smith demonstrated how progress had taken shape over time and how the past is connected to the future (Heffernan 1999: 131). His view of progress is not exclusively a linear process. However, according to Smith the future will be more advanced than the past. In the interval, there are short and long rounds that are a fusion of chaos and barbarism, order and rationality. Overall, there is an ascending sense of progress. This process advances from lower development to higher development since in each future cycle there will be more freedom and less tyranny and control. This notion of cyclical progress was not new. It had its earlier proponents in Europe. Giambattista Vico (1668–1744) also described human progress in cycles (Carlton 2006: 173). This approach conceives of a pattern in which growth and order is followed by disorder and decline. Jacques-Benigne Boussuet (1627–1704) a French scholar also proposed a similar description of progress in his book *Universal History*. He described the cyclical rise and fall of empires from the point of view of the linear progress. In the same vein, Edward Gibbon (1737–94) in his classic book *The History of the Decline and Fall of the Roman Empire*, discusses the pattern of progress in human history. He employs the case study of the Roman Empire to illustrate his views. Gibbon points out that progress has a natural course. However, it can be prevented from following its natural course by hostile forces such as religion.

Progress was a central and growing theme in the age of Enlightenment. It was a concept that was examined and discussed in a wide range of ways from many different perspectives. Bernard de Fontenelle (1657–1757) correlated it with the accumulation of human knowledge. Voltaire in his *Essay on Custom* associated it with the improvement of the human mind. William Godwin linked the idea of progress to the expansion of political freedom and individual liberty. One of the most optimistic thinkers in relation to the future was Marques de Condorcet (1743–94), who demonstrated his concept of progress in a few different stages. Freedom was defined by Marques de Condorcet as the key facilitator of progress. He outlined these concepts in his *Sketch for a Historical Picture of the Progress of the Human Mind.*

Marques argued that the crucial engine of progress was science and reason. However, science and reason cannot be fully applied in the absence of freedom. Human salvation itself is dependent on the essential existence of freedom. He held that an expansion of freedom results in the greater utilisation of science and reason and identified ten important stages in the development of human liberty. Inevitably the gradual establishment of freedom undermined religious bigotry and political tyranny. One of the most important stages in this process was the French Revolution.

The last stage of human development is characterised by the establishment of perfect liberty. In this ultimate stage, the primary guides for human conduct are science and reason. People could create a positive and free future. In time they would construct perfect societies that are founded on moral principles. They would strive to create and develop prosperous and happy social systems.

The proponents of the Age of Enlightenment were emancipationists. They were radical thinkers who opposed the medieval world. This was the time when Christianity dominated all aspects of life in Europe. The unity of state and religion instigated, endorsed and encouraged intolerance. The status quo at this time violated people's basic rights. Two pioneering political philosophers of the age who recognised this fundamental flaw in this unity of the church and state were Niccolo di Bernardo dei Machiavelli (1469–1527), and Thomas Hobbes.

Hobbes argued that an effective government cannot found its authority on religious doctrines. Hobbes regarded religion and politics as two distinct spheres of thought and belief. Religion in its most basic essence stands in opposition to the nature of politics. Religion is concerned with fantasy and delusion. By contrast politics is concerned with concepts such as reality and decision making. Politics strives to establish solutions. Such solutions can be put into practice according to the given conditions of life. Therefore, religion cannot provide us with a workable political system. An effective and functional political system can be drawn from the systematic and precise study of human nature, scruples, aims and conducts. To this end, Machiavelli argued that religion must be subordinated to the dominance of politics. This domination would then allow politics to be effective (Pandy 2017: 36).

Thomas Hobbes in forming his political ideas was greatly influenced by his personal experience. The world that he experienced for most of his adult life was very turbulent. It was marred by wars, religious fanaticism, extreme cruelty and poverty. He experienced disorders and intolerance in every aspect of life. Hobbes laid the blame for the flaming chaos first and foremost upon human nature. Since human beings are naturally selfish, greedy, warmongers and pleasure-seekers—they carry out all these misconducts at the expense of others. Religion is the worst representation of this mob mantra. For Hobbes human nature is wicked. He argued that religion was essentially irrational, fanatical and violent. The combination of these two was disastrous. The separation of religion from the civil law for Hobbes is a necessity (Goldstein 2010: 30). Hobbes expressed profound pessimism about human nature. This belief led him to endorse the concept of absolute monarchy. He argued that absolute monarchy would guarantee order and it would prevent religion from exercising supreme authority.

This period also readdressed the question of what is morally deemed to be good or bad and re-examined the moral concepts of vice and virtue. Bernard Mandeville (1670–1733) recapitulated the prevailing view. In his *The Fable of the Bees* poem, he created a paradoxical interpretation of these concepts. Mandeville wrote a detailed commentary on his poem and published it as a book in 1714. He repudiated religious misconceptions of vice. In his view religion associates sin with harm. Vice is a sin, hence it is regarded as harmful. The prescription of vice then follows from this definition. Mandeville dismissed this as a fallacy. He stated that private vices can result in public good. A society may benefit and flourish because of individual vanity and greed. In reverse, a conduct that is sanctioned as virtuous may be detrimental to the well-being and the welfare of a society. The conceited passion that serves individual self-interest, pride and vanity do not just harm the society but can work for public benefit. Bernard put the essence of his political satire as follows: "thus every part was full of vice, yet the whole mass a paradise" (Mandeville 1795: 5). Bernard's verdict was controversial. His ideas triggered hostility and resentment among believers and agitators at the time. However, for those who were ready to break with the past, Mandeville's irony rekindled their curiosity for further creative thinking. It influenced a diverse range of thinkers including Francis Hutcheson, Jean-Jacques Rousseau, David Hume and most importantly the works of the founder of modern economics, Adam Smith.

For the proponents of the Age of Enlightenment absolute authority, either in the form of religion or state is essentially unnatural. Civil authority is natural when it is legitimate in character. For John Locke (1632–1704) the critical question was what is the nature and the source of the legitimacy of the civil authority? Locke examined whether such authority is derived from God or from people. He questioned whether such authority could derive from brute force or from public consensus. Locke held that the attainment of political power, divine or secular, has no natural legitimacy because one finds oneself in authority. In his search for an answer to these questions, Locke differentiated the legitimacy of authority from the source of the legitimacy of political power. He sought the answer to these issues in human nature. For Locke human nature is defined as being "good." Humanity is gifted with the power of reason. Humanity can resolve their problems under the right conditions. Thus, the problem is not related to human nature but rather with the external conditions in which people live. By the virtue of the fact that human beings are gifted with the power of reason and morality then they should determine their destiny and political authority. Therefore, the legitimacy of political authority comes from the consent of the governed (Dunn 2002: 29).

The enlightenment thinkers situated morality within the grand scheme of nature. They believed the best of humanity can be discovered when humanity is free. It is within the nature of humanity to be free. Being enslaved by religion or any other authority demeans and degrades human potential. That was the philosophical norm that Baruch Spinoza (1632–77) stood for in his relatively short life. For Spinoza rationality is a key characteristic of humankind. Spinoza argued that we can employ rationality to advance and improve our living conditions, knowledge and morality. The capacity to reason is one of the most prized gifts of nature. With this gift, we can discover and understand the true nature of everything. Rational investigation can explain the true nature of morality and religion. However, for Spinoza reason without freedom is lifeless. Reason cannot be put fully into practice unless there is freedom of thought and expression. Freedom, rationality and knowledge are integral parts of true moral actions. These attributes can only be fully utilised in a democratic environment. In his great book, *The Ethics*, Spinoza attempted to formulate a complete code of universal ethics. He strove to outline and define a system of ethics compatible with the principles of freedom and rationality. Spinoza aimed to define an ethical system of values that could be deduced from axioms of geometry and mathematics.

One outstanding aspect of the Age of Enlightenment was the liberation of knowledge. It released knowledge from the captivity of God and religion. The quest for knowledge was rendered democratic. The acknowledgement of the fact that every individual is gifted with the faculty to acquire knowledge and can add to the body of human knowledge was a conclusive break with the past. Besides, this gift was regarded as everyone's natural right. No one should be deprived of this right. This mundane but revolutionary idea cast aside God and priests as absolute owners of knowledge. The implications of this realisation were profound. Indeed, it discredited the conventional view that nothing could be done without God's will.

The Age of Enlightenment effectively repudiated God as the primary source of knowledge. This concept undermined the authority and prestige of the religious establishment. Human beings could determine their own destiny. This idea placed each person at the core of the process of acquiring knowledge. The rejection of religious authority over knowledge freed human civilisation. Progress could be founded on rational and empirical notions.

This new approach was later discussed and developed by David Hume (1711–76) and Immanuel Kant (1724–1804). The starting point of knowledge for both philosophers is anchored in a person. For Hume, the source of knowledge derived from sense impression or reason. Hume maintained that if a supposition cannot be verified either by sensory observation or reason, that statement cannot be qualified as knowledge. Therefore, anything that cannot be substantiated either by sense experience or reason is not real knowledge. Hume was very insistent and spoke firmly that:

> If we take in our hand any volume of divinity or school metaphysics, for instance—let us ask, *does it contain an abstract reasoning concerning quantity or number*? No. *Does it contain any experimental reasoning concerning matter of fact and existence*? No. Commit it then to the flames, for it can contain nothing but sophistry and illusion.
>
> (Hume 1955: 173—italics in original)

Immanuel Kant is arguably the greatest philosopher of the modern era. Hume's insight into the problem of induction has left a lasting impact on his theory of knowledge. Were it not for reading Hume's inquiry, Kant might not have written his greatest book, *The Critique of Pure Reason*. Kant confessed that he woke from his "dogmatic slumber" by reading and thinking about Hume's argument on the bounds of human knowledge. Kant too begins his theory of knowledge from an individual. His epistemology of knowledge begins with a set of necessary "categories of human understanding." He classified these categories as "synthetic a priori" knowledge. But these categories of understanding belong to the world of sense experience that everyone is equipped with a sensory faculty and capable of acquiring such knowledge.

Laisses-faire, the order of nature

Modern economics was born in Europe. It was concurrent with the renewal of the idea of natural law. Hugo Grotius, a Dutch jurist and political philosopher, renewed the quest for the meaning of natural law. The unifying theme of his book, *The Law of War and Peace*, was natural law. The idea of natural law proved timely. It has left a lasting impact on the foundations of modern economics. For reasons which will become clear later, the influence of Samuel von Pufendorf (1632–94) on natural law in economics was considerable. In his book, *Law of Nature and Nations*, Pufendorf discusses the concept of natural law. This was a very influential book in laying the foundation of modern economic thought.

Natural law has a long history. Its origin dates to ancient times. This is an attribute of being as it is meant to be by virtue of its nature. Natural law is grounded in the order of nature. This attribute was extended to humans too. Human beings were assumed to be rational creatures. These rational creatures pursued a rational end. They aspired to a good and happy life. By their nature human beings are rational. By virtue of being rational and social, they can form a just society. They can achieve their ultimate end, which is to experience a good life and happiness. Differences of opinion are merely related to the intricacies of detail rather than actual principles. Hobbes repudiated the teleological view and presupposed a form of existence as natural law. His disagreements related to human nature. One may safely say that he overtly rejected any end in human nature. But if we consider the matter more narrowly, we can see that he subtly assimilated some kind of teleological end in his theory of human nature. He described human nature as being restless that craves not for happiness and a perfect life but for power. The most natural thing in this ruthless struggle for power is self-preservation. The aim is to survive. In Hobbes's view humans inhabit a fierce and competitive world. The fight for power is endless. Humankind is ruthless: competitive, self-centred, egoistic, violent and selfish. In the "state of nature," which is anarchic, repressive and violent, people use their faculty of reasoning and rationality to serve their own power and vanity.

It is no wonder that Hobbes insinuated that the dream of the greater good is merely an illusion. The greater good is contrary to human nature. He described natural law as "a Law of Nature (*lex naturalis*) is a precept or general rule, found out by reason, by which a man is forbidden to do that which is destructive of his life, or which taketh away the means of preserving the same, and to omit that by which he thinketh it may be best preserved" (Hobbes 2005: 98, Italics in original). Hobbes approached this matter in two ways. One was in the form of natural law and another in the form of natural right. In laying out the basic requirements of natural right he appealed to the authority of natural law. If we assume that natural law is the whole, the natural right will be a subset of this whole. Self-preservation is the most obvious expression of the two. Avoiding death is an instinct. Hobbes says it is a self-evident universal truth that "for every man is desirous of what is good for him, and shuns what is evil, but chiefly the chiefest of natural evils, which is death" (quoted from Finn 2006: 50). Then he went on to mark out his division between natural law and natural right. Conjuring that the root of justice cannot be natural justice as justice is "not a duty but a right."

Samuel von Pufendorf (1632–94), a German philosopher and economist, expressed views that were shaped by Hugo Grotius and Thomas Hobbes interpretations of natural law. In his book the *Law of Nature and Nations*, unlike Hobbes, Pufendorf assumes a peaceful state of nature. He presents a secular view of the law that binds all people. Pufendorf resumed Grotius' line. That is the nature of things are good. For Pufendorf the state of nature is peaceful, and the law of nature entails self-preservation. Humanity gets its meaning in social context, in their relationship with one another living in a society. Natural laws and ethical principles are the requirements for the communal interactions. Self-preservation is not just an obligation, but it is a predetermined law of nature. These are two complementary aspects of the same thing. Both are grounded in human nature. They address the entire spectrum of human affairs. In the same manner, human dignity is essentially innate. It is a part and parcel of human nature. Everyone has got the right to appeal to the authority of reason, freedom, peace, universal justice and self-interest as the source of action and pursuit of equality. Pufendorf states that the rule should be to "cultivate and maintain toward others a peaceable sociality that is consistent with the native character and end of humankind in general" (Pufendorf 1994: 10).

The principle of natural law found its way into the universities of Scotland. Gershom Carmichael (1672–1729) introduced the works of Grotius and Pufendorf to Glasgow University. Francis Hutcheson (1694–1746) built upon the foundation of Carmichael's pioneering work. Hutcheson was an original thinker and a forerunner of the European age of enlightenment and an enthusiastic exponent of the idea of greatest good. Pufendorf's book *The Law of Nature and Nations* was one of the textbooks used in the classroom when Adam Smith was a student at Glasgow University. Hutcheson countered the assertion that the knowledge of God is the prerequisite for discerning good and evil. In addition to the basic five senses, Hutcheson contended that there are two additional senses. He added the aesthetic sense or the appreciation of beauty as the sixth sense. He defined morality as the seventh sense. (Frazer 2010: 24). Hutcheson reasoned that the sense of morality is distinguishable from the other five basic senses in two ways. The first one is the palpability of the five sense organs. These sense organs are ears, eyes, nose, tongue, and skin. Second, together they make up the sensory neurons system. Each organ contains receptors that collect and transmit information to the central nervous system and return the commands to different parts of the body. But the sense of morality just like six other senses is a protector that helps us to live, understand and perceive the world.

To many founders of the enlightenment, the maxims of natural law and natural order were self-evident truths. Pierre de Boisguilbert (1646–1714) is best known as an early advocate of laissez-faire. He is known for laying the foundation of physiocratic ideas in France. In his book, *Detail de la France*, he examined the causes of the decline of the French economy. His economic analyses are noteworthy on two accounts. Firstly, he pointed to a relationship between income and consumption. That is, one person's consumption is another person's income. Secondly, he provided a description of the everyday process of buying and selling. He describes the activity as a natural process that is consistent with nature and the natural order. Buying and selling are natural forces that are motivated by a natural desire to make a profit. So he called for minimal government. He was in favour of leaving the process of buying and selling to nature. For Boisguilbert the concept of laissez faire allowed everyone to obtain the most out of their interactions (Backhouse 2002: 91).

The French Physiocrats were the first systematic school in economics. One of the basic tenets of the Physiocratic school of economics is the idea of natural order. Francois Quesnay (1694–1774) was the founder of the school. His famous article was published in the encyclopedia in 1756. This was followed by the publication of his *Tableau e'conomique* in 1758. Quesnay was a physician. The influence of his medical training is very evident in his graphical presentation of the creation and distribution of wealth. He based his Tableau on William Harvey's (1578–1657) discovery of flow of blood in the human body. In a similar way, Quesnay "sought to analyse the pathology of society and to propose remedies" (Backhouse 2002: 101). To the Physiocrats the economy, just like the circulation of blood, is driven by the "rule of nature" since the author of all systems, economic, cosmology or physiology, is the deity. God could not design a system that is imperfect and disorderly. His systems are perfect, orderly and work naturally. In human societies these natural laws are "imprinted on the hearts of man; they form the light which illumines his conscience" (Gray 1957: 100). So no legislator can alter the nature of things. Thus, it is best to leave everything to its natural course. This motto is manifested in Physiocrats' catchphrase of laissez-faire, paissez passer. Natural laws are "established by a benevolent providence for the good of mankind" (Roll 1983: 135). In the absence of government interference, individuals compete freely. This process is in harmony with the natural order. Nature prescribes the economy to be free from regulation, restriction and customs. Free economies ensure equilibrium and harmony. They safeguard a regular flow of income and payment between different classes and sectors of the economy. On condition that the economy is left to its own natural course of action, to the laissez-faire, it ends in improving the well-being of the public.

The extension of the rule of nature to society like the circulation of blood had a number of implications. One was the laissez faire economic system. The term means "allow to do." The French economist Jacques Claude Marie Vincent de Gournay (1712–59), was captivated by this idea. According to Turgot (1727–71), Gournay believed that "in general every man knows his own interest better than another to whom it is of no concern" (Turgot 2011: 106). Moreover, private and public interests can be compatible. On the back of the foregoing assumption, he concluded that when the interest of "individuals is precisely the same as the general interest, every man ought to be left at liberty to do what he likes" (Turgot 2011: 106).

Another implication of the extension of the rule of nature in society related to the concept of change. Human societies change in the same manner as nature. They evolve in stages. The process of evolution moves from the hunting and gathering of fruit to pasture and domestication of animals. In time this leads to property ownership, to the agrarian economy and the exchange and commercial economy. Adam Ferguson (1723–1816) wrote that each stage of natural history develops to greater perfection. It evolves in a manner that "the present age is perfecting what a former age began; or is now beginning what a future age is to perfect" (Ferguson 1792: 47). Natural progress was also central to the Physiocratic system. Jacques Turgot identified three constituents of ideal progress. These categories were the growth of freedom, knowledge and economy.

All these measures prepared the ground for Adam Smith's economic system. Therefore, economics as a scientific discipline was a derivative of the Age of Enlightenment. It was a product of cumulative efforts of a wide range of discoveries and achievements from different branches of human endeavour which culminated in the Age of Enlightenment. The general foundations of Smith's ideas were well established. This foundation stood on well-accomplished enlightenment ideas of rationality, free thought, natural law, the pursuit of interests and commitment to science and progress. Smith's masterpiece was a refined deliberation of such convictions, transformations and discoveries. The economic perspectives of Smith were based on the behaviour of rational and free individuals. Everyone was regarded as being able to acquire knowledge. Most importantly the individual could employ knowledge to pursue his or her interest. The enlightened pursuit of self-interest is not seen as a vice. It is regarded as a natural undertaking. Human societies are natural mechanisms. These societies operate according to specific natural laws. These are natural mechanisms that work according to certain natural commands. They progress and advance to a higher level of development. The law of progress of society is natural. It is not determined by divine law.

Individuals must enjoy their "natural liberty." They must exercise their "economic freedom" to pursue their "enlightened self-interest" in a natural environment. The role of God is negligible in this process. A level playing field of free competition is the key requirement. An individual would benefit but the whole society and economy will benefit as result of the "natural progress." Hence, freedom, equality, justice and knowledge are not only rational and natural but also have profound economic implications. Smith places economic activities among the most common and natural human activities. This activity can be most effective when it is democratised. Smith made the economic undertaking democratic.

The Enlightenment period was a revolutionary period. It ignited radical new concepts and ideas. The French and American revolutions occurred during this period. The Declaration of the Bill of Rights in America and the Declaration of the Rights of Man in France were the great achievements of this era. The central idea of these documents relates to the issue of the natural rights of people. The essence of the idea is that everyone has some fundamental and unalienable rights. These documents specified these rights as the right to dissent and rebel against tyranny, the right to free thought and belief, the right of equality under the law and the right to happiness. Many advocates of the movement called for these rights. John Locke was one of the earliest defenders of these newly asserted rights. Thomas Paine (1737–1809) not only promoted these rights in his *Common Sense* but he applied them. He took part in the American Revolution. The American constitution embraced the ideals of natural rights and progress.

The Enlightenment readjusted several important conceptual relations. It shifted the priority from God to the individual, from religion to reason, from divine scriptures to the book of nature, from blind obedience to dissent, from tyranny to freedom, from absolute power to the rule of law, from the concept of original sin to natural goodness, from misanthropic pessimism to a naturalistic optimism, from self-improvement as vice to self-love as a virtue, from divine morality to natural morality and from fixed destiny to directing the destiny. Emmanuel Kant was the greatest philosopher of the age. He substituted the treatment of human beings as a means to an end in themselves. Kant regarded everyone as autonomous. He believed that naturally, everyone is endowed with the capacity to think and reason independently. But for a person to fully utilise this capacity, that person must be free.

The most critical prerequisite for the power of reason to function naturally and to seek truth effectively is under the condition of freedom. Thus, true progress will take place when free individuals exercise their faculties of reasoning in a free and open society. This is when human societies experience true progress. The best time for humanity lay ahead in the future. This was essentially an optimistic reading of human potential. Reason and free thought were in fact regarded as the agencies of progress and hope. The religious traditions of Europe emphasised the powerlessness of humanity before an all-knowing God. The Enlightenment liberated humanity from this philosophical straight jacket. Individual thinkers gained a new significance. Rational discussion and the examination of knowledge provided a fresh context in which humanity could bloom and develop. Claude Saint-Simon (1760–1825) remarked that "the golden age is not behind us but in front of us. It is the perfection of social order" (quoted from Bury 2008: 185).

The tradition that everything has got a unique nature that is distinguishable from other things dates to Aristotle. The issue of money is an important example. Aristotle defined the nature of money as something that is employed as a medium of exchange, a unit of account and a store of value. Accordingly, using money in any other way was deemed to be unnatural. Lending money to obtain interest was regarded as an unnatural process. Aristotle proclaimed that

> money was intended to be a means of exchange; interest represents an increase in the money itself. We speak of it as a yield, as of a crop or a litter; for each animal produces its like and interest is money produced out of money. Hence of all ways of getting wealth, this is the most contrary to nature.
>
> (Aristotle 1970: 46)

In the new age, nature played a defining role as the crucial frame of reference. It became the standard of measurement for everything. Human beings were not an exception to this predominant trend. Their unique nature was defined as being good or as being self-interested. It was the latter benchmark of validity that has prevailed. The groundwork for the economics of the Enlightenment were laid under these prevailing conditions. Adam Smith was the key proponent of the economics of this period.

During this period there was a widespread philosophical aim to narrow the gap between the realm of nature and the realm of society. This is essentially the gap between natural philosophy and moral philosophy. A new term was invented for this approach. William Whewell (1794–1833) invented the term "scientist" in 1833 for those who adopted this approach. The aim was to study the natural and the social realms in a scientific manner. This was due to the concept that they operated according to similar natural laws, that is, the Newtonian laws (Backhouse 2002: 167). In the realm of human societies natural liberty was held to be one of these laws. It is under the natural order of natural liberty that people can reason naturally. In view of that, it was argued that the optimum outcome can be achieved when we leave rational individuals to act according to natural predispositions. These predispositions are based on their desire to pursue their individual self-interests. In this way, not only individuals benefit but they also promote the general well-being of the whole society.

Implicit in this world view was the belief that the natural order and a well-functioning civil society are compatible. Interfering with the laws of nature and society is contrary to the nature of things. Government intervention, regulations, customs, culture, religion, monopoly privileges and institution would not improve the situation. They would tend to misdirect the natural course of events. The general climate of the time was in favour of a natural justification. Nature and society are said to have their own laws. These laws are not beyond the understanding of people. Such laws are discoverable. By a proper application of systematic reason and scientific methodology, we comprehend these laws, and these methods propel progress to a higher stage of development.

Therefore, the idea of natural order is deeply rooted in the foundations of economics. This idea is expressed in different ways. In essence, it is the same central concept. The most common use of it is in the laissez-faire economics and the idea of natural liberty. It is captured in the premise that if rational individuals are left alone, they will do better. This doctrine in its most general form defined individuals and the government as being opposite to each other. In its purest form, this doctrine claims that "governments can do no better than to do nothing" (Mill 1873: 65). As a rule, government intervention in the economic affairs of individuals is disadvantageous. In contrast in a "system of natural liberty" free individuals advance their interests in a superior manner. As each person does better, consequently the commonwealth of the society will be enhanced and improved. Virtually all the variations of mainstream economics adhere to this general rule. Ludwig von Mises (1881–1973) in his major work, *Human Actions: A Treatise on Economics* put economic efficiency side by side with the laissez-faire system. In view of this, in absence of this system, individual economic actions cannot be coordinated effectively. Owing to this, the diverse and ever-changing needs and desires of individuals cannot be met. Costs for consumers and the suppliers of the goods and services will be higher. As things go, the economy degenerates because the natural motive for making a profit is undermined.

The laissez-faire model is most often equated with the market economy. This is an economic system that is characterised as a spontaneous order. In this model it is believed that the unplanned economic actions of economic agents achieve an order that is spontaneous, harmonious and efficient. This is an economic system that maximises the consumers' benefits and producers' profits. An economic organisation that matches the pattern of consumers' wants to producers' production plan allocates the scarce resources to the best advantage of consumers, producers and the economy (Hayek 2014). No government can achieve this. Governments cannot do any better than what is natural. Indirectly, therefore, the laissez-faire system is taken to be synonymous with nature. Any deviation from the natural course of events will then divert a course of action from its natural path. In the case of the economy, laissez-faire is the natural course of events. Governments or any other outside interference drives the economic course of events out of its natural orbit. This results in the misallocation of scarce economic resources.

The term natural is used frequently in different schools of thought in economics. Smith used it in relation to prices. He divided price into the natural price and the market price. The natural price derives from the ideas of natural liberty and perfect competition. It is the price of a commodity that

> is neither more nor less than what is sufficient to pay the rent of the land, the wages of the labour, and the profits of the stock employed in raising, preparing, and bringing in it to market, according to their natural rates.
>
> (Smith 1986: 158)

At the natural price, the output is at its optimum, producers and consumers maximise their profit and benefits and the resources are most efficiently allocated. Under the domain of natural liberty, when prices deviate from natural prices, competition and the mechanism of the invisible hand would pull the prices back to their natural level.

The usage of the term "natural" in economics has appeared in a variety of different contexts. One of these contexts was described by the Swedish economist, Knut Wicksell (1851–1926). He identified a form of rate of interest that maintains price stability in a certain period (Jonung 1994: 161) and called it the natural or neutral rate of interest. At this level of interest rate, the economy is operating at its maximum potential and full employment. Keynes found some merit in Wicksell's theory of natural rate of interest. He defined the natural rate of interest as

> the rate at which saving and the value of investment are exactly balanced so that the price level of output as a whole . . . exactly corresponds to the money-rate of the efficiency earnings of the Factors of Production.
>
> (Keynes 1965: 155, vol. I)

In the *General Theory*, Keynes argued that saving and investment can be equal at a different level of income and interest. But the natural rate of interest rate is a unique rate. It is the equilibrium rate of interest "which is consistent with full employment" (Keynes 1967: 243). The attribute of "natural" has been extended to other areas such as unemployment and inflation in economics. For instance, Milton Friedman (1912–2006) defined the natural rate of unemployment as the rate that is consistent with a constant rate of inflation. From this premise, he extrapolated that any attempt by any government to alter unemployment from its natural rate would be a futile attempt (Backhouse 2002: 297).

The idea of "natural" in its most emblematic form of economics is expressed in the form of the economic equilibrium. This is an ideal situation, a natural condition. In other words, equilibrium is normal. Logically therefore what is abnormal is disequilibrium. Equilibrium is a longstanding target and a lasting desire of humanity. We can find this concept in all organised systems of beliefs. The Greek Physician Hippocrates (460–370 BC) described a healthy body as one that enjoys a sense of balance. In his explanation of the human body-mind relationship, he identified four elements or four "humors." These are black bile, yellow bile, phlegm and blood. He purported that an illness is caused when these humors are not balanced. Good health can be restored when they are brought into balance (Wolper 2013: 6). Likewise, the idea of equilibrium is manifested in Archimedes' (287–212 BC) law of the lever (Krajewski 1977: 17). However, the concept of equilibrium in economics is, by and large, a derivation of Newtonian cosmology. It is drawn from Newton's theory of gravitation and physics.

The publication of Newton's historic book the *Principia Mathematica* marked the end of the old era. This was a remarkable intellectual achievement. Many scholars were overwhelmed with the detailed analytical reasoning of application of Newton's mechanics. Newton displayed his prediction of planetary motion and the precision of his mathematical models. Here there was the prototype of knowledge to look to and follow. Antoine Augustin Cournot (1801–77), a French mathematician, adopted Newtonian mechanics in his description of market forces supply, demand and market equilibrium (Lawson 2015: 233). Leon Walras (1834–1910) another French mathematician walked in the footsteps of his compatriot, Cournot and published his seminal book, *Elements of Pure Economics*, in which he aimed to show how the general equilibrium in the economy can be achieved. Walras wrote to Paul Matthieu Hermann Laurent and explained his understanding of the nature of economics. He commented that

> all these results are marvels of the simple application of the language of mathematics to the quantitative notion of need or utility. . . . You can be sure that the economic laws that result from it are just as rational, just as precise and just as incontrovertible as were the laws of astronomy at the end of the 17th century.
>
> (Buchanan 2013: 30)

William Stanley Jevons, an English statistician and economist, shared the same view. Buchanan remarks that "equilibrium thinking is so deeply ingrained for most economists that they find it difficult to think in other terms" (Buchanan 2013: 7). Even Alfred Marshall (1842–1924) who was an evolutionary economist and who believed that "nature doesn't make the jump" (Rostow

1992: 193) could not break away from the grip of the idea of equilibrium. He only relegated equilibrium to its partial configuration.

To Newton mathematics was a precise and universal language. It was a language that could convey the laws of nature. It was a means of communication that transcended social, cultural, national and ideological and gender boundaries. In scientific inquiry, maths cannot be the end in itself. Maths is an instrument to communicate scientific information. For many eminent economists, maths is an end in itself. It has an intrinsic value along its use as a means of communication. The archetypal example of this orthodoxy is the economic equilibrium. The frame of reference for a perfect world is economic equilibrium. For those economists supporting this approach, the pursuit of mathematical proof of equilibrium is the end in itself. Kenneth Arrow and Gerard Debreu are in this category. In their model of general equilibrium, economic agents interact voluntarily, and markets coordinate all these diverse activities, interests, prices and knowledge in a manner that is orderly and mutually beneficial. Every seller can sell the goods or services they bring to the market at the right price. Every buyer can obtain the goods and services at the right price. The dealings of all these economic agents are not just mutually beneficial but also each agent can maximise his or her profit or utility and resources are allocated most efficiently at the Pareto efficiency level (Buchanan 2013: 32). From mathematical proof of the general equilibrium, one cannot extrapolate its "relevance to the real world" (Landreth and Colander 1994: 278).

Another extreme form of market equilibrium is the one that was proposed by Robert Lucas Jr, an American economist in the 1970s. In his influential article in 1972, Lucas developed his theory of rational expectations. The idea that individuals are rational and maximise their self-interests was not new. Lucas himself confirmed that this is one of the assumptions in standard microeconomics. What he claimed to have done was apply the same principle in macroeconomics. Lucas based his macroeconomic models on the assumption that "individuals were completely rational and that they took advantage of all opportunities open to them. He interpreted this to imply that all markets must be modelled as being in equilibrium, with supply equal to demand" (Backhouse 2002: 299). The hypothesis of rational expectations is not just sterile, but it is also contrary to its claim of being rational. Let us examine the limitation of the informative content of this theory. Consider what is tacitly assumed: (a) all economic agents have the identical capacity to reason, (b) all economic agents have a like capacity to know and understand and (c) all economic agents are equally capable to take right decisions and act according to them given exact information. The theory of rational expectations is irrational because all individuals do not have equal opportunity and freedom to reason and acquire knowledge. Besides, no individual, without exception, has the time, resources, ability and desire to acquire all the information that is available in a society. They cannot then employ such information precisely in real time and life. This possibility is conclusively improbable. Of course, we do not know everything. What we may consider as true can be revised or rejected with future discoveries, innovations and critical examination of the past assertions. Lastly, people plan and act not just in accordance with exact knowledge but from a combination of reliable information, instinct, beliefs (religious or ideological), customs, culture, interest, expectations, fear and pressure, imitation, envy, the climate of opinion, conventions and many, many other factors.

Conclusion

The Italian navigator, Christopher Columbus (1451–1506) discovered the new world in 1492. This was not an accident. The discovery of the new world was a by-product of the Renaissance in Europe. The Renaissance was a period that generally dated from 1300 to 1600 AD. This period in Europe trigged great social and scientific movements. These movements fractured and challenged the foundations of medieval Europe. Paper was invented in China in 100 BC. This product found its way to Italy in the 13th century. The gunpowder that Chinese alchemists accidentally discovered around 850 found its way through the Silk Road to Europe in the 13th century. In the same way, the magnetic compass, another ancient Chinese invention, appeared in Europe in roughly the same period. Johannes Gutenberg, a German craftsman, invented the printing press in the 15th century. The interest in ancient Greek, science, wisdom and humanism revived after Arab academics introduced the ancient classic texts to Europe. The protestant reformation led by Martin Luther and John Calvin and others widened the rift between western Christianity and the papacy.

The combination and interactions of all these factors triggered vital scientific and social revolutions in Europe. These dynamic, new ideas had germinated in the Age of Enlightenment. The European renaissance was the precursor of the Age of Reason. It laid the foundations for greater exploration, inventions, discoveries and investigation. It led to the repudiation of dogmatism, superstition, corruption, authority and unfounded assertions. It fatally wounded the old world and challenged the established ideas, legal, political, social and economic relations.

New social orders began to replace the old ones. The Renaissance had far-reaching scientific, political and economic consequences. A counter-Aristotelian world view was gradually beginning to be formed. Nicolaus Copernicus (1473–1543) repudiated Ptolemaic astronomy. His ground-breaking belief was that the earth orbits the Sun. Johannes Kepler (1571–1630) described the laws of planetary motion. Galileo Galilei (1564–1642) advanced Copernicus' and Kepler's astronomy. He discovered the rings of Saturn and the moons of Jupiter. All these discoveries and advances paved the way for Isaac Newton's cosmological revolution.

The heliocentric theory contradicted traditional religious texts. The church soon realised the ramification of this challenge. It branded Galileo a heretic. Galileo was arrested and excommunicated for expressing views that were directed against the teaching of the Bible. Galileo was forced to confess to committing a cardinal sin. He was furthermore forced to retract his views.

What Isaac Newton accomplished was not limited within the confinement of astronomy and physics. He changed our understanding of the universe. He transformed our understanding of everything else. He presented us with an automated static and infinite universe, a mechanical cosmology, a clockwork universe that works in accordance with principles of natural laws. The universal law of gravity is the supreme law responsible for this automated mechanical cosmology. Furthermore, gravity is a universal force that is predictable. All matters in the universe are subject to this force. That was the model that all subsequent branches of science aspired to and tried to copy. The Newtonian cosmology model became the ideal scientific model for other scientific subjects. The ideal science was one that dispensed with God and instead resorted to free, open, rational investigation and mathematical order.

The fundamental part of Adam Smith's argument rests on the Newtonian concept of an automated universe. The roots of naturalistic modes of thought such as this can be traced back to antiquity. It is a broad school of ideas that has a long history. In ancient Greece we saw the Stoics. In Rome we saw great thinkers such as Cicero, Seneca and Epictetus. The modern age dawned with naturalist thinkers such as Bacon, Hobbes and John Locke. Smith was educated in the idea of natural order. Besides the Newtonian clockwork automated universe, Smith was inspired by the naturalist philosophy of his favourite teacher, Francis Hutcheson, and the French naturalist economics school, the Physiocrats (Roll 1983: 143). The central idea that is common in all naturalist modes of thought is their conviction in natural laws and forces as the only source by which the world operates. In his first book, *The Theory of Moral Sentiment* (1759), Smith discusses the basis of the nature of morality. He attempted to lay the foundations of natural conduct and moral judgement. This was his first attempt to "formulate the character of a 'natural order' of society." The human conduct was analysed in terms of three pairs of motives: self-love and sympathy; the desire to be free and a sense of propriety; the habit of labour and the propensity to exchange. In Smith's view, these natural sentiments acted as checks and balances on one another. They supported a social order of natural harmonies in which each man, when left to pursue his own interests, unconsciously promoted the common good (Barber 1970: 25–6).

In his monumental work, the *Wealth of Nations* (1776), Smith skilfully and persuasively explains these natural principles that govern the economy and human moral conducts. Natural human motives tend to balance and that is out of natural necessity in the same way the universal law of gravity has created an automated balance in the universe. Human motives act in accordance with principles of natural laws. Smith with the rest of enlightenment thinkers went with the flow. In addressing his natural balance, in the *Wealth of Nations*, he concluded that in "the system of natural liberty" individuals adopt moral standards that are compatible with their natural desires, everyone then pursuing his or her own self-interest "led by an invisible hand."

Jean-Baptiste Say (1767–1832), the French economist, is better known for his rhythmic rhetoric, the Say's law, which Keynes attributed to him. But at the heart of Say's law lays the foundation of a naturally balancing and automated economic system. Say in his major work stressed that natural mechanism of markets does not allow any general gluts or general overproduction. He asserted that:

> Should a tradesman say, "I do not want other products for my woollens, I want money," . . . he may be told . . . You say, you only want money; I say, you want other commodities and not money. For what, in point of fact, do you want money? Is it not for the purchase of raw materials or stock for your trade, or of victuals for your support? Wherefore, it is products that you want and not money. . . . Even when money is obtained with a view to hoard or bury it, the ultimate object is always to employ it in a purchase of some kind.
>
> (Say 1880: 133)

Say remarked that

> a product is no sooner created, than it, from that instance, affords a market for other products to the full extent of its value. . . . Thus, the mere circumstance of the creation of one product immediately opens a vent for other products.
>
> (Say 1880: 134–5)

The order of things in the economy therefore is perceived as much to be natural and balancing as in the Newtonian universe. Supply naturally creates its balancing demand. All income received by different factors of production for the service they provide would be spent. More to the point, "the machinery of production is . . . always fully employed. There is no unused capacity" (Pen 1966: 39). The price system equally and automatically regulates the amounts saved to the amounts invested. Then we will have the foregone conclusion "that income is spent automatically at a rate which will keep all resources employed" (Dillard 1966: 19). The self-adjusting economy is not just natural, but it maximises self-interest where at the point of equilibrium the individual pursuit of self-interest will coincide with the society's maximisation of output, efficiency and well-being. In the words of another recent prominent proponent of this line of thinking, Milton Friedman, freedom can be maximised when individuals are free to spend their income as they wish (Galbraith 1991: 271).

Among other great achievements of the Enlightenment was the secularisation and democratisation of knowledge. These changing habits of thinking and behaviour had a revolutionary effect. New ideas influenced all new branches of science. Humans looked at the world with a new perspective. The new outlook triggered a critical and innovative interpretation of knowledge. Objective knowledge came to be distinguished from unreliable sources of knowledge. The old sources of knowledge were challenged. The exponents of the Enlightenment emphasised the necessity of objective knowledge. This new source of knowledge was secular in character. The Enlightenment invigorated secularism. The idea of acquiring knowledge no longer belonged to any specific group. Every individual was now believed to be equipped with a faculty to acquire knowledge. Individuals who were not free to think could not pursue knowledge. Individuals who do not enjoy free economic and social conditions are deprived of utilising this natural capability to seek knowledge. Diderot and D'Alembert described a secular knowledge seeker as someone who "trampling on prejudice, tradition, universal consent, authority, in a word, all that enslaves most minds, dares to think for himself" (quoted from Law 2011: 19).

In addition, human beings are capable of great thought. The faculty of thinking is not exclusive to a certain elite group of people. Every individual is capable of thinking. By virtue of this fact human beings are rational. Rene Descartes with his dictum "Cogito ergo sum," I think therefore I am, attempted to prove his own existence by reason alone, a conclusion that he believed can be attained a priori. He aimed for ideas that are innate, clear-cut and eternal. No knowledge is valid unless it has all these attributes. Designating mathematics to represent this form of knowledge, Spinoza's *Ethics* centered on Euclidean geometry. It is patterned on Euclidean method. Spinoza applied the Euclidean method to demonstrate that ethics can be constructed from rigorous deductive reasoning. We can start with basic foundations, axioms and theorems through pure logic to construct a system of ethical order that is universal. Such ethical order can be proved without relying on sensory experience or authority except for reason. Gottfried Leibniz was adamant that reality is traceable since it has a rational structure. He placed this contested view in an equally contested dictum that "all is for the best in the best of all possible worlds." The only way we can understand and know this reality and structure is through reason and mathematical principles.

In stark contrast, the Empiricists rejected the theory that the origin of all knowledge is innate and a priori. The leading exponents of the empiricist school were Francis Bacon, John Locke, George Berkeley and David Hume. These thinkers repudiated the rationalist view. They defended the position of the empiricists' account of knowledge. The empiricists argued that the origin of all forms of knowledge is sense experience. Human knowledge is based on experience. It is a posteriori and does not rest on a priori reasoning. John Locke argued that human mind at birth is like a "clean slate." Through their senses, people acquire their knowledge and more complex ideas are formed through sensory experience and inductive reasoning. In a nutshell, ultimately there can be no meaningful knowledge without reference to sensory experience. Irrespective of the validity of these perspectives, for our analysis in this chapter, one point is of the utmost importance. It is the democratisation of knowledge. Everyone has the capability and faculty to acquire knowledge irrespective of whether or not one is born with it or can acquire it with sensory experience.

The most basic elements upon which Kant's theory rests are that human beings are fundamentally rational. In view of this, rationality is the ultimate good. There can be no objective reality or objective morality in the absence of rationality. Free will is indispensable for anyone to utilise effectively and correctly one's rationality. In effect, rationality is ineffective without freedom. Freedom of thought and expression are essential. Kant restored the idea of each human being as a complete being that is master of his own knowledge and moral conduct. A human being was defined as an agent that is solely responsible for his or her understanding and actions. This amounted to the view that each person is an end in himself and herself and should not be used as means at any circumstance. Human beings are social beings. Therefore, ethical rules are vital. These rules will bind us to behave and act ethically. He described his moral laws in his theory of the categorical imperative. In its most general sense, the theory of categorical imperative states that each individual should act in a way that his or her action is compatible with a universal law. It is applicable to everyone doing the same thing in the same circumstances.

All in all, this world view needed an alternative discourse in relation to humanity. Religious concepts that stressed the notion of original sin had to be rejected. Such ideas had condemned humanity to eternity. This alternative discourse centred on the idea of natural progress. This was a common theme among writings of almost all exponents of the enlightenment. Progress is natural. Auguste Comte (1798–1857) and Herbert Spencer (1820–1903) put progress and time parallel to each other. For Spencer, the "beneficent necessity" derives the whole of nature and humanity from chaos to increasing order (Carneiro 2000: 569). Comte also saw progress to greater order but much more in a Baconian tradition that knowledge is power. Influenced by Newton triumph in Physics, he thought the science of sociology, the "social physics," can be developed on similar principles and methods to discover, understand and manipulate the natural laws of society and then direct the society into a desirable course.

Galileo professed that "the universe . . . is written in mathematical language." The emergence of modern science was marked with mathematisation of natural philosophy. Galileo captured the sentiment of the time. Newton in his great work, attests the central role of mathematics in his theory. In this monumental work, Newton described his landmark laws of motion and the universal gravitation in mathematical language. This work was not only the most profound scientific inquiry but also the most influential exemplary book to duplicate and adapt. Its influence spread far and wide. It is a matter of great importance to understand that it was the successes of Newton's theories in their description and predictions that infatuated various branches of science in their attempt to mathematise their scientific disciplines. Moreover, mathematics for these pioneering scientists is not an end in itself. That is, science was not equated with the language of mathematics, but it was considered as an effective instrument and a way of communication to reveal the mysteries of nature. The idea was that nature can be expressed more precisely with mathematical language than with natural language.

Mathematisation of academic disciplines in social sciences has taken place to a different extent during various time periods. Economics has been at the forefront in this regard. Mathematisation of economics in a very systematic way began with the marginalist revolution in the 1870s. The marginalist revolution was initiated by three theorists, William Stanley Jevons (1835–82), Carl Menger (1840–1921) and Len Walras (1834–1910). Jevons, an English logician, and economist published his book *The Theory of Political Economy* in 1871. Menger, the founder of the Austrian economics, published his book, *Principles of Economics*, in the same year. A few years later, in 1874, the French mathematician and economist published his book, *Elements of Pure Economics*. In these three books, the authors separately developed the theory of marginal utility. They laid the foundation of the marginal revolution in economics. Unlike, Jevons and Walras, Menger did not use mathematical language in his exposition of the idea of marginal utility.

In contrast, both Jevons and Walras equated science with maths. In their judgement, the only truly scientific economics is mathematical economics. Jevons purported that economics is governed by economic laws of pleasure and pain. These laws can be reduced to a few mathematical principles. He compared economics laws to the laws of Physics and mechanics and argued that economics is similar "to the science of Statical Mechanics." Jevon was adamant that economics "*must be mathematical, simply because it deals with quantities*. Wherever the things treated are capable of being *greater or less*, there the laws and relations must be mathematical in nature" (Jevons 1970: 78, Italics in original).

The mathematisation of economics has grown over time. There is an unconscious or subconscious desire for unity and harmony in the use of mathematics in economics. The certainty of analytical truth somewhat reassures this longing for the unity and harmony of the mind. This reassurance stems from several directions. First, it emanates from equating science to mathematics and hence capitalising on scientific credibility. Second, analytic propositions are true by virtue of their meaning. These truths are predictable and certain. These truths are tautological, rhythmic that echoes and recapitulates their replications. Thirdly, there is much attraction in the aesthetic nature of mathematical proofs and verification of mathematical theorems. Bertrand Russell (1872–1970) remarked that "mathematics, rightly viewed, possesses not only truth but supreme beauty" (Russell 1981: 49). Fourthly, where the language of mathematics is more adaptable, that is, in natural sciences, technology, and engineering, the outcome has been unthinkable. Joann Karl Friedrich Gauss (1777–1855), a German Mathematician and Physicist, described mathematics as "the queen of sciences" (Bos 1997: 173). Mathematics has a technical language that the common person cannot use and communicate. This grants extra social and intellectual status and prestige to those who are trained and well-versed in this special language.

5 Manageable economic disorders

Introduction

This and next chapter will be on Keynesian and Marxian accounts of economic disorders. There are not historically more influential books in economics than Smith's *Wealth of Nations*, Marx's *Capital*, and Keynes' *General Theory*. Each of these books represents one of the economic classic books of the last three centuries. Smith's book was the economics book of the18th century, Marx's book the book of the 19th century and Keynes's book the book of the 20th century. These books are about economic disorders. They are the narratives and solutions to the biggest economic problems of their time.

Keynes's epoch-making work, *The General Theory of Employment, Interest and Money*, was published in 1936. The time of the publication of this book is of great interest. This was about 7 years after the Wall Street Crash. The book was by-product of the Great Depression. Keynes, during the most formative and productive part of his life, experienced three political and economic systems, three of the greatest historical events and three momentous economic experimentations. He witnessed the post-war hyperinflation, many periodical monetary disorders, and the great depression. He observed the 1917 Russian revolution and the economic experiment of the command economy, the fascist state cooperative economy and the American New Deal experiment.

Leaving the socialist and Marxian denunciation of the industrialised societies aside, the seeds of Keynes's dissent from classical and neoclassical economics are in the same works that he criticised. Economic disorder, as we referred to in Chapter 2, is something that has been acknowledged by all schools of thought in economics. Many also point to the periodic and regular breakdown in the level of economic activity during the 18th century. These irregularities in business activities are said to be a natural part of the course of events. They were external factors caused by misfortune, war, mistakes, misadventure, poor management, miscalculation and matters of such nature. In the 19th century, as the British economy developed at a faster pace, business fluctuations were deeper and more frequent. During a period of about 50 years, 1815 to 1866, there were about six major economic recessions in Britain. These were in

DOI: 10.4324/9781003346364-6

1815, 1825, 1836–9, 1847–8 and 1866. These recessions and their effects were much too visible that they could not easily be overlooked. To many profound thinkers and social critics external factors were an unsatisfactory explanation of the causes of economic fluctuations. The real problem, they thought, was deeper than that and the problem was inherent in modern economic structure and organisation (Marshall 1968: 712).

Despite acknowledging occasional disorders and fluctuations in the economy, the prevalent view was content with the power of natural healing. This general trend was shared in the writings of the most influential economists of the 18th and 19th centuries. Jean-Baptiste Say (1767–1832), however, institutionalised the natural law of markets. In his book, *A Treatise on Political Economy*—which was an attempt to popularise Smith's ideas in France—Say expounded what came to be known as Say's law. Say's law in a nutshell is the idea that any imbalance in the economy would adjust itself automatically. In the long run there will be no glut of goods because in the end goods are exchanged for goods. There will always be an equilibrium between aggregate supply and aggregate demand. Total output or supply will at last be equal to the total demand or expenditures. That being said, Say did not deny oversupply of or demand for a product or service in a sector of the economy in the short term. In viewing the economy in this manner, he could not see any likelihood of general overproduction since production creates its own demand.

This theme, with some slight variation in exposition, is reiterated in the works of the proponents of classical and neoclassical economics. It is echoed in James Mill's (1773–1836) major publication. In his account "consumption is co-extensive with production." In other words: "production is the cause, and the sole cause, of demand. It never furnishes supply without furnishing demand, both at the same time and both to an equal extent" (Mill 1824: 227, 231). David Ricardo followed a similar line. He reaffirmed that "no man produces but with a view to consume or sell, and he never sells but with an intention to purchase some other commodity" (Ricardo 1992: 192). John Stuart Mill was equally adamant on the soundness of automatic adjustment of production and consumption. He postulated that

> all sellers are inevitably and *ex vi termini* buyers. Could we suddenly double the productive powers of the country we should double the supply of commodities in every market, but we should by the same stroke double the purchasing power. Everyone would bring a double demand as well as supply: everybody would be able to buy twice as much because everybody would have twice as much to offer in exchange.
>
> (Mill 1848: 93, Italics in original)

Even though, these economists admitted to occasional disorder and hoarding of money for its own sake, they never cast doubt on the possibility of general overproduction and the collapse of the whole system (Marshall 1968: 713).

In the self-adjusting economic system, all factors of production are subject to the law of markets. The foundation of self-regulating markets rests on perfect information and price flexibility. Given that we have perfect information and prices are perfectly flexible, the excesses and shortages of supply and demand will automatically be eliminated. Overproduction of goods and services result in falling prices and the fall in prices would increase the demand until the excesses and shortages of goods and services would be cleared from the market. The labour market is not an exception from this general rule. In the same way, the market forces of supply and demand determine the level of wages and employment. At the going market wage rate anyone who wants a job would get one. In such conditions there can be no one out of work apart from frictional unemployment. As in all sectors of the economy, producers supply promptly and proportionately to consumers' demand. The essence of the classical and neoclassical theory boils down to this spontaneous and self-regulating economy.

Keynes refuted the classical concept of economic equilibrium, emphasising that "the postulates of classical theory are applicable to a special case only and not to the general case, the situation which it assumes being a limiting point of the possible positions of equilibrium" (Keynes 1967: 3). This special case can only be a theoretical ideal—a likely situation when the resources are utilised fully and most efficiently. This likely situation is the state of full employment. The real interwar economic events seriously contested this world view. The major industrialised economies of the world went through some historic social and political upheavals, deeper monetary disorders (both hyperinflation and deflation), speculative mania and depression. The discourse that prophesied the impossibility of such events lost much of its credibility.

After the Wall Street crash and its aftereffects no sincere economist could only rely on classical and neoclassical descriptions of the economy and their policy prescriptions. Keynes communicated his theory of economic disorder after these events. His success in capturing the general attention was due to the climate of the time and the recognition of the necessities of the time. The novelty of Keynes's theory of economic disorder was his readiness to respond to the changing economic conditions and challenges of the great depression. Keynes broke with what was thought to be sacrosanct both in economic theory and at a governmental level. He questioned the idea that whatever happens in the economy is because it must. Keynes found the defence of masses of unemployed, who were able and willing to work for the market wage rate but could not find jobs on the grounds of some immutable order, deeply disturbing. He demonstrated what life would be like without involuntarily unemployment and framed a concise analytic economic theory that not only sparked off a significant and meaningful controversy in economics but also shaped the implementation of the welfare state in many democratic nations.

This chapter is divided into six parts. In these parts we will provide an overview of Keynes's theory of economic disorder. We will present the layout of his theory of economic disorder, his account of causes and the effects of economic volatilities and his policy solutions to prevent or cure the cyclical fluctuations. Part one provides a synopsis of Keynes's break up with the economic orthodoxy. Part two reviews his theory of the relationship between deficient demand and under-unemployment. Part three addresses specific characteristics of advanced money exchange economy according to Keynes. Part four surveys and examines Keynes's necessary conditions for intense and frequent fluctuations in output and unemployment. Part five reflects on one of Keynes's most important contributions on the causes of economic disorder. The contender here is the pitfall of liquidity preference in organised money exchange economies. This is where the main difficulty rests. This is "because the problems of unemployment are . . . peculiar to a monetary economy" (Stonier and Hague 1958: 361). In the last section, part six, having identified and addressed the causes of economic disorders—the question is about how to tackle and rectify the problem. Keynes's solution is, although capitalist system of production and distribution is imperfect, the alternative economic systems are less efficient and politically desirable. His solution is to keep the system but continuously reform it. The task of reforms is handed over to the state. As a final point, it is well worth mentioning that along the way in discussing Keynes's theory of economic disorder we will look at and explore some of Keynesian and post-Keynesian contributions on the point of discussion.

Parting with economic orthodoxy

The First World War (1914–18) was one of the most destructive, savage and devastating interstate global conflicts in human history. Keynes worked for the British government as a Treasury official from 1915 to 1919 and was the economic adviser to David Lloyd George (1863–1945) in the Versailles Peace Conference (1919–20). Keynes learned his lessons of war finance during this deadly conflict. Germany was defeated and at the Versailles Peace Conference the European allies opted for revenge rather than corrective measures. The allied delegates went for punishment and humiliation of the German nation. Germany was compelled to pay reparations of about 33 billion dollars (Hardach 1981: 290). Keynes found the terms of the treaty inimical and counter to the armistice. He anticipated that not only was the treaty unfair but it was a pretext for the outbreak of another war.

The First World War I was not yet ended before another seismic event occurred. This was the fall of the Tsar in Russia and the victory of the Bolsheviks in March of 1917. The Russian revolution was the greatest social and economic experiment and engineering of the 20th century. The revolution dismantled the Tsar dictatorship and substituted it with a Marxist-Leninist dictatorship of the proletariat. The Russian economy was underdeveloped and mainly agricultural. Most of the Russian population were illiterate peasants. The Bolsheviks transformed the economy into a centrally planned economy. The peasants and other social groups were organised in the form of soviet regiments. The new political, economic and legal model was a shot in the dark. Keynes met a Russian ballerina, Lydia Lopokova (1892–1981), in 1918 and the couple were married in 1925. He visited the Soviet Union for two weeks in September 1925. It was not only to visit Lydia's family but also to attend the bicentennial celebrations of the Russian academy. After this visit, Keynes wrote two articles about the Soviet Union experiment. In one of these articles, he described the system as "unscrupulous" and "colourless" that it persecutes its citizens without justice. He wrote "like other new religions, Leninism derives its power not from the multitudes but from a small number of enthusiastic converts whose zeal and intolerance makes each one the equal in strength of a hundred indifferentists" (Keynes 1972: 256). In his next visit to Russia in 1928, Keynes found the system even more disagreeable.

The 1917 Russian revolution divided the world into two ideological camps, those who fell under the shadow of the command economy and those who fell under the sphere of influence of the laissez-faire economy. Russia led the communist bloc, and the United States headed the anti-communist bloc. Each side was trying to counter and overdo the other side. Countries that were caught in the flames of the First World War were devastated under the strain of war, except the United States. After the wartime economic boom, 1916–20, the US economy experienced a short recession. The recession only lasted for about a year from 1921 to 1922. The US economy soon recovered and from 1922 the economy grew rapidly. The years from 1922 to 1929 were years of unprecedented economic growth and prosperity in US history. The industrial production from January 1920 to July 1929 increased by 40.6 per cent and real income by 4.6 per cent on average per year. In the United States, this period was also marked with fast economic transformation, technological and product innovations (Stabile and Kozak 2012: 80). The year 1929 was the best and the worst year of the decade. In that year the United States had 40 per cent of the world gold reserve, controlled 16 per cent of international trade and was in possession of 40 per cent of the world's industrial production. After the October 1929 crash and the 3 years after the crash, production fell by 50 per cent, exports fell by 60 per cent and unemployment increased from 1.5 million to 12 million (Iriye 1999: 116).

The great economic growth and transformation, most specifically the US economy in the 1920s, reinforced the expectation in the permanent prosperity and the self-adjusting market system. Keynes too was a devotee of this teaching. In 1927 he anticipated no crash and asserted that "we will not have any more crashes in our time" (quoted from Skousen 2007: 142). Likewise, the *New York Times* on 5 September 1929 reported Irving Fisher's sanguine prediction. Fisher anticipated "a recession in stock prices, but not anything in the nature of a crash" (quoted from Walton and Rockoff 2018: 395). In the end, the greatest crash took place at a time when mainstream economics was ideologically disarmed. The conventional economics failed to undertake any practical action to deal with the problem. It chose a hands-off policy under the false pretext of not tampering with the nature of markets. Doing nothing was a deliberate and measured policy, which worsened the situation.

The basis for adopting the hands-off doctrine was the assumption that the downturn and the disruption was a normal situation that was caused by the excesses of the preceding years. The prescribed remedy was the market. In the same way that the markets generate the excesses, the markets could remove them. In time, markets would readjust automatically. Wages and prices can go higher than their natural rates at the time of shortage and then will be pulled back to their natural rates when the level of full employment is achieved, where savings and investment are balanced. So long as the laissez-faire economy is well maintained, free trade is secured, the government budget is kept in balance and the gold standard is upheld, wages and prices are left to be determined in the competitive markets, business cycles would be a self-correcting course of action. It was according to instruction of this sacred writ that the Treasury Secretary of the United States, Andrew Mellon (1855–1937), recommended his policy to deal with the excesses of markets—to "liquidate labour, liquidate stocks, liquidate the farmers, liquidate real estate . . . it will purge the rottenness out of the system. High costs of living and high living will come down. People will work harder, live a more normal life" (quoted from Kindleberger 1986: 119). The policy recommendation of the leading economists of the period were also confined in their scope to the principles of sound finance and strict adherence to laissez-faire economics. Lionel Robbin (1898–1984) in *The Great Depression* and Friedrich Hayek (1899–1992) in *Prices and Production* sought recovery in free trade, orthodox fiscal policy, gold standard and flexibility of all prices and wages (Blaug 1994: 384).

Another infamous event that vindicated Keynes's gradual break from orthodoxy was the rise of fascism in the 1920s and its spectacular seizure of political power in the beginning of the 1930s. The German Nazi party was conceived in 1919 when Adolf Hitler joined the German Workers' Party (Lee 2010: 1–2). The title of the party is misleading. Contrary to its title, this was a far-right party. Anton Drexler (1884–1942) led the party. In 1920, the Party changed its name to the National Socialist German Workers Party and Hitler became the Party public speaker. In 1921, Hitler was elected the leader of the party. The Nazi's philosophy was based on racism and antisemitism, equating the Aryan race as the master race and many other races such as blacks and Semitic races as sub-human. The prevailing social and economic conditions in the 1920s and early 1930s created a fertile ground for fostering Nazi philosophy in Germany and some other European nations. The interwar period is a period in which the public that were affected by the impact of the First World War were desperate, helpless and very angry. The political establishments in most of the countries affected were dysfunctional and hopeless. By the autumn of 1922, Germany defaulted in payment of her war debts. In November 1923 the exchange rate for one US dollar was 4,210,500,000,000 German Marks. The unemployment rate for the period of 1921 to 1929 was 9.2 per cent (Temin 1991: 3). The Nazi demagogues centred their propaganda on fear, ignorance, anger and the despair of the German people.

The share of the national vote in the 1924 elections for the Nazi party was only 3 per cent. In the 1928 elections it decreased to 2.6 per cent. The popularity of the Nazi party quickly increased after the Wall Street crash of 1929. The main reason for this swift rise in popularity of Nazi philosophy was that the German economy and political system was very fragile then. It was too exposed, and the Great Depression hit it hard. In addition, Nazis promised employment, higher income, security, cancellation of the provisions of the Treaty Versailles, protection from communism, restoration of Germany's social, cultural, and political power and a quick transition from the Great Depression. In the July 1932 elections, the Nazi party won 230 seats in Germany's parliament. It became the largest party in Germany that held 37.3 per cent of electorate votes (Nicholls 2000: 75–76). Hitler gradually consolidated his power and position in his party and subsequently in Germany. He was appointed the chancellor of Germany on 30 January 1933.

Keynes was not a devoted conformist economist. Both in his personal life and his intellectual curiosity, he led an unconventional life. He was an unorthodox thinker. He received his first-class BA in mathematics in 1905 from King's College, Cambridge, and his MA a few years later. Keynes was an optimist and a talented debater. He had great faith in the right people finding the right time to resolve the economic and social problems. It was this conviction that diverted him from his study of mathematics and directed him instead to economics. Keynes began his serious studies in economics from 1905 under Alfred Marshall (1842–1924) and Arthur Cecil Pigou (1877–1959). His interests were wide ranging from art, literature, drama, politics and philosophy to economics. Keynes was a member of the British Liberal party and a member of the Bloomsbury group. The latter was a group of radical and liberal intellectuals, artists, writers and philosophers. Like many liberals, he became a devotee of Moore's ethics. George E. Moore (1873–1959) published his influential work, *Principia Ethica*, in which he discussed the knowledge of moral truths. His emphasis was that ethical naturalism was not attainable. Ethical doctrines do not have intrinsic natural roots. In this sense moral claims are indefinable. Properties of ethical claims are non-natural. The truth of moral values cannot be inferred by non-moral properties. Moral truths are intuitive and are based on self-evident moral properties. Moore's moral philosophy rests on common sense realism where moral rules are determined by the effects of actions.

For someone who had public prominence, leading an unconventional life was a big risk to take. The practice of homosexuality was deemed immoral and if the accused were caught engaging in acts of homosexuality he would be arrested and charged with gross indecency. Keynes made a fortune from speculating and nearly lost most of it during the 1929 Stock market crash. He was an inventor, inventing macroeconomics and he was the first great economist who applied economic principles to real macroeconomic problems. He was an academic and practitioner who had no fear of breaking with conformity either from social status or in terms of political power or ideas. Bertrand

Russell commented on the sharpness of Keynes's intellect. He pointed out that whenever he met him, "I felt I took my life in my hands, and I seldom emerged without feeling of a fool" (Russell 1998: 69).

Keynes could be generous and accommodating in his reviews if he found the argument thoughtful and intelligent, irrespective of the author's ideological persuasion. In reviewing Sidney and Beatrice Webb's book, *Soviet Communism*, Keynes praised it and said that "every serious citizen will do well to look into" this book (quoted from Raico 2012: 170). In his review of Hayek's book, *The Road to Serfdom* on the other side of the spectrum, he described it as "a grand book" and said that he was "morally and philosophically" in agreement with the whole book (Fitzgibbons 1988: 178). With these characteristics Keynes simply could not be indifferent about the events and all the economic and political upheavals that encircled him. As much as he was fascinated with all social experiments, he was just as concerned with their failures, successes and their unintended consequences.

The three greatest social engineering experiments took place when he was in his prime. The Soviet experience after the 1917 Russian revolution, the Fascist experiment in Germany and her allies and the New Deal experiment in the 1930s in the United States of America. In reference to these experiments Keynes wrote that "each year it becomes more obvious that the world is embarking on a variety of politico-economic experiments." Keynes did not jump for a definite conclusion before the end of the events. He said "we do not know what will be the outcome. We are—all of us, I expect—about to make many mistakes. No one can tell which of the new systems will prove itself best" (quoted from Raico 2012: 163–4).

Keynes met Lydia Lopokova in 1918. After getting married to her in 1925, he visited Russia once in September of the same year and for the second time in 1928. He described his first impression of the Soviet experiment in an article entitled "what is the communist faith?" He wrote, "like other new religions, Leninism derives its power not from the multitudes but from a small number of enthusiastic converts whose zeal and intolerance makes each one the equal in strength of a hundred indifferentists" (Keynes 1972: 256, CWK, vol. 9). Fascist ideologues too not just were acquainted with Keynes's ideas, but he found some affinity between his and their economic policy recommendations.

Otto Wagner, head of the Nazi research bureau, was certainly familiar with Keynes's works. He read Keynes's book on 'Money" and gave it to Hitler to read and indicated to Hitler that Keynes was on their side but without being fully aware of it. The German edition of the *General Theory*, however, did not only fall on deaf ears but was taken with great hostility. Most of the Nazi reviews of the *General Theory* were very critical, even though Keynes in his preface to the German edition of the *General Theory* pointed out that his economic theory was best adapted in totalitarian systems. It is also believed that Keynes was influenced by the idea and policy implementation of the New Deal in the United States of America. What attracted Keynes in these social experiments was their success in reducing the level of unemployment. The Russians in their First Five Year Plan (1928–32) launched a massive investment expenditure spree in building, industry, infrastructure and public services, as a result of which the unemployment rate was reduced by the early 1930s so low that there was an acute shortage of labour in some sectors of the economy (Lane 2002: 222). Unemployment in Germany was 5.6 million in 1932. It was reduced to 2.7 million in 1934, to 1.6 million in 1936 and to 0.4 million in 1938 (Overy 1982: 29). In the United States the unemployment rate in 1932 was about 22 per cent. As result of the New Deal, it was reduced to 9 per cent by 1937. Within this period about 9.5 to 10 million workers were taken out of the army of the unemployed into the job market (Hiltzik 2011: 431).

Stalinist communism and Hitler fascism were political and ideological experiments of perfect brutality, repression and disaster. In the eyes of Keynes, the two politico-economic experiments failed not in their economic experiment but in their political experiment also. In 1934, he rejected these two historical calamities and argued that "Marxists are ready to sacrifice the political liberties of individuals in order to change the existing economic order. So are Fascists and Nazis. . . . My own aim is economic reform by the methods of political liberalism" (Keynes 1982: 28–9, CWK vol. 28). For Keynes, an economic order that respects individual liberty cannot also be perfect. Besides its other failings, unemployment is its biggest problem. In the *New Statesman and Nation* Keynes wrote the "curse of unemployment" is the cause of all problems including submerging into penitentiary totalitarian experiments. He was convinced that the authoritarian states had solved the problem of unemployment. They achieved this objective "at the expense of efficiency and of freedom." The unemployment, said Keynes, is a systemic problem. It is "inevitably associated with present-day capitalistic individualism." Something that with "a right analysis of the problem" can be cured "whilst preserving efficiency and freedom" in the society (Keynes 1967: 381).

With this realisation Keynes broke away from the classical and neoclassical models of the economy. He repudiated the essence of their economic philosophy, that is, keeping distance from the institution of the market as being natural and self-correcting postulating that the market economy does not go through occasional disorders but corrects itself automatically. The experience of the Great Depression was so strong that it could not be dismissed lightly. The prescription of the conventional theory and what was happening were poles apart. The market was not functioning. The supply and demand were ineffective. These were not the presupposed natural forces that interacted in a naturally functioning market. The given level of the wage rate failed to bring the supply of and demand for labour into equilibrium. Neither was it the case that at the equilibrium wage rate, all the workers who wanted a job could get employed. The conjecture that workers cannot get employed if the general wage rate is high lost its credibility as an applicable theory during the Great Depression. On the contrary, as wages decreased, greater numbers of workers were laid off. What Keynes did was to articulate the reality of the Great Depression and to show the danger of taking the essence of classical and neoclassical economic philosophy for granted and condemning the masses of unemployed for being out of work because they have not adjusted the wage level to the self-regulating market rate. Keynes went against this antidote and remarked that "the characteristics assumed by the classical theory happen not to be those of the economic society in which we actually live, with the result that its teaching is misleading and disastrous if we attempt to apply it to the facts of experience" (Keynes 1967: 3).

Deficient demand and under-employment

Marx coined the term "classical economist." There is unanimity in the use of this designate but for different reasons. For Marx it stands for bourgeois mode of production and for Keynes it represents non-interventionist economics. Keynes's break from the classical and the neoclassical economics was not complete. His biggest point of contention with those schools was on the issue of unemployment. In his judgement, chronic unemployment is not natural, and the blind forces of the market cannot cure it. There are real causes and remedies for chronic unemployment. It was after this realisation that Keynes launched his methodical exposition of causes and remedies of mass unemployment in advanced monetary economies. To this end, he relied on classical and neoclassical literature and narratives. For Keynes as for the neoclassical economics "the wage is equal to the marginal product of labour." In addition, "the utility of the wage when a given volume of labour is employed is equal to the marginal disutility of that amount of employment" (Keynes 1967: 5). That much is commonly assumed. The disagreement between Keynes and his adversaries begins after passing this point of agreement. To neoclassicals and their predecessors if the labour market is left alone, it corrects itself naturally. Keynes did not oppose this presupposition entirely. He argued that more people would be employed if the "whole would agree to the reduction of money wages" (Keynes 1967: 8). This claim of classical economics, Keynes maintained, cannot be disputed. Because "in a given state of organisation, equipment and technique, the real wage earned by a unit of labour has a unique (inverse) correlation with the volume of employment" (Keynes 1967: 17). But Keynes contended that this description is not applicable to the involuntary unemployed. For these workers "the marginal disutility of labour is necessarily less than the utility of the marginal product. Indeed, it may be much less. For a man who has been a long time unemployed some measure of labour, instead of involving disutility, may have a positive utility" (Keynes 1967: 128–9).

So where did classical economists not get it right? First of all, they failed to distinguish between individual and collective economic actions. Serving self-interest does not necessarily entail serving one's society. The invisible hand does not always guarantee the optimum social and economic outcome. Keynes criticised the deduction that is inferred from the invisible hand. He states that "the world is not so governed from above that private and social interests always coincide" (Keynes 1972: 287, CWK, vol. 9). Keynes objected to the soundness of the supposition on the grounds that "there is no design but our own . . . the invisible hand is merely our own bleeding feet moving through pain and loss to an uncertain . . . destination" (Keynes 1981: 474, CWK, vol. 20). An individual pursuit of self-interest does not automatically follow the promotion of common good. If one enriches oneself, this does not lead to enriching the whole society. Keynes remarked that "those who think in this way are deceived, nevertheless by an optical illusion, which makes two essentially different activities appear to be the same" (Keynes 1967: 211). The delusion stems from the conjecture that "there cannot be a buyer without a seller or a seller without a buyer. Though an individual whose transactions are small in relation to the market can safely neglect the fact that demand is not a one-sided transaction, it makes nonsense to neglect it when we come to aggregate demand" (Keynes 1967: 85). It was in this renunciation of the classical theory that Say's law stepped out of obscurity and received its prominence in mainstream economics. The teaching that "supply creates its own demand" according to Keynes dominated economic thought since Ricardo and Say (Keynes 1967: 18), a supposition that is based on a misunderstanding of developed monetary economies. Keynes regrets the victory of Ricardo and Say's argument over Malthus's analysis of effective demand. Keynes upheld that had the economists, policy makers and market practitioners opted for Malthus's argument, the present economy would have been in much more agreeable form. But instead "the great puzzle of effective demand with which Malthus had wrestled vanished from economic literature" (Keynes 1967: 32), and this occasioned serious misapprehension of the economic problems and their remedies.

Keynes held that in a complex exchange economy, markets do not automatically correct everything in the economy. For instance, it does not bring the individual savings into equilibrium to aggregate investment. In contrast, in the classical explanation of markets, the rate of interest and the demand for capital are given. Changes in rates of interest automatically equalise the level of savings to investment (Dome 1994: 217). Keynes repudiated the rationale behind this reasoning on the grounds that income is not constant (Keynes 1967: 179).

The chief source of the problem for Keynes rests in the individualistic capitalist system. Taking no notice of this fact can result in distortion of Keynes's central message. Keynes introduced his theory of effective demand (ED) to show where the main causes of breakdowns in the individualistic money exchange economies are concealed. He describes effective demand as "the aggregate income (or proceeds) which the entrepreneurs expect to receive, inclusive of the incomes which they will hand on to other factors of production, from the amount of current employment which they decide to give" (Keynes 1967: 55). Suppose Q stands for total output at a given price and time and N for the number of workforces employed. The relationship between the output and employment can be expressed as $Q = f(N)$. It simply means output depends on the number of people employed. If Y stands for the income received by the employed, then we can get the aggregate demand function as in $AD = f(N)$. In the light of what has been said, then employers increase the number of workers employed if there is more demand for the output (Q). Provided that the conditions of production—expectations, the state of technology are right—aggregate supply and the level of aggregate demand will balance each other. The point at which aggregate supply (AS) is equal to aggregate demand is the effective demand. In Keynes's words "the effective demand is the point on the aggregate demand function which becomes effective because, taken in conjunction with the conditions of supply, it corresponds to the level of employment which maximises the entrepreneurs' expectation of profit" (Keynes 1967: 55). From this perspective the economy is in a state of acute economic disorder when there are abnormal imbalances between aggregate demand and aggregate supply. That is, when aggregate demand is deficient and continues to be deficient. This is the scenario we find in a situation when able-bodied workers with appropriate skill, knowledge and attitude who are willing to get a job at the market wage rate cannot get a job. Keynes considered this situation as being unnatural and furthermore he sought the cause of it as being entrenched in the developed capitalistic systems of production and distribution. He argued that "the outstanding faults of the economic society in which we live . . . [is] . . . its failure to provide for full employment and its arbitrary and inequitable distribution of wealth and incomes" (Keynes 1967: 372).

The Great Depression diminished the credibility of the classical and neoclassical economic models considerably. No longer, full employment, rational economic agents, perfect information, marginal cost being equal to price, consumer sovereignty, perfect competition, optimum production and distribution of income could be taken as known and indisputable truths. The system failed and Keynes offered his alternative theory of aggregate demand (AD). Keynes defined AD in the closed economy as "the sum which will be spent on consumption when employment is at the given level, and the sum which will be devoted to investment" (Keynes 1967: 90). Given the level of income and employment, AD will comprise aggregate consumption (C) and aggregate investment (I) or simply AD = C + I. From this basic mathematical model, Keynes deduced several far-reaching conclusions about the modern market economies. On the top stands the obvious truth that consumption expenditure is the biggest component of aggregate demand. Consumption spending is fundamental in economic activities as most of the income is allocated to consumption. Changing consumption expenditures can have far-reaching effects on the effective demand, production, and employment. Because consumption "is the sole object of all economic activity" (Keynes 1967: 104).

Among Keynes's factors that will influence a community consumption expenditure are income, objective and subjective factors. On the objective side we have changes in income, wage units, windfall changes in capital and changes in consumer expectations, interest rate and government macro policies and objectives. In the case of subjective factors there are elements such as pride, foresight, precaution, interdependence and enterprise that will influence the level of consumption expenditures. These factors are, collectively, a defence mechanism to ensure one against unexpected future events. Among the motives that encourage one to spend more are generosity, extravagance and short-sightedness, giving greater priority to current enjoyment and miscalculation. The subjective factors consist of "those psychological characteristics of human nature and those social practices and institutions which, though not unalterable, are unlikely to undergo a material change over a short period of time, except in abnormal or revolutionary circumstances" (Keynes 1967: 91). In view of these considerations, Keynes constructed the core element of his theory of crisis. This element is contingent upon the psychological law of consumption. The law that states "as a rule and on the average 'men' increase their consumption as their income increases, but not by as much as the increase in their income" (Keynes 1967: 96).

In Keynes's closed economy, total disposable income (Yd) is equal to total consumption (C) and total investment (I), or Yd = C + I. The crucial question in understanding Keynes's theory of economic disorder is in his psychological law of consumption. On average, this law states, the marginal propensity to consume (MPC) of a community as their income increases will always be between zero and one. It will be $1 > dC/dY > 0$. Keynes referred to the proportion of the additional disposable income that is not consumed as marginal propensity to save (MPS). On average, as disposable income increases, the MPS will increase but less than 1. It follows then that MPC + MPS = 1 and both MPC and MPS are affected by the changes in disposable income. They vacillate between 0 and 1 as disposable income changes. The extent and the frequency to which the MPC and MPS fluctuate are critical in the nature, depth and the position of economic disorder in Keynes's theory.

Aggregate saving in Keynes's model is "the excess of income over expenditure on consumption" (Keynes 1967: 61). Aggregate saving (S) is equal to aggregate disposable income (Yd) minus aggregate consumption (C), or S = Yd – C. The relationship is linear and the greater the disposable income, the greater will be the proportion of the disposable income that will be saved. Thus, "rising income will often be accompanied by increased saving and a falling income by decreasing saving" (Keynes 1967: 97). In another context, richer communities save relatively more of their disposable income than the poorer communities. Keynes says there is a paradox in this economic arrangement that contains the seed of economic disorders.

A plain truth is that with development of economies, incomes of people will grow. The implication of this simple truth is much more profound than it first appears. One implication is the growth of savings. Keynes remarked that there are three important issues about this relationship that classical economists have misread and misinterpreted. The first one is about equating individual interest with the common interest. In a classical system, if an individual saves, his or her action does not just serve the interest of the individual but the interest of the community as a whole. But individuals save for different reasons and those who save are, by and large, are not the same as those who invest. For this reason, then, it does not follow that what individuals save will necessarily be invested. If and only if market forces bring aggregate savings automatically through changes in rates of interest into equality to aggregate investment, then there will be no gap in the effective demand and no unemployed. The income generated remains continuously in the circular flow of income. People use most of whatever income they get for consumption and the rest will routinely be channelled into investment. Aggregate demand repetitively will be equal to aggregate supply. On these terms there can be no deficient aggregate demand and hence no voluntarily unemployment.

In a classical economy, the relationship between aggregate savings and aggregate investment is direct and equal. Keynes disputed this assertion, arguing that the process and the act of saving is much more complex than is assumed in classical teaching. In developed economies there are individuals who dis-save, there are individuals whose savings is zero and there are those whose savings are positive. The social groups that are responsible for economic disorders are among the first and the last group. They are those who use the credit market and those whose incomes and therefore savings will go on to rise. Keynes assumed that saving is

> like spending, a two-sided affair. For although the amount of his own saving is unlikely to have any significant influence on his own income, the reaction of the amount of his consumption on the incomes of others makes it impossible for all individuals simultaneously to save any given sums. Every such attempt to save more by reducing consumption will so affect incomes that the attempt necessarily defeat itself.
>
> (Keynes 1967: 86)

Savings do not automatically trickle down to investment. The economic conditions could be such that it can be more advantageous to keep the additional increase in income in liquid form, instead of spending it or investing it. Hoarding could be more expedient in this case. In the best possible conditions, there can be lags between the amount saved and the amount invested. Nonetheless, in Keynes's view, in a closed economy the ultimate source of investment is savings. A closed economy stagnates and degenerates in case it fails to save.

Monetary economies are complex, and exchanges take place by using a multifaceted range of medium of exchange. Keynes borrowed Marx's basic money exchange economy model where commodities are exchanged with a generally accepted medium of exchange (money) and money is used to buy other commodities. In this form of exchange, by selling labour services and receiving income in money, one does not necessarily immediately after receiving income buy other goods or invest it straight away in income-producing real or financial assets. In a well-established and complex credit system, the transfer of money from savers to investors also depends on the rate of interest, the level of development of financial markets, institutions and instruments. It also depends on the expectations of the rate of return and the expectations of entrepreneurs about the state of the economy. This brings us to the question of investment. Investment in Keynes's economic model is the second most important component of

AD. A regular and increasing level of investment is vital in complex monetary economies because as aggregate real income increases, aggregate consumption will increase but less than the increase in income. Keynes suggested that under such circumstances in order "to justify any given amount of employment there must be an amount of current investment sufficient to absorb the excess of total output over what the community chooses to consume" (Keynes 1967: 27).

In a money exchange economy, there is an additional element that complicates the process of buying and selling and the process of savings to investment. This complication arises from the unique position of money as an asset. The demand for money is not alike to demand for other assets. Keynes identified three main motives for demand for money. These are the transaction demand for money. Individuals and businesses hold a proportion of their incomes in cash for their daily transactions. The transaction demand (Td) depends on disposable income, Td = *f* (Yd). The second motive for holding money is the demand for precautionary purposes (Pd). The precautionary demand for money is the amount of disposable income that is kept in cash for unexpected requirements of unforeseen situations. The precautionary demand for money (Pd) also depends on disposable income, Pd = *f* (Yd). The originality of Keynes's theory of demand for money in relation to economic disorder is associated with his third motive of demand for money, which he designated as speculative demand for money. This motive stems from expected returns and changes in the price of both financial and real assets. If economic agents expect the price of these assets is going to fall, they sell their assets and switch to cash and if they expect that their prices will go up, they forego liquidity and buy assets. So, the speculative demand for money (Sd) depends on interest rate (r) and expectation (E), Sd = *f* (r, E) (Keynes 1967: 199). The speculators speculate because they believe they know better than the market the direction of the change in the prices of the assets or the change in the rates of interest.

On this account, transfer of the community's savings to investment in Keynes's theory of investment is neither smooth nor definite. Savings may or may not be channelled into investment. Even if they are channelled into investment, the money may not be assigned into the most efficient types of investment. What is certain is that savings of a community will never fully be invested for all sorts of institutional, social, psychological and structural reasons. Investment, in Keynes's theory, is an additional unit to "fixed capital, working capital or liquid capital" (Keynes 1967: 28). The incentive to invest depends on "the relation between the schedule of the marginal efficiency of capital and the complex of rates of interest on loans of various maturities and risk" (Keynes 1967: 28). Unlike consumption, investment is a very volatile component of aggregate demand. Investment is not like consumption, a basic biological and survival need. To stay alive we need to eat, drink and we need shelter and other means of protection from the elements. Investment does not fit into this category of needs. Investment is inextricably linked with production. Both processes involve time. The decision to produce and supply any good or service can be taken in one time (A) and the profit return is expected sometime in the future, in time (B). No one knows for sure what the time interval holds. To defeat the force of time, an entrepreneur "has to form the best expectations he can as to what the consumers will be prepared to pay when he is ready to supply them (directly or indirectly) after the elapse of what may be a lengthy period; and he has no choice but to be guided by these expectations" (Keynes 1967: 5).

Advanced money exchange economies

A generally accepted medium of exchange is the foundation of complex developed economies and trade systems. Introduction of a medium of exchange, that is the most liquid and marketable asset, alters the nature and requirements of the economy. Keynes was a monetary economist. He recognised the role and position of money and its implications in money exchange economies. One of the preconditions for the introduction of a generally accepted medium of exchange is an intricate system of production, exchange and distribution. A rudimentary credit system can exist without any generally accepted medium of exchange. The rise and application of a medium of exchange does not only facilitate the expansion of the credit system and markets, but it is a prime catalyst in initiating financial crisis. Economic relations get much more impenetrable and mystifying when we exit the system that is based on borrowing and lending of goods and services without the payment of interest and enter the system where borrowing and lending is based on the payment of interest.

For too long, receiving interest on a loan was regarded widely as a deadly sin. Aristotle described it as the worst and most disliked type of money making (Aristotle 1970: 46). The zealous believers and absolute rulers in the past condemned and subjected those accused of getting interest on loans to gruesome torture and very slow and painful death. Parallels to that were those with power and wealth who lent money at usury rates to the impoverished and dispossessed individuals. Many of these ill-fated individuals who experienced unexpected serious financial hardship turned to the unscrupulous money lenders but were unable to fulfil the terms of the agreements and as a result were reduced to slavery (Homer 1963: 27). By the time classical economics became a decisive social force, receiving and paying interest on loans was generally an acceptable undertaking. The body of modern industrial and commercial systems could not function effectively without the payment of interest. The rate of interest became a dynamic device in the system in regulating the level of savings and investment in the economy. To Keynes interest payments was more than just a robotic levelling device. It was an indispensable condition in money exchange economies. In his opinion, the actual rate "is largely governed by the prevailing views as to what its value is expected to be. Any level of interest which is accepted with sufficient conviction as likely to be durable will be durable; subject, of course, in a changing society to fluctuations for all kinds of reasons round the expected normal" (Keynes 1967: 203–4).

The new economic conditions dictated the modification of interest from a curse into a virtue. It was no wonder that the consensus changed relatively quickly in favour of interest. The emerging industrial and commercial economy gradually cleared the way for private investment. Never before, in the field of human economic activity, were so many individuals permitted to accumulate so much capital and invest in market led initiatives than when interest payment became a norm in the big picture of the economy. In short, the emerging industrial and commercial nations of Europe were systems of private investors. The more individuals could take part in this activity, the more investment fortified its preponderant importance in the economy and the more payment of interest on loans for investment was justified. As much as investment is the engine of economic growth, equally it is the chief cause of economic fluctuations and disorder. The road from savings to the rates of interest to investment and the expected rate of return on investment in the future is a long, uneven, and uncertain road. All these connections and juxtapositions cannot be known before the event with absolute certainty. It is this lack of synchronisation among these joints, bends and processes that produce surprising waves of ups and downs in investment.

Keynes understood the crucial position of investment in the individualistic industrialised economies. He succeeded in disentangling many intricacies of the process of investment and the discoordination between numerous stages of the path between savings and investment. The thrust of his doctrine of investment is stored up in his theory of marginal efficiency of capital (MEC). Keynes defines MEC as the "rate of discount which would make the present value of the series of annuities given by the returns expected from the capital asset during its life just equal to its supply price" (Keynes 1967: 199). In ordinary language, it translates as the situation where entrepreneurs would carry on investing to the point where the MEC is equal to the rate of interest, MEC = r. Implicit in the concept of MEC is the common-sense view that borrowing at the higher rate of interest than the rate of return, in form of profit, is unwise and does not keep anyone in business for long.

There was not much disagreement between Keynes, Marx and the classical economists about long-term investment. The similarity is quite striking. The common ancestor of all theories of investment in the long run was the classical theory of the stationary state. At its core, the result is the same. The points of dispute are on the specific causes and consequences of the ultimate end. Ricardo, in his examination of process of accumulation and economic growth in a closed economy, clearly demonstrated that the rate of profit would eventually fall to zero. Marx got the most out of the central feature of classical theory of economic growth and investment. Keynes also believed that increasing investment in a business, in the long run, leads to the diminishing return of profit. His equivalence to the classical "stationary state" is the "quasi stationary community" that is characterised by constant stability in population, society and employment (Daly 2007: 118).

Investment in complex industrialised money exchange economies can never be certain. We cannot get rid of the lapse of time between the time of deciding to invest and the time the yield from the investment is expected. The available information for undertaking production for the future profit also can never be based on complete facts or else the whole concept of expectation in relation to investment would be meaningless. For Keynes, because of this uncertainty, we need to find a link between the present and the future. That link is "the existence of durable equipment . . . the expectation of the future . . . affect the present through demand price for durable equipment" (Keynes 1967: 146).

In previous chapters we have shown that all schools of thought in economics recognise the possibility of disorder in the money system of production and exchange. The classical school saw the cause of disorder, by and large, as an external factor that derives a sector or number of sectors of the economy out of their natural course, which is the state of equilibrium. For instance, wage rates can deviate from their natural rate and that could derail the market from its natural route temporarily, but the system readjusts itself and returns to its natural setting before too long. Keynes could not agree with this view. He asserted that the system is naturally susceptible not to just temporary disorder but also to long and deep-seated disorders. Moreover, unlike the classical views that linked the causes of disorder primarily to external factors, Keynes considered them to be mainly internal. In his account, any component of aggregate demand, and the variables upon which that component depends, is liable to break and eventually cause the collapse of the determining parts of the system. The initial catalyst of the failure could be because of change in one component of aggregate demand, let us say an increase in consumers' consumption. The increase will create more demand and a positive outlook for making more profit in the future. The optimistic prospect generated draws in more investment as a result of which more people will be employed. If this trend goes on unstopped, it finally ends in chronic economic disorder. The downturn starts with "some bottle-necks" (Keynes 1967: 322–3).

What instigates economic disorder in its initial stage is gradual scarcity of some factors of production. Bottlenecks are the early symptoms of the disorder. These shortages increase the price of bottle-neck factors of production. The increase in prices at this phase of the cycle reinforce the market optimism. The increase in prices is used as confirmation of greater economic activities and the efficacy of economic policies in place. Economic boom remains beneficial up to the point where the rate of expansion of output is greater than the rate of increase in the costs of production. When the increase in the rate of inflation exceeds the rate of expansion of output, we have economic disorder in the true sense of the word. About this stage of the business cycle, Keynes remarks that "when a further increase in the quantity of effective demand produces no further increase in output and entirely spends itself on an increase in the cost unit fully proportionate to the increase in effective demand, we have reached a condition which might be appropriately designated as one of true inflation" (Keynes 1967: 303).

Business cycles are caused by "change in the marginal efficiency of capital, though complicated and often aggravated by associated changes in other significant short-period variables of the economic system" (Keynes 1967: 313). Full employment is the state when all components of aggregate demand are used at their full capacity. This is where aggregate demand and aggregate supply are balanced. Any increase in any component of aggregate demand at this stage only adds to the cost of production, hence to the inflation. Uncertainty will never leave the sight of the economy, but it is accelerated when the economy approaches its full employment equilibrium. As the shadow of pessimism spreads, consumers begin to consume less and producers stop investing, one after another. Aggregate demand contracts and workers lose their jobs at a progressively higher rate. If proper economic measures are not undertaken at the correct time, economic contraction turns into an economic slump and depression.

Two sides of the business cycle are asymmetrical. Misperception about economic boom and depression must be seen in this light. The period from recovery to economic boom is a relatively slow and long phase whereas the turning point from the tip of an economic boom to its descent is sharp and unpredictable. The turning point from the peak of economic activity to economic contraction is brief and precipitating. Suddenly, the rapid economic growth ends and the economy plunges into a sharp decline in output, consumption and investment. The future becomes bleak. Organised markets panic and oversell. The values of equities decline fast, and unemployment rises sharply.

At the stage of the cycle of speculative boom the role of credit markets is critical both in intensifying economic expansion and in precipitating economic contraction. Credit expansion is a barometer of the trade cycle. In ordinary times, it is compatible with the facts. During the phase of economic boom, it progressively detaches itself from reality and takes a form of a frenzy speculation. The companies and individuals that borrow money either to invest, buy equities, bonds or other financial or real assets in good times, at the turning point of the cycle default on the payment of their credit bills. When the economy is out of control, many firms and individuals would not be able to repay the principal and interest on the loans that are due. For the reason that the value of their assets has decreased, their profits have plummeted and their credit rating has sharply deteriorated so they cannot get credit. As markets subside, banks and financial institutions that provided credit face a liquidity shortage. As a result of the shortage of funds and rising business risks, interest on loans will go up and make it harder for struggling firms and individuals to borrow money to withstand the storms. The more developed and organised is the market the sharper this decline can be. This was what happened to the US economy, according to Keynes, during the 1929 Wall Street crash. Keynes states that in such markets

> the dismay and uncertainty as to the future which accompanies a collapse in the marginal efficiency of capital naturally precipitates a sharp increase in liquidity—preference—and hence a rise in the rate of interest. Thus, the fact that a collapse in the marginal efficiency of capital tends to be associated with a rise in the rate of interest may seriously aggravate the decline in investment.
>
> (Keynes 1967: 316)

Keynes's theory of economic disorder begins with the increase in uncertainty about the expected rate of return on certain assets. The uncertainty causes the cost of production of durable goods to rise when economic activities are buoyant, and it is getting out of hand. At this stage all available factors of production and economic resources are fully employed, and the policy makers cannot make up their minds about a right course of action. They do not want the boom to subside but also, they are not happy about the direction in which the economy is heading. The advice they get from the learning community is mixed and the economic indicatives are very perplexing. The policy makers are caught in a state of inaction and panic. On the one hand, aggregate demand is equal to aggregate supply. On the other hand, any increase in AD at this stage triggers the formation of true inflation. It is at this point that the economy subsides with an unexpected sharp downturn. The turning point marks a sharp decline in MEC and turmoil in major stock markets. Markets will crash. Equities and other assets will be devalued, which severely affects the incomes of many asset holders. The asset holders will part with liquidity, sell their assets and desire to hold their wealth in the form of money. Current savings will increase, and current consumption will plummet. Concurrent to the drop in consumption, producers hesitate to invest because of falling MEC and higher rates of interest.

Manifested in an open economy is the great opportunity for specialisation in international trade and the augmentation of AD through export. But inherent in international trade is a fundamental contradiction that we cannot do away with. An open economy compared to a closed economy is more exposed to deeper economic disorders. Trade between two countries can be affected by factors such as the degree of technological development: institutional advances, efficient management, sophistication of credit system, the state of the infrastructure and political stability. These factors determine the competitive advantage of one country in relation to another. A country with these characteristics, either partially or fully, will have a higher level of productivity and because of this, it can produce goods and services at comparatively lower cost and consequently it can export more goods and services to the other country. Therefore, comparative advantage in productivity promotes trade and exports. It boosts economic activity and output, as a result of which the level of employment in the country with higher levels of productivity will increase and that promotes the rate of economic growth and improves the standard of living. The reverse will be the case with countries that lack competitive productivity advantage.

In addition to differences in costs of production between two trading countries, the exchange rate and the prevailing exchange rate system, and interest rates between the countries are important determinants of trade of goods, services and capital between trading countries. Keynes propounded that for his policy of management of aggregate demand to be implemented effectively the exchange rate system should be fixed. So, provided that there is a constant wage, predictable banking conventions and fixed liquidity preference, then the inflow and outflow of precious metals will be regulated by a surplus or a deficit in balance of payments. The level of output and employment will be higher when the balance of trade is in surplus. If the surplus trade persists, that will increase the demand for the currency of the exporting country. The value of the currency, if other factors remain the same, will appreciate and this will lead to the demand for export goods and services to recede.

The economic currents, as the economy approaches its boiling point, are all over. One thing that is clear is the direction of domestic prices. They go upward because of the increase in both domestic and external demand for exported goods and services. The increased demand for export goods and services increases the demand for the domestic currency. The combined rise in domestic and international demand puts pressure on prices and appreciates the value of the domestic currency. In the end we get to a situation where prices, interest rates and the exchange rates are much higher than their normal levels, which cause the demand for export goods and services to drop drastically. The decrease in exports of goods and services eventually reduces the level of effective demand and hence aggravates the level of employment in the economy. Balance of payments occupy an important position in Keynes's theory of economic disorder. He indicated that deficit in the balance of trade "provided it is not too large, will prove extremely stimulating; whilst unfavourable balance may soon produce a state of persistent depression" (Keynes 1967: 338).

Fluctuations in output and employment

Keynes identified three key determinants of the level of output, employment and distribution of income. These are marginal propensity to consume (MPC), marginal efficiency of capital (MEC) and marginal propensity of export (MPX). He related the main causes of fluctuations in modern economies to these determinants. Unlike classical and neoclassical total reliance on the private sector to cure itself, Keynes saw the cure to the economic ills not in the private sector but held the private sector as the prime suspect for chronic economic disorders. For Keynes, in a complex free enterprise economy, it is the profit-seeking private sector that derives the economy in cycles of boom and recession. Amid the crisis, it is the private sector that will be crippled, disheartened and wrecked. It is in the private sector that the wealth holders try to sell and run away. Depending on the private sector, it will not only improve the situation, but it makes worse.

The remedy is with the national government, the most organised institution that has the means of communication, the tools of restoration and the power to put into effect its commands. One of the reasons that the private sector is ineffective during economic downturn is the presence of different social groups. The high-income, the middle-income and the low-income social groups have different MPC and MPS. The MPC of low-income social groups is the highest, followed by the middle-income groups and last by the high-income social groups. In reverse, the MPS of high-income groups is the highest then followed by the middle income and it is the lowest for the low-income groups.

Considering that savings is a withdrawal from the circular flow of income and consumption is an injection, Keynes formed one of his most distinguished macro policy prescriptions out of this relationship. The private sector is neither willing nor has the mechanism to transfer some of their savings to low-income groups whereas the national government is and has this power. It can tax the social groups with high income and then distribute the tax revenue to low-income social groups to boost the AD. With this policy, the government can cure two of the most outstanding problems in advanced free enterprise economies. In the first place, this policy will increase the aggregate consumption as a portion of the savings of the social groups with some of the higher income being transferred to the low-income groups. Most of the transferred income will be used in consumption as the low-income groups have higher MPC. In this way the transfer of income will increase the AD and the level of employment.

In comparing developed and underdeveloped economies, Keynes elaborated that unemployment is more of an issue in developed economies than in underdeveloped economies, the main reason being that in underdeveloped economies the MPC is so high that there is a very narrow gap between national income and national expenditures. Meanwhile, in the developed economies the problem lies not just in relatively lower MPC but also in the falling MEC and in MPX. In the developed economies, the MPS is higher. Besides, developed economies are dominated by organised markets and the psychology of organised markets is quite different from individual buyers and sellers. In organised markets there is a separation between the ownership of the enterprise and the management team and investment decisions are determined by average expectations of dealers.

The component of the aggregate demand that can be affected the most by these factors is investment. Keynes identified two categories of investment: the short- and long-term investment. The short-term investment can be more profitable but may not be socially desirable. In reverse, long-term investment can be less profitable but socially advantageous. Keynes maintained that "there is no clear evidence from experience that the investment policy which is socially advantageous coincides with that which is most profitable" (Keynes 1967: 157). The interval of time between making the decision to invest and receiving all the returns from the investment is the reason for speculation. These markets are built on the back of speculation. Speculation both can stimulate and destroy economies. In a very famous extract, Keynes described the role of speculators as economic agents who may not:

> harm as bubble on a steady stream of enterprise. But the position is serious when enterprise becomes the bubble on a whirlpool of speculation when the capital development of a country becomes a by-product of the activities of a casino, the job is likely to be ill done.
>
> (Keynes 1967: 159)

There is risk in every economic activity, in production, exchange and distribution. Depending on the nature, size and the scope of risks, economic fluctuations can be brief and insignificant or very big and long. Episodic fluctuations are tied to speculation. Large and frequent variations in the economic temperature follows big and frequent swings in speculation. The economic temperature is always going up and down because an economy is always in a state of disorder. In this case taking risk and speculating is quite usual. The economy is always operating in a state of mild anxiety. The economic pulse rate never stays the same. It fluctuates for unknown numbers of reasons. For Keynes, taking risks for the sake of risk is the cause of wild swings in the level of effective demand. The risk is neither taken to earn an income for consumption nor to be invested but for more speculation.

In the main, the wide swings in modern exchange economies are caused by large variations in the level of investment. The main problem regarding abnormal fluctuations in the economy, according to Keynes, lies with investment. Most specifically, it is "the weakness of the inducement to invest" (Keynes 1967: 348). Keynes emphasised that the deviation of economic fluctuations from its normal range does not just stem from the nature of the economic system but also from human nature. One of the biggest contributors of economic fluctuations from high to low output or vice versa is because a large proportion of our economic decisions and actions are based on "spontaneous optimism" or "animal spirits." For Keynes, economic agents are neither completely rational nor are they capable to know the outcome of their actions fully and are not consistent in what they do or believe. Therefore, "there is the instability due to the characteristics of human nature that a large portion of our positive activities depend on spontaneous optimism rather than mathematical expectations, whether moral or hedonistic or economic" (Keynes 1967: 161–2).

The Wall Street crash in 1929 was so destructive that to come out of it there had to be some new inventions in terms of economic ideas. One of these inventions was the idea of a multiplier. Richard F. Kahn (1905–89) formulated the argument in his article in the *Economic Journal* in 1931. It was a requirement of the time. Economists and policy makers had to make up their minds about public expenditure—on what grounds it is beneficial and if not, for what reasons. Kahn's argument was timely. It concentrated on the "employment multiplier" (Kahn 1931). He showed how the initial investment in the public sector increased the income and employment both directly and indirectly. There are some similarities between the idea of a multiplier and the idea of an accelerator. John Bates Clark (1884–1963) first used the term "accelerator." The basic idea of the principle of an accelerator is that any increase in demand for a good will lead to an increase in the demand for the factors of production that will produce that good (Clark 1917). The Clark principle of an accelerator did not receive due recognition because the level of unemployment was not as serious as when the idea of a multiplier came on the scene.

Khan's multiplier principle explains a simple truth. An increase in investment expenditure is not restricted in its initial amount. A small change in investment expenditure will multiply and because of that, incomes and expenditures get bigger and bigger as a result of the sequence of reinvestment, of reduction in unemployment and positive future outlook. However, this was only one side of the story. The multiplier effect also changed the long-held view of the direction of causation between savings and investment. For the classical economists it was the increase in savings that led to more investment. The multiplier effect inverted that order. It is not more savings that create more investment but more investment that generates more savings. These discoveries were essential to Keynes's theory of effective demand and business cycles.

The multiplier effect is a dynamic process. Its discovery was vital to Keynes's theory of the management of effective demand. There are two sides to multiplier effects, the side that stimulates economic activities, that is, speeds up economic expansion and the side that accelerates economic contraction. In both cases the effect is not stationary. It is not aiming for equilibrium. Depending on economic conditions, the direction of the multiplier effect can be ascending or descending. Its pace can be either fast or slow. As the economy enters the phase of economic boom and depression the multiplier effect progressively gains speed and accelerates with the pace of economic growth and depression. As the phase of the economy settles into a depression the pace of the multiplier will slow down but it never stops. Thus, contrary to conventional wisdom, the multiplier effect is not an economic stabiliser. In its slow mode, it is a source of economic disorder and in its very high fast mode it is a cause of chronic economic disorder. The former condition is permanent while the latter situation is only a transitional stage.

The multiplier effect is the necessary constituent of Keynes's theory of effective demand in three important respects. The first one is that it is an internal part of the structure of the economy. It is born with any economic activity in the AD. Secondly, it is a remedy to the economic ills. Thirdly, it is used to validate the theory of the management of effective demand (Keynes 1967: 115). Keynes was captivated with the idea of the multiplier effect to an extent that he found any unproductive activity to be beneficiary to the economy. He suggested that the multiplier is effective even with "wasteful" expenditures. Calvin B. Hoover recalls that:

> While I was preparing to share dinner with Keynes in his hotel suite in Washington in 1934, he genially ridiculed my niceness in selecting a towel from the rack so as not to mess the others. He made a sweep with his arm and knocked two or three to the floor. "I am convinced," he said, jokingly, "that I am more useful to the economy of the U.S.A. by stimulating employment through messing up these towels than you are by your carefulness in avoiding waste."
>
> (Hoover 1948: 397)

Keynes did not think that this would be the most sensible policy for the government to do but even a trivial act such as the one just cited is better for the economy than doing nothing. Blaming classical economics for being incapable of even doing that, in another persuasive passage in *The General Theory*, Keynes argued that wealth can be created by building pyramids, wars and earthquakes. He proceeded on the same line that "if the Treasury were to fill bottles with banknotes, bury them at suitable depths in disused coal-mines which are filled up to surface with town rubbish, and leave it to private enterprise on well-tried principles of laissez-faire to dig the notes up again . . . there need be no more unemployment" (Keynes 1967: 129).

Despite his fixation with the efficacy of the multiplier effect, Keynes was mindful of many countervailing forces in the economy. Among these counterbalancing influences are the market forces of supply and demand, pursuit of self-interest and promotion of public good, animal spirit of spontaneous optimism and pessimism and the instinctive drives of self-preservation and self-protection. There are other elements like traditions, customs, laws, ethics and prevailing institutions that also play a partial role in ensuring relative economic stability. Even though these factors are necessary, they are not sufficient corrective mechanisms to prevent modern economies from descending into deep depression and chronic unemployment. Keynes was less concerned with the long run, proclaiming that in the long run anything is possible. A person's lifespan is too short, and Keynes famously reminded us that "in the long run we are dead." Leaving everything to correct themselves may never happen in one's lifetime and the cost of doing nothing can be inestimable.

Liquidity preference in organised markets

The problem is embedded within the money exchange economy. The same problem does not exist in the so-called barter exchange economy. Keynes took this categorisation of the economy for granted. This was Marx's view too. Keynes also borrowed Marx's symbols and simple models for these two types of economy, although not with full accuracy. In Marx's account barter exchange is represented by C—C, where C stands for commodity. His monetary economy is represented by C—M—C, where M stands for money. Whereas Keynes remarked that

> Karl Marx . . . pointed out that the nature of production in the actual world is not, as economists seem often to suppose, a case of C—M—C, i.e., of exchanging commodity for money in order to obtain another commodity. That may be the standpoint of the private consumer. But it is not the attitude of business, which is a case of M—C—M, i.e., of parting with money commodity in order to obtain more money.
>
> (Keynes 1988: 81)

Despite the symbolic misrepresentation of Marx's models, in one respect Keynes is right. As we shall find out in the next chapter, according to Marx, the aim of the capitalist process of production is not for consumption but for creating more surplus value. The common mistakes that all adherents of barter exchange system share is the assertion that there has been a definite economic system that operated on the principle of barter exchange. This assertion is inaccurate on two accounts. First and foremost, a definite system of barter production and exchange has never existed. It is only a phantom of the mind. Furthermore, a generally accepted medium of exchange is only one form of money. Money can have many forms and these forms can be used in exchange concurrently (Karimzadi 2013).

Marx termed the industrialised economies as a capitalist mode of production. Keynes, more or less, agreed with this characterisation. He too found the system to be "in many ways extremely objectionable" (Keynes 1972: 294). Keynes went on to say that "modern capitalism is absolutely irreligious, without internal union, without much public spirit, often . . . a mere congeries of possessors and pursuers" (Keynes 1972: 267). In the main, it is built on "egotistic atomism." The system lacks not just sufficient effective operative mechanisms, but it is also lacking adequate morality. Keynes implicated the system for not being "intelligent," "just," "virtuous" and for not delivering "the goods" (Keynes 1982: 239).

For Keynes one important characteristic of the capitalist mode of production is its organised markets. This characteristic is vital in understanding Keynes's theory of economic disorder. Organised markets, by and of themselves, are not the cause of chronic disorders but "it is of the nature of organised investment markets . . . that, when disillusion falls upon an over-optimistic and over-bought market, it should fall with sudden and even catastrophic force" (Keynes 1967: 315–16). Markets are not self-adjusting and decisions to invest in these markets are made on a precarious basis that are subject to sudden revision. Economic agents invest in expectations to make profit. No investment is done with the full knowledge of the future. So, there is not any risk-free investment. Investment decisions are made on partial knowledge, on partial expectations and estimations. Since the future is uncertain and our investment decisions are based on estimations, then investment by its nature is subject to fluctuations. Keynes insisted that investment as "the most volatile component of the aggregate demand . . . is most prone to sudden and wide fluctuation" (Keynes 1937). The more distant it is, the less predictable the return on investment will be. Speculative motives arise out of our ignorance. The objective of speculative motive is to secure "profit from knowing better than the market what the future will bring" (Keynes 1967: 170).

Keynes in summary of his theory says, "given the psychology of the public, the level of output and employment as a whole depends on the amount of investment" (Keynes 1937: 121). Those factors that determine the rate of investment are the ones "which are more unreliable, since it is they which are influenced by our views of the future about which we know so little"

(Keynes 1937: 121). The mature industrial economies have one self-destructive element that if not restored will lead to deficient demand and protracted unemployment. It is this self-destructive tendency that "the richer the community, the wider will tend to be the gap between actual and its potential production; and therefore, the more obvious and outrageous the defects of the economic system" (Keynes 1967: 31).

Keynes's law of consumption states that "when aggregate real income is increased," the aggregate consumption will also increase "but not by so much as income" (Keynes 1967: 27). That part of income that is not consumed will be saved. Here lies the problem. It is worth noting that the history of the problem of under-consumption was a problem that was debated long before Keynes. One line of this argument goes back to Marx and a Marxian economist that we will turn to in the next chapter. Lauderdale (1759–1839) in 1804 pointed out that consumption was the most important stimulant of the economy including investment. J. C. L. Simode De Sismondi (1773–1842) saw the central economic problem in divided society as being between the rich and the poor. The problem of under-consumption is inevitable in a system of production where revenue determines expenditure and consumption determines production. In an economic system of such nature, workers and the poor would not be able to purchase the over-produced goods. Johann Karl Rodbertus (1805–75) in 1850 looked at the problem of under-consumption from a different angle. He saw the cause of under-consumption in the two effects because of invention and the application of new technology. Technology increases productivity but it also replaces workers. As a result of the combination of both effects workers' income falls short of the output produced.

Another influential figure in the history of under-consumption theory was Atkinson Hobson (1858–1940). He pointed to the increasing ratio between saving and consumption in contemporary economies. As economies get richer the ratio of savings to consumption will increase. The other side of over-savings, he said, is under-consumption. His remedy was to redistribute some of the oversaved incomes through a progressive taxation system from the rich to the poor. This policy will not only reduce the inequality gap but also it prevents the problem of mass unemployment. Keynes was attracted to the under-consumption theory. He found himself in total agreement with two of their suppositions. Firstly, "unequal distribution of income contributes to an inadequate demand for consumption goods and services" (Dillard 1966: 278). Secondly, under-consumption is one of the most important causes of deficient effective demand. Keynes argued that the advocates of the under-consumption theory are right as long as "the volume of investment is unplanned and uncontrolled" and it is "determined by the private judgement of individuals ignorant or speculative." But Keynes did not share their view when they laid "a little too much emphasis on increased consumption at a time where there is still too much social advantage to be obtained from increased investment" (Keynes 1967: 324–5)

For the classical economists saving was a virtue. Smith advised the public and the policy makers that "what is prudence in the conduct of every private family can scarcely be folly in that of a great Kingdom" (Smith 1909: 34). For Keynes an act of saving does not just affect those who save but everyone collectively. Everyone eventually gets poorer as a result of it. Keynes warned that "the conclusion that [one's saving] also increases aggregate wealth fails to allow for the possibility that an act of individual saving may react on someone else's savings and hence on someone else's wealth" (Keynes 1967: 83–4). For the reason that individuals who save, by and large, are not the same as those individuals who invest. What is more, those who save and those who invest have different motives (Keynes 1967: 210).

Uncertainty, says Keynes, is the main cause of economic fluctuation. He left no room for doubt that "many of the greatest economic evils of our time are the fruits of risk, uncertainty, and ignorance . . . these . . . factors are . . . the cause of un-employment" (Keynes 1972: 291). Since we do not know much about the future and the essence of the economic activities rest on what we expect to happen in the future, the reality and our expectation will never be completely synchronised. Keynes held that "our knowledge of the factors that will govern the yield of an investment some years hence is usually very slight and often negligible" (Keynes 1967: 149).

Economic agents, in Keynes's assessment, make decisions about the future within the boundary of incomplete ignorance and partial certainty. He tried to clarify what he meant by the term uncertainty in his article *The General Theory of Employment* (1937). The uncertain knowledge does not

> mean merely to distinguish what is known for certain from what is only probable. The game of roulette is not subject, in this sense, to uncertainty . . . The sense in which I am using the term is that in which the prospect of a European war is uncertain, or the price of copper and the rate of interest twenty years hence, or the obsolescence of a new invention . . . About these matters there is no scientific basis on which to form any calculable probability whatever. We simply do not know.
>
> (Keynes 1937: 114)

Bearing this in mind, the decisions on long-term expectations owe much to our natural obstinacy of going for action rather than inaction. On this as on other matters of long-term decision making, unless there are sound reasons to the contrary, we rely on our confidence in our most probable predictions. The assurance in our confidence "lies in assuming that the existing state of affairs will continue indefinitely" (Keynes 1967: 152).

In order to cope with uncertainty, Keynes suggests, we put our faith in many factors including prevailing conventions and our power of learning, but time, money and ideas are the most important factors in dealing with uncertainty. The further away are our expectations, the less we trust our current wisdom. Money is a curse as well as an antidote. It is an indispensable instrument of economic communication on the one hand and on the other it is a source of worship and idolisation. In respect of the multi-faceted nature of money, Keynes commented that "the love of money as a passion—as distinguished from the love of money as a means to the enjoyments and realities of life—will be recognised for what it is, a somewhat disgusting morbidity, one of those semi-criminal, semi-pathological propensities which one hands over with a shudder to the specialists in mental disease" (quoted from Mitchell 2012: 113). The love of money in Keynes's estimate is the main "moral problem" that modern economies are immersed with. Money is indispensable because it "plays a part of its own and affects motives and decisions and is, in short, one of the operative factors in the situation, so that the course of events cannot be predicted, either in the long period or in the short, without a knowledge of money between the first state and the last" (Keynes 1972: 408, cw, vol. 9).

In addition to the love of money for its own sake, Keynes recognises two other crucial dimensions of money that are critical in determining economic disorders. First, Keynes argued that "money is not neutral" and "booms and depressions are phenomena to an economy in which" money is not just a veil. It affects real economic variables. Money is the connection between the present and the future. Keynes went on to say that money "is, above all, a subtle device for linking the present to the future; and we cannot even begin to discuss the effect of changing expectations on current activities except in monetary terms . . . So long as there exists any durable asset, it is capable of possessing monetary attributes and, therefore, of giving rise to the characteristic problems of a monetary economy" (Keynes 1967: 294).

To the question of why people on specific occasions prefer money instead of other income earning assets, Keynes responded that money has an extra element of security that other assets do not have. Money is the most liquid asset in an economy. Because of this quality, money is "a barometer of the degree of our distrust of our own calculations and conventions concerning the future. . . . The possession of actual money lulls our disquietude; and the premium which we require to make us part with money is the measure of the degree of our disquietude" (Keynes 1973: 115–16, cw, vol. 14). In the course of economic expansion, due to this characteristic of money, unemployment begins to rise rapidly "because people want the moon;—men cannot be employed when the object of desire (i.e., money) is something which cannot be produced and the demand for which cannot be readily choked off" (Keynes 1967: 235).

For Keynes causes of chronic economic disorders stem from three principal sources. The first one stems from human psychology. Most specifically it stems from the lack of knowledge of the future. But by necessity we are compelled to act. For our psychological satisfaction and for justification of such actions, Keynes maintains, we depend on animal spirits. The second principal source of economic disorder is the nature of the contemporary monetary system of production. In this system selling is not necessarily followed by buying. Money is not just a medium of exchange and a unit of account. It is not a neutral instrument of economic communication. Money does not just influence all aspects of the economy but also it is demanded because money is the most liquid asset in the economy. Another characteristic of the monetary system of production is that the richer it gets the greater will become the gap between consumption and production. As people's income increases their consumption will increase but less than the increase in income. As a society gets richer its savings relative to its consumption will increase. In classical tradition, saving is a virtue since savings are automatically invested. So, the gap between consumption and production is bridged regularly and the problem of unemployment is resolved continuously. Keynes considered this theory to be false on two accounts. First, savings are not automatically transformed to investment. Second, there is a paradox in the act of saving. As individuals collectively save more, they will consume less. The drop in consumption will reduce the aggregate demand and hence their incomes. Lower incomes mean lower savings.

The third general source of economic disorder is believing and applying erroneous theories and policies. Keynes held classical economists responsible for recurring economic recessions and unemployment. He argued that their hands off policy combined with their inability to acknowledge the possibility of a general glut in advanced monetary economies caused most of the ills in modern economies. Instead, he praised Malthus for his insights about the deficiency of effective demand as the cause of longstanding unemployment. Keynes remarked that "if only Malthus, instead of Ricardo, had been the parent stem from which nineteenth-century economics proceeded, what a much wiser and richer place the world would be today! We have laboriously to rediscover and force through the obscuring envelopes of our misguided education what should never have ceased to be obvious" (quoted from Hollander 1997: 9). Despite Keynes's blanket denunciation of classical theory, there is an element of truth in his much broader claim. It stands to reason that wrong theories will not only result in wrong diagnoses, but they also compound the existing problems.

The following two quotes clearly explain Keynes's mistrust of these ideas. Keynes compared classical theories to the

> Euclidian geometers in a non-Euclidian world who, discovering that straight lines apparently parallel often meet, rebuke the lines for not keeping straight-as the only remedy for the unfortunate collisions which are occurring. Yet, in truth, there is no remedy except to throw over the axiom of parallels and to work out a non-Euclidian geometry.
>
> (Keynes 1967: 16)

In another often-quoted passage, Keynes describes the difficulty of parting with erroneous ideas by saying that

> the ideas of economists and political philosophers, both when they are right and when they are wrong, are more powerful than is commonly understood. Indeed, the world is ruled by little else. Practical men, who

> believe themselves to be quite exempt from any intellectual influences, are usually the slaves of some defunct economist. Madmen in authority, who hear voices in the air, are distilling their frenzy from academic scriber of a few years back.
>
> (Keynes 1967: 383)

Superior but imperfect

The concept of capitalism was one of Marx's inventions. Keynes, just like most economists, took the term on faith. What is paradoxical is that Marx's capitalism does not correspond to the rest of those who use the term to represent Marx's invention. Keynes is also in this group. The kind of capitalism that Keynes has in mind is a type of economic system that can be preserved forever. According to Keynes the system is imperfect. It suffers from disorders that can spread not only to one or two sectors of the economy as had been purported by classical and neo-classical economics but to many sectors of the economy. Keynes's capitalism is better than all other available alternatives. Keynes was of the view that the critics' objections against capitalism are misplaced because they object to it "on the ground of its inefficiency in attaining its own objects." Keynes had faith in the system but not in the way it was arranged and administered. The potential is there and if managed wisely it can be "made more efficient for attaining economic ends than any alternative yet in sight" (Keynes 1972: 294, cw, vol. 9). Another objection raised against the system according to Keynes is that the system has lost its dynamism that characterised its rapid growth in the 19th century. Keynes rejected this objection on account of being "a wildly mistaken interpretation of what is happening." He argued, on the contrary, "we are suffering, not from the rheumatics of old age, but from the growing pains of over-rapid changes, from the painfulness of readjustment between one economic period and another" (Keynes 1972: 321, cw, vol. 9).

Many of the defects of the economic system that we referred to in this chapter are issues that cannot be overlooked according to Keynes. Despite of all its weaknesses, Keynes was persuaded that the capitalist economic system can be reformed and can be put on the right track, professing that the alternative solutions are far worse than a sensibly managed capitalist system. The three economic alternatives that Keynes had at hand were the classical free market economy, the Marxian command economy, and the fascist economy. The classical free markets proved to be pretty ineffective during the Great Depression. It proved to behave like "Euclidian geometers in non-Euclidian world." Their solution instead of curing the disease, aggravated it. This is because "the cure lies outside the operations of individuals." Besides, the capitalist system enthusiasts are "unduly conservative, and reject reforms in its technique, which might really strengthen and preserve it, for fear that they may prove to be first steps away from Capitalism itself" (Keynes 1972: 292–4, cw, vol. 9).

About the other alternative Keynes was even less impressed. He compared the Marxian alternative to that of a new religion. In one passage he commented that

> how can I adopt a creed which, preferring the mud to the fish, exalts the boorish proletariat above the bourgeois and the intelligentsia who, with whatever faults, are the quality in life and surely carry the seeds of all human advancement. . . . It is hard for an educated, decent, intelligent son of Western Europe to find his ideals here.
>
> (Keynes 1972: 258–9, cw, vol. 9)

He doubted the efficacy of the class struggle as the right conveying means for reaching any ideal goals. If left with no choice but to select from two competing possibilities, Keynes pointed out that, "I can be influenced by what seems to be justice and good sense; but the *class* war will find me on the side of the educated *bourgeoisie*" (Keynes 1972: 297, cw, vol. 9, Italics in the original).

Keynes considered himself a saviour of capitalism. The type of capitalism he had in mind were the British and the American models. For Keynes these systems were relatively more efficient economic systems but at the same time were prone to deep and long-lasting depression. Therefore, at its very foundation, Keynes's solution was to rescue the capitalist system of production from its ultimate downfall. He saw no other institution than the state that could achieve this aim. The state has the power, the resources, the organisation and the mechanism to carry out and enforce this as one of its principal economic policy mandates. Keynes defended the role of government "both as the only practicable means of avoiding the destruction of existing economic forms in their entirety and as the condition of the successful functioning of individual initiative" (Keynes 1967: 380).

To prevent the economy experiencing violent fluctuations and depressions, government can manage the aggregate consumption through the taxation system and through handling the rate of interest. Banking systems, money and capital markets in a free enterprise economy cannot set interest rates that are consistent with sufficient effective demand and full employment. Under these conditions we would not get the rate of interest that is "sufficient by itself to determine an optimum rate of interest." To overcome this problem Keynes proposed a policy of "a comprehensive socialisation of investment . . . [as] . . . the only means of securing an approximation to full employment" (Keynes 1967: 378).

For the socialisation of investment to be put effectively into practice, Keynes suggested the creation of some "semi-autonomous bodies." These bodies are, in effect, state institutions that are subject to parliamentary control. In his articles in *The Times* (January and March 1937), Keynes described the implementation of his policy of semi-autonomous bodies in two stages. In the first stage "to appoint a board of public investment" and in the second "to make sure that detailed plans are prepared" and implemented (Keynes 1971: 394, cw, vol. 21). The second stage of the implementation of the policy has two parts. These are the effective use of the rate of interest and the instrument of the subsidy. The success of the socialisation of investment and the semi-autonomous bodies will depend on the degree of synchronisation of appropriate rates of interest that is compatible with the various projects that are undertaken. There are projects that need to be subsidised in the private sector provided they are socially beneficial. Keynes was convinced that his theory and policy recommendations were practical, feasible and achievable within the confinement of the existing economic system and exchange. In defence of this proposal, he wrote "the rate of interest must be reduced to the figure that the new projects can afford. In special cases subsidies may justified. . . . If we know what rate of interest is required to make profitable a flow of new projects at the proper pace, we have the power to make this rate prevail in the market" (Keynes 1971: 395, cw, vol. 21).

Reaction to the publication of *The General Theory* was immediate. The reviewers from the older generation of economists, who adhered to the classical and neoclassical doctrines of prices and wage deflation and balanced budget, rejected the validity of Keynes's theory (Spiegel 2002: 607).. In their reviews, D. Robertson (1936), A. Hansen (1936), J. Viner (1936), R. Hawtrey (1937) and B. Ohlin (1937) laid a string of criticisms about the inconsistencies in Keynes's theory. A. C. Pigou (1936) and F. Knight (1937), in their reviews not only rejected Keynes's economic narrative and prognoses but expressed much hostility towards his account of economic malaise, his prescription and remedies, reproving his overemphasised weaknesses of the system.

One of the earliest attempts to reconcile Keynes's monetary theory of disorder to neoclassical economics was J. R. Hicks (1937). He abridged Keynes's theory into a simple model that came to be known as the IS-LM model. In this model IS stands for the equilibrium point in the goods market and LM represents the equilibrium in the money stock and the demand for money. Keynes wrote to Hicks on 31 March 1937 about the IS-LM model and said he "found it very interesting and really have next to nothing to say by way of criticism" (Hicks 1973: 9). Many followers of Keynes have levied their criticisms about this interpretation of *The General Theory*, on two fronts, both of which are anti equilibrium objections. A. Leijonhufvud (1968) and R. Clower (1965) censured this interpretation of Keynes for obscuring Keynes's actual message, contending that Keynes's theory was a departure from the "hydraulic" Walrasian self-adjusting economy (Backhouse 1995: 213–14; Snowdon and Vane 2005: 72). Their objection rests on the premise that in their anti-equilibrium theory, economic agents do not trade at the equilibrium prices. People make choices before the equilibrium price is reached. Unemployment and low output are caused by lack of coordination in different parts and stages of production, exchange and distribution. Trades always take place at lower prices than the equilibrium price. Subsequently, in no instance goods, services and money are cleared at the equilibrium price. For the foregoing reason we will have underemployment because full employment is a special case, and it can only be achieved when all outputs are sold at their equilibrium prices.

The focus of the other disequilibrium interpretation of Keynes lays emphasis on uncertainty and expectation as the cause of fluctuation in output and employment. Among this group of economists, we find Keynes's closet friends and collaborators. Eminent economists such as Joan Robinson (1903–83) and her contemporaries such as Nicholas Kaldor (1908–86) and George L. S. Shackle (1903–92) are among this group. The core argument of this group is the idea that the actual economic conditions are such that economic decision making is far from the equilibrium prices. They refer to Chapter 12 of *The General Theory* and Keynes's article in 1937 as the true reflection of Keynes's theory (Fontana 2009: 7). Keynes, in his 1937 article, concluded his theory by saying that the rate of investment is determined by factors that are "most unreliable, since it is they which are influenced by our views of the future about which we know so little" (Keynes 1971: 121, cw, vol. 14, part 2).

This tradition has evolved into Post-Keynesian economics. On the core essentials all the Keynesian economists agree that the advance free enterprise economies, which stand on the principle of the pursuit and maximisation of individual self-interest will experience violent fluctuations in output and employment. The emphasis in the Post-Keynesian perspective, however, is on the unstable nature of advanced capitalist economies that are aggravated, given Keynes's uncertainty and expectation, by the endogenous supply of money and financial instability. P. Howells referred to two propositions as the core components of the endogeneity theory of the supply of money. "The first is that the money supply is determined by the demand for bank lending. . . . The second . . . the demand for loans is driven by the 'state of trade'" (Howells 2001: 134).

Post-Keynesians see a direct link between the nature of financial structure and the economic breakdown. H. Minsky (1919–92), arguably the most influential Post-Keynesian economist, put borrowers into three categories: the hedge borrowers, those who can cover the principal and the interest on the principal. Then we have the speculative borrowers who can repay the interest, and finally we have the Ponzi borrowers who can neither cover the principal nor the interest payments. They rely merely on rising asset values to meet their obligations. Economic crisis occurs when the Ponzi borrowers dominate the credit markets. Minsky stressed that:

> the economy has financing regimes under which it is stable, and financing regimes in which it is unstable . . . over periods of prolonged prosperity, the economy transits from financial relations that make for a stable system to financial relations that make an unstable system. In particular, over a protracted period of time, capitalist economies tend to move from a financial structure dominated by hedge finance units to a structure in which there is large weight to units engaged in speculative and Ponzi finance.
>
> (Minsky 1992: 7–8)

Conclusion

One third of the 20th century was a period that is unique in human history. The years from 1915 to 1945 are the most violent years in recorded human history. The eminent British historian, Eric Hobsbawm (1917–2012), characterised the 20th century as the age of extremes (Hobsbawm 1995). The ideas of *The General Theory* were formed during these extreme and frantic years. Keynes's ideas were the product of his time. As we indicated earlier many of his ideas in relation to the instability of advanced industrialised economies, business cycles, insufficient aggregate demand and unemployment were discussed by different socialist writers and other economists such as Robert Malthus. The idea of the state assuming an active role in the economy was not a radical suggestion either. It was, in fact, a common practice among leading European states that enabled them to organise their economies and to colonise and divide the world between themselves. Besides, many social reformers called for government intervention in the economy to combat some of the market failures. William Petty (1623–87) appealed to the government to employ the jobless workers in public projects to remedy the problem of unemployment (Ravallion 2016: 31). Charles Fourier (1772–1837) contended that the delivery of protection and security should not be the only duty of the state. The state should also be responsible for creating jobs to help reduce poverty and for provision of a minimum level of subsistence for its citizens (Fumagalli 2005: 437).

The mercantilist writers associated wealth with power and were for strong centralised states and for a strong military. They called for protection of home industries and the promotion of exports. G. Alexander points out that "Mercantilism was a policy of ubiquitous and perpetual governmental activity. There was nothing the Government might not do" (Alexander 1957: 77). Even Adam Smith did not overrule limited government intervention in the economy. He found certain essential and limited roles for government intervention in the economy. These roles are "protecting the society from the violence and invasion . . . establishing an exact administration of justice . . . erecting and maintaining certain publick works and certain publick institutions" (Smith 1875: 545).

The German historical school of economics, which was a considerable intellectual force in the second half of the 19th century targeted their criticism, primarily, against the laissez-faire doctrine and in favour of the role of the state in the economy. Friedrich List (1789–1846), one of the founders of the school, described laissez-faire doctrine as "no less agreeable to robbers, cheats and thieves than to the merchant. It is not the function of the statesman to do nothing" (Gray 1957: 231). Adam Muller (1779–1829), whose ideas influenced the founding fathers of the historical school, defined the state as "not merely a fundamental need" but also as "the supreme human need" (Galbraith 2017: 101). Wilhelm Roscher (1817–94), another founder of the school compared the state to the head in relation to the rest of the body. He purported that "as the physiologist cannot understand the action of the human body, without understanding of the head; so we would not be able to grasp the organic whole of national economy, if we were to leave the state, the greatest economy of all" (Roscher 2018: 77).

Both A. Marshall (1842–1924) and A. C. Pigou (1877–1956) were Keynes's former teachers. The analytical base of Keynes's economics is essentially Marshallian and Pigouvian. Pigou remained loyal to Marshall's teaching to the end, whereas Keynes partially departed from his mentor's primary precepts. Marshall was the founder of neoclassical economics and the most influential economics teacher of his generation. Pigou was one of the founders of welfare economics. Their works are, primarily, in the tradition of the classical liberal philosophy of A. Smith and J. S. Mill. Therefore, Keynes's characterisation of Marshall and Pigou economics is not wholly balanced. Keynes held his former teachers as custodians of a classical school when he directed his criticism against the prevailing theory of unemployment.

Both Marshall and Pigou were mild reformists. Whilst they argued for minimum government intervention in the economy, they acknowledged the obvious defects and shortcomings of the economic system. They were not anti-statist and assigned several economic responsibilities to government, which cannot be delivered efficiently by the private sector. They admitted that economic progress is not an upward linear progression. Marshall pointed that "the commercial storm leaves its path strewn with ruin; when it is over there is calm, but a dull heavy calm" (Marshall and Paley 1879: 152). Such considerations as efficiency, equality and security were matters of great importance in their economic philosophy. The pursuit of self-interest is not sufficient, in their system of economic thought, for common well-being. If the economic system were driven solely by the pursuit of self-interest, it would reward the winners and penalise the losers. Consequently, it creates an unusual level of economic inefficiency, insecurity and inequality. For these reasons they assigned several economic functions that government can assume to protect and improve the economic conditions of the vulnerable members of the society and to promote greater economic efficiency.

Marshall was aware of the general trend towards greater involvement of the state in the economy to relieve the unemployed and the poor from abject poverty. He welcomed the trend and was in tune with economists who desired the increase "intensity of state activities for social amelioration that are not fully within the range of private efforts" (Marshall 1998: 108). Pigou's greatest book is about state intervention in the economy. His book, *The Economics of Welfare* (1920), which was an extended version of his earlier book, *Wealth and Welfare* (1912), is about what the private sector was unable to provide efficiently. The philosophical foundation of these books is anti laissez-faire economics. Pigou, in these books, challenges the laissez faire as an inadequate system that cannot protect the poor and unemployed. So, he justifies government intervention on the grounds of provision of public education, public works and social insurance to promote efficiency, equity and security in the society. To achieve this goal,

Pigou recommended adopting an effective tax and transfer system. He justified this stance because "it is evident that any transference of income from a relatively rich man to a relatively poor man of similar temperament" will "increase the aggregate sum of satisfaction. The old 'law of diminishing utility' thus leads securely to the proposition" (Pigou 1960: 89).

The novelty of Keynes's theory of economic disorder was not about pointing to the defects of advanced industrialised economies or his justification of state intervention in the economy. Either of these matters were one way or another covered in the economic literature before, including the works of classical and neoclassical economics. The novelty of Keynes's theory of chronic economic disorders were in five important areas. Firstly, that conventional economists did not only fail to foresee the 1929 collapse in Wall Street and the subsequent Great Depression, but their prescribed hands-off policy also made matters worse. Keynes launched his attack against the conventional economic theory at the right time, while the mainstream economics was paralysed and was unable to explain the situation and to provide a practical solution to come out of economic depression. The time was ripe for a different economic theory and policy prescription.

Secondly, Keynes not only challenged the philosophical foundations of laissez-faire economics but also the command economy and the fascist corporatist alternative. Thirdly, Keynes went a step further than the classical and neoclassical reading of economic disorder. In the classical and neoclassical account of economic disorder, there can be oversupply and overproduction, that is, a glut, of a good or a few goods and services in one market or a few markets or sectors and no more than that. They did not rule out possibilities of such disorders but they thought they are abnormalities that are self-correcting. They denied that there can be general glut for all goods and services in all markets and all sectors across the economy. Fourthly, the main point of contention between Keynes and the classical school is a matter of form and not the substance on the subject of economic disorders. Keynes recognised the possibility of gluts in many goods, services, sectors and markets simultaneously that are caused by lack of sufficient aggregate demand, which can be prolonged if correct measures are not taken at the right time. The underlying factor in his diagnoses to restore economic stability is government. In Keynes's view, the law of markets cannot resolve the problem of prolonged mass involuntary unemployment but a government, by implementing correct macroeconomic policies, can. Keynes provided practical solutions for the process of transition from depression to economic recovery. Finally, Keynes presented a systematic alternative economic theory. He gave the first rigorous account of the theory of deficient effective demand and unemployment in the history of economic thought.

The central problem in Keynes's theory is the deficient effective demand. This fault, in his opinion is "the public scandal of wasted resources." Keynes's message was "the cure lies outside the operations of individuals . . . the cure for these things . . . would involve Society in exercising direct intelligence . . .

over . . . private business" (Keynes 1967: 380–1). The capitalist system does not just suffer from extreme individualism, deficient effective demand but also from its rentier phase. The rentier phase of capitalism, Keynes maintained, is a transitional chapter that "will disappear when it has done its work . . . the euthanasia of the rentier, of the functionless investor, will be nothing sudden, merely a gradual but prolonged continuance" process (Keynes 1967: 376). What is required until then is a well-planned "skilled investment."

6 The order of self-destruction

Introduction

One cannot set apart Marx's theory of economic disorder from his overall world view. At the time Marx was formulating his grand theory, the developed Europe had already moved out of one of its greatest intellectual movements. The force of circumstances of the two centuries, 17th and 18th centuries, not only reshaped the new Europe but also the modern world. The time changed and the new world was fundamentally at odds with the medieval view. Marx's ideas, in a big way, are a side effect of this period. The age of enlightenment came to its end in the late 18th century. But Marx began his mature writings about mid 19th century. By this time the idea that society can be reorganised along rational and predictable lines was generally accepted as a truism. We would not be able to present an accurate account of Marx's theory of economic disorder unless we allow for the influence of this historical period on Marx's intellectual development. The essential point to be grasped is that Marx's world view is built, primarily, upon the conditions, the scientific findings and contributions of this remarkable movement.

The most recurrent theme of the age of enlightenment was reason, the ultimate triumph of reason over ignorance. Next to it was the indispensability of reason to human progress. Human beings were categorised as a thinking species, who are rational and by virtue of being rational they acquire knowledge that is the highest form of thinking. The exponents of the age of enlightenment not only advocated the use of reason to reveal the truths, but reason was tantamount to creativity. A good deal was said about the connection between rational reasons and discovery of the mysteries of the universe and human societies and inventions of new ideas, technology and institutions in different corners of Europe. One could hardly look too far not to find examples of such notable accomplishments. Newton discovered the universal law of gravity and explained the motions of the planets in a few mathematical equations. The Dutch lens maker, Han Lippersheim (c.1570–1619), invented the telescope in 1608. As soon as Galileo got hold of Han's instruction, he developed a new and better telescope. With his more advanced model, he showed that the moon's surface is uneven.

DOI: 10.4324/9781003346364-7

It is not in the least surprising that Marx insisted that his theory is scientific. One scientist that he was most impressed with his scientific discoveries was his contemporary biologist, Charles Darwin (1809–82). Marx wrote that Darwin's book, *On the Origin of Species*, "is very important and serves me as a basis in natural science for the class struggle in history" (Marx and Engels 1936: 125). Marx tried to dedicate his book, *Capital*, to Darwin but Darwin did not accept his offer. Another scientist that not only Marx but every other intellectual looked up to was Isaac Newton. At that time his book, *Principia*, was widely considered to be the greatest scientific work of all time. Marx did not refer directly to Newton in corroborating the validity of his theory but in three different ways, he implicitly linked his analysis to Newton's scientific achievements. The first link is about the objective truth, something that is real and exists independent of human understanding, just like Newton's laws of planetary motion. Marx purports that wherever "speculation ends . . . real, positive science begins" (Marx and Engels 1991: 48). But science for Marx, like anything else, is a dialectical process. It is a dialectical interaction between human and nature. Marx and Engels asserted that "we know only a single science, the science of history" (Marx and Engels 1973: 15).

Scientists like Newton and Darwin disclosed some regularities of nature. Newton unveiled some unknown riddles of the cosmic motion and Darwin the evolution of species. Marx intended to do the same with human societies. Marx wanted "to lay bare the economic law of motion of modern society" (Marx 1983: 20). In comparing nature with society Marx proclaimed that in society "the behaviour of men in the social process of production is purely atomic" (Marx 1983: 20). He tried to find likeness between cosmic motion and social production and concluded that as the "social production" is set into motion it will go on just like "the heavenly bodies, once thrown into a certain definite motion" (Marx 1983: 593). On this very point Marx only speaks of Democritus, Epicurus, Kepler and Hegel (Burkett 2000: 381–2). He has not acknowledged explicitly Newton's influence on his ideas. But despite this fact, any claim of being scientific at the time when Marx was composing his mature works could not have been free from the influence of the scientific achievements of Newton and Darwin. It was the findings of these scientists and not those of Democritus, Epicurus, Kepler and Hegel that dominated the world of science at the time.

The other two contexts in which Marx claimed his theory to be scientific in the same way as Newtonian cosmic motion and Darwinian theory of natural selection is his claim to natural laws. There are two sides to this claim. Firstly, it implies that just like in the realm of nature, there are hidden universal laws in human societies and economy that govern modes and social relations of production. Secondly, these laws can be studied objectively and can be discovered and managed to improve the conditions of the masses. Marx supposed that Hegel's law of transformation of quantitative into qualitative applies in society just as in natural sciences. Engels wrote that historical events may appear as accident but "the course of history is governed by inner general laws . . . it is always governed by inner, hidden laws, and it is only a matter of discovering these laws" (Engels 1941: 48–9). Vladimir I. Lenin (1870–1924) also affirmed that Marx exposed "objective laws governing the development of the social relations" of capitalism and deduced from that "the inevitability of the transformation of capitalist society into socialist society wholly and exclusively from the economic law of the movement of contemporary society" (Lenin 1930: 39).

Marx predicted that finally "there will be one science. . . . Natural science will in time incorporate into itself the science of man, just as the science of man will incorporate into itself natural science" (Marx 1977a: 105). He then went on to say "the first premise of all human history is, of course, the existence of living human individuals. Thus, the first fact to be established is the physical organisation of these individuals and their consequent relation to the rest of nature" (Marx and Engels 1991: 42). Marx identified two distinctive features of human science that are different from natural science. Human science is not about the history of "some individual person" but it is about the history of "the actions of men in pursuit of their ends." On the same topic Engels added that:

> the history of the development of society proves to be essentially different from that of nature. In nature . . . there are only blind unconscious agencies acting upon one another and out of whose interplay the general law comes into operation . . . In the history of society . . . the actors are all endowed with consciousness, are men acting with deliberation or passion, working towards definite goals; nothing happens without a conscious purpose, without and intended aim . . . Thus, the conflict of innumerable individual wills and individual actions in the domain of history produces a state of affairs entirely analogous to that in the realm of unconscious nature. The ends of the actions are intended, but the results which actually follow from these actions are not intended.
>
> (Engels 1941: 48)

Marx extrapolated the following deductions from the reasoning singled out here. That there is a goal in human history. Communism is the end, an end that can be explained by means of dialectical materialism. People "make their own history, but they do so not under conditions of their own choosing, rather under conditions given and transmitted from the past" (Marx 1977b: 15). There are hidden laws within human societies. Human beings are capable to discover and master these laws. This verdict persuaded Marx to have a high hope for philosophers to change the world for the better. Theories have very little validity unless they are proved to be right in practice. The objective truths can only be verified or falsified when tested in practice. It is in practice, noted Marx, that "man must prove the truth" (Marx and Engels 1991: 121). Lastly, progress gets its meaning in relation to the class-based modes of production. As in any phenomenon, progress is caused by the unity of negations and negation of negation. In the class-based modes of production, there are always two main classes that are in constant struggle. Marx declared that "the history of all hitherto existing societies is the history of class struggles" (Marx and Engels 2008: 6).

Moreover, at any stage in human history "definite individuals who are productively active in a definite way enter into . . . definite social and political relations" (Marx and Engels 1991: 46). Over time the coexisting means of production (technology) and the social relations of production diverge and become incompatible. The social relations of production prevent the development of means of production to advance. The laws of dialectic apply to all modes of production. It is always the case that "within the old society, the elements of a new one" can be created and nurtured and eventually subdue and prevail over the old as the old system conforms to the desires and needs of the new mode of production. One example of this phenomenon was the capitalist economy, which was conceived in feudalism. It came into being concurrently with its own antagonist class, the working class. The capitalist mode of production does not only organise its own class but also its negation, the working class. It organises the working class and arms it with the science of communism. As the industrial capitalism draws to its close, it polarises the entire society and reduces the working class into a state that they will have "nothing to lose but their chains." It is within this theoretical framework that Marx explained his theory of permanent economic crisis and the eventual collapse of the capitalist mode of production.

The main task of this chapter is Marx's theory of economic disorder. The chapter is divided into five parts. Part one explores the teleological concept of history that Marx adopted in his theory of economic disorder. The teleological perspective maintains that human history is purposefully heading to a specific direction and goal. This goal in Marxian economics is communism. The second part will look at the laws of development of human societies that are proposed by different thinkers and how they have justified the idea of social and economic progress from these dynamic laws. Part three, the dialectic of economic fatalism, discusses how with changing circumstances of production, the economy develops into a higher level of development and shows how each mode of production contains the seeds of its own undoing. Against this background, it explains the role of the economy as the base in any mode of production. This is the base that determines all components of superstructure according to the Marxian theory of economic disorder. In part four, we will show how Marx considered technology as the most dynamic lever that not only propels the capitalist production forward but also creates the reserve army of unemployed, overproduction and under-consumption. The final part discusses the process of falling rate of profit and Marx's theory of the inevitability of the demise of the capitalist mode and social relations of production.

The teleological dialectic of history

Karl Heinrich Marx (1818–83) was a follower of Hegel. His radical views got him into trouble with German authorities. Marx went into exile to France in

1843 where he met his lifelong collaborator, Frederick Engels. In France, after meeting French communists, he became a communist. Communism was the most radical political philosophy then. This conversion turned out to be riskier for the German government. So, the German state put the French under pressure to remove Marx from France. Marx was expelled from France and in 1844 he went to Brussels where he stayed for 3 years. His historical materialism took shape during this period in Brussels, an idea that he in collaboration with Engels developed in their book, *The German Ideology*. This concept, historical materialism, is indispensable to Marx's theory of economic disorder.

The essence of history for Marx is the real life of people. It is the real conditions in which they live. The nature of humanity is not an abstract matter but something that is determined by real material conditions of production, exchange and distribution (Marx and Engels 1991). The real history is not a long list of kings and queens. The history comprises all the struggle between different social classes and the entire humanity against nature. In this struggle human history follows a linear and ascending path. It follows a specific pattern that passes through five successive stages, each stage with its specific laws and trends. Marx presupposes five definite ascending stages of development of human societies. These stages are primitive communism, slavery, feudalism, capitalism and communism (Cox 2007: 1). Progressing through these distinct historical stages, according to the foregoing theory, is inevitable.

The idea of economic transformation was not a novel theory at the time when Marx was articulating his ideas. As we have explained in the preceding chapters, the idea of social and economic transformation has got a long history. A form of an ideal life awaiting in some distant future for humanity has been one main source of attraction for the rise of virtually all religions and their followers. The most plausible account of the ideal society in the ancient time was the one given by Plato in his *Republic*. But the thinkers of the enlightenment went for planning, layout and construction of such a society.

Marx's stages of development of human history are teleological. It is a concoction of Hegelian dialectic and his concept of history. Marx began his philosophical quest when he first entered the university. As a left-wing young Hegelian, he was much influenced by Hegel's theory of dialectic and historical progress. Georg Wilhelm Friedrich Hegel (1770–1831) was then a dominant figure in German philosophy. Two of Hegel's ideas are crucial in understanding Marx's system of thinking in general and his theory of economic crisis. These are Hegel's dialectical system and his concept of history. Neither of these ideas were original. Their origins can be traced back to ancient Greek philosophy (Morrison 2006: 139; Preston 2013: 18). Nevertheless, Hegel used them as integral parts of his philosophy.

There is no consensus on the meaning of the term "dialectic." Broadly speaking, we find two trends that have evolved over time: The dialectical method is used to explain the relation between thought and the relation between objective realities. For Socrates, Plato, Aristotle and their followers in the scholastic tradition, dialectic is an exercise of mind to find the truth. In the other school we have Heraclitus, Zeno, Hegel and Marx who see dialectic as being entrenched in everything that exists. Heraclitus (born about 540 BC) did not use the concept but what he proposed is in line with the dialectical method. In his view, fire is the origin of everything, and fire is a self-consuming process. It exists and expires simultaneously. From the property of fire Heraclitus deduced that everything is made of opposites and the only permanent thing is change. He remarked that "no man ever steps in the same river twice, for it's not the same river and he's not the same man" (quoted from Christian 2012: 97). Zeno of Elea (c. 495–430 BC), in Aristotle's view, was the inventor of the dialectical method (Walton 2007: 50). Sophists too found the dialectical method as a useful tool in their rhetorical arguments. Protagoras (486–11), the best-known Sophist, raised the rhetorical dialectic to the status of the art of persuasion by seeking a counterargument in each statement.

The term "dialectic" means "to debate" in Greek. This is the meaning that a modern reader mostly likely associates dialectic to—something that is not accidental. In this sense, it is a Socratic legacy that has continued its resilience to this day. This is the very method that Socrates (470–399 BC) used in his search for the ultimate truth, a method of discovery of truth by means of exposing the inconsistencies of a claim or statement through a relentless cross-examination debate and questions. Plato applied this method in his *Republic*, a tradition that he passed to his student, Aristotle. In their hands dialectical method was gradually transformed, as a process of discovering the ultimate truth, into a system of logical thinking. Both the teacher and his pupil applied the dialectical method to the precepts of form and essence. Plato, for example, pointed to variation in form and unity in essence asserting that there can be many forms of beauty, tree, house, dog and so on. But no single instance of a form can represents all forms, concluding that the perfect form, the essence, does not exist. Perfection is merely an ideal state of mind. The essence of all different forms is the idea of perfection that is not what we find in reality. Hegel endorsed Plato and Aristotle's dialectical method with one important exception. He discarded Aristotle's formal logic. Instead of ideas as fixed entities, he saw ideas in continuous motion from a state of less perfection to a higher perfection (Megill 2002: 28–9).

Hegel's dialectical method is constructed upon several "categories" such as quality, quantity, substance, causality, essence and existence. Central to all categories is the state of motion (Shand 1994: 177–8). Rooted in each category is a goal. The aim is moving forward towards the idea of the absolute. This type of history is predetermined, and we can discern its path only through our minds. History has a purpose, which is teleological. The history is the journey of the spirit that slowly and continuously exposes its perfection through time until its ultimate reality. This reality is expressed in the idea of the absolute. In Hegel's scheme of history, the beginning of this journey was in primitive societies and ever since it has been progressing upwards. Its highest form, the ultimate reality, is the nation state (Shand 1994: 180–90).

The lever that drives ideas to go forward is the triadic dialectical system of thesis, antithesis and synthesis. The voyage is initiated with the thesis. The thesis comes with its opposite, the antithesis. This unity of opposites cannot be confined to thesis or its negation, the antithesis. One side of the unity of opposites always predominates the other. The constant clash between these two forces will result in a qualitative transformation, the synthesis. The new is born from the old because of the conflict and the unity of the opposites (Cornforth 1952: 76, 96). Each successive transition from unity of the opposites of thesis and antithesis into synthesis is one step closer to the goal. The transition and the progress follow strict laws of dialectics. It goes through (a) the transformation of quantity into quality, (b) the law of the unity of opposite and (c) the law of the negation of the negation.

The core idea of Marx's theory of economic disorder is rooted in Hegel's laws of dialectics. In the transformation of quantity into quality, Marx discovered the force of economic, social and political transformation. He saw the hidden potential for historical progress and radical change. All microscopic and constant quantitative changes accumulate and then turn into a major power that cannot be restrained in its old outfits. It must break away and it will. Then it assumes a qualitative transformation. The qualitative changes occur through revolution. In the laws of dialectic and Hegelian teleological concept of history, Marx found the beginning and the end of human social, economic, legal and political organisations. Based on these laws and the notion of history, he divided the entire human history into what he called five modes of production. Starting with primitive communism to slavery, to feudalism, to capitalism and finally to scientific communism.

The gradual struggle (quantitative change) transforms one mode of production to another (qualitative transition). The primitive communism was transformed into a slave ownership mode of production. Then the form of struggle altered. The slaves and slave owners were the beginning of class struggle, which gave birth to feudalism. In the feudalist mode of production, the struggle was between peasants and landowning feudal lords. This struggle continued until the victory of the capitalist mode of production. Capitalism is another class-based mode of production. It is made up of two main antagonistic classes, the capitalist class, and the working class. In the modes of production that are class-based, the dominant class owns the means of production and the other class has nothing or very little possessions. In the capitalist mode of production, which was Marx's main concern, the capitalist class owns the means of production and the working class has got nothing except their labour power to sell. Because capitalism is a class-based mode of production, it eventually and inevitably falls victim to the law of the transformation of quantity into quality. In Marx's order of modes of production, capitalism is the last class-based mode of production. In the next mode of production, communism, social classes will be abolished and there will be unconditional equality among all citizens.

Marx applied all three laws of dialectics in his theory of history. Gradual struggle and changes in each mode of production then will result in a qualitative change. Through revolution the whole system of production, exchange and distribution will change. The transformation is caused by the unity of opposites. Due to this law, there is a never-ending struggle that drives each mode of production to its destruction. Whenever the dominant force gives way to the subordinated force, a new mode of production will emerge with a new form of struggle. In primitive and advanced communism, the opposite forces are human beings against nature. In the class-based mode of production the struggle is between the opposite classes. Let us take the capitalist mode of production as an example to demonstrate how this struggle takes place. We begin with the formation of capitalism as the thesis. As soon as the capitalist mode of production came into being it created its antagonistic classes (the capitalists and workers), and antithesis. The interests of these classes are incompatible. The economic system is unable to resolve this antagonism. Whatever the dominant class does, at the end of the day, is self-defeating. The capitalist class gradually loses its power and the working class gradually gains more power. Eventually the working class becomes the dominant class and the old mode of production will be replaced with a new mode of production. This is the stage that antithesis gives way to synthesis and thereafter the whole process of thesis, antithesis and synthesis will renew itself in an entirely different structure and format. Accordingly, economic disorder changes its form.

Marx took Hegel's laws of dialectic in their entirety, except in one respect. He labelled Hegel's dialectic as idealism. For Hegel, ideas are the ultimate reality, whereas for Marx, reality exists independently of ideas. So, for Marx the cause of change is not ideas. The real conditions in nature and life necessitate change. Real conditions are the source of reality. Marx believed that dialectical idealism "is standing on its head" and he has turned it the "right side up" (Marx 1983: 29). Dialectical laws are necessities that explain the natural motion of human societies. These laws exist independently of our beliefs. They can be discovered and understood in the same way as the laws of nature can be discovered. Marx inserted his concept of materialism to Hegel's dialectic of history. In Hegel's teleological dialectic, history will advance towards the absolute idea. Just like in Hegel's history, in Marx's transformation of modes of production, history follows its dialectical progression from thesis to antithesis to synthesis. For Hegel this struggle is manifested in the dialectical struggle of ideas. In Marx's approach it is expressed in the struggle of social classes and human beings with nature. In Hegel's dialectical teleology of history, there is an ultimate end in this struggle. The history is directed to an end, which is the absolute idea or spirit.

Hegel's starting point about his "absolute mind" was Kant's contention that we can never know "things—in—themselves." What is real for Hegel is the spirit, the mind. There is a collective mind or sprit, which is the absolute mind. Each person's mind (consciousness) belongs to this absolute mind or spirit. The end goal of history is the realisation of absolute idea or mind. History is the total and perfect demonstration of absolute spirit. Each stage of human development is a state closer to this absolute idea. Each period has its own spirit of age. History, Hegel held, "is mind clothing itself with the form of events" (quoted from Thompson 2000: 3). It is a rational process that takes itself to its own annihilation, to the time when there is no history or need for history, a state of perfection that lacks ideological oppositions. All individuals in a nation collectively reflect the common spirit of the nation. The absolute idea is a self-contained entity that covers everything. The realisation of absolute spirit is the envelope of all events in history. Absolute idea is the unity of the theoretical and the practical ideas. With the theoretical idea we will have a complete concept of the world and the practical idea is the way this concept is expressed and practised. The unity of the two gives us full consciousness, awareness and above all complete fulfilment. People will have full self-awareness and freedom to achieve self-fulfilment and act then according to their true nature. It is when the mind and the nature become one indivisible whole. The same also goes for Marx but he expressed it differently in a different context. In his teleological concept of history, history advances towards the perfect society (communism) but from tracking a different route from that of Hegelian dialectical idealism. The point that both Hegel and Marx have in common about their teleological concept of history is that history is the hostage of some predetermined laws and these laws propel history to a somewhat ultimate end.

The inevitable laws of economic development

To Marx reality and idea is not a chicken and egg situation. His view on this point is clear-cut and definite. Reality precedes and exists independent of ideas. You have the planet earth and people first, then ideas and not the other way around. Likewise, human constructions are real, be that a machine, a bridge or a society. These constructions are assembled according to certain natural laws. These laws are real and exist independently of human beings. Marx thought that he discovered the fundamental laws of society and economy. His predictions are based on these underlying laws. One example should suffice to clarify the general idea about these fundamental laws. For instance, Marx argued that the development of the capitalist mode of production is inevitable. The capitalist system sooner or later will spread throughout the world. All countries in due course will be capitalist. He wrote:

> it is not a question of the higher or lower degree of development of the social antagonisms that spring from the natural laws of capitalist production. It is a question of these laws themselves, of these tendencies working with iron necessity towards inevitable results. The country that is more developed industrially only shows to the less developed, the image of its own future.
>
> (Marx 1983: 19)

As has been pointed out earlier, human, technical and economic progress were not novel ideas at the time when Marx was writing his revolutionary books. In his time, the effects of industrialisation were prevalent in most urban parts of England. Its impacts were widespread. In particular, the scale and scope of social and economic conditions of the poor and working class were such that it was impossible to overlook such effects. Masses of dispossessed labourers and their families downpoured and inundated the urban areas. The number of people living in abject poverty was increasing rapidly while a small section of society was getting richer by the day. Marx was not the first to pin down the problems of the poor. Many thinkers before him wrote about the effects of industrialisation and the plight of the poor. However, the difference between Marx and his predecessors and his contemporaries was his visionary and all-encompassing approach. Marx was a polymath who dedicated his life to the study of the first industrial economy to change it.

He built his theory of economic disorder on the social, economic, political and technological conditions of his time. The period when Marx was writing his most important books was one of the most volatile periods in the 19th century. This was the dawn of a new economic system, a period that was characterised by dispossession of masses of rural peasants, mass poverty, increasing population, mass migrations, colonialism, extreme exploitation, revolution and concentration of wealth and power among a small group of people. It was during these social, political and economic upheavals that Marx and the earlier socialist thinkers and anarchists articulated their criticisms against the most excruciating drawbacks of industrialisation.

Works of many thinkers have influenced Marx's blueprint for his communist society. One of these thinkers was Henri de Saint-Simon (1760–1825), the founder of Christian socialism. Saint-Simon was in the French regiments helping the Americans in their war of independence. He was imprisoned during the reign of terror in France. In the last 17 years of his life, he lived in abject poverty and in 1823 he had a failed suicide attempt. His teachings revolve around rejection of the excesses of the French revolution and Napoleon's military aggression. He advocated the cause of the poor and brotherhood. Engels described him as a "genius." Saint-Simon, in many respects, was ahead of his time, who understood many challenges and repercussions of the scientific revolution and emerging industrial societies. The new world, in his view, was beyond the power of understanding of priests and the power of religious conviction. The new world needed experts to manage it. The chaotic new world could only be directed into an efficient, prosperous and just society if scientists and engineers replaced the priests and kings and took over the responsibility of solving the modern social and economic problems scientifically (Ball, Dagger and O'Neill 2017: 152). The social and economic disorders that are caused by advanced commerce and industry can only be put into order effectively through planning by scientists and engineers. He thought that justice cannot be served unless the work is based according to the principle of one's ability and the pay according to one's needs.

Another pioneering socialist thinker who influenced Marx's ideas was Charles Fourier (1772–1837). The title of his book *The Social Destiny of Man* gives much away about the author's core beliefs in this and his subsequent books. His central idea is about the existence of a natural social order that has the same reality as in the Newtonian planetary order. There are corresponding laws in the social world to that of the laws in the physical world (Beecher 1986: 225). In the context of human societies, this order passes through eight different stages—the last stage is the stage of harmony. In this stage, the intention of the deity will be realised, and humanity transcends and surpasses everything else. People can express themselves in every sense of the term—intellectually, emotionally and in their other needs. This stage is organised by cooperatives that are planned and consciously designed to serve human needs. This was a kind of political philosophy that Robert Owen (1771–1837) tried to put into practice. He set up the New Lanark Textile Mills cooperative, preaching that humans are inherently good. People are born good, but it is the external circumstances and conditions that determine their moral characters (Packard 1866: 66). The problem is not, therefore, the poor but the economic system that is based on monopoly and concentration of wealth among a small group of people, private property, individualism and competition. In a good and cooperative environment people will live and work in harmony in pursuit of a common good. To this end, in his cooperative, he introduced what he always professed.

Other early socialist thinkers whose ideas had a profound influence on Marx's theory of economic disorder were Auguste Blanqui (1805–81) and Louis Blanc (1811–82). There are two overriding themes in Blanqui's system of thought. Firstly, any form of ownership of earth cannot be natural. Secondly, and closely related to the first principle, is that ownership of earth is seen as the cause of division in society between the rich and the poor classes. Seizing land inevitably goes together with violence. Thus, the usurpers of land are not only the instigators of violence but also, they take away the right to live from those who are left with no land. In this unnatural division the law takes the side of the few wealthy and goes against the interest of the majority poor. Under such conditions the poor would not be able to improve their conditions, while they create most of the wealth of the nation. Blanqui contended that "there can be no society without labour!" and "the man who makes the soup should get to eat it" (Blanqui 1992: 193–9).

Blanqui was fully aware of the emerging industrial economy and the formation of the modern working class as an increasing social force. He was true to his revolutionary ideals. Wherever there was a popular insurrection in France he took part in it. During his lifetime, he spent over 33 years in prison for his political activities. He held the view that the interest of the rich and the poor is irreconcilable. The gap between the emerging dominant classes, the working class and the bourgeoisie class, get deeper and deeper with industrialisation of the economy. The class struggle is inevitable and will intensify with the growth of workers' movements. Creation of a just and equal society is possible but the transition from the class-based society to classless society is conditioned to a transitory period of dictatorship of the proletariat (Callinicos 2011: 51). During this period the wealth of the rich will be nationalised and put into the hands of the state to manage. The government then plan large national industries to serve the whole society.

Louis Blanc was also a leading figure in the early socialist movement. After failure of the workers' revolt in 1848, he fled France and went into exile in England. He stayed in England for over 20 years and returned to France in 1871. During the time he was in exile he wrote a 12-volume history of the 1789 French Revolution and a history of the 1848 Revolution. While in England he personally observed the effects of large markets, big business organisations, fierce competition, low wages, long working hours and unemployment. Blanc saw the solution for economic and social problems of his time in large state owned, managed and financed cooperatives, insisting that there is no need for the workers to be at the mercy of circumstances. Scientific organisation and management of cooperatives can absorb the entire workforce and direct production to serve the needs of the society. Blanc argued that the "right to work" should be the aim of the economic system. A just and efficient economic system is the one that the principle of "from each according to his abilities, to each according to his need" is guaranteed and enforced (Laidler 2000: 63).

In addition to the contributions of thinkers previously cited, Marx's theory of economic crisis is also much indebted to anarchist ideas. The origin of the term "anarchy" goes back to the Greek term "anarchos" which means without ruler. There are two complementary sides to the anarchists' cardinal moral principle. On one side it is freedom—total individual liberty and self-reliance. A free individual, free from all forms of oppression, can utilise his or her full potential and can live in complete uniformity to his or her will. On the other side of their moral principle, we have the state as the master of organised coercion. Anarchists are against all forms of organised institution. All types of organised institution, religion, business and political, are said to restrict individual freedom. The state as the pinnacle of all organised institution is not only superfluous but has no moral legitimacy. No organised institution has the right to compel individuals to obey its unnatural laws. Effective societies are those that have no states. Willian Godwin (1756–1836) was a pioneering anarchist thinker but unlike most anarchists he believed that state is a "necessary evil" that eventually will disappear (Taylor 1980: 35).

The principal source of power for anarchists is land. The alliance of land and power comprise the bare bones of all forms of coercive institutions. The only workable remedy is complete individual liberty. Joseph Proudhon (1809–65) blamed property ownership for coercive organised power. Power and exploitation go hand in hand and are integral parts of the state. He stressed that "property is theft" (Proudhon 1970: 124–5). In his ideal society there is neither private property nor a central authority. The society functions according to a form of "spontaneous order." In this social structure free individuals conduct themselves naturally, conferring to their natural motives to attain their natural moral duties. Other founding fathers of anarchist theory such as Mikhail Bakunin (1814–76) put more emphasis on communal societies, but they all called for abolition of private property and the state. Moses Hess (1812–75), another thinker who influenced Marx, contended that there can be no equality without true freedom.

Marx arrived at the same conclusion on the necessity of the state to that of the Anarchist interpretation, that the state is neither necessary nor has a moral legitimacy. His account was closer to Godwin's view perceiving the state merely as a "necessary evil" at least for a relatively short period of time. In the long run Marx's concept of the state and the Anarchist version are well matched—a vision of state that is positioned at the extreme end of liberal individualism. The last stage in Marx's theory of history is communism. This is a "spontaneous order" mode and social relations of production. Here we have the ultimate development of humanity and economy. Individuals live in total freedom, optimise their potential fully and enjoy a most fulfilling life in a perfect egalitarian and stateless society. A mode of production that Marx in his *Critique of the Gotha Program* summarised in the epigram: "from each according to his ability, to each according to his needs" (Marx 2008: 27). However, the dictum was not Marx's invention, but Marx popularised it. We can trace its origin in the work of Etienne-Gabriel Morelly (1717–78), a French novelist and a forerunner socialist in his book *The Code of Nature* (published in 1755) and in the writings of August Becker, a German journalist and politician in 1844 and in Louis Blanc's writings in 1851.

In contrast to anarchists and earlier socialist thinkers, Marx felt that his teleological concept of history was already confirmed by the work of anthropologists, most specifically the work of American anthropologist Lewis Henry Morgan (1818–81). Morgan began his studies of Native Americans in 1840. By observing and closely studying these groups of people, Morgan published one of the first comprehensive theories of social evolution. His book, *Ancient Society* explored the primary cause of advances in human societies. Morgan pointed to the changes in the means of food production as the leading cause. The evolution is slow and gradual. What is more, it is as the result of humans' "mental and moral powers through experience, and of their protracted struggle with opposite obstacles while winning their way to civilization" (Morgan 1907: 4). Morgan divided the stages of progress in human societies into three stages. These are the hunting and gathering (the savage stage), the settled agriculture (the barbarism stage) and the urban society (the civilisation stage).

Three aspects of Morgan's findings worked as a magnetic field for Marx's revolutionary social theory. Firstly, human history evolves and progresses upwards (it has evolved from savagery into civilisation). Secondly, the primitive societies were egalitarian and stateless social organisations. Thirdly, the role of technology, the means of production, are the main forces of progress. Marx expressed his high appreciation for Morgan's book. In the preface to the *Origins of Family*, Engels described it as "one of the few epoch-making works of our time." He went on to say that "Morgan rediscovered in America, in his own way, the materialist conception of history that had been discovered by Marx forty years ago" (Marx and Engels 1962: 170). We can also see the footprints of Morgan's ideas even in the title of Engels's book, *The Origin of Family, Private Property, and the State* (1884).

In Marx's theory, economic disorder and the force that propel the society into a higher stage are symbiotic. The one and the foremost force that propels change to a higher stage in all modes of production is the means of production. This is the constant struggle of humanity with the nature to provide the means for their survival. In the class-based modes of production there is an additional force. That is the force of class struggle. One issue worthy of reflection at this junction is the state. We have no state and class structure in both the primitive and the developed communism. It is in a class-based society that we have the institution of the state. For Marx the state was created with the formation of the class-based society. The state is an instrument of repression at the hands of one class against the disadvantaged classes. The class that has the means of production is the class that will have the state under its monopoly. In slavery, the state protected the interests of slave owners, in feudalism the interests of feudal lords and in capitalism the interests of capitalists. Hence, the state is a transitory phenomenon, and it will disappear with the abolition of a class-based mode of production. The last time we see the state is during the passage from capitalism to communism. This period is defined by the dictatorship of the proletariat.

Engels posited that "the state is nothing more than a machine for the oppression of one class by another" (Marx 1977c: 13). Marx postulated that the state and dictatorship are two sides of the same coin. Lenin held that Marx's theory of the state can only be understood "by those who understand that the dictatorship of a *single* class is necessary not only for every class society in general, not only for the *proletariat* which has overthrown the bourgeoisie, but also for the entire *historical period* which separates capitalism from . . . communism" (Lenin 1975: 262, Italics in original). Stalin equated the essence of Leninism to dictatorship of the proletariat.

It was in Paris and Brussel that Marx broke off with his young Hegelian past and became a communist. Adopting communism was the impetus that brought him to the study of economics. The first indication of Marx's interest in economics is in late 1843. At this time, he started to read the work of his compatriot, George Friedrich List (1789–1846). Engels says "Marx began his economic studies in Paris, in 1843, staring with the Great Englishmen and Frenchmen. Of German economists he knew only Ran and List" (Marx 1986: 7).

He came to England in 1845. Once more he also visited England shortly before the publication of *Communist Manifesto* in 1848. In 1849 Marx was expelled from Belgium. He returned to France, but he was not wanted there anymore. So he had to leave Paris for London. Britain did not give him citizenship but allowed him to stay until his death in 1883. After turning to study of political economy in late 1843, Marx was absorbed in the subject and devoted most of his study to the British economy. England then was the world factory and the first industrialised economy. It was the richest nation and the largest empire. England had the largest working-class population, the vast majority of whom lived in extreme poverty, in squalid and rundown neighbourhoods.

Engels in his classic book, *The Condition of the Working-Class in England* (in 1844), described such conditions most vividly.

After turning to the study of economics, Marx saw his role as a saviour and a visionary. His comprehensive critique of classical political economy intended to show that the contemporary economy was neither natural nor eternal. He tried to show that the economic system is full of contradictions and because of its contradictions it would eventually collapse. To this end, he was in the search of the key to disentangle the conundrum of social and economic metamorphosis. After a decade and half of reading about British economy and political economy, Marx was convinced about his discovery. In *A Contribution to the Critique of Political Economy*, his first major work in economics, he explains the determining factor in human societies that transforms a lower society to a more advanced society. He reasoned that the totality of relations of production:

> constitutes the economic structure of society, the real foundation, on which arises a legal and political superstructure and to which correspond definite forms of social consciousness. The mode of production of material life conditions the process of social, political, and intellectual life. It is not the consciousness of men that determines their existence, but their social existence that determines their consciousness.
>
> (Marx 1971: 20–1)

His target in the *Contribution* is the political economy of Adam Smith and David Ricardo. Smith's *Wealth of Nations* (1776) and Ricardo's *The Principles of Political Economy and Taxation* (1817) were the focus of his criticisms. Smith and Ricardo's emphasis was on the creation and augmentation of wealth of developed nations—under what circumstances the wealth of a nation diminishes and under what conditions it expands. Their main concern was to explain how the medieval restrictions, be that from economic ideas—policies, regulations, cultural, religious and political—prevent a nation from becoming more developed and wealthier while maintaining that a nation is an assembly of many individuals and increase or decrease in individual wealth corresponds to the rise and fall of the wealth of a nation. If there is free trade and individuals can persue their economic self-interest, the wealth of the nation will be augmented. Otherwise, the economy will recess backward.

The forefathers of the classical school had to start their economic analysis with the riddles that they inherited from the former thinkers. The economist had not cracked the long-lasting enigma yet. What makes the two goods or services to be exchanged? This was a much-debated topic in the 17th century. John Locke tried to answer it by suggesting that every person is entitled to a product to which he employs labour for its production (Haworth 2004: 125). Smith provided two explanations about the reason why goods can be exchanged. In one explanation two commodities are exchanged because they have equal value. The reason for having equal value is because equal labour is used in their production. If it takes, for example, one hour to hunt a deer and one hour to hunt four rabbits, the value of one deer will be equal to four rabbits. In the *Wealth of Nations*, Smith also says that this scenario applies only to early stages of economic development. In more advanced stages of economic development, the value of a commodity is determined by the cost of factors of production. Ricardo elaborated the cost of factors of production theory further and wrote that "the value of a commodity, or the quantity of any other commodity for which it will exchange depends on the relative quantity of labour which is necessary for its production" (Ricardo 1992: 5). He divided society into three major social classes—the landlords, the capitalist, and the workers. Out of the value of a commodity, profit goes to the capitalist, rent to the landlord and wage to the worker. For Ricardo the task of political economy should be the study of distribution of income between these classes. Marx embraced Ricardo's theory of distribution of income and with some modification placed it at the heart of his theory of the capitalist mode of production and economic disorder.

The irrevocable economic destiny

The ascent of humanity is coalesced into a perpetual struggle, the struggle between human and nature. The fight for all living things will always be for food and protection. Early humans were merely armed with their senses, with their limbs, brain and with their clans. They gathered their foods, built shelters and protected themselves from the elements and wild animals or from other clans with this primitive defence mechanism. It was the extension of these natural instruments that led to the creation of more advanced technologies. All types of technology somehow are an upgrade to the power of our legs, hands, sight, hearing, smell, taste, brain and so on. The first pedal of progress began when human species either invented or discovered the first instrument of production. Hunting and gathering communities employed the instruments of production that were specific for hunting animals and for gathering food.

With development of greater division of labour, that is, hunting and cultivation, new instruments of production had to be invented or discovered for cultivation. So, for Marx, in order to live humanity must work. Living and work are real and inseparable. This reality determines one's very existence. Second, work and living cannot last long if individuals live in isolation. The human race is a social animal and work is a social undertaking. Third, to work in order to produce for the needs and for the protection—instrument of production is invented or discovered. Fourth, as human species are social, and work is a social undertaking—there would be a unique relationship between work and people. Either you work or you do not. This connection forms a relation between the means of production and those who work and those who do not work. It creates a relation between those who own the means of production and those who have no possession.

According to this perspective, economic and social changes come after advances in instrument and techniques of production. Improvement in instrument and techniques of production led to division of labour and specialisation of employment. This in turn, according to Marx, led to the production of surplus products. The monopoly of the surplus products is the origin of private property and the formation of the class relations of production. In the first class-based social relation of production, the slavery mode of production, the slave owners have monopoly over the surplus product and employ their economic power to enslave others. As means and techniques of production improved, a new mode of production was conceived and nurtured within the slavery mode of production. The feudalist mode of production replaced slavery and land substituted slave as the main source of production. The economic, political, religious and cultural power were shifted from the slave owners to the landowners. In the same way, the means and techniques of production continued to develop and in the meantime the foundations of a new mode of production were born and grew within feudalism. That eventually led to the collapse of feudalism and the rise of the capitalist mode of production.

In England Marx observed a totally different economic system. He called it "capitalism." But what caused industrialisation in England? For Marx the primary cause was invention and application of military and navigation technologies. These advances in Europe empowered relatively more developed European nations to colonise North America and then stretch their colonial reign to the rest of the world. Exploitation of these colonies generated enormous wealth for the individual colonists and their states. This wealth is the source of the embryonic accumulation of capital in Europe. The extraordinary upsurge of consumption of the wealthy people and unparalleled accumulation of capital paved the way for larger scale production and trade. The mass production for mass consumption one after another required application of science, more advanced technology and skilled management. These changes in turn extended the division of labour and hence created more surplus product. The emerging class, the bourgeois to use Marx's term, was a progressive class when it fought for its emancipation against feudalism. The medieval world restricted individual freedom and security for capitalist investment. The medieval laws limited the trade, the movement of labour, capital and goods.

These factors in combination with other changes in the economy and society created industrial cities with a large urban population. The time that can be marked as the birth of the capitalist mode of production is:

> when each individual capital employs simultaneously a comparatively large number of labourers, when consequently the labour-process is carried on an extensive scale and yields, relatively, large quantities of products. A greater number of labourers working together, at the same time, in one place . . . in the same field of labour . . . in order to produce the same sort

> of commodity under the mastership of one capitalist, constitutes both historically and logically the starting point of capitalist production.
>
> (Marx 1983: 305)

The key prerequisites for capitalist production, prior to concentration of capital in the hands of a small number of capitalists and congregation of a large number of workers under one roof are: (a) private property—the means of production are owned and controlled by a small number of individual capitalists; (b) very advanced and refined division of employment and specialisation; (c) domination of trade by a generally accepted form of money; (d) a relatively large number of dispossessed and landless individuals who are thrown out of rural areas and catapulted to cities; (e) domination of production not for personal consumption but for exchange; and finally, (f) the supremacy of commodity production over production of goods. Marx remarks, capitalism "first makes the production of commodities general then, by degrees, transforms all commodity production into capitalist commodity production" (Marx 1986: 36).

Marx stressed that "capital is not a thing." Capital is:

> a definite social production relation, belonging to a definite historical formation of society, which is manifested in a thing and lends this thing a specific social character. Capital is not the sum of the material and produced means of production. Capital is rather the means of production transformed into capital, which in themselves are no more capital than gold or silver in itself is money. It is the means of production monopolised by a certain section of society, confronting living labour-power.
>
> (Marx 1984: 814–15)

Marx identified two main characteristics that distinguish the capitalist mode of production from the former modes of production. "First, it produces its products as commodities . . . the fact that commodity is the dominant and determining characteristic of its products . . . The second distinctive of the capitalist mode of production is the production of surplus-value as the direct aim and determining motive of production" (Marx 1984: 879–80). At the outset we need to explain that for Marx products and commodities are two different economic entities. Products are produced for consumption and commodities for exchange. Commodities and products are produced in all class-based modes of production. However, the capitalist mode of production is the only mode of production that is dominated by commodity production.

Commodity is the most basic building block of the capitalist mode of production. Each commodity is made up of two elements: the use value and the exchange value. The use value represents the utility attribute of a commodity. The exchange value is the "common property" of all commodities. The common property that all commodities share is labour (Marx 1983: 45). The use value is the specific utility that each commodity satisfies a specific human need. Each commodity is also a product of a certain amount of abstract human labour, "the social necessary labour time." In this respect commodities are homogenous. They are a product of mass of value. When commodities are exchanged, it is the equivalent amount of abstract labour that is exchanged from one hand to another. Therefore, commodities are produced for sale, not for personal consumption. In the capitalist mode of production "commodities are non-use-value for their owners and use-value for their non-owners" (Marx 1983: 89).

Capitalist production comprises three main components: the constant capital (K). Constant capital consists of technology, land and raw materials. The second component is the variable capital (V). Variable capital is the living labour power that is sold to the capitalist in return for the wage they receive. The last component is the surplus value (S) that the labour produces that goes to the capitalists. So, the capitalist production is put into motion by the capitalist organising the means of production and labour power and putting them into the production process to produce commodities for sale. Marx explains the fundamental difference between the constant capital and the variable capital in the following way:

> constant capital is the part of capital . . . which is represented by means of production, by the raw material, auxiliary material, and the instrument of labour, does not, in the process of production, undergo any quantitative alteration of value . . . that part of capital, represented by labour power, does, in the process of production, undergo an alteration of value. It both produces the equivalent of its own value, and also produces an excess, a surplus-value.
>
> (Marx 1983: 202)

The constant capital reproduces itself and the variable capital in addition to its reproduction, produces surplus value. The entire capitalist production rests on this central objective. This is the reason for the existence of capitalist production. Marx maintains that "the production of surplus value is the chief end of capitalist production" (Marx 1983: 220). Besides, "the entire character of capitalist production is determined by the self-expansion of the advanced capital value, that is to say, in the first instance by the production of as much surplus value as possible; in the second place by the production of capital, hence by the transformation of surplus-value into capital" (Marx 1986: 81). In view of this, the creation of surplus value and its transformation into capital are at the heart of Marx's theory of economic disorder.

So, what constitutes the sources of wealth? For Mercantilists it is gold, for classical economists it is free trade and for Marx it is surplus value, which is the product of the living labour. Surplus value is the product of variable capital (V). That is the product of mental and physical capabilities of workers, something that Marx designated as labour power (LP). One distinctive feature of the capitalist mode of production, according to Marx, is that it has converted LP into a commodity. Just like any other commodity, LP comprises use value and exchange value. As a use value it can produce new value and as an exchange value it embodies LP that enables it to be exchanged with other commodities that contain equivalent LP. The big difference between LP, as a commodity, with the rest of other commodities is that for other commodities you pay first then receive the commodity, but in the case of LP you get the commodity first and then pay for its service.

Like other commodities, the value of LP is determined by the necessary volume of labour time used for its production. The capitalist mode of production cannot carry on its production unless there are workers who can sell their LP and can raise the next generation of workers. What workers get is solely the means of subsistence. For the capitalist economy workers have two main functions, to produce the means of subsistence for themselves and the surplus value for the capitalists. One day of working time is divided into two different times. The necessary labour time (NL) is the time that a worker works for his or her wage and surplus labour time (SL) is the time that she or he works for the capitalist. The NL is the source of concrete or use value and the SL is the source of abstract or exchange value.

Capitalism comes into being as LP becomes not just a commodity, but it predominates the mode of production. For the capitalist class to go on living it must act like a vampire. It must live "by sacking living labour, and lives the more, the more labour it sucks" (Marx 1983: 224). In *Capital* volume three, Marx demonstrates this vampire-like nature of the capitalist class. In this volume he defines the cost price of a commodity as constant capital plus variable capital (K+V). This is what costs the capitalist. But the capitalist class gets more than that. The surplus value that is created by the workers also goes to the capitalist class. Given that the cost price is Z = K+V and the value of a commodity is K + V + S then the capitalist takes more than what it costs him or her. Surplus value (S) is what costs the labour (Marx 1984: 26). This is the extra value created by labour, but it is appropriated from him or her. Surplus value is the amount of unpaid labour. Marx argued that the capitalist class exploits workers by appropriating the surplus value. He defined the rate of exploitation (RE) as the ratio of surplus value to the variable capital, RE = S/V or SL/NL. The rate of exploitation of labour by capital can be either absolute or relative. In case of absolute rate of exploitation, it is increased by increasing the hours of work in a day and in case of relative rate of exploitation, it is when the NL is reduced.

Marx described capitalism as an anarchic system with its own specific circulation structure. It is different from the barter exchange (C—C) and the simple circulation of commodities (C—M—C). In these forms of circulation either a commodity is exchanged for a commodity or money and money for another commodity. The purpose of exchange in both cases is for consumption. Money here is a medium of exchange and the circuit ends with consumption. In capitalist circulation of commodities, we start with money then buy commodity to sell it for more money. At the two ends of circuit, we have money. Buying is not for satisfaction of the immediate wants but for sales and more money.

In *Capital* volume two, Marx has divided the circular movement of capital in capitalist production into three different stages. In stage one, the capitalist enters the market with money (M) to buy dead and living labour, the means of production (MP) and labour power (LP). This part is represented by M—C. The second stage is the production process (P), in which the commodities purchased are put into production. This is one of the most crucial stages in the capitalist mode of production. It is at this junction that surplus values are created. In the third stage, new commodities are produced and will be taken to the market for sale. In this part the role of the capitalist alters from a buyer to a seller. They sell their commodities for money, C'—M. The whole circular movement of capitalist production can be presented as: M—C . . . P . . . C'—M'. M is the money capital. It is original money that the capitalist initially invests. C is made up of two commodities, the means of production (MP) and the labour power (LP). P is the production process and after this process the "commodity is pregnant with surplus value" (Marx 1986: 38). C' represents the new commodities that are produced which have higher value than initial commodities that are used in the production process. The last stage is M' that is received after selling the new commodities produced. The M' is higher than money capital M. The difference is the surplus value in money capital. The entire process consists of "the transformation of money-capital into productive capital" (Marx 1986: 28).

The general circuit of capital comprises two stages of circulation; M—C and C'—M' and one stage of production, P. Marx laid much stress on the sphere of production (P) as the stage where surplus value is created. The economists whom Marx labelled as vulgar do not acknowledge creation of surplus value or wealth in production. They seek it in exchange, in trade. In Marx's extended circuit of capital one process of production is followed by another with each successive production being greater than the one before. Successive accumulation of surplus value is both good and bad for the capitalist mode of production. If everything remains the same, the capitalist economy continues to expand, but this is a self-defeating process. The seeds of economic crisis are geminated in this self-expanding nature of the capitalist system of production. In the anarchic capitalist production, many capitalists compete to make more profit. The desire to make more profit finally will not match with actual conditions of the capitalist mode of production. Since the capitalist production develops large-scale production because of "the thirst for profits on one hand, and competition on the other." At the same time this process "compels the cheapest possible production of commodities" (Marx 1984: 86).

When the aim is to produce surplus value, the capitalists do not reinvest their money capital unless they are confident that they can make more profit. The level of profit is neither even nor regular. It fluctuates with different stages of business cycles. When the economy is working at its full capacity, the expectations of making profit are very high. In the recession, the opposite is the case. In boom, Marx says there is an "intense expansion, acceleration and vigour of the reproduction process, labourers are fully employed . . . there is also a rise in wages which makes up in some measure for their fall below average during other periods of business cycle" (Marx 1984: 446). Capitalist is a system of boom-and-bust economy. Economic booms are followed by economic busts. When the economy plunges into recession "prices fall, similarly wages; the number of employed labourers is reduced, the mass of transactions decrease" (Marx 1984: 448).

Composition of capital and labour redundancy

In Marx's theory of employment, the level of employment is determined by organic composition of capital (OCC). This is the ratio between constant to variable capital K/V. In other words, it is the ratio of the dead labour to the living labour. Marx employs two more related terminologies in relation to OCC. These are technical composition of capital (TCC) and the value composition of capital (VCC). The TCC is the definite ratio of constant capital to variable capital at any given stage of economic activity. The OCC is TCC if it is measured in old values. If it is measured in new values, it becomes VCC. In the capitalist economy these compositions of capital are the signposts of the degree of economic productivity at any given time (Marx 1983: 574).

Capitalists' aims and actions collectively are the cause of the change in the OCC. The chief aim of all capitalists is to make more profit. Different capitalists, to make more profit, enter a self-destructive competition. This competition, in the course of time, will reduce the number of capitalists into a few capitalists. As a result, the national capital would be concentrated in fewer hands. Smaller and less productive enterprises would go bankrupt or would be swallowed up by bigger rivals to avoid bankruptcy. For Marx there is a positive correlation between concentration of capital in fewer hands and application of more and better technology in the business. Therefore, over time the K/V will rise and the dead labour substitutes and dominates the living labour. The effects of the increase in K/V are mainly twofold; it increases labour productivity as well as it replaces the machine in place of workers. The higher the organic composition of capital, the higher will be the level of output and the reserve army of unemployed.

It is the capitalist mode of production to bring workers under one roof. By this act the capitalist system facilitates its own destruction. It organises and fosters its own negation. Congregation of workers under one roof creates several conditions that go against the very existence of the system. Sharing a common interest and getting together at a large number under similar conditions generates a communal power. It generates a force that can be organised and demand the rights that individually are not attainable. These very conditions have been responsible for workers learning about their common interests, building camaraderie in the workplace, creating cooperative associations, trade unions and workers' political parties. On the other side of the coin there is a constant fear of redundancy. Workers' conditions, therefore, teach them the art of class struggle and gradually improve their consciousness about their power and rights. In addition to the reserve army of unemployed caused by application of more advanced technology, Marx also referred to the agricultural labourers who are hard-pressed and leave the rural areas and head towards cities for a better life. Marx states that capitalist production destroys feudalistic agricultural relations of production and as a result "the demand for an agricultural population" will be "constantly on the point of passing over into an urban or manufacturing proletariat" (Marx 1983: 601).

The economic system that Marx observed was cruel and pitiless. It exploited "women and children . . . on a large scale." The entry of women and children into the labour market and the flow of agricultural labourers into urban areas increased the reserve army of unemployed and kept wages low (Marx 1983: 601). All these changes supplemented the existing tension between the ever-increasing army of unemployed and the employed workers. The capitalist class uses and exploits this tension to reduce further workers' wages. Marx proclaims that this tension "allows the capitalist to beat down the price of labour whilst the falling price of labour allows him on the other hand, to screw up still further the working time" (Marx 1983: 513). However, low wages are not a one-way street. A fraction of unemployed will be "diverted into new channels of industry: and become absorbed in other branches" of the economy (Marx 1983: 415). The reserve army is "kept in misery in order to be always at the disposal of capital" (Marx 1983: 458).

During the appropriation of the means of production by capital two distinctive relationships would develop. One of these relationships is the technical relationship between productive forces of production. This is the relationship between labour power and the means of production. The second relationship is the social relationship of production between the capitalists and labourers. On one side of this relationship, we have the direct producers, the workers, and on the other side are the capitalists. By virtue of owning the means of production, capitalists not only appropriate a segment of the products produced by workers but they also can control and dominate the entire social superstructure of society that is comprised of the state, culture, conventions, morality and religion. About this relationship Marx notes that:

> It is always the direct relationship of the owners of the conditions of production to the direct producers—a relation always naturally corresponding to a definite stage in the development of the methods of labour and thereby its social productivity—which reveals the innermost secret, the hidden basis of the entire social structure, and with it the political form of the relation of sovereignty and dependence . . . the corresponding specific form of the state.
>
> (Marx 1984: 791)

Production process is the second phase in Marx's circuit of capital. It is a very complex process that depends on many factors. It depends on price of factors of production, the state and level of technological development, organisation and management of production process, the time lag between the decision to start a production to the production of commodities, that is, capitalists' planned expectations and actual market conditions after the goods being produced. It depends on how organised and informed the working class are. It also hinges on the general state of national, international economy and cultural and natural elements.

The final stage in the circuit of capital is C'— M'. This is the second circulation phase, the exchange of commodities produced in the production stage and their exchange for money. In this phase the surplus value is realised and distributed between different sub-capitalist classes. From production of C' it does not follow that the commodities produced can be exchange to M'. First there must be a market for these goods or else they remain in the form of goods in the market. Marx says these commodities "are produced specially for the market and must be sold, transformed into money" (Marx 1986: 38). Equally it does not follow that wherever production takes place there is a market for the goods in the same location. Marx remarks that the "periods of turnover" depend on "the distance of the market in which a commodity is sold from its place of production" (Marx 1986: 253). Even if all these preconditions are met, there may not be enough demand for the commodities produced to clear the market. One reason for this is that "the demand of the capitalist for labour-power and thus indirectly for necessary means of subsistence, steadily decrease compared with his demand for means of production" (Marx 1986: 121).

As we have cited earlier, investing more in the means of production increases productivity on the one hand and on the other substitutes the machines for labour. More commodities are produced because of higher productivity and at the same time we will have a larger reserve army of unemployed. The commodities produced C' is greater than the money income of the working population to buy all the commodities that are brought into the market for sale. Therefore, under this situation not all C' is going to be exchanged with M'. In this relationship, money is another factor that affects the exchange of C' to M'. Money is "the measure of value in as much as it is the socially recognised incarnation of human labour; it is the standard of price in as much as it is a fixed weight of metal" (Marx 1983: 100). The exchange of C' to M' fluctuates by the rise and fall in the value of money. This could be as a result of discovery of a new gold mine or cost-push inflation.

In Marx's view, money is a real commodity. As a commodity it is a product of labour. It has use value and exchange value. Its use value is the utility that we obtain from consumption of precious metals and its exchange value is the amount of abstract labour that is embodied in production of precious metals used as a form of money. Thus, the price of money just like any other commodity fluctuates from its natural value. The price of a commodity may or may not correspond to the value of the commodity. It can be equal to the value of the commodity, or higher or lower. That can happen for two reasons. The value of money changes while the value of commodities stays the same. In reverse, value commodities do not change while the value of money changes. The value of commodities, Marx claims, is "the centre of gravity around which their prices fluctuate" (Marx 1984: 178). The force behind the market price of commodities and their actual value is supply and demand. Marx comments that:

> should the market . . . value rise, this would entail a drop in the society demand, and a smaller mass of commodities would be absorbed. Hence, if supply and demand regulate the market price, or rather the deviations of the market-price from the market value, then in turn, the market value regulates the ratio of supply to demand, or the centre round which fluctuation of supply and demand cause market prices to oscillate.
>
> (Marx 1986: 181)

Falling profit and capitalist production

In Marx's theory profit is the oxygen of the capitalist mode of production. Profit sustains its life. Industrial capitalists organise production. This class represents "the capitalist as functioning capitalist, as representative of working capital as opposed to the capitalist as mere personification of capital, as mere owner of capital" (Marx and Engels 1990: 490). At the end of each circuit of production, industrial capitalists obtain a certain amount of surplus value. The surplus value first appears in form of commodity C' but this needs to be converted into M'. After C' is converted into M' industrial capitalists encounter several challenges. This group of capitalists like other groups of capitalists are not a homogenous group. There are those industrial capitalists who own all factors of production. In this case, all profit goes to this group of capitalists. There are those industrial capitalists who borrow capital and rent land for their production. In this case, out of the profit they must pay rent to the land-owning capitalists and interest to money-lending capitalists. In addition, they must sell their commodities at lower prices to merchant capitalists for their commodities to be circulated into different markets. According to Marx, there are two types of merchant capital: the commercial capital and money lending capital. The commercial capital is "a transmuted form" of capital that is "constantly to be found in the market" in circulation (Marx 1984: 268).

Money lending capitalists lend money and procure interest on money. Marx considered interest as an irrational price. For the reason that "if all capital were in the hands of the industrial capitalists there would be no such thing as interest and rate of interest" (Marx 1984: 377). Money capitalists make money out of money M—M'. M' is greater than M and the difference is what the industrial capitalists pay in the form of interest to money lending capitalists. Making money out of money, M—M', is one of the peculiar characteristics of money according to Marx. This capacity "to expand its own value independent of reproduction . . . is a mystification of capital in its most flagrant form" (Marx 1984: 392).

Profit consists of different shares of the surplus value that will be allocated to different subsets of the capitalist class. Marx's theory of profit in the long run was inspired by the classical economists. Classical economists anticipated the rate of profit to fall with the economic development. Marx's law of the rate of profit to fall is a variation of their theory of diminishing rate of return. Marx's formula for the rate of profit in a capitalist economy is S/K + V, where S stands for surplus value. In this equation, any change in S, K and V can change the rate of profit. An increase in K, if other factors remain constant, will decrease the rate of profit. In the same way if there is an increase in V, and other factors remain the same, the rate of profit will fall. But if the ratio of K/V decreases and wages fall, the rate of profit will increase. Marx holds that the rate of profit depends "on the low or high prices of raw materials and the experience of the buyer, on the relative productivity, efficiency and cheapness of the machinery, on the greater or lesser efficiency of the aggregate arrangement in the various stages of the productive process, elimination of waste, the simplicity and efficiency of management and supervision" (Marx 1984: 138).

The rate of profit in the short run differs from the rate of profit in the long run. In the short run, the rate of profit can increase, decrease or remain the same depending on countervailing forces that operate within the capitalist mode of production in different stages of circulation of capital. For example, from the quotation cited previously, in the short run the surplus can be increased if there is a more effective management of resources, less waste, more advanced technology and longer working days. But in the long run, as the capitalist mode of production progresses, the rate of profit will fall. This law is inevitable. Two other effects of the fall in the rate of profit are a corresponding fall in the rates of interest and the gradual rise in land rent. The interest rates fall because of development of credit system, institutions, and instruments. Also, because there will be less profit to be made and less demand for credit. Marx believes in the course of time as rate of profit falls, the rate of interest also falls in "so far as it is regulated by the rate of profit . . . furthermore, the interest rate shows a tendency to fall in consequence of the growth of loanable capital" (Marx 1984: 623).

As the capitalist mode of production progresses, in the long run, the portion of profit of industrial capitalists that goes in the payment of rent to the land-owning capitalists will rise with time. For Marx land is a gift of nature. It cannot have a value. The rent is paid merely for the monopoly of land. Rent is "the lease money paid under the heading of ground-rent to the landlord for the use of the land for purposes of production or consumption" (Marx 1984: 633). The price of rent will increase because of the increase in population, concentration of investment and production. So, the increase in rent is also one of the reasons for rate of profit to fall in the long run.

After surplus value is realised at the final circuit phase of capital, it will be divided between different capitalist classes. The surplus value will be divided further as different capitalist classes use a segment of their share of surplus value for their own consumption and the rest either to lend on interest, buy land to rent, to use it for circulating commodities, and in case of industrial capitalist to reinvest it. The only productive capital in this sequence is the surplus value that is reinvested by industrial capitalists. This surplus value is not only the source of wealth but also it is the engine of economic growth. Unless there is a constant flow of reinvestment of a segment of surplus value by the industrial capitalists, there will be no growth in the economy. Marx says, "no society can go on producing . . . no society can reproduce, unless it constantly reconverts a part of its products into means of production" (Marx 1983: 531). Yet, investing a portion of surplus value in means of production and labour power is not a certain and straightforward process. First and foremost, "all the circumstances that determine the mass of surplus-value operate to determine the magnitude of accumulation" (Marx 1983: 561). The rate of accumulation of capital also depends on what proportion of surplus value goes to unproductive capitalist sub-classes. In addition, how much of this is used for unproductive consumption. Marx said classical economists were right for maintaining that "the consumption of surplus products by productive, instead of by unproductive labourers, is a characteristic feature of the process of accumulation" (Marx 1983: 552).

Marx divided consumption into two categories, productive and unproductive consumption. In unproductive consumption, the value of the commodity "disappear during its consumption." Whereas, in productive consumption "its value is transferred as an additional value to the commodity itself" (Marx 1986: 54). For instance, when a large part of surplus value is used in consumption of luxury goods then "accumulation and the rate of reproduction will stagnate" (Marx 1972: 246). The amount of accumulation of capital also depends on the amount of surplus value that is spent on unproductive labour. The productive labour produces surplus value and unproductive labour only consumes surplus value. Marx listed social groups such as clergy, state officials, servants and actors in the category of unproductive labour. An unproductive labourer is someone whose labour is not "exchange with capital, but *directly* with revenue, that is, with wages or profit (including . . . the various categories of those who share as co-partners in the capitalist' profit, such as interest and rent)" (Marx 1978a: 157, Italics in original).

Circuit of capital in a capitalist mode of production tracks several periods and phases. Overall, these periods and phases can be divided into production of capital and circulation of commodities. Both these phases side by side comprise a full capital turn over. This turn over can be long, short or average. In its short form the faster the capital turnover, the higher will be the rate of accumulation of capital and economic growth. Even if the capital turnover goes smoothly and efficiently, there will always be a portion of money left idle outside different stages of the circuit of capital. This is a percentage of M' that is "withdrawn from circulation and stored up as a hoard by selling commodities without subsequent buying" (Marx 1986: 495). The higher the portion of money capital hoarded the lower the rate of accumulation of capital and economic growth.

Economic productivity produces the opposite effect to that of hoarding. It expands accumulation of capital. That is "the productive power of labour increases the mass of the products" (Marx 1983: 570). But in turn increase in the organic composition of capital K/V will intensify competition among the capitalist class, which in turn leads to reduction in the number of smaller capitalists and concentration of wealth in the hands of a fewer number of large capitalists.

For Marx these are not the only contradictions in the capitalist mode of production that keeps it in state of unbroken cycle of disorders that drives it to its ultimate destruction. Every component of the system conflicts with itself. The economic system only is here to fulfil its historical mission. Capitalism belongs to a specific historical period. He criticised those economists who viewed the system as being eternal. Marx believed that the downfall of the economic system is inevitable because there is disorder in all different components of the economy. The parts of the economy are neither compatible nor synchronised. Dialectical and historical materialism are set in and operate in the entire structure of the system. It is possible at any time for the economic distress to commence in any component or the stage of circuit of capital. Let us now consider the possible sources of disorder in three different stages, M—C, P and C'—M', of circuit of capital.

The first stage of the circuit of capital is productive commodity capital, M—C. The problem with the start of any complete turn over of capital could be the shortage of M. The cause of this could be low savings, high uncertainty and poor and underdeveloped credit system. Given that there is enough money capital (M), there could be problems with the labour market (LP), in the commodity markets (MP) or in combination of both markets. In the case of the labour markets, workers can be ignorant of their rights, power, dispersed and disunited or they can be conscious of their rights, organised and united. They are either a "class in itself" or a "class for itself." A well organised and informed working class increases the necessary labour time and reduces the surplus labour times that go to the capitalists. Higher wages mean lower profit and lower accumulation of capital. Marx remarks that the increase or decrease in wages "influences the rate of surplus value inversely" (Marx 1984: 65).

Marx divides the means of production (MP) into two clusters. These are the raw materials, machines and buildings. Means of production can be acquired from the domestic and foreign markets. If all other factors remain the same, investing in the means of production results in outcomes that are crucial in understanding Marx's theory of economic disorder. Adopting new technology enables the capitalist or capitalists to produce super surplus value. This increases the level of productivity of production of capitalists who are equipped with new technology on the one hand and on the other will bankrupt the capitalists who do not have the same advanced technology. As less productive businesses go bust, the wealth will be concentrated with a smaller number of capitalists. Other repercussions of this effect are an increase in the level of unemployment consisting of the workers who were substituted by machines and the capitalists who went bankrupt. Besides, increase in productivity increases the total output and increases in the number of unemployed decreases the effective demand. This is a striking feature of the capitalist production that we often encounter—the dilemma of overproduction and under-consumption. In relation to means of production Marx states that the rate of profit depends on the ratio of surplus value to:

> the variable capital plus constant capital. If the *rate of surplus value is given, the amount of surplus value* does indeed depend on the amount of variable capital, but *level of profit* . . . depends on the ratio of this surplus value to the total capital advanced . . . the rate of profit will thus be determined by the price of the raw material . . . and the value of machinery of a particular efficiency.
>
> (Marx 1978b: 87, italics in original)

Clearly all possible proportionate combinations of MP and LP cannot be equally efficient. Out of all these combinations there is one that will yield the most optimal result. From this right mixture of MP and LP we will get the highest output at the least cost. The right proportional blending of MP and LP is not an easy task to measure and more than that to apply accurately. Technology wears out and becomes obsolete, workers become deskilled or can be organised and demand higher wages and better conditions at work. The business can be managed by the owners of the business or it can be detached from ownership. Marx referred to this disproportionality as a possible cause of economic disorder.

The second stage of the circuit of capital is production. Production process (P) involves time-lags. From the time MP and LP are organised and put into production process, a certain amount of time elapses to the time commodities are produced and ready to sell. During this interval of time so many things may change, and the capitalist's plans and objectives may or may not be realised. There are three possibilities associated with this period. The situation may remain as expected. The situation may turn in favour of the capitalists in that sector. Then the expectation of making more profit attracts a greater number of capitalists to invest in this sector and consequently increases the level of competition among them. The third possibility is the situation may turn against this sector and what is expected will not be realised. Under these circumstances many capitalists leave the sector or become bankrupt. So, Marx remarks that from whatever angle we look at capitalist production, we find it in a state of anarchy and in haste to escape from its current bounds. Because it is "in the nature of capitalist production to produce without regard to the limits of the markets" (Marx 1978b: 522). One must not lose sight of the fact that production in the capitalist economy is mostly out of proportion and that causes capital to migrate "from one branch of production to another" (Marx 1978b: 521).

Disproportionality in production is not exclusive to Marx's theory. Even Say's law of markets that Marx dismissed as "childish babble" refers to over- or underproduction in different sectors of the economy. But Marx's theory differs both in its causes and effects of disproportionality in production. Marx puts more stress in disproportionality in accumulation of capital for the reason that all sectors of the economy are not equally profitable at the same time. Marx claims that "overproduction of capital always includes overproduction of commodities" (Marx 1984: 251). In the capitalist system, the capitalist credit system also deteriorates the situation further. The credit system is "the main lever of over-production and over-speculation in commerce solely because the reproduction process, which is elastic by nature, is here forced to its extreme limits" (Marx 1984: 441).

Three main factors, according to Marx, contribute to the expansion of the credit system in the capitalist economy. The first factor is the most determining factor that not only determines the expansion of the credit system but everything else in the economy and society. This factor is production. Along with development of production develops the expansion of the credit system. Marx writes that the size of credit "grows with the growing volume of value of production. . . . A mutual interaction takes place here. The development of the production process extends the credit, and credit leads to an extension of industrial and commercial operations" (Marx 1984: 481).

Another cause of expansion of the credit system in the capitalist economy is the development of large-scale production and the growing distance between the locations of production to the markets. Marx says, "with the development of the productive power of labour, and thus of production on a larger scale: 1) the markets expand and become more distant from the place of production; 2) credit must, therefore, be prolonged; 3) the speculative element must thus more and more dominate the transactions" (Marx 1984: 481). An additional cause that augments the expansion of credit markets is the growing separation of ownership and management. On this point Marx remarks that "a large part of the social capital is employed by people who do not own it and who consequently tackle things quite differently than the owners, who anxiously weights the limitations of this private capital in so far as he handles it himself" (Marx 1984: 441).

The capitalist economy is built on booms and busts. Cumulative fluctuation of disproportionality and anarchy in production over time make the cycles of over-production and under-production more frequent, longer and deeper. The system goes repetitively through cycles of expansion and contraction until its final day. Marx was the first outstanding economist who described the basic causes and effects of business cycles of the industrialised economies. Over-production and under-production come and go together. The periodic economic decline and recession is characterised by significant reduction in economic activity, high unemployment, and low accumulation of capital. Meanwhile, the hallmarks of a period of economic expansion and growth are high profits, overconfidence, high volume of buying and selling, high consumer demand, over-accumulation of capital, full or nearly full employment, over-expansion of money supply and high and rising inflation rate. Marx notes that:

> In times of prosperity, intense expansion, acceleration and vigour of the reproduction process, labourer is fully employed. Generally, there is also a

> rise in wages which makes up in some measure for their fall below average during other periods of the business cycle. At the same time, the revenues of the capitalists grow considerably. Consumption increases generally. Commodity prices also rise regularly, at least in the various vital branches of business. Consequently, the quantity of circulating money grows at least within defined limits.
>
> (Marx 1984: 446)

All in all, these periodic and irregular movements get deeper and longer over time. These cycles get so long and so deep that in the long run they will destroy the system. The structure of the capitalist economy contains an incurable contradiction that grows in time and leaves no other way out except the destruction of the system itself. Marx maintains that "the bourgeois mode of production contains within itself a barrier to the free development of the productive forces, a barrier which comes to the surface in crises and, in particular, in *over-production* the basic phenomenon in crises" (Marx 1978b: 528, part II). Marx criticised economists before him for denying the cycles of expansion and contraction and deepening of these cycles over time. Marx holds that "in a situation where men produce for themselves, there are . . . no crisis, but neither is there capitalist production" (Marx 1978b: 502, part II). Economic disorders in the capitalist mode of production become a commonplace. During deeper economic disorders selling predominates buying. This rule applies to most goods and most capitalists. Under such circumstance, Marx says "a man may be very pleased, if he has sold his commodities without immediately thinking of a purchase" (Marx 1978b: 503, part II).

The exchange in capitalism is not what the classical economists believe it to be. The production is neither for personal consumption nor is the exchange dominated by exchange of commodities for commodities. The capitalist production is set for making profit. It does not operate on the exchange relationship of commodities for commodities (C—C) but based on money capital to make more money (M—C—M'), based on exchange. In the latter scenario "no one can sell unless someone else purchases. But no one is forthwith bound to purchase because he has just sold" (Marx 1983: 115). The economic disorder emerges when the interval of the time between sells and purchase is the predominant trend in the economy.

Conclusion

The prophecy that the industrialised economies eventually degenerate and fall is not exclusive to the Marxian theory of economic disorder. Classical economists argued that in the long run the economic growth would in the end be terminated and the economy would finally stagnate at a stationary state. Keynes also anticipated the end of the system. Joseph Schumpeter (1883–1950) too expected a similar outcome. Unlike Marx's prediction, Schumpeter envisaged the fall of the system not from its failures but from its overachievements. But just like Marx, he saw the chief cause of the end of capitalist production in the dynamic motion of capitalist production. He borrowed Marx's characterisation of the "destructive" and "regenerating" nature of the capitalist economy and from that he deduced the eventual demise of the system. His version of the theory is known as "creative destruction" or Schumpeter's gale theory. Schumpeter asked the question "Can capitalism survive?" In his reply, he said, "No. I do not think it can." The reason being that "its very success undermines the social institutions which protect it, and 'inevitably' creates conditions in which it will not be able to live" (Schumpeter 1966: 61).

Marx's theory of economic disorder is not confined solely to economics. His theory of economic disorder is engrained in his philosophical, political, sociological, historical, methodological and anthropological system of thought. Short of these prerequisites, his theory is incomplete. One of the key and most determining premise in Marx's theory of disorder is the presupposition that the capitalist mode of production is a transitory historical period. It is a system that is full of contradictions. The element of self-destruction is entrenched in the very nature of the mode and social relations of production. The economic system is a prisoner of dialectical and historical materialism. It is the hostage of class struggle and a captive of economic determinism.

Capitalism is created from unities of negation. On the top of all the unities stands the unity of negation of the capitalist and the working classes. There can be no capitalist class without the working class and vice versa. Profit is the overruling link between these classes. For this purpose, the system congregates masses of dispossessed men, women and children under one roof. The capitalist economy first deprives large crowds of people, then organises and exploits them. For the individual capitalists to make the highest profit and remain in the market, they enter a fierce competition. The fight for survival compels them to invent and apply new technology in their sectors of the economy. Application of technology in the business increases productivity. As a result of the increase in productivity the output will rise. Automation not only cause job losses, but it exacerbates wage reduction. All these events occur parallel to each other. Owing to these factors the capitalist mode of production "establishes an accumulation of misery, corresponding with accumulation of capital. Accumulation of wealth at one pole is, therefore, at the same time accumulation of misery, agony of toil, slavery, ignorance, brutality, mental degradation, at the opposite pole" (Marx 1983: 604).

The system introduces some countervailing reforms, but these reforms do not go far enough to save the system. Marx remarks that capitalism "owing to its very nature, excludes all rational improvement, beyond a certain point" (Marx 1983: 453). At the same time, among commodity modes of production capitalism is the most dynamic system of production. Quantitative build-up of all these contradictions and the gradual and increasing gap between the means of production and social relations of production reach to a defining breaking moment, to a point of no return. At this juncture, the base and the superstructure become incompatible. Marx argues that this is the time the system succumbs and crumbles. In Marx's words:

> Along with the constantly diminishing number of the magnates of capital, who usurp and monopolise all advantages of this process of transformation, grows the mass of misery, oppression, exploitation; but with this too grows, revolt of the working class, a class always increasing in numbers, and disciplined, united, cited, organised by the very mechanism of the process of capitalist production itself. The monopoly of capital becomes a fetter upon the mode of production, which has sprung up and flourished along with, and under it. Centralisation of the means of production and socialisation of labour at last reach a point where they become incompatible with their capitalist integument. Thus, integument is burst asunder. The knell of capitalist private property sounds. The expropriators are expropriated.
>
> (Marx 1983: 715)

The motive of profit takes the capitalist economy far and wide. The system started in England and then spread to the rest of the world. Wherever capitalism goes it destroys the old and regenerates a new economic system. Marx gave the example of India to corroborate this point. He said England's missions in India were "one destructive, the other regenerating" (Larain 1999: 173). Global capitalism creates a "global working class." Marx's case study was England. From it he drew many general conclusions, placing industrialisation of England in a specific historical category, as a definite mode of production, a mode of production that is dominated by two classes—the capitalist class and the working class. The capitalist class owns the means of production. So, they oversee the state, culture, law, religion, art, literature and every other aspect of the superstructure. Capitalists have one aim in life and that is to make as much profit as possible. The more they appropriate the workers' labour time the richer they will get. The system is built on a fixed target. To reach its target it over time accelerates the rate of exploitation of the working class. During the development of capitalism, the productive forces, and the productive relations of production reach to a turning point. The system unites all its "contradictions into a single group, where they will stand face to face" that will "eventuate in the emancipation of the proletariat" (Marx and Engels 1976: xxiii). The conflict between the productive forces and the existing relations of the production will intensify in due time and reach the point where revolution becomes the only way out of the conflict.

It is then that the capitalist mode of production completes its historical cycle and mission. The transition into a new mode and relations of production becomes inevitable. In the new mode of production, communism, "the question then comes down to the need of society to calculate beforehand how much labour, means of production, and means of subsistence it can invest" (Marx 1986: 318). Communism liberates humanity from old forms of economic repression. It is at this mode of production that people fulfil their humanity. Class differentiation, violence, private property, greed, theft, repression, hunger, deceit, treachery, state, police and religion will all disappear. The means of production will be owned by the community and everything would be managed and administered rationally on voluntary civic instincts. Science and technology would be employed in the interest of all. Social justice and equality would become the cornerstones of the new society. The economy would be organised in accordance with scientific laws and methods. The economy would function in the interests and the needs of the masses. Every required means of existence would be supplied in abundance. This new reality would eliminate competition and greed. People would then cooperate naturally. Each individual citizen would contribute according to his or her ability. Each individual citizen would take from the social output according to his or her needs.

To Marx this is the final destiny of the human race. The upcoming of a perfect life is inevitable. No one can stop this outcome. Marx purported that communism is different from all other modes of production. Communism:

> overturns the basis of all earlier relations of production and intercourse, and for the first time consciously treats all-natural premises as the creatures of hitherto existing men, strips them of their natural character and subjugates them to the power of the united individuals. Its organisation is, therefore, essentially economic, the material production of the conditions of this unity; it turns existing conditions into conditions of unity. The reality, which communism is creating, is precisely the true basis for rendering it impossible that anything should exist independently of individuals, insofar as reality is only a product of the preceding intercourse of individuals themselves.
>
> (Marx and Engels 1991: 86)

Bibliography

Addison K. N. (2009) *We Hold These Truths to be Self-Evident . . .*, Indian, University Press of America, INC.

Adel G. H., Elmi J. and Taromi-Rad H. (2012) *Pahlavi Dynasty: An Entry from Encyclopaedia of the World of Islam*, London, EWI Press Ltd.

Akira H. (1998) *A History of Indian Buddhism*, trans. and ed. P. Groner, Delhi, Motilal Banarsidass Publishers.

Alesina A., Matuszeski J. and Easterly W. (2011) Artificial States, *Journal of the European Economic Association*, vol. 9: 2.

Alexander G. (1957) *The Development of Economic Doctrine*, London, Longmans, Green and Co.

Allen G. (1977) *The Evolution of the Idea of God: An Inquiry into the Origins of Religions*, Pomeroy, Heath Research.

Annas J. (1993) *The Morality of Happiness*, New York, Oxford University Press.

Aristotle (1970) *The Politics*, trans. T. A. Sinclair, Harmondsworth, Penguin Books.

Aristotle (1984) *The Complete Works of Aristotle*, vol. 2, ed. J. Barnes, Princeton, Princeton University Press.

Aristotle (1996) *The Politics and the Constitution of Athens*, ed. S. Everson, Cambridge, Cambridge University Press.

Aristotle (2016) *Aristotle's Politics, Writings from Complete Works*, ed. J. Barnes, Princeton and Oxford, Princeton University Press.

Aspromourgos T. (2009) *The Science of Wealth: Adam Smith and the Framing of Political Economy*, London, Routledge, Taylor and Francis Group.

Assandri F. (2014) Impermanence and Immortality, in I Theodor and Z. Yao (eds.) *Brahman and Dao*, Lanham, Lexington Books.

Auker M. R., Sparks R. S. J., Siebert L., Crosweller H. S. and Ewert J. (2013) A Statistical Analysis of the Global Historical Volcanic Fatalities Record, *Journal of Applied Volcanology*, vol. 2: 2.

Ausubel K. and Harpignies J. P. (2004) *Nature's Operating Instructions: The True Biotechnologies*, San Francisco, CA, Sierra Club Books.

Axworthy M. (2017) *Iran: What Everyone Needs to Know*, Oxford, Oxford University Press.

Backhouse R. E. (1995) *Interpreting Macroeconomics: Explorations in the History of Macroeconomic Thought*, London, Routledge.

Backhouse R. E. (2002) *The Penguin History of Economics*, London, Penguin Books.

Bacon F. (1999) *Selected Philosophical Works*, ed. R. Sargent, Indianapolis, Hackett Publishing Company, Inc.

Bader R. M. (2015) Kant's Theory of the Highest Good, in J. Aufderheide and R. M. Bader (eds.) *The Highest Good in Aristotle and Kant*, Oxford, Oxford University Press.

Ball T., Dagger R. and O'Neill D. I. (2017) *Political Ideologies and the Democratic Ideal*, 10th edn, New York, Routledge.

Baloch A. Y. K. B. (1975) *Inside Baluchistan: Autobiography of the Khan-e-Kalat, Mir Ahmad Yar Khan Baluch*, Karachi, Royal Book Co.

Baqer M. (2000) *Life of the Ayatollah*, New York, Thomas Dunne Books.

Barber W. J. (1970) *A History of Economic Thought*, London, Penguin Books LTD.

Barker E. (2010) *Greek Political Theory: Plato and his Predecessors*, Abingdon, Routledge.

Bates D. W. (2012) *States of War*, New York, Columbia University Press.

Beccaria C. B. D. (1804) *An Essay on Crimes and Punishment*, London, Printed for H. D. Symonds.

Bedrij O. (2007) *Celebrate Your Divinity*, 2nd edn, Bloomington, Xlibris.

Beecher J. (1986) *Charles Fourier: The Visionary and His World*, Berkeley, University of California Press.

Belliotti R. A. (2009) *Roman Philosophy and Good Life*, Lanham, Lexington Books.

Bentham J. (1816) *The Works of Jeremy Bentham*, part IX, Edinburgh, William Tait.

Bernstein W. (2009) *A Splendid Exchange—How Trade Shaped the World*, London, Atlantic Books.

Blanqui A. (1992) The Man Who Makes the Soup Should Get to Eat It, in A. Fried and R. Sanders (eds.) *Socialist Thought*, New York, Columbia University Press.

Blanton S. and Kegley C. W. (2017) *World Politics—Trend and Transformation*, Boston, Cengage Learning.

Blaug M. (1994) Second Thoughts on the Keynesian Revolution, in C. Wood (ed.) *John Maynard Keynes, Critical Assessments*, 2nd edn, vol. viii, London, Routledge.

Blaug M. (1996) *Economic Theory in Retrospect*, 5th edn, Cambridge, Cambridge University Press.

Blum P. R. (2012) *Giordano Bruno: An Introduction*, trans. P. Henneveld, Amsterdam, Rodopi.

Bodin J. (2006) Response aux Paradoxes de Malestroit touchant l'Encherissement de toutes Choses et le Monyen d'y reedier, in A. E. Monroe (ed.) *Early Economic Thought: Selected Writings from Aristotle to Hume*, Mineola, NY, Dover Publications.

Böhm-Bawerk V. E. (1930) *The Positive Theory of Capital*, trans. W. Smart, New York, G. E. Stechert and Co.

Bos H. J. M. (1997) Lectures in the History of Mathematics, in *History of Mathematics*, vol. vii, US, American Mathematical Society.

Bovard J. (2005) *Attention Deficit Democracy*, New York, Palgrave Macmillan.

Bowley M. (1973) *Studies in the History of Economic Theory Before 1870*, London, Palgrave Macmillan.

Boyce M. (2001) *Zoroastrians: Their Religious Beliefs and Practices*, London, Routledge.

Brannigan A. (1981) *The Social Basis of Scientific Discoveries*, Cambridge, Cambridge University Press.

Brenner Y. S. (1983) Sources of Inflation: Old and New, in N. Schmukler and E. Marcus (eds.) *Inflation Through Ages: Economic, Social, Psychological and Historical Aspects*, New York, Brooklyn College Press.

Breseeg T. M. (2004) *Baloch Nationalism: Its Origin and Development*, Karachi, Royal Book Company.

Broadwater J. (2012) *James Madison: A Son of Virginia and Founder of the Nation*, Chapel Hill, The University of North Carolina Press.

Brown H. G. (1913) The Marginal Productivity Versus the Impatience Theory of Interest, *The Quarterly Journal of Economics*, vol. 27: 4.

Brownmiller S. (1993) *Against Our Will: Men, Women, and Rape*, New York, Ballantine Books.

Brue S. L. and Grant R. R. (2013) *The Evolution of Economic Thought*, 8th edn, Mason, South Western, Cengage Learning.

Buchanan M. (2013) *Forecast: What Extreme Weather can Teach us about Economics*, London, Bloomsbury Publishing Plc.

Buddha (2005) *In the Buddha's Words: An Anthology of Discourses from the Pali Canon,* ed. B. Bodhi, Somerville, Wisdom Publications, Inc.

Bulliet R. W., Crossley P. K., Headrick D. R. and Hirsch S. W. (2015) *The Earth and Its Peoples: A Global History,* vol. 2: *Since 1500*, 6th edn, Stamford, Cengage Learning.

Burkett J. P. (2000) Marx's Concept of an Economic Law of Motion, *History of Political Economy*, vol. 32: 2.

Bury J. B. (2008) *The Idea of Progress: An Inquiry into its Origin and Growth*, New York, CosimoClassics.

Bury J. B. (2015) *A History of Greece*, Cambridge, Cambridge University Press.

Cairnes J. E. (1875) *The Character and Logical Method of Political Economy*, New York, Harper and Brothers Publishers.

Callinicos A. (2011) *The Revolutionary Ideas of Karl Marx*, Chicago, Haymarket Books.

Cantillon R. (2001) *Essay on the Nature of Commerce in General*, trans. H. Higgs, New Brunswick, Transaction Publishers.

Carlton E. (2006) *Politeia: Visions of the Just Society*, Madison, Fairleigh Dikinson University Press.

Carneiro R. L. (2000) Herbert Spencer as an Anthropologist, in J. Offer (ed.) *Herbert Spencer Critical Assessment,* vol. II, London, Routledge.

Chase G. (2018) *Redemptor Domus*, Leicestershire, Gamelyn Chase.

Chen L. (2017) *The Core values of Chinese Civilization*, Trans. Paul J. D'Ambrosio, R. Carleo, C. Meyers and J. Guzowska, Bejing, Springer.

Child J. (1751) *A New Discourse of Trade*, 4th edn, Printed for J. Hoges.

Christian J. L. (2009) *Philosophy: An Introduction to the Art of Wondering*, 10th edn, Belmont, Wadsworth Cengage Learning.

Christian J. L. (2012) *Philosophy: An Introduction to the Art of Wondering*, 11th edn, Wadsworth, Cengage Learning.

Clark J. B. (1899) *The Distribution of Wealth: A Theory of Wages, Interest and Profit*, New York, Palgrave Macmillan.

Clark J. M. (1917) Business Acceleration and the Law of Demand: A Technical Factor in Economic Cycles, *Journal of Political Economy*, vol. 25: 3.

Clodfelter M. (2017) *Warfare and Armed Conflicts*, 4th edn, Jefferson, NC, McFarland and Company, Inc. Publishers.

Cloudsley-Thompson J. L. (2005) *Ecology and Behaviour of Mesozoic Reptiles*, Berlin, Springer.

Clower R. W. (1965) The Keynesian Counter-Revolution: A Theoretical Appraisal, in F. H Hahn and F. Brechling (eds). *The Theory of Interest Rates*, International Economic Association Series, New York, Macmillan.

Cohen M. R. and Cohen F. S. (2002) *Readings in Jurisprudence and Legal Philosophy*, vol. 1, Washington, DC, BeardBooks.

Commons J. R. (1931) Institutional Economics, *American Economic Review*, vol. 21: 4.

Congressional Research Service Report (2021) *Global Economic Effects of COVID-19,* 9 July. https://crsreports.congress.gov/product/pdf/R/R46270/76.

Copleston F. (2003) *A History of Philosophy: Late Medieval and Renaissance Philosophy,* vol. 3, London, Continuum.

Copleston F. S. J. (1946) *A History of Philosophy*, vol. I, Westminster, MD, The Newman Bookshop, Greece and Rome.

Cordell K. and Wolff S. (2010) *Ethnic Conflict, Causes—Consequences—Responses*, Cambridge, Polity Press.

Cordesman A. H. (1999) *Iran's Military Forces in Transition*, Westport, Praeger.

Cornforth M. (1952) *Dialectical Materialism*, vol. 1, London, Lawrence and Wishart LTD.

Costanza R., Cumberland J., Daly H., Goodland R. and Norgaard R. (1997) *An Introduction to Ecological Economics*, Boca Raton, FL, St. Lucie Press.

Cox J. (2007) *The Concise Guide to Economics*, 3rd edn, Auburn, Ludwig Von Mises Institute.

Cregg C. T. (1985) *Plague: An Ancient Disease in the Twentieth Century*, Albuquerque, University of New Mexico Press.

Cubeddu R. (1993) *The Philosophy of the Austrian School*, Abingdon, Routledge.

Daly H. E. (2007) *Ecological Economics and Sustainable Development*, Cheltenham, Edward Elgar.

Darwin C. (1958) *Autobiography of Charles Darwin*, New York, Norton.

Daudi I. (2014) *Civilization and Violence*, Bloomington, Xlibris.

Davenant C. (1695) *An Essay upon Ways and Means of Supplying the War*, 2nd edn, Printed for Jacob Tonfon.

Davidson N. (1994) Rome, in Porter and M. Teich (eds.) *The Renaissance in National Context*, Cambridge, Cambridge University Press.

Delitala M. and Marsan G. A. (2014) *Managing Complexity, Reducing Perplexity: Modelling Biological Systems*, New York, Springer.

Demand N. H. (2011) *The Mediterranean Context of Early Greek History*, Chichester, Wiley-Blackwell.

Descartes R. (1996) *Meditations on First Philosophy*, 2nd edn, ed. J. Cottingham, Cambridge, Cambridge University Press.

Descartes R. (2000) *Philosophical Essays and Correspondence*, ed. R. Ariew, Indianapolis, Hackett Publishing Company, Inc.

Diderot D. (2016) Three Aphorism from Diderot, 'Letter to My Brother', 1760; Voltaire, Treatise on Metaphysics, 1735; and Rousseau, The Citizens, or An Address on Political Economy, 1765, in C. Warman et al. (eds.) *Tolerance: the Beacon of Enlightenment*, Cambridge, OpenBook Publishers.

Dillard D. (1966) *The Economics of John Maynard Keynes: The Theory of a Monetary Economy*, London, Crosby Lockwood and Son Ltd.

Dome T. (1994) *History of Economic Theory: A Critical Introduction*, Cheltenham, Edward Elgar.

Doniger W. (2014) *On Hinduism*, Oxford, Oxford University Press.

Dreisbach D. L. (2011) Virginia's Contributions to the Enduring Themes of Religious Liberty in America, in P. Rasor and R. E. Bond (eds.) *From Jamestown to Jefferson: The Evolution of Religious Freedom in Virginia*, Charlottesville, University of Virginia Press.

Dunn J. (2002) *Political Obligation in its Historical Context*, Cambridge, Cambridge University Press.

Dwivedi D. N. (2005) *Macroeconomics: Theory and Policy*, 2nd edn, New Delhi, Tata McGraw-Hill Publishing Company Limited.

Economist (2016) *Ebola in Africa: the end of a Tragedy? Background on the Ebola Outbreak in West Africa,* 14 January. https://www.economist.com/graphic-detail/2016/01/14/ebola-in-africa-the-end-of-a-tragedy.

Edgeworth F. Y. (1881) *Mathematical Psychics: An Essay on the Application of Mathematics to the Moral Sciences*, Chesterland, C. Kegan Paul and Co.

Edsall N. C. (1971) *The Anti-Poor Law Movement 1834–1844*, Manchester, Manchester University Press.

Ekelund R. B. Jr. and Herbert R. F. (2007) *A History of Economic Theory and Method*, 5th edn, Long Grove, Waveland Press Inc.

Engels F. (1941) *Ludwig Feuerbach and the End of Classical German Philosophy*, London, Lawrence and Wishart.

Ferguson A. (1769) *Institutes of Moral Philosophy*, 2nd edn, Edinburgh, A. Kincaid, W. Creech and J. Bell.

Ferguson A. (1792) *Principles of Moral and Political Science*, vol. I, Edinburgh, Printed for A. Strahan and T. Cadell.

Fine B. (2012) Exploitation and Surplus Value, in B. Fine, A. Saad-Filho and M. Boffo (eds.) *The Elgar Companion to Marxist Economics*, Cheltenham, Edward Elgar.

Finn S. J. (2006) *Thomas Hobbes and the Politics of Natural Philosophy*, London, Continuum.

Fisher I. (1997) *The Works of Irving Fisher,* vol. 4, *the Purchasing Power of Money*, ed. W. J. Barber, London, Pickering and Chatto.

Fitzgibbons A. (1988) *Keynes's Vision: A New Political Economy*, Oxford, Clarendon Press.

Flower R. (2012) *Chianti: The Land, the People and the Wine*, Garrett County Digital Edition.

Fontana G. (2009) *Money, Uncertainty and Time*, London, Routledge.

Frazer M. L. (2010) *The Enlightenment of Sympathy*, Oxford, Oxford University Press.

Freudenthal G. (1986) *Atom and Individual in the Age of Newton,* Dordrecht, D. Reiddel Publishing Company.

Friedman M. (1972) *An Economist's Protest: Columns in Political Economy*, New Jersey, Thomas Horton and Company.

Fumagalli A. (2005) Bio-Economics, Labour Flexibility and Cognitive Work: Why Not Basic Income, in G. Standing (ed.) *Promoting Income Security as a Right: Europe and North America*, London, Anthem Press.

Fusfeld D. R. (2002) *The Age of the Economists*, 9th edn, Boston, Addison Wesley.

Galbraith J. K. (1988) *Economics in Perspective*, Boston, Houghton Mifflin.

Galbraith J. K. (1998) *Created Unequal: The Crisis in American Pay*, New York, The Free Press.

Galbraith J. K. (1991) *A History of Economics*, London, Penguin Books.

Galbraith J. K. (2017) *Economics in Perspective: A Critical History*, Princeton, Princeton University Press.

Gassendi P. and Thill O. (2002) *The Life of Copernicus (1473–1543),* Maitland, Xulon Press.

The Guardian (2016) *Iran Executed all Adults in one Village for Drug Offences*, 26 February. http://www.theguardian.com/world/2016/feb/26/all-adult-males-in-one-iranian-village-executed-for-drug-offences-official-says.

Gholi Majd M. (2001) *Great Britain and Reza Shah*, Gainesville, FL, University Press of Florida.

Ghose S. (1991) *Mahatma Gandhi*, New Delhi, Allied Publishers Limited.

Glassman B. (2002) *Benjamin Disraeli: The Fabricated Jew in Myth and Memory*, Lanham, University Press of America Inc.

Goldschmidt A. (1991) *A Concise History of the Middle East*, 4th edn, Boulder, Westview Press.

Goldstein N. (2010) *Religion and the State*, New York, Facts On File, Inc.

Gomes G. J. (2012) *Discovering World Religions*, Bloomington, iUniverse.

Gomes L. O. (1992) Nonviolence and Self, in K. Kraft (ed.) Early Buddhism, in *Inner Peace, World Peace – Essays on Buddhism and Nonviolence*, New York, State University of New York Press.

Goodson F. E. (2014) *The Evolution and Function of Cognition*, Greencastle, Psychology Press.

Goranko V. (2016) *Logic as a Tool: A Guide to Formal Logical Reasoning*, Chichester, Wiley.

Gordon H. S. (2002) Alfred Marshall and the Development of Economics as a Science, in J. C. Wood (ed.) *Alfred Marshall: Critical Assessments*, vol. 4, London, Routledge.

Grana S. J. (2010) *Women and Justice*, 2nd edn, Lanham, Rowman and Littlefield Publishers Inc.

Gray A. (1957) *The Development of Economic Doctrine*, London, Longmans, Green and Co.

Griffith-Dickson G. (2005) *The Philosophy of Religion*, London, SCM Press.

Grimm G. (1999) *The Doctrine of the Buddha: The Religion of Reason and Meditation*, New Delhi, Motilal Banarsidass Publishers.

Grotius H. (2007) *The Rights of War and Peace*, New York, CosimoClassics.

Grousset R. (2002) *The Empire of the Steppes*, trans. N. Walford, New Brunswick, Rutgers University Press.

Gualtieri A. R. (1994) *Search for Meaning: Exploring Religions of the World*, Toronto, Guernica.

Hajari N. (2015) *Midnight's Furies—The Deadly Legacy of India's Partition*, Boston, Houghton Mifflin Harcourt.

Handa J. (2000) *Monetary Economics*, London, Routledge.

Hanley L. H. (1922) *History of Economic Thought*, London, Palgrave Macmillan.

Hansen A. H. (1936) Mr. Keynes on Underemployment Equilibrium, *Journal of Political Economy*, vol. 44: 5.

Hansen A. H. (1951) Classical, Loanable-Fund, and Keynesian Interest Theories, *The Quarterly Journal of Economics*, vol. 65: 3.

Hardach G. (1981) *The First World War 1914–1918*, Berkeley, University of California Press.

Harees L. (2012) *The Mirage of Dignity on the Highways of Human 'Progress'—The Bystanders' Perspective*, Bloomington, AuthorHouse.

Harrison S. (1981) *In Afghanistan's Shadow: Baluch Nationalism and Soviet Temptation*, New York, Carnegie Endowment for International Peace.

Harvey W. (2003) An Anatomical Study on The Motion of the Heart and the Blood in Animals, in D. J. Rothman, S. Marcus and S. A. Kiceluk (eds.) *Medicine and Western Civilization*, New Brunswick, Rutgers University Press.

Hawke G. R. (1980) *Economics for Historians*, Cambridge, Cambridge University Press.

Haworth A. (2004) *Understanding the Political Philosophers: From Ancient to Modern Times*, London, Routledge.

Hawtrey R. G. (1937) Alternative Theories of Rate of Interest: Three Rejoinders, *The Economic Journal*, vol. 47: 187.

Hayek F. A. (2014) *The Collective Works of F. A. Hayek—Market and Other Orders*, vol. 15, ed. B. Caldwell, Chicago, Chicago University Press.

Heffernan M. (1999) Historical Geographies of the Future: Three Perspectives from France, 1750–1825, in D. N. Livingstone and C. W. J. Withers (eds.) *Geography and Enlightenment*, Chicago, The University of Chicago Press.

Herder J. G. (1803) *Outline of a Philosophy of History of Man*, vol. II, London, Printed for J. Johnson, by Luke Hansard.

Hergenhah B. R. and Henly T. B (2014) *An Introduction to the History of Psychology*, 7th edn, Belmont, Wadsworth Cengage Learning.

Herman A. (2008) *Gandhi and Churchill*, New York, Arrow Book.

Hesiod (2006) *Hesiod: Theogony, Works and Days, Testimonia*, ed. and trans. G. W. Most, Cambridge, Harvard University Press.

Hicks J. (1937) Mr. Keynes and the "Classics"; A Suggested Interpretation, *Econometrica*, vol. 5: 2.

Hicks J. R. (1973) Recollections and Documents, *Economica*, vol. 40: 157.

Hiltzik M. (2011) *The New Deal: A Modern History*, New York, Free Press.

Hinkley B. (2015) *Atheism, Religion and Life—A Layman's Perspective*, Morrisville, Lulu.com.

Hobbes T. (1976) *Leviathan*, ed. J. Plamenatz, New York, Fountain Books, Collins.

Hobbes T. (2005) *Leviathan*, Part I and II, ed. A. P. Martinich, Canada, Broadview Edition.

Hobsbawm E. (1995) *The Age of Extremes*, London, Abacus.

Hobsbawm E. (1999) *Industry and Empire*, London, Penguin Books.

Hochschild A. (2006) *King Leopold's Ghost: A Story of Greed, Terror, and Heroism in Colonial Africa*, London, Pan Books.

Hollander S. (1997) *The Economics of Thomas Robert Malthus*, Toronto, University of Toronto Press.

Homer S. (1963) *A History of Interest Rates*, New Brunswick, Rutgers University Press.

Hoover C. B. (1948) Keynes and the Economic System, *Journal of Political Economy*, vol. 56: 5.

Horvath J. (1983) A Theory of Institutional Inflation, in N. Schmukler and E. Marcus (eds.) *Inflation Through Ages: Economic, Social, Psychological and Historical Aspects*, New York, Brooklyn College Press.

Howells P. G. A. (2001) The Endogeneity of Money, in P. Arestis and M. Sawyer (eds.) *Money, Finance and Capitalist Development*, Cheltenham, Edward Elgar.

Hulsey T. L. and Frost C. J. (2004) *Moral Cruelty*, Lanham, University Press of America.

Hume D. (1955) *An Inquiry Concerning Human Understanding*, Indianapolis, The Library of Liberal Arts.

Hume D. (1998) *Selected Essays*, eds. S. Copley and A. Edgar, Oxford, Oxford University Press.

Hume D. (2003) *Hume: Political Essays*, ed. K. Haakonssen, Cambridge, Cambridge University Press.

Ibn Khaldun (1958) *The Muqaddimah: An Introduction to History*, trans. Franz Rosenthal, New York, Antheon.

Ikram S. M. (1992) *Indian Muslims and Partition of India*, New Delhi, Atlantic Publishers and Distributors.

Iriye A. (1999) *The Cambridge History of American Foreign Relations*, vol. 3, Cambridge, Cambridge University Press.

Ivanhoe P. J. (1991) Character Consequentialism: An Early Confucian Contribution to Contemporary Ethical Theory, *The Journal of Religious Ethics*, vol. 19: 1.

Jayapalan N. (2002) *Comprehensive Study of Plato*, New Delhi, Atlantic Publishers and Distributors.

Jefferson T. (1854) *The Writings of Thomas Jefferson*, vol. viii, Washington, DC, Taylor and Maury.

Jevons W. S. (1871) *Theory of Political Economy*, vol. I, London, Macmillan and Co.

Jevons W. S. (1888) *Theory of Political Economy*, 3rd edn, London, Macmillan and Co.

Jevons W. S. (1970) *The Theory of Political Economy*, ed. R. D. Collison Black, Harmondsworth, Penguin Books.

Jevons W. S. (1971) *The Theory of Political Economy*, ed. R. D. Collison Black, Harmondsworth, Penguin Books.

Johnstone D. (2002) Q and A: Ayatollah Khomeini, in C. Aaron (ed.) *Appeal to Reason—25 Years in These Times*, New York, Seven Stories Press.

Jonung L. (1994) Knut Wicksell and Gustav Cassel on Secular Movements in Prices, in J. C. Wood (ed.) *Knut Wicksell Critical Assessments,* vol. II, London, Routledge.

Kahn R. F. (1931) The Relation of Home Investment to Unemployment, *Economic Journal,* vol. 41: 162.

Karimzadi S. (2013) *Money and Its Origins*, London, Routledge.

Karimzadi S. (2015) *Methodology of Deception*, London, Humgaam Press.

Kasambe R. (2020) *Birds in Agriculture*, Mumbai, Google Play Books.

Kasper S. D. (2002) *The Revival of Laisses-Faire in American Macroeconomic Theory*, Cheltenham, Edward Elgar.

Keane N. (2015) On the Origins of Illness and the Hiddenness of Health: An Hermeneutic Approach to the History of a Problem, in *Medicine and Society – New Perspectives in Continental Philosophy*, ed. D. Meacham, Bristol: Springer.

Keddie N. R. (2003) *Modern Iran: Roots and Results of Revolution*, New Haven, Yale University Press.

Kelbessa W. (2011) Indigenous Environmental Philosophy, in G. J. L. Garfield and W. Edelglass (eds.) *The Oxford Handbook of World Philosophy*, Oxford, Oxford University Press.

Kelly M. J. (2005) *Nowhere to Hide*, New York, Peter Lang Publishing.

Kennedy D. F. (2013) *Antiquity and the Meaning of Time*, London, I. B. Tauris.

Keynes J. M. (1937) The General Theory: Fundamental Concepts and Ideas, *Quarterly Journal of Economics*, vol. 51: 2.

Keynes J. M. (1965) *A Treatise on Money*, vol. I. London, Macmillan and Co Ltd.

Keynes J. M. (1967) *The General Theory of Employment Interest and Money*, London, Palgrave Macmillan.

Keynes J. M. (1971) *The Collected Writings of John Maynard Keynes, Activities 1931–1939, World Crises and Politics in Britain and America*, vol. 21, ed. D. E. Moggridge, London, Palgrave Macmillan.

Keynes J. M. (1972) *The Collected Writings of John Maynard Keynes,* vol. 9, *Essays in Persuasion,* New York, St. Martin's Press.

Keynes J. M. (1973) *The Collected Writings of John Maynard Keynes*, vol. 14, The General Theory and After, Part 2, Defence and Development, Cambridge, Cambridge University Press.

Keynes J. M. (1981) *The Collected Writings of John Maynard Keynes, Activities 1929–1931, Rethinking Employment and Unemployment Policies*, vol. 20, ed. D. E. Moggridge, London, Macmillan.

Keynes J. M. (1982) *The Collected Writings of John Maynard Keynes, Social and Literary Writings,* vol. 28, ed. D. E. Moggridge, London, Macmillan.

Keynes J. M. (1988) *The Collected Writings of John Maynard Keynes*, vol. 29, ed. D. E. Moggridge, Cambridge, Cambridge University Press.

Khilnani S. (2009) Nehru's Judgement, in R. Bourke and R. Geuss (eds.) *Political Judgement: Essays for John Dunn*, Cambridge, Cambridge University Press.

Khwaja J. R. (2013) *Toward a General Theory of Exchange: Strategic Decisions and Complexity*, Bloomington, iUniverse LLC.

Kindleberger C. P. (1986) *The World in Depression 1929–1939*, Berkeley, University of California.

Kirazli S. (2016) Roots and Causes of Terrorism in the Middle East, in A. R. Dawoody (ed.) *Eradicating Terrorism from Middle East*, Switzerland, Springer.

Kirzner I. M. (2007) *Market Theory and the Price System*, Auburn, The Mises Institute.

Kjellberg P. (1996) Sexus Empiricus, Zhuangzi, Xunzi on 'Why Be Skeptical?' in P. Kjellberg and P. J. Ivanhoe (eds.) *Essays on Skepticism, Relativism, and Ethics in the Zhuangzi*, New York, State University of New York Press.

Knight F. H. (1937) Unemployment: And Mr. Keynes's Revolution in Economic Theory, *The Canadian Journal of Economics and Political Science*, vol. 3: 1.

Knobloch E. (2002) The Sounding Algebra: Relations between Combinatorics and music from Mersenne to Euler, in A. Assayag, H. G. Frichtinger and J. F. Rodrigues (eds.) *Mathematics and Music: A Diderot Mathematical Forum*, Verlag Berlin Heidelberg, Springer.

Koehler C. S. W. (2000) Bring out Your Dead! *The Time Line*, vol. 3: 9.

Kozuskanich N. R. (2015) *Benjamin Franklin: American Founder*, New York, Routledge.

Krajewski W. (1977) *Correspondence Principle and Growth of Science,* Boston, D. Reidel Publishing Company.

Kristof N. D. (1995) Unmasking Horror–A Special Report, Japan Confronting Gruesome War Atrocity, *New York Times*, 17 March.

Kirzner I. M. (1989) Economic Harmony, in J. Eatwell, M. Milgate and P. Newman (eds.) *The Invisible Hand*, London, Macmillan Reference.

Laidler H. W. (2000) *History of Socialism*, Abingdon, Routledge.

Lamb C. (2001) 'Khomeini Fatwa' Led to Killing of 30,000 in Iran, *The Telegraph*.

Landreth H. and Colander D. C. (1994) *History of Economic Thought*, 3rd edn, Boston, Houghton Mifflin.

Lane D. (2002) Full Employment and Labor Utilization of the Soviet Economy, in M. P. Sacks and J. G. Pankhurst (eds.) *Understanding Soviet Society*, London, Routledge.

Larain J. (1999) Classical Political Economists and Marx on Colonialism and 'Backward Nations', in B. Jessop and R. Wheatley (eds.) *Karl Marx's Social and Political Thought*, vol. 6, London, Routledge.

Larrere C. (2009) Montesquieu and Liberalism: The Question of Pluralism, in R. E. Kingston (ed.) *Montesquieu and his Legacy*, New York, State University of New York Press.

Law D. (2006) *The Secret History of the Great Dictators*, London, Magpie.

Law S. (2011) *Humanism: A Very Short Introduction*, Oxford, Oxford University Press.

Lawrenz L. (2012) *Life and Mind: A Philosophical Quest*, Newcastle Upon Tyne, Cambridge Scholars Publishing.

Lawson T. (2015) Essays on the Nature and State of Modern Economics, London, Routledge.

Leakey R. R. B. (2017) *Multifunctional Agriculture*, Oxford, Academic Press.

Lebow R. N. (2003) *The Tragic Vision of Politics: Ethics, Interests and Order*, Cambridge, Cambridge University Press.

Lee S. J. (2010) *Hitler and Nazi Germany*, 2nd edn, Abingdon, Routledge.

Leibniz G. W. (1989) *Philosophical Papers and Letters: A Selection*, ed. L. E. Loemker, 2nd edn, Dordrech, Kluwer Academic Publishers.

Leijonhufvud A. (1968) *On Keynesian Economics and the Economics of Keynes: A Study in Monetary Theory*, New York, Oxford University Press.

Lenin V. I. (1930) *Collected Works: Imperialism and the Imperialist War*, New York, International Publishers.

Lenin V. I. (1975) *V. I. Lenin Selected Works*, vol. 2, Moscow, Progress Publishers.

Leonard C. S. (1993) *Reform and Regicide—The Reign of Peter III of Russia*, Bloomington, Indiana University Press.

Letwin W. (2003) *The Origins of Scientific Economics: English Economic Thought 1660–1776*, London, Routledge.

List F. (2005) *National System of Political Economy*, vol. 1, New York: CosimoClassics.

List F. (2006) *National System of Political Economy*, vol. 2–3, New York, CosimoClassics.

Locke J. (1751) *The Works of John Locke*, vol. 2, London, Mr. Desmaizeaux.

Locke J. (1824) *The Works of John Locke*, vol. 4, 12th edn, London, C. Baldwin Printer.

Locke J. (2004) *Second Treatise on Government*, New York, Barnes and Noble Books.

Lombardo T. (2008) *The Evolution of Future Consciousness*, Blooming, AuthorHouse

Long H. S. (1998) *The Order of Nature in Aristotle's Physics: Place and Elements,* Cambridge, Cambridge University Press.

Loposer B. (2008) *Seven is the Perfect Number*, Blooington, Author House.

Ludington Daily News (26 April 1926) *Persian Hostler now Rules Country*. https://newspaperarchive.com/ludington-daily-news-apr-26-1926-p-1/.

Magliocco S. (2014) Pagans, in G. Harvey (ed.) *Religions in Focus: New Approaches to Tradition and Contemporary Practices*, Abingdon, Routledge.

Malešević S. (2017) The Rise of Organised Brutality: A Historical Sociology of Violence, Cambridge, Cambridge University Press.

Malthus T. R. (1872) *An Essay on the Principle of Population*, London, Reeves and Turner.

Malthus T. R. (1985) *An Essay on the Principle of Population*, London, Penguin Books.

Malthus T. R. (1986) *The Works of Thomas Robert Malthus*, vol. 1–2, eds. D. Souden and A. Wrigley, Glasgow, W. Pickering.

Malthus T. R. (1989) *An Essay on the Principle of Population*, vol. 2, ed. P. James, Cambridge, Cambridge University Press.

Malthus T. R. (1996) *Population: The First Essay*, Ann Arbor, MI, The University of Michigan Press.

Mandeville B. (1989) *The Fable of the Bees*, London, Penguin Books Ltd.

Mandeville B. D. (1795) *The Fable of the Bees: or, Private Vices, Public Benefits*, London, Printed for C. Bathurst.

Marballi G. K. (2014) *The Vedanta Primer*, 2nd edn, New York, Azure Publishing.

Markham J. D. and Zarzeczny M. (2017) *Simply Napoleon*, New York, Simply Charly.

Marshall A. (1996) *The Correspondence of Alfred Marshall, Economist*, vol. 3, ed. J. K. Whitaker, Cambridge, Cambridge University Press.

Marshall A. (1998) *Alfred Marshall—Critical Responses*, vol. 2, ed. P. Groenewegen, New York and London, Routledge.

Marshall A. (2009) *Principles of Economics*, 8th edn, New York, CosimoClassics.

Marshall A. and Paley M. (1879) *The Economics of Industry*, London, Palgrave Macmillan.

Marshall B. V. (1968) *Comprehensive Economics*, London, Longman.

Marx K. (1967) Toward the Critique of Hegel's Philosophy of Law, in L. D. Easton and K. H. Guddat (eds.) *Writings of the Young Marx on Philosophy and Society*, New York, Doubleday and Company, Inc.

Marx K. (1971) *A Contribution to the Critique of Political Economy*, trans. M. Dobb, London, Lawrence and Wishart.

Marx K. (1972) *Theories of Surplus-Value*, part 3, Moscow, Progress Publishers.

Marx K. (1977a) *Economic and Philosophic Manuscript of 1844*, Moscow, Progress Publishers.

Marx K. (1977b) *The Eighteenth Brumaire of Louis Bonaparte*, New York, International Publishers.

Marx K. (1977c) *The Civil War in France*, Peking, Foreign Language Press.

Marx K. (1978a) *Theories of Surplus-Value*, part 1, Moscow, Progress Publishers.

Marx K. (1978b) *Theories of Surplus-Value*, part 2, Moscow, Progress Publishers.

Marx K. (1983) *Capital*, vol. 1, London, Lawrence and Wishart.

Marx K. (1984) *Capital*, vol. 3, London, Lawrence and Wishart.

Marx K. (1986) *Capital*, vol. 2, London, Lawrence and Wishart.

Marx K. (2007) *Capital*, vol. 1, New York, CosimoClassics.

Marx K. (2008) *Critique of the Gotha Program*, Rockville, Wildside Press.

Marx K. and Engels F. (1936) *Karl Marx and Friedrich Engels, Correspondence, 1846–1895*, New York, International Publishers.

Marx K. and Engels F. (1962) *Karl Marx and Friedrich Engels Selected Works*, vol. 2, Moscow, Foreign Languages Publishing House.

Marx K. and Engels F. (1973) *Feuerbach*, London, Lawrence and Wishart.

Marx K. and Engels F. (1976) *Karl Marx and Friedrich Engels: Collected Works*, vol. 6, New York, International Publishers.

Marx K. and Engels F. (1990) *Karl Marx and Friedrich Engels: Collected Works*, vol. 32, New York, International Publishers.

Marx K. and Engels F. (1991) *The German Ideology*, 2nd edn, ed. C. J. Arthur, London, Lawrence and Wishart.

Marx K. and Engels F. (2008) *The Communist Manifesto*, Auckland, The Floating Press.

Masters R. D. (1976) *The Political Philosophy of Rousseau*, Princeton, Princeton University Press.

Megill A. (2002) *Karl Marx: The Burden of Reason*, Lanham, Rowman and Littlefield Publishers Inc.

Menger C. (2007) *Principles of Economics*, trans. J. Dingwall and B. F. Hoselitz, Auburn, Ludwig von Mises Institute.

Mill J. S. (1824) *Elements of Political Economy*, 2nd edn, London, Printed for Baldwin, Cradock, and Joy.

Mill J. S. (1848) *Principles of Political Economy*, vol. 2, Boston, Charles C. Little and James Brown.

Mill J. S. (1873) *Dissertations and Discussions: Political, Philosophical and Historical*, vol. II, New York, Henry Holt and Company.

Mill J. S. (1985) *Principles of Political Economy*, vol. 4–5, ed. D. Winch, London, Penguins Books.

Miller C. L. (2008) *Triangle: Literature and Culture of the Trade*, Durham, Duke University Press.

Minsky H. P. (1992) *The Financial Instability Hypothesis*, Working Paper no. 74, Bard College, The Jerome Economics Institute.

Mirowski P. (1999) *More Heat Than Light*, Cambridge, Cambridge University Press.

Mises L. V. (1962) *The Ultimate Foundation of Economic Science*, New York, Van Nostrand.

Mises L. V. (1998) *A Treatise on Economics—Human Action*, ed. The Scholar's, Auburn, Ludwig von Mises Institute.

Mises L. V. (2003) *Epistemological Problems of Economics*, 3rd edn, trans. G. Reisman, Auburn, Ludwig von Mises Institute.

Mitchell M. T. (2012) *The Politics of Gratitude*, Washington, DC, Potomac Books.

Mitchell W. C. (1930) *Business Cycles, the Problem and Its Setting*, New York, National Bureau of Economic Research.

Monter E. W. (1999) *Judging the French Reformation*, Cambridge, Harvard University Press.

Montesquieu (1766) *The Spirit of Law*, trans. Nugent, vol. I, 4th edn, London, J. Nourse and P. Vaillant.

Montesquieu (1977) *The Spirit of Law*, ed. D. W. Carrithers, Berkeley, University of California.

Montesquieu (2007) *The Spirit of Law*, vol. I, New York, Cosimo Classics.

Moosa I. A. (2014) *Quantitative Easing as a Highway to Hyperinflation*, Singapore, World Scientific Publishing Co. Pte. Ltd.

Morgan L. H. (1907) *Ancient Society*, New York, Henry Holt and Company.

Morrison K. (2006) *Marx, Durkheim, Weber: Formations of Modern Social Thought*, 2nd edn, London, Sage Publications.

Murray W. and Woods K. M. (2014) *The Iran-Iraq War: A Military and Strategic History*, Cambridge, Cambridge University Press.
Nabhan D. (2017) *Earthquake Prediction*, New York, Skyhorse Publishing.
Nazish K. (2014) Balochistan's Missing Persons, *The Diplomat*, 6 January.
Nicholls D. (2000) *Adolf Hitler: A Biographical Companion*, Santa Barbara, ABC-CLIO.
Nicolini J. P. (2009) Hyperinflation, in S. N. Durlauf and L. E. Blume (eds.) *Monetary Economics*, Basingstoke, Palgrave Macmillan.
Nicolson I. (1999) *Unfolding our Universe*, Cambridge, Cambridge University Press.
Nisbet R. (2009) *History of the Idea of Progress*, New Brunswick, Transaction Publishers.
Noraiee H. (2011) Globalization and Islam: Modernity, Diversity and Identities, in F. Moradi and I. Siriner (eds.) *Globalization, Religion and Development*, London, IJOPEC Publication.
North D. (1997) *Discourse upon Trade, in Monetary Theory, 1601–1758*, vol. 3, ed. A. E. Murphy, London, Routledge.
O'Connor J. M. and Costa J. E. (2004) *The World's Largest Floods, Past and Present: Their Causes and Magnitudes*, Reston, U.S. Geological Survey.
Ohlin B. (1937) Alternative Theories of Rate of Interest: Three Rejoinders, *The Economic Journal*, vol. 47: 187.
Oppong J. R. (2006) *Africa South of the Sahara*, Philadelphia, Chelsea House Publishers.
Oresme N. (2006) Traictie de La Premiere Invention des Monnoies, in A. E. Monroe (ed.) *Early Economic Thought: Selected Writings from Aristotle to Hume*, Mineola, NY, Dover Publications.
Overy R. J. (1982) *The Nazi Economic Recovery*, London, Palgrave Macmillan.
Paarlberg R. L. (1999) Politics and Food Insecurity in Africa, *Review of Agricultural Economics*, vol. 21: 2.
Pack S. J. (2010) *Aristotle, Adam Smith and Karl Marx*, Cheltenham, Edward Elgar.
Packard F. A. (1866) *Life of Robert Owen*, Carlisle, Applewood Books.
Palmer M. (2013) *Atheism for Beginners*, Cambridge, The Lutterworth Press.
Palmer M. and Palmer P. (2008) *Islamic Extremism: Causes, Diversity, and Challenges*, Lanham, Rowman and Littlefield Publishers, Inc.
Pandy S. (2017) *Western Political Thought*, Bhopal, Horizon Books.
Pascal B. (2018) *Pensées*, vol. 2, Woodstock, Devoted Publishing.
Payne S. G. (1973) *Massacre: The Tragedy of Bangla Desh and the Phenomenon of Mass Slaughter Throughout History*, New York, Macmillan.
Payne S. G. (1995) *A History of Fascism 1914–1945*, Madison, WI, The University of Wisconsin Press.
Pen J. (1966) *Modern Economics*, Harmondsworth, Penguin Books.
Penprase B. E. (2011) *The Power of Stars: How Celestial Observations have Shaped Civilization*, New York, Springer.
Perry M. (2016) *Western Civilization: A Brief History*, vol. II, 11th edn, Belmont, Wadsworth Cengage Learning.
Pesic P. (2014) *Music and Making of Modern Science*, Massachusetts, MIT Press.
Petty W. (1899) *The Economic Writings of Sir William Petty*, vol. 1, ed. C. H. Hull, Cambridge, Cambridge University Press.
Pigou A. C. (1912) *Wealth and Welfare*, London, Macmillan.
Pigou A. C. (1920) *The Economics of Welfare*, London, Macmillan.
Pigou A. C. (1936) J. M. Keynes' General Theory of Employment, Interest and Money, *Economica*, vol. 3: 10.
Pigou A. C. (1960) *The Economics of Welfare*, 4th edn, London, Palgrave Macmillan.
Plato (1871) *The Dialogues of Plato*, vol. 4, trans. B. Jowett, London, Macmillan and Co.

Plato (1965) *The Republic*, trans. H. D. Lee, Harmondsworth, Penguin Books.

Plato (1981) *The Works of Plato*, vol. 2, trans. B. Jowett, Minneapolis, Franklin Library.

Plato (1992) *The Trial and Death of Socrates: Four Dialogues*, New York, Dover Publications, INC.

Plato (2010) *Dialogues of Plato*, vol. 4, trans. B. Jowett, Cambridge, Cambridge University Press.

Pomeranz K. and Topik S. (1999) *Society, Culture, and the World Economy, 1400-the Present*, New York, M.E. Sharpe.

Potter K. H. (1991) *Presuppositions of India's Philosophies*, New Delhi, Motilal Banarsidass Publishers Pvt. Ltd.

Preston P. W. (2013) *Theories of Development*, Abingdon, Routledge.

Price J. (2010) *Sacred Scriptures of the World Religious: An Introduction*, London, Continuum International Publishing Groups.

Procopius of Caesarea (2015) *History of the Wars*, Books I and II, Kindle edition.

Proudhon P. J. (1970) *Selected Writings of Pierre-Joseph Proudhon*, ed. S. Edwards, London, Palgrave Macmillan.

Pufendorf S. (1994) *The Political Writings of Samuel Pufendorf*, ed. C. L. Carr, Oxford, Oxford University Press.

Rabie M. A. (2001) *The Making of History*, San Jose, Authors Choice Press.

Raic D. (2002) *Statehood and the Law of Self-Determination*, The Hague, Kluwer Law.

Raico R. (2012) *Classical Liberalism and the Austrian School*, Auburn, Mises Institute.

Rata E. (2012) *The Politics of Knowledge in Education*, Abingdon, Routledge.

Rauh N. K. and Kraus W. H. E. (2017) *A short History of the Ancient World*, Toronto, University of Toronto Press.

Raup D. M. (1991) *Extinction: Bad Genes or Bad Luck?* New York, W.W. Norton and Company.

Ravallion M. (2016) *The Economics of Poverty: History, Measurement and Policy*, Oxford, Oxford University Press.

Ray J. K. (2011) *India's Foreign Relations, 1947–2007*, Abingdon, Routledge.

Reale G. (1990) *A History of Ancient Philosophy: II Plato and Aristotle*, ed. and trans. J. R. Catan, New York, State University of New York Press.

Reinhart C. M. and Rogoff K. S. (2011) *This Time is Different—Eight Centuries of Financial Folly*, Princeton and Oxford, Princeton University Press.

Reisman D. (2012) *The Social Economics of Thorstein Veblen*, Cheltenham: Edward Elgar.

Réville J. (1905) Anticlericalism in France, *The American Journal of Theology*, vol. 9: 4.

Rhodes C. (2011) Lakshmi: Hindu Goddess of Abundance, in P. Monaghan (ed.) *Goddesses in World Culture*, vol. I, Santa Barbara, Praeger.

Ricardo D. (1992) *The Principles of Political Economy and Taxation*, London, Everyman's Library, Phoenix.

Ricardo D. (1810) *The High Price of Bullion: A Proof of the Depreciation of Bank Notes*, vol. 10, London, Printed for John. Murray.

Rieffer-Flanagan B. A. (2013) *Evolving Iran*, Washington, DC, Georgetown University Press.

Roll E. (1983) *A History of Economic Thought*, 4th edn, London, Faber and Faber.

Robertson D. (1936) Some Notes on Mr. Keynes' General Theory of Employment, *Quarterly Journal of Economics*, vol. 51: 1.

Robertson D. M. (2009) *An American Warning*, New York, iUniverse, Inc.

Roscher W. (2018) *Principles of Political Economy*, vol. 1, Frankfurt, Outlook.

Rosen W. (2007) *Justinian's Flea: The First Great Plague and the End of the Roman Empire*, New York, Viking Penguin.

Rostow W. W. (1992) *Theories of Economic Growth from David Hume to the Present*, New York, Oxford University Press.

Rothbard M. N. (2011) *Economic Controversies*, Auburn, Ludwig Von Mises Institute.

Rothlin S. and McCann D. (2016) *International Business Ethics: Focus on China*, Heidelberg, Springer.

Rousseau J. J. (2016) *The Social Contract and Discourses*, ed. A. Uyl, Woodstock, Devoted Publishing.

Ruggiero V. (2013) *The Crimes of the Economy—A Criminological Analysis of Economic Thought*, Abingdon, Routledge.

Rummel R. J. (1994) *Death by Government*, New Brunswick, Transaction Publishers.

Russell B. (1981) *Mysticism and Logic*, Totowa, Barnes and Noble Books.

Russell B. (1998) *Bertrand Russell Autobiography*, London, Routledge.

Saha K. (2008) *The Earth's Atmosphere – Its Physics and Dynamics*, Verlag Berlin Heidelberg, Springer.

Sarkar K. R. (1978) *Public Finance in Ancient India*, New Delhi, Abhinav Publications.

Say J. B. (1880) *A Treatise on Political Economy*, Philadelphia, Claxton, Remsen and Haffelfinger.

Schrems J. (2007) *Understanding Principles of Politics and the State*, Revised edn, Lenham, University Press of America.

Schuler K. (1992) The World History of Free Banking: An Overview, in K. Dowd (ed.) *The Experience of Free Banking*, London, Routledge.

Schumpeter J. A. (1966) *Capitalism, Socialism and Democracy*, 4th edn, London, Unwin University Books.

Schumpeter J. A. (1994) *Capitalism, Socialism and Democracy*, London, Routledge.

Schuster J. (2017) Did Descartes Teach a 'Philosophy of Science' or Implement 'Strategies of Natural Philosophical Explanation', in S. Gaukroger and C. Wilson (eds.) *Descartes and Cartesianism – Essay in Honour of Desmond Clarke*, Oxford, Oxford University Press.

Schwarz H. (2002) *Creation*, Michigan, William B. Eerdmans Publishing Company.

Scott R. A. (2011) *The Gothic Enterprise: A Guide to Understanding the Medieval Cathedral*, Berkeley, University of California Press.

Sedlacek T. (2011) *Economics of Good and Evil*, Oxford, Oxford University Press.

Senior N. W. (1939) *An Outline of the Science of Political Economy*, New York, Farrar and Rinehart, Inc.

Shand J. (1994) *Philosophy and Philosophers*, London, Penguin Books.

Shand J. (2014) *Philosophy and Philosophers: An Introduction to Western Philosophy*, London, Routledge.

Sharma S. D. (2012) *India Marching, Reflections from a Nationalistic Perspective*, Bloomington, iUniverse, Inc.

Siddiqi F. H. (2012) *The Politics of Ethnicity in Pakistan*, Abingdon, Routledge.

Skousen M. (2007) *The Big Three in Economics—Adam Smith, Karl Marx and John Maynard Keynes*, London, Routledge.

Skousen M. (2010) *Economic Logic*, Washington, DC, Capital Press.

Smith A. (1827) *An Inquiry into the Nature and Causes of the Wealth of Nations*, Edinburgh, Thomas Nelson and Peter Brown.

Smith A. (1869) *An Inquiry into the Nature and Causes of the Wealth of Nations*, vol. 2, ed. J. E. T. Rogers, Oxford, Clarendon Press.

Smith A. (1875) *An Inquiry into the Nature and Causes of the Wealth of Nations*, London, Bradbury, Agnew Printers.

Smith A. (1909) *An Inquiry into the Nature and Causes of the Wealth of Nations*, vol. 10, ed. C. J. Bullock, Cambridge, Harvard Classics.
Smith A. (1976a) *An Inquiry into the Nature and Causes of the Wealth of Nations*, Chicago, University of Chicago Press.
Smith A. (1976b) *An Inquiry into the Nature and Causes of the Wealth of Nations*, eds. A. H. Campbell, A. S. Skinner and W. B. Todd, Oxford, Clarendon Press.
Smith A. (1979) *The Wealth of Nations*, London, Penguin Books.
Smith A. (1986) *The Wealth of Nations, Books 1–3*, London, Penguin Classics.
Smith A. (2006) *The Theory of Moral Sentiments*, Mineola, Dover Publications, Inc.
Smith B. (2015) *Back to School*, Avon, MA, Adamsmedia.
Snooks G. D. (1997) *The Ephemeral Civilization—Exploding the Myth of Social Evolution*, London and New York, Routledge, Taylor and Francis Group.
Snowdon B. and Vane H. R. (2005) *Modern Macroeconomics: Its Origins, Development and Current State*, Cheltenham, Edward Elgar.
Somervill B. A. (2010) *Empires of Ancient Mesopotamia*, New York, Chelsea House Publishers.
Sowell T. (1972) *Say's Law: An Historical Analysis*, Princeton, Princeton University Press.
Spiegel H. W. (2002) *The Growth of Economic Thought*, 3rd edn, Durham, Duke University Press.
Spinoza B. D. (2007) *A Theologico—Political Treatise and a Political Treatise*, trans. R. H. M. Elwes, New York, CosimoClassics.
Stabile D. R. and Kozak A. F. (2012) *Markets, Planning and the Moral Economy*, Cheltenham, Edward Elgar.
Stamatellos G. (2012) *Introduction to Pre-Socratics*, Chichester, Wiley-Blackwell.
Stanlake G. F. (1976) *Introductory Economics*, 3rd edn, London, Longman.
Sternhell Z. (2010) *The Anti-Enlightenment Tradition*, trans. D. Maisel, New Haven, Yale University Press.
Stewart M. (1991) *Keynes and After*, 3rd edn, London, Penguin Books.
Styers R. (2004) *Making Magic: Religion, Magic, and Science in the Modern World*, Oxford, Oxford University Press.
Stuckrad K. V. (2014) *Western Esotericism: A Brief History of Secret Knowledge*, trans. N. Goodrick-Clarke, London, Routledge.
Stonier A. W. and Hague D. C. (1958) *A Textbook of Economic Theory*, London, Longmans Green and Co.
Tabak J. (2004) *The History of Mathematics and the Laws of Nature*, New York, Facts On File, Inc.
Tamanaha B. Z. (2004) *On the Rule of Law*, Cambridge, Cambridge University Press.
Tangain A. (2014) *Mathematical Theory of Democracy*, Dusseldorf, Springer.
Taylor H. and Mill J. S. (2004) Enfranchisement of Women, in C. C. Nelson (ed.) *Literature of the Women's Suffrage Campaign in England*, Peterborough, ON, Broadview Press.
Taylor M. (1980) On 'Normative' Rational-Choice Theories of Politics, in L. Lewin and E. Vedung (eds.) *Politics as Rational Action*, Dordrecht, D. Reidel Publishing Company.
Temin P. (1991) *Lessons from the Great Depression*, Cambridge, The MIT Press.
Teraji S. (2016) *Evolving Norms: Cognitive Perspectives in Economics*, New York, Palgrave Macmillan.
Thompson W. (2000) *What Happened to History?* London, Pluto.
Tuchman B. W. (1978) *A Distant Mirror: The Calamitous 14th Century*, New York, Alfred A. Knopf.
Turgot A. R. J. (2011) *The Turgot Collection*, ed. D. Gordon, Auburn, Mises Institute.

Udehn L. (2001) *Methodological Individualism—Background, History and Meaning*, London, Routledge.

Van Cauwenberghe E. H. G. (1983) Inflation in the Southern Low Countries, from the Fourteenth to the Seventeenth Century: A Record of some Significant Periods of High Prices, in N. Schmukler and E. Marcus (eds.) *Inflation Through Ages: Economic, Social, Psychological and Historical Aspects*, New York, Brooklyn College Press.

Van der Veen M. (2011) *Consumption, Trade and Innovation*, Journal of African Archaeology Monograph Series, vol. 6, Frankfurt, Africa Magna Verlag.

Veblen T. (1943) *The Theory of the Leisure Class*, New York, Random House, Modern Library Edition.

Veblen T. (2005) *The Vested Interests and the Common Man*, New York, CosimoClassics.

Viner J. (1936) Mr. Keynes on the Causes of Unemployment, *The Quarterly Journal of Economics*, vol. 51: 1.

Walton D. N. (2007) *Dialog Theory for Critical Argumentation*, Amsterdam, John Benjamins Publishing Company.

Walton G. M. and Rockoff H. (2018) *History of the American Economy*, 13th edn, Boston, Cengage.

Webster A. (2003) The Contribution of the Scottish Enlightenment to the Abandonment of the Institution of Slavery, *The European Legacy*, vol. 8: 4.

Wicksell K. (2007) *Interest and Prices*, trans. R. F. Kahn, Auburn, The Ludwig Von Mises Institute.

Whittaker E. (1950) *A History of Economic Ideas*, New York, Longman, Green and Co.

Wolper L. F. (2013) *Physician Practice Management*, Burlington, Jones and Bartlett Learning.

Worden S. (2010) *Godliness and Greed—Shifting Christian Thought on Profit and Wealth*, Lanham, Lexington Books.

Wray T. J. and Mobley G. (2005) *The Birth of Satan*, Basingstoke, Palgrave Macmillan.

Xenophon (2013) *Xenophon Complete Works*, Hastings, Delphi Classics.

Yao X. (2000) *An Introduction to Confucianism*, Cambridge, Cambridge University Press.

Zeidan R. (2018) *Economics of Global Business*, Cambridge, The MIT Press.

Zeigler P. (1969) *The Black Death*, Godalming, Surrey, Bramley Books.

Index